Recent changes in the British civil service ~~~~~~~~~~
reaching for 150 years. A book describing the ~~~ ~
lysing their implications has long been needed. Campbell and
Wilson have now provided it. This is one of the books one can
honestly describe as indispensable. It gains enormously from
placing Britain's experience in the context of the international
bureaucratic revolution.

Anthony King
University of Essex

Colin Campbell and Graham Wilson, two notably astute observers of executive systems in general and of Whitehall in particular,
have collaborated to produce a most impressive book on the
changing mores and norms of the Whitehall system. Utilizing
extensive interviews with British civil servants and other officials
and their wide-ranging knowledge of the relationship between
civil servants and politicians in other systems, the authors bring
both depth and comparative perspective to the task of assessing
the nature of change in the Whitehall paradigm.

This is a wise and very readable book of great value not only
to observers of Whitehall but to those tracking similar trends in
other administrative systems.

Bert A. Rockman
University of Pittsburgh

A must for students of Whitehall and Cabinet. Its strengths are
its analytical comparisons across five countries and the out-
spoken interviews with civil servants. It will infuriate tradition-
alists and spur on reformers.

G. W. Jones
*The London School of Economics
and Political Science*

COMPARATIVE POLITICS
Edited by Gillian Peele
Lady Margaret Hall, Oxford

Books in the Series:

Forthcoming:

The End of Whitehall

Death of a Paradigm?

Colin Campbell and Graham K. Wilson

BLACKWELL
Oxford UK & Cambridge USA

The right of Colin Campbell and Graham K. Wilson to be identified as authors of this work has been asserted in accordance with the Copyright, Designs and Patents Act 1988.

First published 1995

Blackwell Publishers Ltd
108 Cowley Road
Oxford OX4 1JF
UK

Blackwell Publishers Inc.
238 Main Street
Cambridge, Massachusetts 02142
USA

British Library Cataloguing in Publication Data

A CIP catalogue record for this book is available from the British Library.

Library of Congress Cataloging-in-Publication Data

Campbell, Colin, 1943–
    The end of Whitehall : death of a paradigm? / Colin Campbell and Graham K. Wilson.
        p.   cm. — (Comparative politics)
    Includes bibliographical references and index.
    ISBN 1–55786–139–0. — ISBN 1–55786–140–4 (pbk.)
    1. Administrative agencies—Great Britain. 2. Executive departments—Great Britain. 3. Great Britain—Politics and government—1945– I. Wilson, Graham K. II. Title. III. Series: Comparative politics (Oxford, England)
JN318.C36   1995
354.41—dc20   94–39180
                                                                    CIP

Typeset in 11 on 13 pt Sabon
by Graphicraft Typesetters Ltd., Hong Kong
Printed in Great Britain by T.J. Press Ltd., Padstow, Cornwall

This book is printed on acid-free paper.

The authors dedicate this book to

Moya Langtry
Virginia Sapiro and *Adam Wilson*

Contents

Preface to the Series

This series in comparative politics has been designed with three broad objectives in mind. In the first instance it is hoped that, by focusing on a number of contemporary themes and issues in comparative politics, the individual studies may cumulatively make a contribution to the subject. Comparative politics has never been an easy discipline; and the subject has become more difficult as conceptual approaches have proliferated and the weight of material available to scholars has increased. As a result there has been a certain fragmentation as the task of refining the conceptualization has become separated from the detailed studies of institutions and processes across political systems. This tendency for discussions of the framework of comparative politics to become divorced from the subject's empirical research agenda has been debilitating for the discipline. But it has also been misleading for students.

A second aim of the series is therefore to fill a gap in the literature by providing volumes that will combine empirical and theoretical material in easily accessible form. Each study will introduce students to the current debates between political scientists about the major issues involved in the comparative study of a particular subject. However, each study will also deploy sufficient information from a range of political systems to enable readers to evaluate the academic debates for themselves.

A third goal of the series is to take account of recent developments which make it necessary to look at governmental systems in new ways. The enhanced importance of supranational and international institutions (such as the European Union) and new partnership arrangements between the public and private sectors are but two examples of changes in the political landscape with profound implications for the organization and understanding of government. Therefore, in addition to the familiar topics of comparative politics, the series contains studies exploring themes less frequently handled in a comparative manner. Thus, as well as the study of interest groups (by Graham Wilson) and party systems (by Bruce Graham), the series contains studies of regulation (by John Francis) and of taxation (by B. Guy Peters).

Although the series has been designed with clear goals in mind, authors have been allowed to exercise their judgement about how much comparative material to include in their discussions. The only requirement is that they should both address the theoretical debates about their chosen topics and devote attention to the way the issues present themselves in the context of modern government.

The study of modern bureaucracy by Colin Campbell and Graham Wilson is an intriguing and important one. The authors examine the traditional 'Whitehall model', which has been exported to a number of other countries and which has come under strain in recent years. They show how the civil service in a number of countries including both Britain and the United States has been at the cutting edge of reforms designed to roll back the state and to give the bureaucracy greater political direction. Many of these reform initiatives have come from right-wing governments, although the authors' analysis suggests that the association between the transformation of civil service structures and the right is far from perfect.

One of the book's many valuable contributions is the extent to which it compares recent developments in the bureaucratic systems of the United Kingdom, Canada, Australia, New Zealand and the United States in a way that is alert to the *political* role of the civil service. Thus Professors Campbell and Wilson link the understanding of bureaucratic culture with efficient executive leadership and, ultimately, effective government. This is an impressive and rich work of comparative political science. I am delighted to be able to include it in the series.

Gillian Peele
Lady Margaret Hall
Oxford

Preface

When President Nixon visited Britain in 1969, one of the entertainments arranged for him by the British Prime Minister of the day, Harold Wilson, was a mock Cabinet meeting. Members of the Cabinet sat around the cabinet table in 10 Downing Street and pretended to have a normal meeting. Consciously, or unconsciously, this episode epitomized the pride that the British political class (and probably the British more generally) took in the workings of the executive branch of their system of government. Like the Brigade of Guards, the workings of the British executive branch were worth showing off to foreigners, with pride. A professional bureaucracy, the higher civil service, would analyse and develop policy initiatives with a tough realism and skill that their experience, high intellectual ability and independence from partisan politics made possible. Civil servants would identify the difficult choices that ministers needed to make, both individually within their departments and collectively through cabinet meetings and in the Cabinet itself. The machinery of government in Britain would maximize the likelihood that policies were adopted only after thorough analysis and discussion. How very different, Britons would muse, this was from the situation in the United States. Both Johnson's blundering in Vietnam and Nixon's Watergate débâcle resulted to a significant degree from failures to structure the executive branch effectively. Johnson's White House staff diminished his awareness of the failure of his Vietnam policy, while Nixon's helped him commit the criminal acts that resulted in his disgrace.

In 1994, however, two events demonstrated that a remarkable change had occurred in the standing of the British executive.

The first and most dramatic was the Scott Inquiry into matters relating to secret sales of equipment to manufacture arms to the brutal dictator of Iraq, Saddam Hussein; sales ended only a few months before British troops participated in the allied campaign against Saddam in 1991. The sale of arms to Iraq had been concealed from Parliament. Even worse in the eyes of many Britons, the Government had attempted to prevent evidence of this secret policy being made available to the lawyers defending three business executives; they had been charged with infringing regulations controlling the export of arms and equipment to manufacture arms to Iraq, regulations that the Government was pretending to enforce as part of its fraudulent policy of denying military supplies to both Iran and Iraq while they were at war with each other. The Scott Inquiry raised serious questions about the willingness of ministers and civil servants to mislead Parliament, the courts and the public. The supposedly great potential of the British system to reconcile competing or conflicting policies and agencies was thrown into question by the astonishing fact that at least one of the hapless business executives prosecuted for breaching export controls by one part of government, Customs and Excise, had been cooperating closely and at some risk to his safety with MI6, the overseas intelligence agency that reports to the Foreign Office.

A second, and less dramatic event in 1994 was the publication of a government White Paper, *The Civil Service, Continuity and Change* (Cmnd. 2627). The content of the White Paper, which attempted to stress continuity more than change, was less important than the fact that it had appeared at all. Discussion of the civil service had been very much a minority interest in Britain in the twentieth century. In the 1980s, it became if not exactly a popular topic of conversation then at least one that was discussed regularly in political circles. As we describe below, the relationships between bureaucrats and civil servants in Britain, long stable and promoted around the world as the Whitehall model of how to link bureaucrats and politicians, had come under intense pressure in the 1980s and 1990s. Convinced that the Whitehall model was inadequate and unsatisfactory, the Conservative governments led by Margaret Thatcher and John Major pushed through a series of radical changes to the structure and workings of the bureaucracy. The 1994 White Paper was not so much part of these changes as a result of the questioning that developed in Parliament about what aspects of the Whitehall model were left after the reforms of the radical Conservative governments.

Our analysis of the nature and causes of the changes in the British civil service and Whitehall model of executive politics that have occurred since the Conservatives came to power in 1979 constitutes a large part of this book. We wish to emphasize at the outset, however, that we intend this book to be of relevance not only to those who are interested in British politics but to those who are interested in studying executive branches comparatively. The Whitehall model of cabinet government supported by a high-status civil service has been of considerable importance to academics and reformers in countries other than Britain. Discussions of the Presidency and of the practice in the United States of filling thousands of government positions with political appointees are frequently influenced by an understanding or, we would argue, a misunderstanding of the Whitehall model. While we have hoped to contribute to a greater understanding of British government for its own sake, we have also tried by analysing the travails of the Whitehall model to contribute to the more general study of the evolving relationship between governing politicians in advanced democracies and the bureaucrats with whom they must collaborate.

We decided to cooperate on this book after discovering that we were working independently on much the same topic. Indeed, we heard of each other's work in part from those we were interviewing. Our interests were slightly different, however. Wilson came to study Whitehall through a general and comparative interest in the relationship between bureaucrats and politicians. Campbell came to the study from his interest in the strategies and styles of chief executives. We decided therefore to divide responsibility for drafting the book, with Campbell writing Chapters 3, 4, 5 and 6 while Wilson wrote Chapters 1, 2, 7 and 8. Naturally, we have exchanged and discussed each other's drafts.

It is difficult to conduct interview-based research in Whitehall. Unlike in the United States, officials rarely give interviews without consulting with a central authority in their department – normally the permanent secretary or the principal establishment officer. Unlike in Canada and Australia, these central authorities ration access, so that 'sampling' in the strict sense of the word becomes difficult if not impossible.

Campbell's interviews were conducted with Whitehall officials between 1978 and 1994. He employed an open-ended instrument (Campbell, 1983). On average, the interviews lasted 90 minutes.

In all but a few cases, they were taped and transcribed. The interviews were conducted pretty well consistently throughout the entire 16-year period. In all, 212 interviews were conducted – forty-seven in 1978–9, nine in 1980, four in 1982, eighty-nine in 1986–7, ten in 1988, thirty in 1989 and twenty-three in 1993. From 1986–7 onward, an effort was made to include a large number of respondents in operational departments as well as interviewees from central, coordinating departments (i.e. no. 10, the Cabinet Office and the Treasury). During the 1986–7 round of interviews, there occurred a very substantial haemorrhaging of senior officials – mainly assistant secretaries – from the public service. Close to 20 per cent of the interviewees in that period included individuals who had recently left their Whitehall positions. This was a one-off tack adopted in an attempt to tap the views of people departing the public service at that time.

Wilson similarly employed a structured interview schedule but with a larger proportion of closed-ended questions. He interviewed fifty senior officials between September 1989 and February 1990. Officials were selected randomly from lists of willing respondents compiled by the permanent secretaries of various departments. During spring 1990, Wilson interviewed twenty-five current or former ministers (two-thirds of the respondents were in the former category). In the cases of both the official and ministerial groups, interviews lasted on average about 75 minutes. About half the sessions were taped. Wilson has followed up with informal background sessions with civil servants and ministers conducted in the summers of 1991–4. In these sessions Wilson took pains to ensure that his materials would take into account changes that had taken place in Whitehall dynamics since the resignation of Margaret Thatcher and in the various phases through which the Major Government has passed.

Acknowledgements

We have incurred many debts in writing this book. Georgetown University (through Campbell's chair) and the University of Wisconsin (through both its Graduate School and the Hawkins bequest) provided essential and much appreciated financial support. Gillian Peele has been a tolerant and encouraging series editor. And we have greatly appreciated the encouragement and help offered by those at Blackwell who have taken a strong interest in the book. These include Sean Magee, Simon Prosser and Jill Landeryou, the original and current commissioning editors, Emma Gotch, our production controller, and David Green, our desk editor.

We are profoundly grateful to the numerous (nearly 300) politicians and civil servants who gave so generously of their time when we interviewed them. Although it was not always easy to gain access to officials for our research, we found that we were almost invariably greeted in a gracious and forthright way by those we actually interviewed. We also received considerable assistance from the permanent secretaries, establishment officers and private secretaries who helped us with the mechanics of selecting respondents and arranging interviews.

The British civil service has often been thought of as distant and aloof in its relationship with scholars. We have not found it so. And we have detected a steady improvement under the present Head of the Home Civil Service, Sir Robin Butler, who has done much to encourage links between academics and Whitehall. It is conventional to emphasize that those who help with a book are not responsible for its content. We would go further. We know that some of our interviewees will disagree with much of what we have to say and will feel that at times we have been over-critical. However, precious few of them let internal papers and the interventions of colleagues at meetings pass without stiff critical review. We have tried our best to bring the same level of critical analysis to this outsiders' assessment of Whitehall, made possible through interviews with many of its key players.

We have dedicated this book to Campbell's wife Moya Langtry, who did much to inspire him to finish the work so that together they could enjoy more weekend drives in the country, Wilson's wife Virginia Sapiro, who provided both intellectual and emotional support to him, and Wilson's son Adam Wilson, who, as he passed through a wonderful stage in his childhood, has given Wilson senior almost constant delight.

Colin Campbell
Graham K. Wilson

1

The Force of the Whitehall Model in the World of Executive–Bureaucratic Politics

There was a period in the history of modern democracies when faith in the wisdom and capacity of government was widespread. Between the Second World War and some time probably in the 1970s, only those intellectuals inspired by ideas that were no doubt intellectually fascinating but politically irrelevant, such as anarchism, marxism or the Chicago school of economics, doubted the capacity of governments to overcome problems that had long been thought part of the human condition. Inspired by the successes of the democracies in organizing for victory in the Second World War, armed intellectually with Keynesian economics and the concept of the welfare state, people across a wide section of the political spectrum had few doubts about embracing the state as a vehicle for social improvement. Not only the British Labour Party and American liberals but nearly all British Conservatives and Eisenhower Republicans accepted as entirely normal and desirable a level and range of state activity that as recently as the 1930s had been regarded as wild radicalism. By the 1960s, it was hard to imagine that there had been a Britain without a National Health Service, or a United States without Social Security. In 1965, when the British Labour Government launched its National Plan to increase economic growth and the American War On Poverty was just beginning, faith in the capacity was profound.

The last third of the century, however, witnessed a dramatic growth in scepticism about the capacity of government. The political successes of President Reagan and Margaret Thatcher were the most dramatic signs of these changes in attitude. More subtle and in a sense more profound signs included the adoption of policies similar to Reagan's or Thatcher's by *Labo(u)r* governments

in Australia and New Zealand. The 'neo-liberal' agenda of trying
to reduce government spending on social welfare programmes,
deregulation, privatizing government-owned concerns and shifting towards economic programmes that placed greater reliance
on the role of markets (and, through monetary policies, central
banks) rather than elected politicians in guiding the economy left
its mark on nearly all democracies. Even Swedish governments
undertook a reconsideration of the welfare state.

Although most social scientists remained to the left of centre
personally, their academic work took on a more conservative
cast. As John Schwarz noted (Schwarz, 1983), the prevalent assumption in policy analysis argued that government policies fail,
and the task of the analyst was to explain why. The dominance
of Keynesian economics was challenged successfully by monetarists. Within political science the 'realistic' assumptions of the
rational choice writers, that bureaucrats strove to maximize their
budgets and personnel while politicians were motivated by the
desire to be re-elected, became commonplace (Niskanen, 1971,
1973a and 1973b). This was ironically during a period in which
politicians like Reagan and Thatcher were pursuing radical policies, such as abandoning commitments to full employment, that
seemed fraught with electoral danger.

Our book is about an aspect of this general collapse in confidence in the wisdom and capacity of governments, the decline in
confidence in the system of executive leadership that Britain exported to every corner of the world, what we term the Whitehall
model. We have chosen this term to make clear our focus on
executive–bureaucratic, not legislative or party politics that the
more common term 'Westminster model' emphasizes. Yet we are
acutely aware that the crisis of executive leadership extends beyond the Whitehall model countries. Here we need determine
neither the causes of this collapse in faith in the capacity of
governments, nor its accuracy. No doubt scepticism about government capacity can be as excessive as the faith of the 1960s. We
are conscious, however, that we write against the background of
a period in which it has become commonplace that governments
fail as well as succeed even when acting on the highest motives. The
capacity of governments to analyse complex situations and devise
coherent, effective solutions to them has become more questioned
than since the pre-Keynesian, pre-social-democratic era.

Not all of this scepticism is rooted in doubts about the capacity of the machinery of government. Some of the scepticism is rooted in doubts about the adequacy of our social or economic knowledge. Whether there exist effective solutions to some of the problems that governments were thought capable of solving in the recent past may be questioned; it is not clear what advice should be given to well-intentioned politicians trying to reduce the American murder rate, to raise the economic growth rate in Britain or to end the plight of the underclass in both countries. We are less inclined to believe that convincing solutions exist to the problems that confront government. Even if such solutions exist, however, we are less sure that governments will find and implement them effectively.

The reasons for our doubts about the capacity of governments to find and implement effective solutions to our problems are numerous, constituting in a sense the agenda of institutional political science. No doubt each country has its unique set of problems and circumstances that help explain these doubts. However, a number of concerns are common to western democracies. We may label these the problems of obtaining advice, the problems of heeding advice, the problems of coordinating solutions and the problems of delivering solutions.

The most basic problem that faces governments is the problem of learning, of discovering the true nature of the problems that confront them and the solutions to these problems that might be pursued.

We have learned that governments will frequently fail this first test in the policy process. Neither permanent bureaucracies nor politically appointed advisers necessarily have the appropriate skills or knowledge to analyse problems. Twenty years after Keynesianism was officially adopted and steering the economy became a central concern of British governments, economists were few and far between in the higher civil service. Even if the appropriate expertise exists, mistakes will be made. Problems will be misdiagnosed, available evidence and expertise ignored and plausible solutions buried by politicians or bureaucrats whose interests or preferences they threaten. George Reedy's stories of how President Johnson's 'courtiers' shielded him from bad news that he needed to hear are famous (Reedy, 1970). A basic question in the study of the Presidency is how staff can be organized in such a way as to increase rather than diminish the flow of information and useful ideas. But the problem is not confined to the United States. It is reported that a British Labour politician in the 1930s complained after the succeeding, Conservative dominated government escaped the economic problem that had destroyed the Labour government, by devaluing the pound: 'They never told us we could do that.'

Advice needs to be heeded as well as offered. A wide variety of work in political science offers reasons why good advice may be discarded. The psychology of the individual decision maker, conflict between the advice offered and the standard operating procedures of the agency, and ideological blindness of decision makers may explain the rejection of policies that would work.

Even if decision makers have an accurate understanding of the problems facing them and plausible solutions to them, they face one of the most basic problems of contemporary government, reconciling the different goals and ambitions of government. Many contemporary officials and politicians feel a deep frustration that any desirable policy in one area conflicts with equally desirable policy goals elsewhere. Improving environmental protection damages economic growth. Halting the decline in educational achievement may require more resources at a time when the top priority is supposedly balancing the budget. Calls for intervention to halt the slaughter of Bosnian Muslims or Iraqi Kurds sit awkwardly with aspirations of cutting the military budget. Modern governments almost never face discrete policy problems that have no impact on other policy areas; the interconnectedness of policy issues is a recurring feature of modern governance. The specification of priorities is all the more difficult because governments invariably have the character of coalitions, including people of differing viewpoints. In a celebrated interview before she became prime minister, Margaret Thatcher announced that she would not appoint any members of the cabinet who did not agree with her because she could not be bothered arguing with them. As her memoirs make clear, often to her annoyance Thatcher was forced to appoint people who did not agree with her to every one of her cabinets (Thatcher, 1993). Policies that collide with each other must be reconciled by people who are likely to have disagreements, before they start making them.

A fourth problem concerns effective implementation. Political scientists such as Wildavsky and Pressman (Wildavsky and Pressman, 1973) have made us so aware of the problems of implementation that we have reached the point of being surprised that policies are ever implemented effectively. Numerous governmental and extragovernmental agents – different levels and institutions of government, bureaucrats, foreign-exchange dealers, business corporations and at times, trade unions – have the capacity to block implementation of government policies.

These well-known problems of modern governance afflict all advanced democracies. Yet the hope that somewhere a system of government exists that avoids the pitfalls that befall the others has been very common. Securing the cooperation of the bureaucracy, obtaining useful policy advice, reconciling different goals and viewpoints and implementing decisions may be difficult here, so goes the argument, but in other countries they do things better. The debate among American political scientists in the 1980s over the causes and consequences of 'divided government' (Mayhew, 1991; Jones, 1994) (one party controlling Congress and the other party the Presidency) has often seemed to be based on the idea that other countries have unitary governments in which conflicts, disagreements and deadlocks do not happen. Japanese and French bureaucrats have been endowed by some political economists with almost mystical powers to foresee economic developments and steer their countries' industries accordingly.

In the recent past, Britain appeared to offer other countries an example of how to resolve the difficulties of modern governance. The prestige of the British model was at its greatest during the quarter century following the Second World War. British governments seemed to have the institutional capacity to carry out their campaign promises; as King has noted, the correspondence between the 1945 Labour Party manifesto and the record of the 1945–51 Labour Government was almost total (King, 1975). British governments had the institutional unity, thanks to the combination of legislative and executive leadership in the cabinet, to implement Keynesian economic policies, whereas hopelessly fragmented American institutions could not. The professional civil service provided politicians with both fearless advice, thanks to a security of tenure comparable to that of university professors, and a smoothly running machine for implementing decisions once they had been made. A career bureaucracy was willing 'to speak truth to power' in a way that American political appointees were not, and, imbued with a strong sense of serving the public interest, was able to overcome the tendencies for the self-interest of individual agencies, so common in the United States, to block the adoption of good public policy. The cabinet and its committees provided a mechanism for reconciling conflicting policy views, goals and departmental interests that countries with political systems other than the Westminster model could only envy. Finally, electoral competition between disciplined political parties ensured the accountability of government to electors more completely and satisfactorily than coalition governments in Europe, or the sharing of powers between institutions in the United States.

Britain's comparatively low rate of economic growth in the 1980s has made the Westminster model much less attractive than it used to be to commentators in other countries. The economic grounds for the diminution in the popularity of the British model in intellectual circles are questionable. It is unclear whether Britain's comparatively low rate of economic growth was the fault of the political system. Some – such as Rubinstein – even question whether the British growth rate has been unusually low (Rubinstein, 1993). It is also possible to argue that an evaluation of the entire British political system should not be based on a single variable, the economic growth rate.

It is our contention, however, that what we call the Whitehall model of interaction between ministers and civil servants has not brought Britain the advantages that are usually associated with it. Our criticisms of the Whitehall model are based not on its economic performance but on its failure to achieve those advantages in governance that have been claimed for it. We are therefore (to our dismay) among the currently fashionable writers who are critical of the British system unlike those in the recent past who praised and admired it. Yet, though the British political system is no longer fashionable, it is still interesting to ask why its apparent advantages in solving the problems of modern governance that we have identified are not greater. The advantages claimed for the Whitehall model in the past were not implausible. British institutions did provide a structure that made coordination easier than in, for example, the United States. The permanent civil service did provide advantages in securing policy advice and implementation. The apparent advantages of the Whitehall model were sufficiently plausible to make the question why it has failed interesting. Why has the permanent civil service not provided politicians with satisfactory policy advice when it seems so manifestly superior to the government by cronies and ambitious, inexperienced youth that characterizes the Clinton White House staff? Why have British politicians seemed so dissatisfied with the implementation of their policies by the civil service machine that American reformers used to admire? And why has the apparently impressive machinery of the cabinet and its committees not secured that harmony between politicians and policies that admirers in other countries have associated with it?

The puzzle that some political systems offer is why they work at all. The American political system, for example, seems almost bound to fail given its fragmented institutions and weak political parties. The British political system and the Whitehall model it has generated provide a more challenging puzzle. Why, in spite of all its apparent advantages, does it fail? That is the challenge that we confront in this book.

The Whitehall Model

As experts on British politics will recognize, the title of this book is a variation of a better-known phrase, the Westminster model. Political scientists use the phrase Westminster model to describe the basic features of parliamentary government as practised in Britain and exported to nations in every inhabited continent. The basic features of the Westminster model include the principles that the governing party should be able to command a majority in the House of Commons, that members of the government are collectively responsible for all its policies, that party discipline should almost always be maintained, that voters should be offered a choice between the competing, disciplined parties. The British, but not the Canadians or Australians, would add that in the Westminster model Parliament is 'supreme', so that no other institution such as the courts can override its legislation (Mount, 1992; Jennings, 1966; Johnson, 1977; Marshall, 1984).

The Westminster model is of course named after the part of London in which the Houses of Parliament are located. Past Parliament Square from the public entrance to the Houses of

Parliament is Whitehall, the street which has given its name to the executive branch of British government. Major departments such as Environment, Transport, Trade and Industry have been banished to modern office blocks on different streets. But the most central departments – Treasury, the Cabinet Office, the Foreign and Commonwealth Office and, a few dozen yards down Downing Street, the Prime Minister's office all adjoin Whitehall and there is no doubt that it is the spiritual heart of British government; after a lengthy period during which they suffered the ultimate indignity of being exiled to a modern and therefore ugly office building that was even south of the Thames, the Departments of Health and Social Security were thrilled to secure a headquarters building, Richmond House, that is actually on Whitehall itself.

It is in the government buildings off Whitehall that British policy making is generally conducted. This is not to deny that the people in those offices are responding to pressures from a variety of people and institutions. The European Union, the governments of other nations, foreign-exchange dealers, public opinion polls and of course Parliament itself have all at times exercised decisive influence. Members of the House of Commons have probably become more willing in recent decades to reject party discipline. Whereas in the 1950s, back-bench revolts were confined to the opposition Labour Party (and viewed with great anger by party leaders), in modern times even members of the governing party have been willing to reject government proposals (Norton, 1974 and 1978). Yet almost invariably, whatever the pressures from inside or outside Britain to which government responds, the actual decisions about public policy are almost always made in the government offices to which Whitehall has given its name. In contrast to practice in the United States, major legislation is rarely drafted or redrafted in Parliament; though courts may exert an increasing influence on public policy, British policy is less likely than American to be made by judges. British policy making is executive branch policy making.

The British executive branch consists of two very different elements, of people who have chosen very different types of career and who almost never switch from one to the other. The first element, and, at least in constitutional theory, the dominant element, is composed of the ministers selected from the ranks of the majority party in Parliament, or if there is coalition government formed of more than one party (as during the Second World War) from the ranks of parties in coalition. Ministers in contemporary Britain are career politicians who have climbed the 'greasy pole' from the back-benches into ministerial office, but who are unlikely to stay long in their posts. When appointed to their first cabinet-level posts, ministers typically have considerable experience of Parliament, limited experience as junior ministers in the ways of Whitehall in general and almost no knowledge of the work of the departments they are appointed to lead. The second element in executive politics consists of the career bureaucrats who share in the formulation and implementation of public policy. Career bureaucrats who work with ministers are typically graduates of elite universities (in the past nearly always Oxford or Cambridge) who have entered the civil service on a 'fast track' to the most senior posts, expecting to spend their working lives in professions that are secure, prestigious and, if not as well paid as in the private sector, reasonably remunerative compared with professions such as university teaching or medicine. Earlier work (Aberbach, Putnam and Rockman, 1981) suggested that British bureaucrats and politicians followed separate and distinctive career paths and had an understanding of their roles that was more clearly distinguished from each other's than in other democracies. In a famous simile, Hugh Heclo and Aaron Wildavsky described Whitehall as a village (Heclo and Wildavsky, 1973). However, rather like pretty English villages where the professional classes are buying up half-timbered cottages, the village contains two very distinctive sets of inhabitants, the bureaucrats and the politicians. To understand British executive politics, one needs to understand the world of the politician, the world of the bureaucrat and the interaction between the two. Each world – and the interaction between the two – is guided by certain principles and expectations that together constitute the Whitehall model. We turn first to the world of the politicians.

Politicians in the Whitehall Model

The famed informality of the British constitution is nowhere more evident than in defining the role of ministers. There is little in

legislation on the role of ministers, and the most detailed guidance available on their duties is a Cabinet Office memorandum
given to new ministers that was kept secret until the 1990s. None
the less, in practice there used to be widespread agreement on the
general outlines of the role of ministers within the Whitehall
model. We may summarize these expectations under the headings
of individual responsibility and collective responsibility.

Individual Responsibility

There was no doubt in the old Whitehall model that the most
senior minister – now generally but not always known as a Secretary of State – was responsible for the policies and actions of
his or her department.

The practicality of this doctrine might seem dubious from the
outset; in addition to the general disadvantages that Weber identified for politicians trying to control a career bureaucracy, British ministers suffered from the additional disabilities of having
been socialized during their careers into the ways of Westminster
(i.e. Parliament) not Whitehall (i.e. executive departments), of
almost always having no substantive background in the work of
their departments and of moving to a new post after, on average,
two and a half years. The theory of the Whitehall model made
the senior minister in each department accountable for its actions
and policies, however. Ministers were assumed to be capable of
establishing guidelines for their departments, ensuring that the
departments followed their policies and ensuring that their officials did not commit egregious abuses or errors in their work. As
recently as 1954, in the Crichel Down affair (discussed in Chapter 7 below), the doctrine that a minister is responsible even for
the conduct of officials of which he or she is unaware was apparently confirmed. Only if an official acted illegally or in direct
contravention of the minister's decision would he or she be identified publicly.

For ministers were the only legitimate representatives of their
departments in public. Only ministers could answer to Parliament for their departments' policies and performance. Civil servants were neither seen nor heard in public in the days before first
the Crossman then the St John Stevas reforms in the late 1960s

and late 1970s respectively made select committees a prominent feature of parliamentary life. Access to civil servants for journalists or academic researchers was sharply restricted. The present Head of the Civil Service, Sir Robin Butler, has probably made more speeches than all his predecessors since the Second World War combined.

Departments were also represented by ministers in the most important negotiations within government. Civil servants might prepare the ground, narrowing areas of disagreement between ministers and their departments. Ultimately, however, the issues between departments, such as conflicts in policy or in competition for scarce resources such as money from the Treasury or time for legislation, would be settled in negotiations between ministers in committees or in the cabinet itself. Not surprisingly, an important determinant of a minister's prestige was said to be his or her success in winning such fights. Indeed, in a sense, the government's major priorities could be said to be determined in such negotiations.

The Centrality of Collective Decision Making

The most important organizing principle of the role of politicians in the Whitehall model was that decision making should be collective. There have of course been many occasions when collective decision making may have fallen by the wayside; the old debate about the relative power of the prime minister and cabinet (Mackintosh, 1977; Crossman, 1972) provides numerous important examples of the cabinet being bypassed, including the decisions to build a British H-bomb, to cooperate with Israel in invading Egypt in 1956, modernizing British submarine-based nuclear weapons in the late 1960s and the direction of economic policy in the 1980s.

Yet the belief that policy should be made collectively has remained embedded in British constitutional thought. The requirement that the Minister of Agriculture be prepared to vote in the House of Commons or speak in the country in favour of the government's defence policy is based in part on the reciprocal belief that he or she should be given the opportunity in cabinet to speak on the topic even though it is not Agriculture's direct responsibility. The British doctrine of collective responsibility contrasts vividly with President Kennedy's puzzled question why anyone should think he would want to hear the views of the Postmaster (then a member of the US cabinet) on foreign policy. British doctrine also contrasts with practice in the coalition governments of continental Europe, where no one would suggest seriously that the cabinet members from the different coalition partners should be equally supportive of different government policies.

The British emphasis on collective decision making reflects in part the requirement that the government stand united in Parliament. British governments are supposedly – we leave aside for now whether this reflects reality – comprised of politicians with independent political positions so that the government can survive only if it remains united. The emphasis on collective responsibility in discussion of the British constitution also reflects the belief that the work of government can be carried out effectively only if the policies and perspectives of different departments are brought together effectively. The Whitehall practice of 'copying' every minute to numerous officials and politicians in numerous departments reflects this emphasis on the importance of coordination. Yet beside these constitutional and practical advantages of collective decision making lies the belief that decisions are better if they are made collectively; Wheare's book, *Government by Committee* (1955) would most likely be imagined by an American to be a blistering attack on the delays and complications inherent in running government by committees – the grandest of which is the cabinet. In fact, Wheare's book was a celebration of government by committee, a setting in which disadvantages of policy proposals could be discovered, and alternatives weighed effectively. Collective decision making has been a goal that the organization of government should attempt to attain as well as (supposedly) a description of British government practice.

What of the relationship between ministers and the prime minister? The theory of the Whitehall model, which we shall have occasion to question, is that the government is led collectively by ministers, not the prime minister. Gladstone doubted whether the prime minister had the right to dismiss cabinet minsters except in cases of gross misconduct. While few prime ministers or even ministers would hold such a view today, several important limitations on the power of the prime minister to direct the government were well established before the 1980s. The first was the expectation that the cabinet would be given the opportunity to discuss major policies before they were announced. The second was that the cabinet should be generally representative of the ruling parliamentary party. The third was that the prime minister should not attempt to reach over a minister's head and make policy within his or her department. Whether or not the prime minister or cabinet took an interest in the work of a department varied. Lord Boyle reported that the only educational issue discussed by the cabinet during his time at the Department of Education and Science was whether to build a road through Christ Church Meadow in Oxford (Kogan, 1971); Roy Jenkins reported that he was left to pursue his own policies in peace as Home Secretary in the 1970s (Jenkins, 1991).

In all events, if either cabinet or prime minister wished to intervene they had to do so through the relevant minister. Though no one doubted that the prime minister was more than first among equals (*primus inter pares*, as it was usually expressed), these constraints on the power of the prime minister were thought by most observers to be sufficient to ensure that leadership remained collective. Odd exceptions did arise, such as Neville Chamberlain's almost single-handed pursuit of appeasement or Anthony Eden's Suez policy, but these departures from the norm scarcely encouraged emulation.

The Centrality of Parliamentary Style

The politicians involved in collective decision making are not just any old politicians, of course. The Whitehall model, unlike the American, has claimed the advantages of an apprenticeship system. Those responsible collectively for government policy are people who have acquired knowledge and experience of government, progressing from the backbenches to the cabinet room, acquiring *en route* not only the political strength independent of the prime minister's that we have noted but also knowledge of Parliament, the workings of government and experience of public policy. If there has been one recurring theme in criticisms of the American presidency by commentators from Whitehall model countries until recently it has been that the presidential selection process and the massive number of political appointments a new president makes places power in the hands of inexperienced amateurs, who, to make matters worse, often have limited experience of working in Washington. In contrast, government in the Whitehall model is in the hands of people who have served a lengthy apprenticeship in Parliament, government and public life more generally and who, in the process have become figures of substance politically so that they are, unlike both White House staff and American department secretaries, not mere creatures of the President.

But what is the experience that ministers acquire in the Whitehall system? It is above all parliamentary experience. It is by making a mark in the House of Commons that ministers escape the back-benches, and it is the reaction of back-benchers to their performance in office that helps determine their prospects for promotion, demotion or dismissal. One of the primary concerns of ministers – as it was when they were back-benchers – is looking good in Parliament. Senior ministers may have served as junior ministers, but how much training that provides for serving as a Secretary of State can be questioned.

If political leaders are equipped primarily with parliamentary experience, are short of executive experience and knowledge of the subjects for which they are responsible, important responsibilities must fall on the permanent bureaucracy. It is to that bureaucracy we now turn.

The Bureaucrats

All modern governments rely on bureaucracies, but the characteristics of the bureaucracies they rely on vary (Suleiman, 1984). It is often supposed in Britain that its professional, career civil service contrasts only with the American system of filling senior posts with political appointees. In fact, the British system differs in important respects from continental European bureaucracies as well. In short, there are a number of characteristics of the British bureaucracy that contribute to the distinctiveness of the Whitehall model. We may summarize them by saying that British bureaucrats at the most senior level constitute a prestigious profession expected to work with equal enthusiasm for any duly constituted government and enjoying a virtual monopoly on advice to it. None of these characteristics are unique to the Whitehall model; it is the combination that is exceptional. All the elements in the Whitehall model need some elaboration.

That the senior civil service in Britain constitutes a profession may seem surprising to some, particularly those who are critical of it. One of the most wounding descriptions of the higher civil service in the critical report of the Fulton Committee (Fulton, 1968) was that it was composed of *amateurs*. By this pejorative term the Committee, echoing earlier criticism made by the economist Thomas Balogh, (1959) meant that the higher civil service was composed of generalist administrators who received little or no technical education, training or experience. British higher civil servants have usually obtained a degree in the humanities and, even in the case of the Philosophy, Politics and Economics (PPE) degree at Oxford, have received an education very different from the American pattern of a liberal arts education followed by specialized graduate training in a subject related to subsequent employment. British practice also contrasts with the French tradition of intensive, specialized education for future senior officials in the *grandes écoles* in the ways in which government works (Suleiman, 1978). Instead, higher civil servants in Britain have obtained degrees – until recently, generally from Oxford or Cambridge – in subjects such as PPE (Philosophy, Politics and Economics), Classics, History. Even once recruited, officials receive little technical training and instead are expected to 'learn on the job'. The amount of knowledge acquired in a post is limited, however, by the practice of moving civil servants regularly; in the late 1960s, the Fulton Committee found that most officials in the highest class of the civil service, the Administrative Class, spent just over three years in a post before being moved again.

Yet in other crucial respects, the higher civil service in Britain has met the criteria for being a profession – a clearly defined, self-governing occupation with restricted entry whose members believe that they are serving an important public purpose. To be an Administrative Class civil servant has been a career option that the best undergraduates from the most prestigious universities have considered along with entering a learned profession such as law or working in financial institutions in the City of London; it is perhaps to Britain's disadvantage that the brightest and best of its undergraduates were more likely to consider the civil service as a career than become executives in manufacturing industry (Weiner, 1981). The higher civil service was a profession, too, in that recruitment and promotion were determined largely by the senior civil service itself. Final selection boards for aspiring civil servants did contain representatives of business, other professions or other non-governmental interests, but the largest part of the selection process was in the hands of current or retired civil servants. Similarly, although the approval of the prime minister had long been required for appointments to the highest ranks of the civil service, in practice even these promotions were determined by other civil servants after a process of informal consultation between them. Ministers and Secretaries of State were expected to work with whomever the system had produced; getting rid of a troublesome permanent secretary was difficult, and there was no guarantee that the replacement would be congenial. After 1968, the process was regularized and a committee was formed of permanent secretaries and the head of the civil service to make recommendations about top-level appointments. Just as in a university a faculty expects to choose a person to hold a prestigious professorship even if the choice has to be formally ratified by the university's Council or Regents, so the senior civil service expected to determine promotion to its highest ranks.

The higher civil service in Britain also has a distinctive professional ethos. Its members feel that they share a common culture; indeed, many higher civil servants cite the feeling of collective, almost collegial life in the service as one of its main attractions (Bridges, 1950). As in all professions, the civil service has evolved its own style, a style that reflects its constitutional position, its work, its educational background and the social class of its members. The exact composition of that style is difficult to define. Many civil servants define the style in terms of a concern for fairness and justice when dealing with the public and honesty and integrity when advising ministers; critics emphasize caution, a tendency to criticize proposals rather than create new ideas and other less desirable features. As Christoph (1993) notes, when British civil servants work in Brussels either for or with the European Union, there is no doubt that their style contrasts with that of bureaucrats from other member states. The emphasis on working by exchanging carefully drafted memoranda, for example, is a characteristic that distinguishes the British civil service from many others.

Interaction with Ministers

The interaction between the two very different groups that make up the British executive, the bureaucrats and the politicians, is the final crucial aspect of the Whitehall model.

One of the most distinctive elements in the Whitehall model is the expectation that civil servants will work with equal enthusiasm in the same posts for successive duly constituted governments of competing parties. The clear expectation of civil servants is that while they have their own opinions on desirable policies, they are prepared to act on behalf of any duly elected government in performing their tasks. As Campbell and Wyszomirski write, 'A neutrally competent public service has earned its title not because it is utterly devoid of political conviction and design. Rather, its legitimacy is based on its relative preparedness to change clients from one party to the other' (Campbell and Wyszomirski, 1991, p. 15). This expectation can produce well-known, apparently perverse situations. The same civil servants who helped draw up plans for the nationalization of the ports for the Labour government worked to reverse those plans for the succeeding Conservative government. The same civil servant who helped a Conservative minister draft replies to parliamentary questions or speeches refuting the criticisms of the Labour Shadow Minister may find after an election that the Shadow Minister is now the minister for whom the civil servant drafts responses to the criticisms of the Conservative opposition.

As these examples indicate, it is quite wrong to think that civil servants are separated from politics. As Richard Rose has noted, the Whitehall model demands not that civil servants be non-political but that they be politically promiscuous (Rose, 1987). Ministers rely on civil servants for assistance in a variety of ways that are quite clearly political. Civil servants not only are expected to help governments develop policies that are in line with its values but are also expected to help the government of the day explain and justify its policies to Parliament. Relatively young 'fast track' civil servants are entrusted with preparing the answers to parliamentary questions that will allow the minister to defuse the criticisms of the opposition; a variety of levels of senior civil servants are involved in drafting speeches for ministers that not merely describe but also justify their policies. During the Thatcher years officials drew up over thirty changes in the definition of unemployment, all of which had the effect of making the government's economic record look better by making the rate of unemployment seem lower.

The final key element of the Whitehall model is that senior civil servants enjoy a virtual monopoly on giving advice to ministers. Of course in a relatively free society a virtual monopoly is not a total monopoly. All sorts of people and institutions give the government of the day advice. Newspaper editorials, the opposition spokesmen and orators at Speakers' Corner give governments advice in public; hundreds of interest groups are in regular close contact with government departments giving advice in private. Senior civil servants and ministers in Britain, unlike their colleagues in Washington, work in a city that is more than a centre of government and interact frequently with members of other elites from business, finance and the prestigious professions. However, much of this advice is mediated through the civil service and it is in the company of senior civil servants that ministers sit down to decide what to do, what advice to take and what advice to reject. Indeed, although (as the public has learned in recent controversies about payments to MPs) interest groups are using backbench MPs on retainers to press their cases on ministers, most interest groups still rely primarily on contacts with officials, not ministers; the officials report to the ministers what the interest groups recommend. It might be said more precisely that the civil service has enjoyed a virtual monopoly on giving to ministers the *final* advice that precedes decision making. When British chancellors of the exchequer in the midst of periodic economic crisis sat down to decide whether to raise or lower taxes and interest rates, the advisers present were civil servants.

The Whitehall model has therefore rested on a very close partnership between politicians and civil servants. It has maintained a clear distinction between the political career and the profession of being a senior civil servant (Aberbach, Putnam and Rockman, 1981). Yet close cooperation day to day, hour to hour between ministers and bureaucrats following two very distinct career paths has been the main feature of the Whitehall model. In no other model, including those models from continental Europe with prestigious career bureaucracies, have the politicians been so dependent on it.

What is the Whitehall Model a Model of?

The phrase 'the Whitehall model' invites a fundamental question: what is it a model of? At first sight, this question is easily answered. The Whitehall model has three purposes. These are to give democratic direction to the machinery of government, to reconcile the differences between the various goals and priorities of government and to solve the problem of the relationship between bureaucrats and politicians identified by Max Weber. Weber had predicted that twentieth-century politics would be dominated by career politicians and bureaucrats but that bureaucrats, with superior knowledge and experience, would tend to dominate the politicians (Weber, in Gerth and Mills (eds), 1958).

The capacity of the Whitehall model to provide for democratic control of the executive is determined primarily by the degree to which the system can achieve the accountability in practice that it promises in theory. Are ministers in practice as well as in theory in control of their departments and their policies? Are ministers in fact held accountable today for the behavior of their officials? There are obvious challenges in achieving democratic accountability in the Whitehall model. Ministers should depend for policy advice, help with parliamentary duties in nearly all staff functions such as drafting speeches and letters, on a career civil service, composed of people selected through a competitive process who cannot be fired or removed for political reasons. The Whitehall model, as we have noted, is highly distinctive in this regard. It contrasts not only with the American practice of having numerous political appointees at the top of each agency, but with the German and Swedish systems of moving bureaucrats in politically sensitive posts after the party in power changes. The Whitehall model is an extreme example of a common problem in democracies, the relation between bureaucrats and politicians. British politicians are dependent to a quite extraordinary degree on permanent bureaucrats not only for policy advice and administrative support but for staff and political assistance.

In his 1918 lectures Weber had identified the two most important trends in the modern state as the increased importance of the professional politician whose career rested on one of the mass parties that dominated modern politics, and the rise of the bureaucracy that provided expertise and administrative capacity without which the modern state could not function (Weber, 1918, in Gerth and Mills (eds), 1958). Though not uncritical of bureaucracy, Weber admired its rational, hierarchical structure; he also identified the fundamental problem in bureaucratic-political relations; politicians with little technical training or expertise would have difficulty in controlling the bureaucracy. In constitutional terms politicians were in command of the bureaucracy but, in practice, they would be unable to tell whether the advice given by the bureaucracy was a neutral assessment of the situation, or whether it was strongly influenced by the bureaucracy's own political preferences. Whether Weber thought that in the end politicians could find means to overcome the advantages of the bureaucracy or whether he believed that the bureaucracy would dominate is a matter of some debate among scholars (Silberman, 1993).

The extreme dependence of British politicians on permanent bureaucrats makes Weber's question (whether politicians could control the bureaucracy or whether they would be dominated by it) central for students of the Whitehall model. Yet, as we shall see in the next chapter, the role of the permanent bureaucracy in the Whitehall model long seemed unproblematic, as British politicians of both main parties found the service provided by what they often termed a 'Rolls Royce' of a civil service entirely satisfactory, even though they had little control over it. Indeed, like many other aspects of the Whitehall and Westminster models, the British exported their model of the bureaucracy to other nations, and American reformers often argued it deserved emulation. By the 1990s, however, the Whitehall model had come under such stress that its survival seemed questionable.

2

Bureaucrats and Politicians in Britain: the Model Breaks

We ended the previous chapter with Weber's argument that an expert bureaucracy will always dominate politicians, who typically, and in Britain most definitely, cannot equal its technical knowledge. Further reflection indicates, however, that the Whitehall model cannot be analysed solely in terms of Weber's construction of the relationship between bureaucrats and politicians. For, whatever description we might settle on for the senior British civil service, it would be extraordinarily inappropriate to describe it as a group of hierarchically organized technical experts. The senior civil service is composed of generalist administrators – often educated in the humanities rather than in the law or social science, moving jobs quite frequently and traditionally emphasizing 'on the job' rather than professional training. There are of course large numbers of highly expert civil servants in Britain in economic and scientific services. But the experts, as the British senior civil servants like to say, are 'on tap not on top'. The failings and virtues of this approach to organizing a senior bureaucracy will be recurring themes in this book. But there can be almost universal agreement that the British bureaucracy does not match the Weberian vision of a rationally organized hierarchy of experts. Nor does the organization of the British civil service constitute a clear hierarchy. The highest ranking civil servants in each Department, the Permanent Secretaries, enjoy considerable autonomy in relation to the Head of the Civil Service (who is usually also the Secretary to the Cabinet). As with the relations between cabinet ministers, so relations between very senior civil servants are closer to equality than to hierarchy. Much the same is true of relations between the highest ranking officials within a single department.

If the British senior civil service is not a rational Weberian hierarchy of experts, what is it? What purpose does it serve? These fundamental questions that the Fulton Committee neither asked nor was required to ask in its highly influential study of the civil service are fundamental to understanding the character of the higher civil service, and deciding whether it fulfils the functions expected of it. Yet there are no generally accepted answers to these questions, and indeed the variety of jobs that have existed within the senior civil service make it unlikely that a single answer can be provided.

On the rare occasions that British politicians and ministers are forced to overcome their distaste for the activity and engage in constitutional thought, the purpose of the civil servants is said to be to assist ministers. This is the phrase used by the then Head of the Civil Service, Sir Robert Armstrong, in a memorandum circulated to all officials in the aftermath of a political crisis, the Westland Affair, which turned in part on whether civil servants had been used to engage too directly in political manoeuvring. Civil servants were servants of the Crown; the Crown was represented for all practical purposes by ministers. Civil servants should therefore do what ministers asked them to do, subject only to the right to complain to superiors if they felt they were being asked to act wrongly (Armstrong, 1986). Yet the shallowness of constitutional thinking in contemporary Britain is nowhere more evident than in Armstrong's reiteration that civil servants exist to assist ministers. What kind of assistance should civil servants provide ministers? For that matter, what kind of assistance should they *not* provide ministers?

The first type of assistance that civil servants provide ministers is obviously and highly political. Civil servants, as we have seen, draft parliamentary speeches and replies to parliamentary questions that will show their ministers in the best possible light. The achievements of the government are emphasized, setbacks minimized and the weaknesses of the opposition's policies pounced on eagerly. The Scott Inquiry into Britain's supply of arms to Iraq heard that civil servants regularly construct replies to Parliamentary questions that, though strictly accurate, mislead by omitting any information to the government's disadvantage. Civil servants also play a major role when dealing with interest groups. It is usually civil servants who meet representatives of interest groups and assess the chances that they will endorse or oppose the government's policies.

The second type of assistance that civil servants provide is policy analysis and advice. Some years ago *The Times* opined that the relations between bureaucrats and politicians in Britain was entirely clear and satisfactory. 'Civil servants propose. Ministers decide. Civil servants execute.' (*The Times*, 15 February 1977.) As this formulation realistically states, many ministers do not come into office with specific policy proposals in mind. One of the jobs of the civil servants is to provide them. Of course, as civil servants emphasize, the potential policies provided must be consistent with the basic approach of the government; there would have been no point suggesting nationalization of industries to the Thatcher Government (though the previous Conservative Government, under Heath, was adept at nationalizing). Still, the civil service enjoys the opportunity to set the agenda by proposing specific ideas that ministers might adopt. One important characteristic of modern British politics makes this opportunity all the more important. Whereas *governments* in Britain are relatively stable so that they stay in office much longer than in, for example, Italy, individual *ministers* keep their jobs for astonishingly brief periods, on average about two and a half years. Whereas an Italian minister might hold office for many years while serving under different Prime Ministers, British ministers keep their jobs briefly, while Prime Ministers serve lengthier terms than Italian counterparts. In consequence, British ministers have little experience or knowledge of the policy areas for which they are responsible.

When ministers have policy proposals of their own – which has happened, particularly during the Thatcher years – the role of the civil service in the traditional Whitehall model is not merely to plan how to implement them but also to analyse their strengths and weaknesses. Ministers often think they favour a policy; once they realize its consequences, they do not. A major task for the civil service is to make sure that ministers realize the disadvantages of policies before they are heavily committed to them. Ministers need to be talked out of impracticable plans with which they have become infatuated during weekends in their constituencies. Yet fulfilling this task requires skill. Too little determination in emphasizing the difficulties of ministers' favourite but unworkable projects may mean those ministers will stumble into disaster; too much determination shades into obstructionism, which ministers may believe reflects a political hostility to their policies. Sometimes the system fails, perhaps because of the obstinacy of the politicians involved; it is scarcely likely that the Conservative Government would have pressed ahead with the Community Charge (Poll Tax), which contributed significantly to Thatcher's fall, had the Prime Minister and her Cabinet appreciated fully the consequences of their proposals.

Civil servants pull together a variety of material in providing policy options and evaluating any policy ideas that ministers suggest. Economic analyses, estimates of administrative feasibility, scientific advice, cost estimates, a host of technical considerations and estimates of political consequences are combined in recommendations and options for ministers. The genius of the good senior civil servant lies in being able to consolidate not only a vast amount of information but also a vast variety of information. The argument for generalist administrators is that they are able to combine a wide variety of analyses and expert advice, any one of which alone is inadequate for reaching a full decision.

The last form of assistance that civil servants provide is to run existing, often non-controversial policies, of which ministers may be almost totally unaware. Civil servants are inevitably decision makers; it was Margaret Thatcher, renowned for her ability to work through massive quantities of memoranda, who emphasized to the Scott Inquiry the sheer impossibility of ministers' reading every document put in front of them, of their working through the 'snowstorm' of paper (the *Independent*, 9 December 1993). One of the tasks of the civil servant is to make decisions that ministers would make if they had the time to do so. It is in this context that civil servants have been expected to fulfil a different role, to be managers, running prisons or organizing the smooth delivery of pensions, drivers' licenses and passports in the most efficient way. Although a few ministers take a temporary interest in such administrative work, it is generally only when something goes wrong and a political storm threatens that most ministers can be persuaded to take an interest in such continuing and dull, if important work.

The Whitehall model is not therefore solely a model of how to resolve relations between politicians and a hierarchical, rational and expert bureaucracy responsible for administration; it is also a model of how to provide politicians with what in the United States might be termed staff support. Not surprisingly, the civil servants we interviewed thought of their work as 'most definitely' political in character. The relationship between the very senior bureaucracy and ministers in Britain should not be compared to a Weberian hierarchy of experts but to the relationship between the president and the White House staff in the United States. In consequence, evaluation of the Whitehall model must proceed in terms not only of administrative efficiency but also of the needs of politicians to obtain policy ideas, advice and evaluation.

Explaining the Whitehall Model

Readers familiar with systems in other countries that link bureaucrats to politicians will probably by now be somewhat puzzled about why the Whitehall model exists at all. It is not a model that conforms with any model of decision making, advising or administration; no one asked to design a system of support for senior politicians would produce the Whitehall model. It is a system in which people recruited to give policy advice have been expected to manage large agencies, and, most strangely of all, is one in which the people who give ministers highly political assistance come from the ranks of a career civil service over whose personnel decisions the politicians traditionally have had little control.

The truth is of course that no one did design the Whitehall model. The Whitehall model was shaped by the history of the British state, not by abstract principles. At no point, not even in the aftermath of the Northcote-Trevelyan report in the mid-nineteenth century that is rightly seen as the foundation of the modern civil service, was the civil service subjected to immediate and thoroughgoing reform; Northcote-Trevelyan recommendations were adopted, as Peter Hennessy rightly emphasizes, over an extended period, not being fully implemented until after the First World War (Hennessy, 1989).

Several important features of the history of the British state have shaped the Whitehall model. For the style and traditions of the civil service existed before the modern state took on its current form.

As is often noted, the range and scale of duties of nineteenth-century government were much narrower than today's. Most of the responsibilities that preoccupy modern government were not seen as the government's business in the nineteenth century. The nineteenth-century British state was in domestic policy primarily a regulatory state, which avoided even more than its contemporaries in other lands extensive involvement in social, economic and industrial problems. Britain is one of the very few countries in the world that has a concert hall named after an economic doctrine (the Free Trade Hall in Manchester). The triumph of free trade, *laissez faire* economics in Britain predated the creation of the modern civil service and helped limit the expectations of it. The civil service – and its traditions – were created in the service of a non-interventionist state.

As British governments accepted wider responsibilities, they generally did so with an administrative framework that kept them at one stage removed from responsibility for implementation. British administration has a habit of transferring responsibility for implementation to someone else. No system of *intendants* on the French model had been created in Britain; prior to the nineteenth century such local administration as existed was carried out by local gentry, the Justices of the Peace. One of the features of British colonial policy was to rule if possible through local power figures such as the native princes of the Indian empire. As domestic responsibilities expanded, central government continued to look for 'local princes' to whom responsibility for implementing policies could be delegated. Local government often filled the bill. In education, for example, while central government largely paid the bill, it had little direct control over what or how children were taught until the great centralization of power by the Thatcher Government changed the situation totally. Similarly, the provision of public housing, roads and their maintenance and the enforcement of many forms of regulation (such as hygiene regulations) were devolved upon local governments even though central government established a policy framework and provided the necessary finance.

The habit of avoiding direct involvement in administration prompted British governments to rely also on a variety of non-governmental organizations. Surface sea rescue, in the United States part of the mission of the coast guard, in Britain has been provided by a private, voluntary organization, the Royal National Lifeboat Institution (RNLI). The care of animals and children has been watched over by the Royal Society for the Protection of Animals (RSPCA) and (perhaps significantly less grandly titled) the National Society for the Prevention of Cruelty to Children (NSPCC) respectively. Both organizations maintain inspectorates that could as easily be operated by central government. During the high point of the government's involvement in farming during and immediately after the Second World War, the draconian powers that it enjoyed were wielded in large part by the local officers of the National Farmers' Union (Self and Storing, 1962; Wilson, 1977). Britain has had a smoothly functioning arrangement for making policy on safety and health at work largely because successive governments have devolved the responsibility to a Health and Safety Commission (HSC), which is dominated by the employers' Confederation of British Industry (CBI) and the Trades Union Congress (TUC) (Wilson, 1985). Although several central government inspectorates do exist, such as Her Majesty's Factory Inspectors and Her Majesty's Inspectors of Schools, the British style of regulation has emphasized cooperation with those inspected in stark contrast to the more adversarial American approach.

Perhaps the ultimate example of the preference of British central government for keeping a distance from detailed involvement was the early, deep and lasting attachment to Keynesian economics. The Keynesian approach, based on the belief that government could help the economy best by manipulating aggregates such as taxation and total government spending, contrasted vividly with the French and Japanese stress on the advantages of close government involvement in addressing the problems and goals of specific industries through indicative planning. As Hall has described, British government focused on policies that were intended to control the total level of economic activity, avoiding the development of policies for specific industries such as chemicals, automobile manufacture or electronics that would require detailed central government involvement at the grass roots in contradiction of the traditions of British administration (Hall, 1986). The attempts of both Conservative and Labour governments in the 1960s and 1970s to intervene more directly in industry in order to promote efficiency were handicapped by a lack of appropriate state capacity; British government, in contrast to French and Japanese, had not acquired the apparatus or even the skills in the bureaucracy required for the task. In the higher civil service only officials in the Ministry of Defence had much experience of working in partnership with industry on detailed practical problems. In this respect if in no other the higher civil service viewed with some relief the move away from interventionism in the Thatcher years.

Thus the traditions of the British state were to discourage the direct involvement of central government agencies in the provision of goods and services. Naturally there were some exceptions to this generalization. The Ministry of Defence was much more closely involved in high technology industry for weapons procurement than this generalization would suggest. Many welfare state payments such as pensions and unemployment pay are not routed through local government but are paid more or less directly to the citizen. However, such examples are too recent in origin and too limited to contradict the generalization that there is a preference for indirect rule in British governance.

Indirect rule and direct administration require very different bureaucracies. In particular, indirect governance emphasizes policy development and monitoring rather than actual administration. It favours the generalist administrator who helps plan what we are trying to do rather than the practical administrator or expert who is charged with making things happen.

If the administrative style of the British state has been indirect, the lines of political accountability have not. As is well known, thanks to the constitutional doctrine of Parliamentary supremacy and political realities of disciplined political parties and the 'first past the post' electoral system, British governments are institutionally free to do what they wish. External economic pressures may block a government's programme, but courts and the legislature are unlikely to. Ministers in consequence have no institutional hiding place from policy problems in their areas. The British government minister faces constant pressures to explain and defend policy choices. These pressures in turn mean that ministers, relatively inexperienced in their departments' policy areas, need to generate politically defensible answers to the policy problems they confront. British ministers face a constant political imperative and the help they need is necessarily political in character.

However often British ministers have expressed admiration for bureaucracies that are more 'expert' in character at their highest levels, in practice they demand and get the help of politically sensitive generalists who can help them generate politically advantageous (or at least not damaging) policy ideas.

The higher civil servant in Britain has therefore worked in a situation where the need for highly technical ability has been relatively low and the demand for politically attuned advice high and frequent. It is this situation, not (as British critics have supposed) the background or education of higher civil servants, that has shaped the Whitehall model. Generalist administrators with degrees in classics, philosophy, politics and economics (the ultimate jack-of-all-trades-master-of-none degree) or history have suited the needs of the system better than engineers or economists. The proof of this, and the ultimate reason for the persistence of the Whitehall model, is that most British ministers have liked the service the Whitehall model has given them. Politicians used to a system such as the American in which a newly elected administration can purge the bureaucracy of senior officials with uncongenial views may wonder how their British counterparts are able to work with a bureaucracy they are almost powerless to change. British politicians believed that they secured several advantages from the Whitehall model.

First, the Whitehall model provided an answer to the problem of how to find people who could 'speak truth to power'. A perennial problem for systems in which political appointees provide policy advice is how to obtain blunt advice that a politician's favourite policy is not working and needs to be abandoned or changed. British civil servants, with their security of tenure, are better able to 'speak truth to power' than political appointees with no security of tenure, who may fear losing status, proximity to power or even their jobs if they are too critical. Sir Alec Douglas-Home, for example, praised the civil service in his memoirs not only because it 'advises the politician how the law can best be put into shape, so that it can pass the scrutiny of Parliament, and will work in practice when it becomes the law of the land' but also because 'The good civil servant, too, will provide his minister with the pros and cons in any situation, and, if he is to earn respect, will not modify a view he feels to be right until he is overruled by his minister.' (Douglas-Home, 1976.)

Second, the existence of a permanent Whitehall machine enabled politicians to move swiftly to implement their campaign promises after winning power. The problem of the transition during which a new administration is constructed, which is so acute in the United States, could be avoided in Britain. The permanent civil service machine would be ready to turn the victorious party's programme into policy as soon as the election was over. Harold Wilson, not always an admirer of higher civil servants, valued the speed with which the civil service could advance his policies after the 1964 election: '. . . the civil service is . . . as sharp as any other body of men in recognizing political realities. They had read the election manifesto and the first draft of the Queen's Speech was ready within days' (Wilson, 1971, p. 20). Wilson echoed here the satisfaction of the Attlee Government, arguably Britain's greatest radical government this century, with the permanent civil service. As Kenneth Morgan notes, the left wing of the Labour Party had long feared that the higher bureaucracy would obstruct the work of a Labour government. But in practice 'evidence of civil service obstruction to the activities and policies of the Labour government is very hard to uncover'. Indeed, ministers received crucial assistance from the civil service hierarchy. Aneurin Bevan 'found his Permanent Under Secretary, Sir William Rucker, to be an invaluable ally in framing and forcing through the national Health Service in 1946 . . . the civil service expertise and practical knowledge afforded by experienced operators such as Bridges and Brook were vital in seeing the government through many desperate crises . . .' (Morgan, 1984, p. 88).

Third, with the exception of some but not all leaders of the far left of the Labour Party, British politicians have been confident in their ability to impose their policies and priorities on the permanent civil service. Ministers thought that they could take control of their Departments; civil servants would not in practice cause more than minor, temporary annoyance when blocking their policies. Even the Home Office, accused by critics of being a nest of reactionaries, has its defenders, who argued that it is responsive to its ministers' values. James Callaghan argued that he was soon able to shape his officials' approach at the Home Office: '. . . it is a Department where the social attitudes of its ministers can have an effect on policy more surely and more quickly than in many other Departments.' (Callaghan, 1987, p. 278). It should be noted, however, that according to his critics, Callaghan was always more likely to agree with his officials than his predecessor Roy Jenkins, precisely because he was less liberal.

Complaints about the civil service from ministers before Thatcher are not difficult to find either, and not just from critics of Whitehall such as the politician and scholar Richard Crossman. Harold Macmillan complained that once the extraordinary circumstances of the Second World War were over, 'The "Trade Union" of officials is back in power . . . Ministers are treated politely but with firmness as temporary nuisances.' (Macmillan, 1969, p. 397.) However, such grumbling was usually followed by tributes to what most politicians as well as officials considered to be the best bureaucracy in the world. Thus 163 pages later Macmillan paid tribute to the loyalty of his civil servants. 'All through the ranks of the Ministry and among the regional officers there grew up during these years a sense of comradeship and even enthusiasm. . . . I was indeed fortunate both in the appointed task and in my fellow labourers.' (Macmillan, 1969, p. 460.)

Politicians' general satisfaction with the Whitehall model before the 1980s is also manifest in our interviews, except with some but not all followers of the left wing Labour leader, Tony Benn. We shall return to this topic later. It suffices to note here that the British senior civil servants are acutely aware of how tenuous is their power constitutionally. The civil service will indeed endure as long as British government. But whether or not it can retain the close proximity to decision making and the effective monopoly on policy advising that the Whitehall model gives them depends in the long run on giving ministers the service they want. For example, had British governments felt that they were denied sufficient policy advice, without changing institutions or the constitution the influence of the senior civil service could have been reduced drastically by appointing more policy advisers and working with think tanks. The extraordinary opportunities given to the British civil service to influence policy decisions in the Whitehall model are conditional on not provoking the politicians sufficiently into changing the system. As we shall see, this possibility came close to reality in the Thatcher years.

In the remainder of this chapter we shall suggest that the Whitehall model of political–bureaucratic relations has been subjected to such intense pressures that it is a matter for debate whether it has survived or not. Yet if we are to say whether or not a model has ceased to exist, we need to specify the conditions to be fulfilled for its demise or continued existence. In the case of the relations between bureaucrats and politicians within the Whitehall model, there are four crucial conditions.

The first is whether the career civil service is able to sustain that belief we noted earlier among politicians that it is indeed a neutrally competent service willing to adopt as its client whichever party or parties constitute a duly elected government. To the degree that ministers cease to believe they can work through and with the civil service and turn instead to political advisers, policy units and non-governmental units such as think tanks for help or advice, they are moving away from the Whitehall model.

A second crucial test for the continuance of the Whitehall model is that the civil service maintains its professional integrity. A number of proposed changes in the civil service threatened to undermine this professional integrity. It was incompatible with the Whitehall model that senior jobs be awarded to political appointees from outside the civil service or even to civil servants on the basis of their political beliefs. As we shall see, there was indeed much discussion of whether there had been 'politicization' of the civil service under Thatcher. The Major Government's white paper *The Civil Service, Continuity and Change* (Command 2627) suggested that all senior civil servants should be placed on individual contracts, raising the prospect that assignments and even employment in the civil service could come to depend on the goodwill of the government of the day.

A third condition for the maintenance of the Whitehall model of bureaucratic political relations is that the politicians continue to accord civil servants a near monopoly on providing policy analysis and advice. Were British politicians to start to rely on outside advisers, political appointees or a *cabinet* of personally selected advisers, the bureaucratic–political relations would have changed fundamentally.

A fourth condition for the continued existence of the Whitehall model is that the lines of accountability be maintained. Ministers accept that they, not individual civil servants, are accountable politically; civil servants in return accept that they have no legitimate basis for making decisions that are not in accord with the policy views of their ministers. This aspect of the Whitehall model is threatened both by ministers who refuse to accept responsibility for their departments' actions and by civil servants acting independently of their ministers' policy wishes. At the heart of the Whitehall model is a bargain between bureaucrats and politicians which serves both their interests. Bureaucrats will never divulge publicly advice they gave ministers, which would make it easier for the opposition to criticize ministers because it would know what the options before ministers were; while politicians will take responsibility for policies that go wrong, protecting civil servants from public criticism or obloquy.

The British political system generally changes slowly and undramatically. Relations between institutions and between the people in institutions change more than the institutions themselves. Changes in what politicians and civil servants consider to be their appropriate roles are the key to understanding changes in the Whitehall model. For, like other staffing systems such as the Executive Office of the President, it is defined more by how people relate to each other on a daily basis than by laws or formal rules. The marriage of permanent bureaucracy and politics that the Whitehall model creates can change its meaning without changing its legal forms. If we look for evidence that the Whitehall model has changed, we shall find it as much in the day-to-day relations between ministers and civil servants as in formal institutional changes. Much of this book relies therefore on interviews with senior officials and politicians. Before that, however, we examine the criticism of the Whitehall model that developed from the late 1950s onwards, and then the degree to which the principal components of the Whitehall model were shattered.

Rising Difficulties

Is it only a few decades since the British displayed a confidence approaching arrogance about their political institutions? It might have been a characteristic of nineteenth-century rather than twentieth-century Britons to believe that their entire constitution, including the House of Lords, was one of the most perfect in the world. Confidence in what Bagehot would have called the effective parts of the constitution survived until the late twentieth century, however. Whatever the imperfections of the concept, research on the 'civic culture' in Britain showed considerable trust in the political system until the 1970s (Almond and Verba, 1965) when, as Kavanagh has shown, that trust declined significantly (Kavanagh, 1980).

The Whitehall model of bureaucratic–political relations has shared in the general decline in confidence in British political institutions. The trust and confidence that politicians and the public placed in the Whitehall model has declined under the pressure of sustained criticism. The frequency with which, as we saw, British politicians proclaimed that the country had the best civil service in the world, a veritable Rolls Royce of a bureaucracy, has declined, giving way to a consensus that whatever the virtues of the Whitehall model it is now at least partially outmoded.

There has always been criticism of the civil service. In the 1950s and early 1960s, what was then the BBC Home Service carried a series 'The Men from the Ministry', which satirized the civil service. The programme's humour was fairly unsophisticated, however, and its caricatures of civil servants as lazy, tea-swilling bumblers were never taken seriously. The 1980s BBC TV satire on Whitehall 'Yes, Minister' was both less hostile and more serious in that it developed humorously suspicions of the excessive power of the civil service that, as we shall see, were indeed influential in politics. Fifteen years of extensive government controls in wartime and recovery fostered fears that the bureaucracy would rule both inefficiently and unfairly over citizens. One of the reasons why the convoluted Crichel Down affair (discussed in Chapter 7 below) had such significance was that it defined the doctrine of ministerial responsibility; it had an altogether disproportionate impact on public opinion because it came to epitomize the dangers to individual liberty of an overbearing administrative state. Yet not until the late 1950s, after the 'bonfire of controls' of the Conservative governments had shrunk the power of central government, did the drum beat of informed criticism of the civil service become audible to all.

As we saw above, politicians in the past, including one of Britain's few radical governments, the 1945–51 Attlee Government, seemed entirely satisfied with the Whitehall model. Yet by the 1980s bipartisan support existed for a crucial change in the Whitehall system, the Next Steps programme, and even very senior civil servants embraced a radical recasting of their profession. Why had sufficient criticism of the Whitehall model arisen to secure major changes in a Whitehall model that had seemed to enjoy such approval?

It is easy to assume that in many areas of British life Thatcherism is responsible, for better or for worse, for the enormous changes that are taking place in British society. Given Thatcher's hostility to the civil service as an institution (discussed below), it is certainly easy to assume that the problems of the civil service are consequences of Thatcherism. Long before the Thatcher years, however, there were grounds for concern about whether the Whitehall model provided an adequate model of bureaucratic–political relations.

We would argue that many of the problems of the Whitehall model result from the structural difficulty of trying to graft radically different functions onto a bureaucracy developed for other purposes as the character of the British state itself changed. The Fulton Committee (Fulton, 1968) had argued that the civil service had retained the character it had acquired following the Northcote-Trevelyan Report of 1854, when the extent and scale of administrative responsibilities were much smaller, requiring little in the way of managerial skill. Fulton, without considering how to combine managerial skills with traditional civil service roles, suggested the need for change. In the modern era, responsibility for administrative efficiency and providing policy analysis or advice have imposed conflicting needs on the British civil service. The British civil service, shaped in the nineteenth century to supply ministers with assistance such as advice in the preparation and presentation of policy to Parliament, has been obliged by the development and expansion of the domestic role of the state in the twentieth century to implement and administer a vast government apparatus charged with tasks such as paying retirement pensions and social security, and running Europe's largest employer, the National Health Service. The challenge to the Whitehall model has not been that those who operate it have to give advice on technological or economic issues. Civil servants have always had to give advice on very complicated subjects and the justification for a career civil service composed of generalists rather than specialists is that they can organize the collation of advice from many different perspectives – economic, legal, scientific and political – for politicians who themselves are not capable of absorbing highly technical information. The problem is more that the same people need also to meet the requirements of complex management structures. The skills required to organize, motivate and in general manage people in vast government organizations such as the Department of Social Security are by no means the same as those required to provide policy guidance to ministers about the options open to them. Yet the tradition in the higher civil service in Britain has been to require the same people to do both jobs.

Most of the criticisms of the civil service focused not so much on the problems of grafting new and very different responsibilities onto an old bureaucratic structure as on the characteristics and backgrounds of civil servants themselves. For criticisms of the civil service were in practice often inconsistent; indeed had any one set of reforms been acted upon they would have worsened rather than helped the situation from the viewpoint of other critics of the civil service. Unfavourable comparisons between the British higher civil service and the French (or later Japanese), for example, implied that the bureaucracy should play a leadership role that would scarcely have been welcome to those who thought that the civil service was already too influential. We therefore distinguish several different lines of criticism.

Amateurism

One line of attack on the civil service focused on what the Fulton Committee was to call its 'amateurism'. Amateurism in turn rolled together several different criticisms of the civil service. For some critics, the proof of the amateurism of the civil service lay in its background. What professional guidance could senior administrators give to the management of a modern state if their undergraduate degrees were in classics or history at Oxford or Cambridge? Perhaps such an educational background might be forgivable if it were followed by training in an American-style graduate school, in a subject such as economics. It was not. Nor did the civil service itself provide an in-house training course for its recruits until the late 1960s. Even in the 1980s, a Permanent Secretary of unusual distinction could recall only three days of formal training in his entire career (Part, 1990). Rather British civil servants exalted a tradition of learning on the job. As the limited number of senior civil servants such as Bridges (1950), Dale (1941) and Sisson (1966) who wrote books about their profession approvingly described, the British administrative tradition disparaged training. True skill and knowledge was acquired by doing, not by studying.

The civil service tradition of learning by doing reflected broader strands in British culture. For the British upper classes even an undergraduate degree was desirable but not essential. British lawyers, unlike their American counterparts, did not train in postgraduate law schools at universities but as clerks or 'pupils' working with established lawyers. An intense commitment to the mastery of a skill has not been highly regarded in upper-class British culture. A now notorious annual cricket match staged at Lords until the 1970s pitted amateur against professional players; the two sides were known as Gentlemen and Players, as though the amateurs were not players, and, more significantly for our purposes, one who made a career out of cricket could not be a gentleman.

No doubt apprenticeship and experience can be as effective as professors in inculcating practical skills. Whether learning by doing is any worse a preparation for a senior post in, for example, the Treasury than a training in economics at a top graduate school may be doubted; economic theories taught in such departments are never universally accepted and are usually discredited rapidly. A British civil servant steeped in the Keynesian approach that dominated British university economics departments until the 1980s would not have been equipped to operate the monetarist policies that Labour and Conservative governments favoured after 1976. None the less, learning by doing is a difficult practice to defend in the modern world and certainly contains dangers of its own. As Keynes himself wrote, the practical person who thinks he or she is voicing mere common sense is usually unconsciously quoting a long-dead writer.

The tradition of learning by doing might also have carried greater authority had it provided for rather more – or at least lengthier – doing than the British civil service in practice supplied. A bureaucrat who remains in place for decades may indeed acquire practical knowledge that is not easily taught. In practice,

however, as the Fulton Committee emphasized, the British civil
service moved its personnel frequently from one post to another
both within departments and even among them. High fliers might
start their careers in the Treasury, but a career in a spending
department might be followed by a transfer back to the Treasury
before the full glory of a permanent secretaryship in a spending
department was achieved.

It is again easy to advance arguments in favour of this practice.
Rapid movements of administrators between posts balanced
the habit of successive British prime ministers of changing the
politicians in command of departments with bewildering speed.
Had civil servants remained in the same posts for longer, the
imbalance between their knowledge and influence and that of
transient ministers with little or no prior knowledge of their
ministries' responsibilities would have been greater. As Heclo and
Wildavsky emphasized (1973), British administrative tradition
has created an atmosphere comparable to a village (or at least a
fictional village such as Robert Blythe's *Akenfield*) (Blythe, 1969).
Important traditions of honesty and moderation in interdepartmental negotiations handled by officials are fostered by the fact
that the officials involved might be trading places in the relatively
near future; the official defending Transport's budget against the
Treasury today might be in charge of cutting it in the Treasury
tomorrow. American administrators, who do tend to spend their
entire careers within single units, are often accused of having
tunnel vision in consequence. Frequent moves within the civil
service help broaden administrators' outlooks.

British civil servants reject the argument that they are amateurs
on the grounds that they are professionals in government procedures. Their professionalism is not based on knowledge of
specific or detailed issues but on knowledge of how to work the
government machine and the skill to condense complex issues
into a form that can be understood by ministers with little background or training in the policy areas for which they are responsible. British bureaucrats see the Whitehall model not as an
independent variable shaping British government, but as a dependent variable shaped itself by the demands of ministers.
Frequent moves between posts or even departments enhance
professional skills by giving the senior civil servant a wider experience and appreciation of how issues are seen and handled in
different parts of the government.

Yet the practice of frequent career moves and the lack of formal training did indeed together leave the British senior civil service open to the charge of amateurism. It is one thing to defend the virtues of learning on the job as a form of training if that job, and therefore the learning, last for decades. It is another thing to defend learning on the job if the job lasts for months. The rapidity with which civil servants were moved between posts inevitably raised major questions about the degree to which they acquired practical information that compensated for their lack of formal training. For critics of the civil service such as Balogh (1959, pp. 99–100), the result was that ministers were dependent on advice from 'dilettantes' who lacked the skills and knowledge to give useful advice. Britain's decline was explained to a significant degree by this.

'The impact of the war and the revolutionary changes in international and economic relations all demand increased strength for increased effort. The fact is that in internal administration, and policy and external relations, Ministers of both parties had no chance of mastering the growing troubles as they were at best not supplied with all the facts and at worst supplied with misleading appreciations.'

In economic policy, for example, the Treasury civil servants 'reared on mathematics at Cambridge or Greats at Oxford, have only a limited outlet. . . . they can express themselves by transferring decisions from the realm of economic realities into the sphere of pseudo-moral philosophy' (p. 111).

Social Class

It is a characteristic of political debate in Britain that nearly all issues are thought to involve social class. The debate over the role of the civil service in the Whitehall model was no exception. One reason why the criticisms of the civil service carried emotional force was that the civil service 'amateurs' were accused of being disproportionately from the upper classes. The civil service recruited most of its intake from Oxford and Cambridge until the 1980s when the proportion of the intake from Oxbridge dipped below 50 per cent for the first time. It was unclear even then whether the decline in the proportion of high fliers recruited from Oxford and Cambridge in the 1980s was due to the efforts of the Civil Service Commission to expand the range of the universities from which civil servants were recruited or to the greater attractiveness of jobs in financial institutions during the frenetic boom of the late 1980s and the disdain for public service the Thatcher Government encouraged. None the less, even in the late 1980s, the percentage of civil servants recruited from Oxbridge was wildly disproportionate to the percentage of all university graduates who come from those institutions. Oxbridge therefore dominated civil service recruitment throughout this period. A senior civil servant we interviewed recalled that it was thought so exceptional and exciting that someone from his university, Newcastle, would be accepted for the high flier administrative group that he felt an obligation to accept a post when it was offered to him. Oxford and Cambridge in turn took a disproportionate share of their entry from fee-paying schools rather than from the state system. Thus the apparent bias of the civil service toward Oxbridge and Oxbridge's apparent bias toward fee-paying schools produced an administrative elite that was highly unrepresentative socially.

No one involved in this process believed that he or she was operating a biased system. Oxbridge admissions tutors often believe that they are operating a system of mild affirmative action in favour of applicants from state schools by taking slightly less qualified candidates from state schools in preference to applicants from private schools. The civil service selection process that starts with a series of anonymized tests and ends with an interview is thought by those involved to be a genuine, neutral test of ability. Private sector employers who recruit a large number of graduates have looked on the civil service selection procedures as a model from which they can learn much. The civil service has therefore defended its selection procedures as a neutral, fair test of ability. If Oxbridge applicants fare best, that is simply because Oxbridge attracts the ablest students and devotes more effort to undergraduates' education than any of the other British universities. Moreover, the typical administrative group recruit who has attended a fee-paying school prior to Oxbridge is not upper class in background but rather professional class; his (now her) father is more likely to be a successful lawyer than to have inherited wealth. Critics reply that no examination system is neutral. The civil service selection system is bound to favour Oxbridge students in its early stages because Oxbridge students are required to write essays more regularly than other British (let alone American!) students and because in its final interview stages the system favours Oxbridge applicants because of their greater poise and confidence.

Like most educational controversies, arguments about Oxbridge and civil service selection processes are in the end irresolvable. More important for our purposes than the argument itself is the belief that British civil servants were amateurs was reinforced with the belief that they were drawn from privileged backgrounds. The French higher bureaucracy is not at all socially representative either. However, the rigorous training provided in *grandes écoles* before admission into the French civil service insulates senior bureaucrats from allegations that they are amateurs; rather they are seen as an embodiment of the republican virtue of a career open to talents. The French higher bureaucracy is not in fact composed of experts in particular subjects or problems; it has, however, a technocratic image that the British senior civil service lacks. The combination of a meritocratic selection system and the intensive training of the grandes écoles has spared the French bureaucracy the criticism of being composed of superannuated gentlemen rather than skilled professionals (Suleiman, 1978; Armstrong, 1973).

Managerialism

Balogh's attack on the dilettantes of the higher civil service focused on their alleged inability to provide useful policy analysis and advice. A further attack on the senior civil service was based on complaints that it neglected managerial tasks and skills. The latter might at first sight seem puzzling. British central government, as Rose has emphasized, has a fondness for delegating practical tasks to others. Important spending programmes such as education have been administered on behalf of central government by local authorities with, until the great centralization of government during the Thatcher years, little interference from the Department of Education and Science. Whoever runs the National Health Service (a puzzle in an enigma), it has not been the

Department of Health. The maintenance of major highways has been subcontracted to County Councils. Public housing has been administered or maladministered by city councils. Britain's nationalized industries were administered not by their 'sponsor' departments but by boards appointed by the relevant ministers. Thus much of the growth of government in Britain meant that ministers needed help to monitor developments in their areas of responsibility and to formulate policy, rather than to manage resources directly.

What, then, has been administered directly by central government that it should require managerial skills from the civil service? In fact, several major and minor spending programmes are administered directly by central government. Britain maintained relatively high defence expenditures throughout the Cold War. In consequence, the government operated large armed forces and placed massive contracts for equipment to supply them. Central government also operated two main welfare programmes directly, social security (the British equivalent of the American welfare system) and payments and advice for the unemployed. The administration of the national insurance (social security) system requires a huge bureaucracy; the administrative centre at Newcastle upon Tyne was described graphically by one official as 'the sort of outfit where the stationary gets moved around on fork lift trucks'. The collection of VAT (Value Added Tax) also requires a considerable administrative effort. In addition to these major programmes were many much smaller ones – Vehicle and Driver Licensing, the Forestry Commission, agricultural subsidy and advisory services, prisons and the courts. Together these services employed a sufficiently large number of people and accounted for a sufficiently high level of expenditure to make managerial skills necessary.

The need for managerial skills created problems for the senior civil service. Many senior civil servants had chosen the service for a career almost to *avoid* management. Almost none of the civil servants we interviewed had been attracted to the civil service by a wish to be managers; almost all saw the higher civil service as a way to pursue an almost academic interest in policy or government. The attraction of the senior civil service was closer to that of academic life or the learned professions than to the attractions of business management, which nearly all the civil servants we interviewed had rejected as a career. When we asked senior civil servants what they would miss most if they left the civil service, nearly all mentioned the intellectual challenge of their work, a challenge that they believed would be absent in private sector management, and the collegiality of the service. A remarkable number said they would like to have been – and could have been – academics if they had not been senior civil servants. The spirit of the higher civil service had shown remarkable continuity from the atmosphere that struck Beatrice Webb during the preparation of the Haldane Report; 'This informal review of our bureaucracy leaves an impression of good temper and good manners, of native capacity and no systematic training. . . .' (Bray, 1970.) The work of the civil service appealed because it gave opportunities for the analysis of problems and situations, not because it required leadership and the capacity to analyse cash flows. Moreover, management skills are often learned, not acquired through the experience at work that has amounted to Whitehall's concept of training. After the Second World War, management became a more developed profession, with an increased number of courses offered in it by universities and polytechnics. The growing emphasis on skills in management faced the civil service with the uncongenial contrast between increased emphasis on training in management and the perception in its own ranks that managing was the least, if necessary, aspect of its duties.

The failure of the civil service to resolve the tension between its emphasis on policy advising and managing led to a steady stream of criticism, notably the Fulton Committee's report (Fulton, 1968). Its criticism of the lack of expertise in the civil service was motivated in large part by the belief that what it saw as the Northcote-Trevelyan civil service, which has survived since the nineteenth century, was incapable of managing effectively the large public sector of late twentieth-century Britain. The higher civil service as shaped by the Northcote-Trevelyan reforms had never been intended to manage a large public sector. The product of a period when the role of the state was restricted to its 'night watchman' functions, the civil service long escaped the need to manage because the implementation of programmes was delegated to bodies such as local authorities, local education committees and the boards of nationalized industries. In a number of policy areas that involved vast expenditure, however, British government after the Second World War became directly involved in the provision of services. The National Health Service, retirement pensions and welfare and, throughout the Cold War era, vast military expenditures created a need for managerial skills that could not be ignored. Indeed, Lord Bridges, the apotheosis of a mandarin, had convened two meetings of all permanent secretaries in the early days of the Attlee Government to consider the possibility that the creation of the welfare state would require the creation of a different type of civil service. Nothing was done (Hennessy, 1989, Chapter 4).

One of the main concerns of the Fulton Committee had been to strengthen the commitment to improving managerial skills. The creation of the Civil Service Department in 1968 in line with the Fulton Committee's recommendations was intended to strengthen that commitment. Although the Fulton Committee reported to a Labour government, the succeeding Conservative government shared the feeling that a more technocratic approach was needed in Whitehall. The Heath Government's White Paper, 'A New Style of Government', called for innovations in policy analysis, such as the use of PPBS; it also confirmed Fulton's recommendation that the management of the civil service should be kept out of the Treasury and in the Civil Service Department. The Treasury was inevitably too preoccupied with the management of the economy and the need for economy to propagate reforms and changes of attitude such as an increased emphasis on management skills.

In fact, the history of the Civil Service Department showed how difficult it was to graft onto British government concern with management issues. The Civil Service Department limped along as a lesser ministry usually headed by a relatively junior politician or a politician with other, more pressing responsibilities until 1981 when it was abolished by the Thatcher Government; its most senior civil servant and the Head of the Civil Service, Sir Ian Bancroft, was forced into early retirement. Thatcher's dislike of Bancroft and the CSD was due to several factors. Bancroft himself had the detached style of the traditional mandarinate of higher civil servants rather than the 'can do' style Thatcher wanted. The CSD had clearly mismanaged labour relations with lower-rank civil servants, contributing to the first ever strike by civil servants in 1981 against Thatcher's decision not to provide an adequate pay increase. The Department also seemed to Thatcher more a defender of the vested interests of the civil service than a spur to change. Yet the abolition of the CSD also reflected the Department's failure to establish itself as a real force in Whitehall.

The drumbeat of criticism of civil service efficiency continued to be heard after the 1960s. Knowledgeable MPs such as Dr Jeremy Bray lambasted the civil service for its lack of interest in sophisticated management techniques (Bray, 1970). Conservative prime ministers seemed to act on the belief long expressed in settings such as the bars of golf clubs that the government could be run much more efficiently if they got a few good businessmen in as advisers. One of the few examples of Margaret Thatcher emulating Edward Heath was her decision to appoint an Efficiency Unit to reduce waste in the public sector. But Thatcher's initiative was much more important than Heath's because it evolved from conducting reviews of single programmes into proposals for radical *institutional* change. Kate Jenkins, a member of the Efficiency Unit, wrote a report that won the support of Sir Robert Ibbs, its Director, and the Prime Minister, arguing for a move beyond the worthy inquiries into particular examples of government inefficiency, and developed the revolutionary Next Steps initiative (*Improving Management*, 1988).

Next Steps developed the seeds planted in the report of the Fulton Committee by arguing for removing from departments the responsibility for implementing policy. Over two-thirds of the civil service would be placed in agencies separated from the parent departments. An agency would have a contract with its parent department that would specify goals and objectives rather than be part of an integrated hierarchy linking the permanent secretary to the lowliest clerk. The Next Steps programme promised (or threatened) to change the Whitehall model fundamentally. First, the separation of Next Steps agencies from parent departments could break the unity of administration and policy advising that had been a feature of the Whitehall model. The seamless web that linked the minister and permanent secretary to the clerks in a local office was broken. Second, the selection of chief executives for the agencies could disrupt the traditional Whitehall career path. High fliers in the administrative class tended not to apply for chief executive posts and, if they did apply, were not successful. Third, Next Steps agencies would break up the unity of the civil service. Agencies were intended to be able to have their own pay and career structures that could differ significantly from each other. The greatest fear about the Next Steps programme at the highest levels of the civil service was that it could bring about the end of the integrated, unified civil service so central to the Whitehall model. The hope of the Head of the Civil Service, Sir Robin Butler, was that it would be 'unified but not uniform' (MacDonald, 1992).

Ironically, in view of its radical potential, the Next Steps programme had come from a small group at the very centre of government. Whereas the Fulton Committee conducted an open inquiry into the civil service seeking advice from all interested groups and people, the Next Steps initiative was the product of the small Efficiency Unit, and perhaps of only a few people within that unit. It is an interesting question why the radical Next Steps programme aroused so little opposition from the higher civil service. Perhaps one answer is that the Prime Minister was known to back the proposal enthusiastically. Whether the potential radical impact of the Next Steps initiative on the Whitehall model was fully appreciated may also be questioned. It is most likely, however, that very senior civil servants felt that a tactical retreat was necessary. Criticism of the civil service had reached such a point that simple defence of the existing order was impossible. Next Steps involved the senior civil service losing some control over agencies; possibly even career opportunities as chief executives for the agencies might be recruited from outside the service. Yet Next Steps agencies were responsible for the task the senior civil servants valued and enjoyed the least, management, and the agencies were at least still in the public sector, not privatized.

Enthusiasts for the change, such as Graham Mather of the Institute of Economic Affairs, believed that the Next Steps programme was merely the beginning of a fundamental change in administration: 'Government by contract is on the way.' (Mather, 1992.) Within a few years, Mather's view seemed plausible. In December 1993, the Major Government announced that it would attempt to privatize all Next Steps agencies, including the Employment and Prisons agencies. The possibility of contracting out even that most valued of civil service roles, policy analysis and advice, was raised, though it seemed less likely than the privatization of administration (Boston, 1994). In all events, criticism of the managerial skills of the higher civil service had resulted in important challenges to the Whitehall model.

Neutrality and Commitment

As we have seen, management is something that the higher civil service has seen as a necessary rather than exhilarating task. The heaviest blow to the Whitehall model came however from the threat to the civil service's dearest role, policy advising.

As we noted above, the strangest feature of the Whitehall model for outsiders is its belief that career civil servants can take on the perspectives and even political interests of politicians sufficiently to provide them with a satisfactory alternative to the work done by personally appointed political staff in other countries. Yet from the Second World War until the 1970s, criticisms of the adequacy of the civil service as a source of advice to ministers were confined to academic discussion or the far left of the Labour Party. Beatrice Webb had noted what she saw as '. . . a moderately felt loyalty to the ideals of the British ruling class. . . . Contempt for Parliament . . . a steady depreciation of parliamentary chiefs are almost universal in the higher ranks of the civil service' (Bray, 1970). Labour thinkers in the 1930s were much concerned with the possibility that a future Labour government would be sabotaged by disloyal civil servants who, after all, were recruited disproportionately from a class background that could be expected to imbue them with hostility to the policies of a socialist government (Morgan, 1986, pp. 86–87). The experience of the 1945–51 Labour Government seemed in this as in so many things to show that the system worked. Labour ministers were apparently entirely satisfied with the quality of advice they received from civil servants, and the loyalty of those civil servants to them.

This is not to say that civil servants were powerless. Hugo Young noted how Sir John Colville, a former senior civil servant, memorialized his colleague, the Cabinet Secretary Sir Norman Brook. 'He was wise in his advice and while appearing to fall in at an early stage with ideas he privately thought wrong and extravagant, he presented the counterarguments so skilfully and so tactfully that they were nearly always approved.' (Young, 1990.) Dame Evelyn (later Baroness) Sharp has been immortalized in

Crossman's diaries as a woman with very clear and strong views
on the direction that policy should take. Crossman also noted
how politicians also endangered their own influence over the civil
service by practices such as frequent cabinet reshuffles.

> I am now convinced that one of Harold's [Wilson's] greatest
> mistakes is his constant reshuffling. Too many job changes in
> three years means a tremendous decline in the power of the poli-
> tician over the civil service and a tremendous growth in the power
> of Whitehall Departments both to thwart central Cabinet control
> and to thwart departmental ministers' individual control. The truth
> is that a Minister needs eighteen months to get real control of his
> Department. I had just about got it when I was moved from
> Housing . . . (Crossman, 1975, p. 78).

Doubts about the neutrality of the civil service, the neutral part
of its 'neutral competence' to use Heclo's phrase, re-emerged in
the Labour Party in the 1970s. No doubt this re-emergence of
distrust was connected to the widespread frustration in the party
over the failure of Labour governments to achieve their objectives. The 1964–70 Labour Government had been trapped by
economic circumstances and misjudgements into pursuing policies that resulted in expenditure cuts and unemployment; the
1974–79 Labour Government was trapped by even more disastrous economic circumstances, misjudgements and the absence of
clear majority support in either the electorate or Parliament.

The minority report of Labour MPs on the Expenditure Committee constituted a full-scale assault on the loyalty of the civil
service to Labour governments.

> The role that they [civil servants] have invented for themselves is
> that of governing the country. They see themselves, to the detri-
> ment of democracy, as politicians writ large. And of course as
> politicians writ large, they seek to govern the country according to
> their own narrow well-defined interests, tastes, education and
> background, none of which fit them on the whole to govern a
> modern technological, industrialized, pluralist and urbanized
> society. (Expenditure Committee, 1976–7, para. 5.)

The minority report contained some memorable attacks on particular departments:

The Department of Trade contains civil servants who are steeped in nineteenth century Board of Trade attitudes. . . . The Home Office, the graveyard of free-thinking since the days of Lord Sidmouth early in the nineteenth century is stuffed with reactionaries ruthlessly pursuing their own reactionary policies. . . . some Foreign Office officials interpret being a good European as being synonymous with selling out British interests. The Vichy mentality . . . undoubtedly exists in some parts of our Foreign Office establishment . . . (Expenditure Committee, 1976–7, para. 6).

The minority Labour report reflected the animosity that had developed between some left-wing Labour ministers and their civil servants. The most famous example of this animosity was the tension between Anthony Wedgwood Benn and his senior civil servants. Benn's permanent secretary, Sir Anthony Part, has described the frigid meetings that took place between Benn and the civil servants who were supposed to be his aides and advisers.

. . . the seating arrangements for his *tête-à-tête* several times a week with his Permanent Secretary emphasized his approach. Usually for such informal talks the Secretary of State and his Permanent Secretaries would sit in armchairs in a corner of the office. Mr Benn wished us to face each other across the long narrow conference table next to his desk. . . . he put a block of paper in front of him and drew a line down the middle. As the conversation proceeded, he noted my remarks to the left of the line and any comment or counter-argument of his to the right of the line. This did not make for a relaxed atmosphere and occasionally it was as though he were pointing a pistol at my head. (Part, 1990, p. 172.)

Benn's civil servants felt that they had been placed in particularly invidious positions by the decisions of Wilson and Callaghan to keep in their cabinets a man who clearly and fairly openly dissented from the major policies of the government. Was their loyalty to the government or their minister? Although Part argued that their loyalty was to their minister, not the government as a whole (Part, 1990, p. 174), the knowledge that following Benn's wishes would involve officials in developing policies that the cabinet as a whole would reject or disapprove of resulted in an impossible position for many civil servants. Should they follow government policy or their minister's? For Benn and sympathetic junior ministers, the position was clear; hostile civil servants were using their Whitehall contacts to mobilize opposition to his policy initiatives. His advisers were part of the problem and not the solution.

Benn probably never used the phrase 'one of us'. Yet the politician who did, Margaret Thatcher, shared much of Benn's mistrust of the civil service. The reasons for Thatcher's dislike of the civil service are varied, and many of her biographers attribute it in part to personal motives such as a distrust of what she understood to be 'establishment' institutions, for example the BBC, the Church of England and possibly the monarchy itself (Young, 1989; Jenkins, 1987; Hennessy, 1989). Thatcher's temperament was at odds with most senior civil servants'. As one who had a good working relationship with Thatcher said, 'You have to realize that for all her abilities, she was not at all intellectual. The dispassionate consideration of ideas that is prized in the civil service culture was the antithesis of her own style.' (Interview, 1991.)

Yet Thatcher was reflecting wider, more enduring forces in her antipathy to the civil service than merely her own beliefs or attitudes. The rise of the 'new right' had brought to power politicians such as Thatcher who viewed civil servants with as much antipathy as Labour left wingers and who had equally developed intellectual reasons for doing so. Civil servants were both contingently and necessarily enemies of the Thatcher revolution. Civil servants were imbued with attitudes that reflected the policy consensus that had prevailed since the Second World War. Civil servants were also imbued with 'departmental attitudes' that could easily conflict with Thatcherite beliefs. The Department of Employment had developed policy views that stressed the desirability of maintaining the so-called voluntary system of industrial relations that prevailed in Britain until the 1980s. The Department of Education and Science (DES) had developed a tendency under both Labour and Conservative governments to share the approaches and values of progressive educationalists. Lord Young, one of Thatcher's favourites among the many Secretaries of Trade and Industry she appointed, considered that the links between his department and Industry were so close that they were 'neocorporatist', a view that surprised most political scientists. In brief, civil servants were suspect because they could be assumed to carry either the virus of the postwar consensus or because they carried the often equally dangerous virus of the 'departmental view'. One minister told the *Daily Telegraph*, '. . . unless we break out of the civil service straight jacket we'll never get a chance to rule. It is beginning to look to many of us that civil servants are a breed who really believe that they run the country and that all they've got to do is to knock new ministers into shape.' (Summerton, 1980.) Sir John Hoskyns, one of Thatcher's fervent supporters, argued that the traditional civil service was an inappropriate vehicle for the Thatcher revolution precisely because of its prized traditions of detachment and scepticism about policy proposals. The Thatcher revolution required commitment, not dispassionate analysis (Hoskyns, 1982).

Civil servants were not just accidentally out of sympathy with Thatcherism according to its proponents. Armed with the simplistic views of the rational choice approach to the study of politics and government, Thatcherites believed that civil servants were necessarily their enemy. Bureaucrats were motivated by the quest for larger staffs and budgets; with some conspicuous exceptions, such as the police and armed forces, Thatcherites were committed to shrinking government. Civil servants could be expected to oppose Thatcherism because its basic goals were at odds with the material self-interest of civil servants (Niskanen, 1971).

It is tempting therefore to see the advisory role of the higher civil service as one of the casualties of the polarization of British politics. In a period in which the Labour Party moved to the left and the Conservatives to the right, the problems of maintaining confidence in the 'neutral competence' of civil service advisers increased. Conviction politicians of the left and the right did not prize dispassionate analysis or criticism of their proposals. Civil service neutrality seemed close to centrism, to sympathy for the Social Democrats, for whom many senior civil servants voted in the 1980s. As Hugo Young wrote (1990), 'Objectivity for example is considered by many of those closest to Mrs Thatcher to be the last refuge of procrastinators and other scoundrels.' The *Guardian* thought that for Mrs Thatcher the Whitehall machine was '. . . the enemy to be chided, kickstarted and bounced out of its lethargy . . .' (9 January 1989).

Ironically, in view of the suspicion of civil servants that Thatcher and her ministers so often conveyed, one of the new issues that arose during the Thatcher years was how far civil servants should work in partisan manner for ministers. In systems in which politicians receive staff support from political appointees, the only limitation on the services staff should provide is the law, and, as Watergate showed, even the law can be broken. When staff support comes from a career, permanent civil service, the answer is less clear. The norms of a professional bureaucracy, of the constitution, can create a feeling on the part of the bureaucracy that there are certain jobs that a civil servant should not be asked to do, and if asked should refuse. The civil service owes a duty to the state or the constitution that goes beyond its duty to the government of the day. Politicians and officials in Britain whom we interviewed argued that there were well-known limits to the work that civil servants should carry out for ministers as politicians. The favourite example was that civil servants should not attend party meetings, or write speeches to be delivered at party conferences. Yet these boundaries are hazy and unmodified. Does providing the draft of a policy statement that a minister will turn into a speech by adding a few rhetorical flourishes count as writing a speech? Remarkably, in view of the inherent ambiguity of these issues, there were few problems until the Thatcher years.

In the Westland affair, the Prime Minister Margaret Thatcher and the Industry Secretary Leon Brittan were heavily criticized because they had used permanent civil servants to give confidential briefings to the press to discredit the Secretary of State for Defence, Michael Heseltine, who had opposed the Government's policy of allowing an American rather than a European corporation to acquire Britain's last helicopter manufacturer, Westland. The Government's critics argued that such manifestly political work was inappropriate for career civil servants. Thatcher's press secretary Bernard Ingham, a civil servant, was so identified with her that her successor, John Major, replaced Ingham as soon as he took office; Ingham's successor Gus O'Donnell was warned by the Head of the Civil Service Sir Robin Butler to avoid Ingham's fate and to remain a civil servant, not an acolyte; Ingham, for his part, rushed out his memoires in which he claimed to have been merely his (Prime) Minister's faithful servant (Ingham, 1991). Similarly, civil servants in the Department of Employment were required to produce over thirty changes in the definition of unemployment during the Thatcher years, each one of which changed the official statistics on unemployment in a way that improved the government's record. The delicate and ambiguous conventions governing the boundary between the civil servants' duty to help ministers in their official tasks and their duty to help them as party politicians was overridden by the Thatcherite determination to prevail. Reluctance by civil servants to cooperate in political manoeuvring merely strengthened the Thatcherite belief that the permanent bureaucracy was a problem, not a solution.

From the 1960s onwards, British ministers had wanted to bring advisers with them into government. The Wilson Government brought in two economic advisers, Kaldor and Balogh, the 1950s critic of the civil service, as outside advisers. Although their appointment was seen as an innovation, British prime ministers as far back as Churchill and Lloyd George had brought in outsiders or irregulars to assist them. Yet such earlier examples had been seen as unusual, temporary departures from the practice of relying on the civil service for advice, departures from the norm usually justified by special circumstances such as war. The systematic appointment of advisers began with the Labour Government of 1964–70 and was confirmed by the 1970–4 Heath Government. The latter also created a unit to carry out policy analysis and review within the Cabinet Office, the Central Policy Review Staff (CPRS), which was half composed of people other than civil servants, though some, such as the economist John Odling-Smee, stayed on in government after leaving the CPRS. The Wilson Labour Government took the process further by creating a Policy Unit dominated by outsiders to provide continuing assistance to the prime minister in the form of policy analysis and advice. What did British politicians miss in the civil service that led them to look for advice outside its ranks?

The answers to this question are as varied as the types of politician who have appointed advisers. Some political advisers have been brought in to question and challenge the advice provided by the civil service. Such advisers have had a difficult and generally unsuccessful time finding ways to fit into the policy-making machine. Policy-oriented advisers have been relatively few, in part because ministers generally lack sufficiently developed views on the policies for which their ministries are responsible to make it possible to pick suitable advisers. Most advisers have been intended to provide more political perspectives than civil servants are thought capable of supplying and to carry out tasks such as writing speeches for party conferences, which civil servants are supposed not to carry out. Advisers who have fulfilled these roles have been welcomed by civil servants as a way of escaping unwelcome tasks; instead of merely refusing to carry out a very partisan task, civil servants can suggest it be handed over to the adviser. Perhaps one of the less attractive roles taken on by an adviser was playing the Labour leader Neil Kinnock in practice sessions before Thatcher's prime minister's question time. 'Quite frequently she gets quite agitated and gives him a very hard time. . . . She asks him how dare he say these things. He has to explain that he has to put the counter arguments. (The *Independent*, 13 September 1988.) Advisers have in general therefore done little to challenge the civil service's monopoly on policy advice.

The story of the Policy Unit is more interesting. Originating in the Wilson Government (Donoughue, 1986), it took on greater importance after Thatcher abolished the Central Policy Review Staff, CPRS (Jones, 1987). The CPRS, created by Heath, had been intended to provide dispassionate analysis at the centre of government. It encountered a variety of practical problems in carrying out this task, including the absence of a minister to speak for its reports in cabinet and the inevitability that highly controversial analyses would be leaked to the press in a form that would raise a political storm from a minister whose department's interests were threatened, thus precluding dispassionate discussion. Thatcher's decision to abolish the CPRS and to rely on a more committed Policy Unit that would develop her policy ideas and monitor Whitehall's compliance with them once again reflected her own style; dispassionate advice from the CPRS was no more welcome than from the civil service. A former member of the Policy Unit under Thatcher saw its role as being 'the grit in the machine', the challenge to the normal advice from the civil service. The Policy Unit, he believed, had a special role to play under a radical prime minister, to think in terms of the 'bigger jump' as opposed to the incremental advice from the civil service. 'Take the Health [Service] review. If you want to improve the NHS a bit the Department of Health is fine. But if you want more profound reform you need other people.' (Interview, 1990.)

Yet once again, Thatcher's actions identified a problem more enduring than the problem of creating machinery to suit her somewhat unusual style. Without a Policy Unit, a British prime minister, supposedly the supplier of direction to the government as a whole, had no satisfactory source of advice. Cabinet Office briefings summarized problems and perspectives rather than supplied potential solutions; after the embarrassments William Armstrong suffered while Head of the Civil Service through being identified as Heath's Chief of Staff (or even Deputy Prime Minister) (Hennessy, 1989, pp. 239–41), his successors have been reluctant to take on the role of supplying prime ministers with analysis and advice that is based on an understanding of their needs and goals. The departure of Thatcher did not result in the decline of the Policy Unit. Although Major did not feel the same urge to drive his ministers towards his ideological goals as Thatcher did, he did feel a pressing need for central advice that would help him monitor the work of departments and the policy choices they were making in order to carry through his political goals. 'Behind that nice appearance, Major is a very nice man but also a highly political man', commented one senior civil servant: 'He needs the Policy Unit to make sure he is in control of the political situation. He uses the Policy Unit to make sure he is kept in touch with what is happening in departments.' (Interview, 1992.) The transition from a highly ideological leader to a more pragmatic prime minister had not reduced the need for a central unit dominated by outsiders. In brief, the Whitehall machine itself left prime ministers with a feeling that they were not adequately supported. The rise of the Policy Unit and other 10 Downing Street staff such as the economic or foreign policy adviser was the consequence. At the very highest level, the civil service's dominance of policy advising was threatened. To understand fully why politicians were less content to rely on the advice of their civil servants, we have to look at the changes that had been taking place in the ranks of politicians.

The Changing Demand Side: the Politicians

British civil servants, as we have noted, often claim that the character of their work is shaped by the needs or demands of the politicians. Yet politicians are not a homogeneous group that generates the same demands on the civil service year in, year out.

British politicians have changed in ways that have created major strains on the Whitehall model.

The two main changes in the character of British politicians since the Second World War appear at first glance contradictory. British politicians have been considered both more likely to be career politicians (King, 1981; Riddell, 1993) and, from 1970 until the 1992 general election, more ideologically committed (or at least differentiated or, to use the then vogue word, polarized) than their predecessors.

In calling politicians 'career politicians', commentators are not merely saying that contemporary MPs and ministers expect to be paid for their work, but are claiming that politics has become a career to which people commit themselves in the expectation that they will spend most of their working life within it. Naturally, it follows that the professional politician also aims to rise as high as possible within the profession. The House of Commons used to contain many members of limited ambition. The ranks of Conservative back-benchers contained retired military officers and gentleman farmers for whom membership of the House was an agreeable way to pass late middle age. The Labour back-benches contained former union officials who enjoyed a spell in the House before retiring completely from public life. These groups provided a ballast welcomed by chief whips; they provided loyal support for their leaders and expected very little in return in the way of ministerial office.

In contrast, the typical contemporary MP is someone who expects and intends to spend a career in the House of Commons and is anxious for promotion. Chief whips today see a dearth of loyal, undemanding back-benchers and a plethora of ambitious, importuning MPs. 'We suffer from what I call pol-flation', one chief whip of the period complained. 'We have too many MPs – and they all want office.' (Interview.) If the practice of moving ministers frequently from post to post in Britain has any defence, it is that it is necessary to open up jobs for 'unemployed' back-benchers.

Career politicians are often thought to be less interested in ideology or policy than in retaining office; the American machine politicians of the past cared little about policy as long as it did not prevent them from retaining office. The professionalization of the British politician coincided, however, with a shift to more ideologically differentiated politics in Britain. The Conservative Party's move to the right from the mid-1970s and the Labour Party's almost simultaneous shift to the left ushered in an era in which the contrast between the parties' policies was greater than at any time since the Second World War, and possibly ever. The Major Government adopted an image very different from the Thatcher government's, but its policies in most areas showed great continuity with its predecessors'.

Yet, though the trends towards career politicians and more ideological politics might seem to be in conflict with each other, they had a similar impact on ministers' concepts of their roles. In his path-breaking work discussed in Chapter 1, Bruce Heady described how British ministers understood their roles in government in the early 1970s. Although a few defined their role as that of a policy initiator, a much larger number saw their role as representing the interests of their departments to the rest of the government; the minister was the department's ambassador. Heady's description of British government fits with the picture of the Whitehall village in which the prestige of ministers is determined by their success in bringing their departments resources. The minister is a hunter who sets out in search of sustenance for the department; if he kills his deer (after fighting off the Treasury) and brings it home, his prestige within his ministerial 'family' rises (Heclo and Wildavsky, 1973).

The advent of the career politician and ideological politics changed this picture of the role of the minister significantly. The more professional the politician, the more eager he or she is to make a mark. Ministers must be seen to be making an impact on departments. The role model becomes not the hunter who brings his family its food, but the colonial administrator who subdues the wild tribe; departments such as Employment and Education are brought to heel. To continue the analogy a little further, in the 1980s ministers were very anxious to please the Queen-Empress in Downing Street by forcing the wayward tribes of Whitehall to amend their thinking. Subject to some constraints (particularly until her second general election victory), Thatcher rewarded politicians who imposed her values on departments and fired ministers who were too understanding of the customs and mores of the natives whose 'departmental view' was incompatible with Thatcherism. Survival as a minister – let alone prestige –

depended on being, in the words of the Prime Minister, 'one of us', even if that meant adopting policies that overturned the traditional view of one's department or accepting gracefully fewer resources in negotiations with the Treasury than the department wanted. The minister anxious to retain office or be promoted – two goals that the professional politician might have – was ill advised to act as the departmental ambassador that Headey (1974) had described.

Stripped of analogies, the preceding argument can be summarized thus. In an age of career politicians, MPs are anxious to become, remain and be promoted as members of the cabinet. In order to succeed, they need to make an impact. They are therefore less likely to accept roles in which they are merely servants of their departments. Moreover, ministers' tenure in office depends on the prime minister (even if he or she is in turn subject to some constraints). Thatcher, and even in some crucial areas such as economic policy and education, Major, have had clear beliefs about the policies they wish their ministers to pursue. It has been important, therefore, for politicians who want to retain office or be promoted to make a mark in their departments, but to do so in a manner that pleases the prime minister, even if it displeases their officials. Whereas studies of British government written in the 1970s had emphasized the importance of ministers engaging in behaviour (e.g. fighting hard for a larger budget) that raised their prestige within their departments, thereafter it became crucial for ministers to make a mark on their departments that pleased the prime minister even if the cost of doing so involved displeasing their departments. In an era that combined professionalization and more ideological politics ministers were both less willing to fall in with their departments' expectations and more eager to please the prime minister. Nicholas Ridley, one of Thatcher's favourite ministers, went to the extreme of suggesting that the constitution had changed to the point where the prime minister should be seen as a president: 'The Prime Minister alone carries the responsibility of the Executive, just as the President of the United States does.' (Ridley, 1993, p. 27.)

The changes in the roles of ministers had implications for the Whitehall model that we have already encountered. First, the likelihood of ministers accepting that their role was to represent the attitudes and interests of their departments to the rest of government was much diminished. Second, ministers eager to make a mark, to be seen to be changing things and not merely presiding benignly over their departments, wanted more advice and advice more geared to change than they were likely to receive from the traditional civil servant. Third, a prime minister who believes that her role is to oversee the policies of her ministers has staffing requirements very different from those of a prime minister who believes that ministers should be left to get on with their work in peace. Thatcher wanted to be able to make sure that the specific policy proposals of her Education and Employment Secretaries conformed to her own values. She needed, therefore, her own sources of advice on what policy options were viable, and her own mechanisms for monitoring what the Department of Education was doing. We turn in the next chapter to the implications for executive leadership of the decline of the Whitehall model.

The End of the Model?

There can be little doubt that the Whitehall model came under increasing fire during the fifty years after the Second World War. By 1994, the civil service was, in the words of William Plowden, '. . . in a state of crisis unprecedented in its history. . . . A significant number of senior officials feel that their professional skills are being ignored or abused.' (Plowden, 1994, p. i.) Doubts about the civil service's interest and competence in management culminated in reforms, the Next Steps programme, that had great potential to end such prized features of the British civil service as a unitary service (i.e. crossing department boundaries) with an integrated career pattern. Even more worrying for the civil service was erosion of its near monopoly on supplying policy analysis and advice to ministers. The era of conviction politics in Britain created suspicion of the civil service among politicians of both the left and the right. That most central and prized role of the higher civil service in Britain, advising ministers, was called into question.

The importance of these trends for civil servants and arguably the entire British political system is clear. Hugo Young welcomed the subordination of civil servants to ministers during the Thatcher years in that '. . . it is not fanciful to say that the constitutional textbooks are truer now than they have been for some time . . .'. Officials '. . . have been brought obediently to heel by the mighty hand of three successive democratic mandates.' But Young noted the danger in this too. 'What we have lost and are in danger of losing forever is institutionalized scepticism.' (Young, 1990.) The Thatcherite insistence on obedience had resulted in numerous errors, such as the introduction of the poll tax, identity cards for soccer fans (that proved to be unworkable as well as an assault on civil liberties) and extraordinarily costly nuclear power policy, because not only was civil service advice disregarded, but sceptical analysis had been discouraged.

Young's analysis fits with the results of our interviews. Civil servants were increasingly defining their role as being implementers rather than policy analysts, people who gave ministers what they said they wanted, rather than functioning as what they disparagingly called 'quasi academics' who tried to show politicians the full consequences, adverse as well as positive, of their policy proposals. These trends will remind students of American executive branch politics of similar trends. In the United States, too, 'neutral competence' has been less prized by executive branch officials in recent decades. Power has passed increasingly into the hands of political appointees whose main qualification is their loyalty to the president. Some political scientists have defended this trend as an understandable, even desirable response to presidential needs (Moe, 1985). Others, such as Campbell (1986) and Rockman (1984), like Hugo Young, have worried that institutionalized scepticism is being lost.

The Whitehall model had provided a closer, apparently more enduring partnership between politicians and neutrally competent but sceptical officials than any other system. One of its main claims to fame was that it provided for that institutionalized scepticism that Young valued. British politicians had long accepted with good grace a partnership with senior civil servants in governing that could be irritating in the short term, as some of their favourite schemes and plans were subjected to analysis and criticism but which politicians knew often saved them from errors and trouble. If the Whitehall model is in decline, the strongest example of a successful partnership between career politicians and neutrally competent bureaucrats in democratic countries will be displaced.

Have the pressures we have encountered indeed resulted in the breaking of the Whitehall mould of bureaucratic political relations? We return to the conditions we suggested above for assessing whether the Whitehall model still existed in regard to bureaucratic–political relations. These were that the civil service is able to maintain the belief that it is a neutrally competent service willing to work in a partisan way for any legitimate government, that it is able to maintain its professional integrity and that it is able to maintain its near monopoly on advising ministers. An additional crucial concern – accountability – is addressed in a separate chapter.

Neutral Competence for Partisan Assistance

At first glance, the Whitehall model of bureaucratic–political relations survived the Thatcher years. Although Thatcher's initial hostility to the civil service in general is well known (Hennessy, 1989; Young, 1989; Jenkins, 1987), no major institutional change had been made in the role of the higher civil service (to provide policy analysis and advice) by the time she left office after a record-breaking period as prime minister. Optimistic civil servants might have concluded that if the Whitehall model could withstand Thatcher, a prime minister who combined unusually strong beliefs about an unusually wide range of policies, instinctive antipathy to the civil service and great determination, it could withstand anything.

Yet in practice the Thatcher years did witness a further erosion in the acceptance of the neutral competence of civil servants. The Whitehall model implied a relationship of mutual trust and respect between bureaucrats and politicians. That respect was not present in the 1980s and 1990s. Thatcher herself set the tone; in her memoirs she describes a dinner she gave for the Permanent Secretaries of all major departments in 1981 as 'one of the most dismal experiences of my entire time in government' (Thatcher, 1993, p. 48). As we have seen, advisers close to Thatcher, such as Sir John Hoskyns, saw the civil service as part of the problem, not the solution. Civil servants we interviewed throughout the

1980s complained frequently that the well intentioned advice and warnings they gave were regarded as obstructionism or negativism. Senior civil servants noted an attitude among ministers that, in the words of one senior official, '. . . if you were any good, you would be working in the private sector'. (Interview, 1989.)

To make matters worse, while ministers disparaged the competence of the civil service in providing policy advice, they demanded more of the civil service in terms of political assistance than had previous governments. The long-standing problem of how far civil servants in Whitehall model systems should provide political assistance to ministers became much more pressing. The frequent revisions in statistics such as the unemployment rate in order to improve the government's record, the use of civil servants to manipulate media coverage to further the prime minister's goals and to conceal government decisions from Parliament all raised acute questions of conscience for civil servants. Not until after the fall of Thatcher did the proceedings of the Scott Inquiry make clear how civil servants had been required to deceive Parliament over decisions to supply arms to Iraq in the late 1980s. In testimony to the Inquiry a Mr Eric Beston, head of export controls at the Department of Trade and Industry in the late 1980s, said that civil servants had drafted replies to Parliamentary Questions intended to mislead (*Guardian* 24 November 1993).

It had been evident long before that many civil servants were desperately concerned about the degree to which they were expected to further the government's short-term advantage. Few followed the example of Clive Ponting, who felt that his duty to the constitution required him to leak documents showing that the Government had deceived Parliament over the sinking of the Argentine cruiser, the *General Belgrano* during the Falklands War. But a growth in the concerns of civil servants about pressures to cross the long-established boundaries between their work and what was regarded as too partisan for career officials was evident in both our confidential interviews and more, publicly, in the calls by their 'union', the First Division Association, for a code of ethics to protect its members against ministerial requests for overly partisan or unconstitutional acts.

The replacement of Thatcher by John Major was expected to improve relations with the civil service. It did so only temporarily. Major, as we have seen, retreated from Thatcher's level of involvement in civil service promotions, and took care to express more frequently and forcefully his admiration for the civil service. Yet civil servants continued to feel that their advice was taken seriously only if fitted with ministers' preconceptions. One senior official complained that '. . . this lot are even worse than under Thatcher. At least she had an instinct for self-preservation we could appeal to; this lot don't even have that.' (Interview, 1993.) In late 1993, a series of events showed how bad relations between ministers and civil servants had become. The Permanent Secretary of the Department of Education, Sir Geoffrey Holland, resigned because ministers would not take his advice seriously, while Home Office officials complained that years of careful policy development had been tossed aside without serious discussion by ministers seeking a few minutes' applause at the party conference. When ritual claims were made that the traditional policy-making process was alive and well at the Home Office, William Plowden, a former civil servant and researcher in a London think tank, reported in a letter to the *Guardian* that '. . . something is badly awry with the relationship between ministers and officials. Many ministers are not interested in frank advice from civil servants.' Plowden quoted from interviews he had conducted that mirrored our own. ' "The government knows what it wants and needs no advice." "What's new is the number of ministers who won't listen to advice." ' (*Guardian* 20 November 1993.)

The Integrity of the Profession

How well did the civil service as a profession survive Thatcherism?

Once again, the initial impression is that the senior civil service preserved most but not all of the civil service's integrity as a profession. Indeed, one interpretation of the developments in the 1980s is that the senior civil service executed a strategic retreat. The Next Steps initiative separated important posts and functions from the high-level civil service. Next Steps agencies were intended to be outside the structure of their parent departments, linked to them by contracts and framework agreements rather than being organically parts of the departments themselves. One-third of Next Steps agency chief executives were recruited from outside the civil service, and of the remainder none came from the traditional 'fast track' civil servants being groomed for the highest civil service posts. Next Steps therefore looked like a major setback for the traditional civil service.

But the Next Steps initiative was a compromise in two crucial respects. First, its agencies were still government agencies, not private sector organizations carrying out government functions. Second, its agencies were entrusted with the very activities – management, efficiency, the delivery of services – that the traditional civil service had regarded as the least prestigious and important activities.

At first, and to the dismay of critics of the civil service such as the Labour MP John Garrett, it looked as though the mandarins had executed a brilliant strategic retreat, abandoning their least favoured activities and maintaining their favourite, working with ministers on policy development. By the mid-1990s, however, the strategic retreat looked more like a mere delaying action. In 1993, the Government announced that it would attempt to privatize the Next Steps agencies, and debate moved on to the possibility of contracting out policy analysis and advice. The responsible minister, William Waldegrave, announced that the Government would advertise all senior vacancies so that people who were not civil servants could apply. The end of the civil service as a distinct profession seemed in prospect.

The integrity of the higher civil service as a profession had also been threatened by politicization. Thatcher's intense interest and involvement in promotions to the higher civil service raised fears that the civil service's non-partisanship was being undermined as the Prime Minister favoured her supporters. Again, as we have seen, the initial reports were reassuring (Royal Institute for Public Administration, 1987). The Working Party found no evidence that promotions in the civil service were being awarded on the basis of whether or not a candidate was an active member or supporter of the Conservative Party.

Again, however, the comforting conclusion was too comforting. Our interviews provide no basis for any argument that civil servants had to be Conservatives to be promoted. Our interviews do suggest that civil servants perceived that in order to succeed they had to change their understanding of their roles. The ambitious civil servant was well advised to play down policy advising, particularly if it challenged the desirability of government policy, and to play up the role of civil servants in implementing ministers' wishes, no matter how poorly considered they were. The clearest public statement of how this process worked is given by Nigel Lawson in his memoirs, in which he describes the appointment of Peter Middleton as Permanent Secretary at the Treasury (Lawson, 1992). One candidate was passed over because of his unwillingness to make a total commitment to Thatcherite doctrines; another who was actually a Conservative lacked the 'can do' style that Lawson and Thatcher favoured. Middleton was promoted because of his willingness to take orders and follow the Government's line less critically than his rivals, not always a desirable characteristic in a senior government economic adviser but one that proved effective in winning him one of the best jobs in the civil service.

> . . . the choice lay between two up and coming Deputy Secretaries, David Hancock and Peter Middleton. Hancock would almost certainly have won in a Treasury vote. I have no idea of what his politics were. *But the majority of Treasury officials, as indeed of Whitehall generally, saw themselves for want of a better description as social democrats. David Hancock certainly fitted that description, however he actually voted.* Discreet, civilized and knowledgeable in the ways of the Treasury and very Oxbridge, he was very much the mandarin's mandarin. He had been immensely sceptical of George Brown's Department of Economic Affairs and National Plan and was probably as sceptical of Tory radicalism. He was clearly not Margaret's type. In her view, the choice lay between Middleton and the Second Permanent Secretary in charge of Public Expenditure, Anthony Rawlinson. He was not only the best looking . . . something that always cut ice with her. He was also the one undoubted Tory of the three, Middleton . . . was not only an enthusiast for monetary policy. *He strongly believed in supporting the government of the day* – for instance in not thrusting an incomes policy down the throat of a Conservative government . . . *Moreover his interpretation of the Constitution was essentially Prime Ministerial, believing that all other Ministers and officials should toe the line.* (Lawson, 1992, p. 267, emphasis added.)

A major supposed advantage of the Whitehall model had been the ability of civil servants to give advice to politicians without fear that their careers would be harmed if that advice contained unwelcome truths. Now their career prospects were improved by their giving advice that ministers wanted to hear, not necessarily what they needed to hear. The considerable significance of Middleton's 'Prime Ministerial' interpretation of the constitution will be discussed further in Chapter 6.

Again, this tendency did not end with the Thatcher Government. In an episode replete with ironies, the civil servant who had won unusual public prominence as the creator of the Next Steps agencies, Sir Peter Kemp, was forced into early retirement because he was unacceptable to his minister, William Waldegrave. As Plowden has noted (1994), in a system such as the British one, where ministers average only a couple of years in each post (and in the Department of Trade and Industry, Thatcher went through twelve secretaries in twelve years), removing senior officials because they are disliked by their ministers opens up the opportunity for frequent turnover.

Maintaining a Monopoly on Advice

We might suppose in view of the other blows to the Whitehall model we have described that the civil service's monopoly on advice was also broken during the 1980s and 1990s. After all, as we have noted, its monopoly on promotion to the chief executiveships of Next Steps agencies was ended, and market testing attempted to move much of the implementation of policy into the private sector. The prisons, managed by an agency run by a former television executive and increasingly contracted out to private companies, were a case in point. If the civil service could no longer run even such a traditionally governmental institution as prisons, it seemed likely to lose its monopoly on policy advising. Certainly, there were a number of trends in that direction.

The first was the rise of the political official. Thatcher created a small-scale version of the White House staff, and three of her officials attracted the prominence and hostility that often go with those posts. These were Bernard Ingham, the Press Officer, Charles Powell, the foreign policy adviser, and Alan Walters, who served as economic adviser in several different periods. Ingham achieved notoriety for his briefings of the press in which he would denigrate not only opposition policies and politicians but members of the cabinet who had been rash enough to disagree with Thatcher or her policies in supposedly confidential cabinet meetings. Ingham's role became most visible during the Westland affair, when he ordered civil servants to leak confidential documents in order to undermine the Secretary of Defence, Michael Heseltine. Powell served so long as a private secretary in Downing Street that he became totally identified with Thatcher. Alan Walters, a holder of an American professorship in economics, became one of the most visible of the Downing Street staff when Thatcher's refusal to replace him at the behest of her Chancellor of the Exchequer, Nigel Lawson, with whom Walters disagreed on the appropriate form of monetary policy to follow, led to Lawson's resignation.

Powell and Ingham were civil servants, and Ingham, though a late entrant into the civil service, had served the Labour Government in the 1970s. Yet Powell and Ingham were totally identified with Thatcher and were removed by Major soon after he became prime minister. Though Powell was a civil servant by background, he had worked his way out of the Whitehall mould. This phenomenon can also be seen in the staff of the Policy Unit, created by Wilson but developed more fully by Thatcher. Thatcher used the Policy Unit not only as an antidote to advice from government departments but to reach over the heads of her ministers to intervene in the details of departmental policy formulation. The Unit was composed half of people outside the civil service – itself a major widening of a breach in the Whitehall model begun with Heath's Central Policy Review Staff – and half of civil servants. Many of the more important civil servants within the Unit, such as David Willett, found it impossible to return to civil service careers, however, and, like Powell and Ingham, felt obliged on leaving the Unit to move on to other careers. Both the importance of the Unit under Thatcher and the politicization of civil servants appointed to it were signs of a major departure from the Whitehall model. The Unit has remained of great importance under Major. Although it has not had as strong an ideological character under its director from 1991 to 1995, the former journalist Sarah Hogg, Major has depended on it greatly in his attempts to develop his own style and programme.

A further blow to the civil service's monopoly on policy advising came from the rise of think tanks in Britain. The Thatcher revolution was remarkable in British politics not only for the strength of its ideological convictions but for the detail in which those proposals were worked out by allies in the think tanks. Without the work of friendly think tanks, Thatcher and her ministerial allies would have been much less able to insist on changes in attitude and policy by government departments such as Education, Employment and Health. Where there was a clash between Thatcherite views and the established 'departmental view', the think tanks helped the process of shattering the departmental view. In departments crucial to the Thatcherite agenda, such as Environment, Employment, the Treasury and Education, the departmental attitudes towards what made for good public policy that had lasted through both Labour and Conservative governments were changed fundamentally. Advice from think tanks was crucial in this process.

As noted above, the challenge to the Whitehall model has not stopped with the demise of Thatcherism. It is now a matter for serious debate whether even the most central and traditional role of the civil service – the provision of policy analysis and advice by a professional, career service – will survive into the next century. The civil service may be composed of people who move in and out of government service rather than people who seek a lifetime career in the service; shorter-term contracts and contracting out advisory functions are real possibilities. The appointment of Terry Burns to lead the Treasury – a man who had spent most of his working life in a different profession (academic life) – has established a pattern of the most prestigious permanent secretaryship going to a person who has not had a normal Whitehall career.

The cracking of the Whitehall model of bureaucratic–political relations is very evident. There is no doubt that the creation of the Next Steps agencies and the pressure for contracting out traditional governmental functions to the private sector were sharp blows to the civil service's monopoly on implementing government policy. The more traditional and central function of the higher civil service in the Whitehall model – giving policy analysis and advice to ministers – has also come under intense pressure. The decline in the faith in the neutral competence of the civil service, its professional integrity and its monopoly on providing policy advice is clear.

Yet, as in much of contemporary British government and life, it is clearer that traditional ways are in decline than that adequate replacements are at hand. Think tanks have helped the challenge to the civil service's monopoly on policy advice, but they did not develop in Britain to the point where a satisfactory volume of advice or supply of 'in and outers' who could be brought into government temporarily was available. Indeed, the signs are now that British think tanks are in decline. Whether this is because of ideological confusion, shortages of money during the recession or internecine strife within the Conservative Party over Europe and the ideal form of monetarism has been debated, but there is widespread agreement that '. . . in the 1990s, think tanks have found themselves on the political periphery.' (*Financial Times*, 22 September 1993.)

The decline in the standing of think tanks has not been followed by a revival in the standing of the bureaucracy as a source of advice, however. As we have seen, civil servants felt as frustrated under Major as under Thatcher about what they feel is a failure to take their advice seriously. The weakening of the Whitehall model has not been accompanied by the development of an alternative. The 1994 White Paper *The Civil Service Continuity and Change* left these important questions unanswered; its main proposal, placing senior officials on fixed-term or rolling contracts, would merely amplify the problems identified here. The question is increasingly: Where, if anywhere, is serious policy thinking done in Britain?

Conclusion

The very nature of discussions about the changing relations between politicians and bureaucrats tends to focus assessments on developments in a specific country. This is largely because of the tendency for knowledgeable observers of executive–bureaucratic politics in a given country to view their system as almost unique. Keen American students of the US system seem especially subject to this reflex. They argue that the separation of powers so distinguishes executive–bureaucratic politics in their country that comparisons prove virtually impossible.

Britons can succumb to a similar inclination. As we will see in the next chapter, some British scholars become nearly apoplectic at the proposition that certain parallels exist in the centralization of power in the hands of US presidents and the 'prime-ministerialization' of cabinet government. Many scholars and practitioners have probed the possibility of upgrading British cabinet ministers' offices to proper coordinative staff units like their French opposite numbers' cabinets. However, one derives a sense that invariably such discussions end with conclusions like 'This might well be fine for Mars, but would it work on Earth?'

Among the Anglo-Westminster systems, i.e. those in the UK, Canada, Australia and New Zealand, one finds a phenomenal amount of cross-fertilization. Normally, when one or other system entertains major changes in the machinery of government or policy, delegations of visiting officials fan out to discover how things are done elsewhere. In the dynamics of these exchanges, the British often bring to their inquiries scepticism about what colonials can contribute. On the other hand, Canadians, Australians and New Zealanders tend to view their visits to London as 'touching base' with 'mother Whitehall' rather than dipping into a font of managerial genius. Yet, even in cases when such visits become almost entirely ritualistic, they still play important legitimizing roles when politicians and/or bureaucrats recommend change or the retention of the status quo.

Those undertaking such projects invariably cite their experiences in other countries in their rationales for prescriptions for change. However, one finds that such reports do not always withstand close scrutiny from those best acquainted with how things actually operate in the countries being observed. The hosts to visiting officials often tell fairy tales about how marvellously their innovations have worked. However, these glowing self-assessments frequently take place just as insiders and well-informed observers in the host country have come to the conclusion that the reform effort has fallen dramatically short of expectations. The visitors return with impressions at clear variance with the reality. Further, their unfamiliarity with how their host system functions exacerbates any distortions they may bring home.

Thus, for two reason, this book employs a comparative perspective as it evaluates change in Whitehall. First, we cannot fully understand what has occurred there unless we place it in a wider context. For the purposes of this analysis, we have chosen to focus on Anglo-American systems. We include the US because its model – negative or positive – looms so large in any consideration of the dos and don'ts of executive-bureaucratic politics. Also, its status as the pre-eminent presidential system – few of these work – makes it a potential reality check for bold assertions about the uniqueness of Whitehall or other Anglo-Westminster systems. We also examine the Anglo-Westminster systems because they all operate variants of the Whitehall model and spend a great deal of time discussing with one another how best to pursue change within this type of structural framework.

Second, we believe it is crucial to convey to the reader a sense of good and bad practices. A great amount of reform has occurred in the Anglo-American systems over the period of Conservative hegemony in the UK. What can we say about approaches that have worked and those that have failed? In our assessment of the UK, can we conclude that certain innovations were doomed to success or failure?

3

Executive Leadership in the Age of Minimalism: a Comparative Perspective

In examining change in Whitehall since the late 1970s, this book has chosen to focus on a period of extraordinary turmoil. In virtually all advanced democracies, immense changes have taken place in the entire context of executive leadership. These ultimately have put severe pressures on formerly stable relationships between politicians and bureaucrats.

Behind the turmoil we recognize very substantial shifts in the entire project of governance – from an emphasis on policy inventiveness and expansiveness to pragmatism and/or contraction. In no small part, these developments relate to a sharp decline in the expectations of the electorates of advanced democracies and their support of government involvement in their lives.

Richard Rose and B. Guy Peters, writing in 1978, anticipated a backlash to government intervention (pp. 33–4). They maintained that electorates had supported the rapid expansion of government programmes in the postwar years because their net impact increased the average voter's disposable income. In the 1970s, governments were approaching the threshold beyond which the funding of additional programmes would bite into disposable income.

To add to their difficulties, the two main energy shocks – in 1973 and 1979 – deeply impaired the capacity of advanced industrial nations to sustain growth. Sluggish economies that laboured simultaneously under high unemployment and inflation denied governments the new wealth which would enable them to expand their roles. In addition, neo-conservative and neo-liberal political leaders began to rally support for the view that both the size and pervasiveness of government had become millstones around the necks of national economies.

William F. Grover (1989) has argued that executive leaders have become prisoners of the market – ever fearful that any proposals to address problems with additional funds will result in a decline of 'business confidence'. In the minds of the electorate, small government has become beautiful.

British, Canadian, Australian and New Zealand prime ministers, along with US presidents, have over the past decade abandoned expansive views of government and – by extension – their roles. In four of the Westminster systems and the US, each party that controlled the executive branch at the beginning of 1979 had lost power by 1984 – with the reins changing hands in New Zealand in 1984, in Australia in 1983, in the UK and Canada in 1979 and in the US in 1980. Of course, Canada's Liberal Party regained power in 1980 only to lose it again to the Progressive Conservatives in 1984. The latter won a renewed mandate in 1988 and then 'self-destructed' – its two members did not even qualify as a party in 1993. The US returned the Democrats to the Presidency – barely that is – in 1992. Still, we would be hard-pressed indeed to find in this century another nine-year period during which the party-of-government remained the same in all four of our countries. New Zealand, of course, embraced the Labour Party only from 1984 to 1990. However, the National Party has largely pursued neo-liberal policies initially put in place during the period of Labour government.

Scholars have tended to characterize significant swings to the left or right as realignments. However, they associate these occurrences with 'critical elections' in which cathartic or epochal experiences cause electorates to shift their preponderant allegiances from one party to another (Key, 1955, pp. 3–18; Sundquist, 1983; Crewe and Sårlvik, 1983). We can see, for instance, why the Great Depression occasioned a realignment from the Republicans to the Democrats in the US. The catastrophic economic conditions put the nation under siege. The public embraced the interventionist politics of the New Deal because the dire circumstances seemed to warrant radical action.

The resilience of the parties which took power in our four nations between 1979 and 1984 undoubtedly stems in a substantial degree from the trauma through which their electorates passed during the period of economic stagnation of the late 1970s and early 1980s. While all four nations' economic decline pulled up considerably short of a depression, their voters appear to believe that they missed one just by a hair.

Concerns about the personalization of executive leadership, the deinstitutionalization of cabinet and bureaucratic systems and the emphasis on responsive, rather than policy, competence do loom large in the UK, Canada, Australia, New Zealand and the US. The exact contexts and parameters of these problems, however, vary greatly from system to system. The presence of cabinet government (rather than presidential leadership), permanent (rather than appointed) bureaucracies and – in the case of Australia – left-centre (rather than right-centre) parties does not immunize Westminster systems from executive styles which downplay the engagement of the conventional institutions for leadership. These approaches on the part of prime ministers – whatever the dys-functions – reflect the prevalent public mood about government. They also exploit the electronic technologies which allow prime ministers and presidents alike to go over the heads of their institutional antagonists and short-circuit standing operating procedures.

A Sense of Malaise, Outsider Politics and Some Second Thoughts

Almost upon cue a sense of malaise began to enshroud contemporary executive leadership in the UK, Canada, Australia, New Zealand and the US as we moved into the 1990s. Margaret Thatcher faced an unceremonious ousting and her successor – after a brief honeymoon – barely pulled his party out of an electoral dive in 1992. Many Conservative policies had clearly angered the public. Since the September 1992 débâcle over sterling, John Major's Government has slid steadily deeper into a quagmire. In the latter days of his 1988 mandate, Brian Mulroney struggled to maintain his approval ratings above the minimum lending rate while his country appeared close to disintegration. His successor of three months – Kim Campbell – led the Conservatives into electoral oblivion in the autumn of 1993.

Bob Hawke met the same fate as Mrs Thatcher did and his successor, Paul Keating, has found bashing the British monarchy a potent device for distracting the electorate from their economic ills. New Zealand's Labour Party put in place the most radical set of neo-liberal policies introduced in any of the Anglo-American systems. However, internal dissension so divided the Party that it lost power in 1990. After his triumph in the Persian Gulf, George Bush stepped down from his white horse to find that the war had only momentarily distracted the people from their growing concern with his lack of leadership in domestic affairs – a preoccupation that led ever-growing numbers of voters to assert that the country was on the wrong track. Bill Clinton initially seemed the beneficiary of a swing in the public mood that might sustain a genuine search for change in domestic policy. However, he has found it difficult to devise the types of understandable yet comprehensive solutions that will galvanize public attention and support.

Bert Rockman has stressed that students of executive leadership have increasingly questioned whether executive leadership itself is on the right track. Their unease stems from a shift in advanced political cultures from a collectivist to an individualistic or entrepreneurial age (Rockman, 1991a). The former system favoured the 'insider politics' which sustains a relatively high degree of salience for cabinet members, the standing bureaucracy, and institutionalized support systems for prime ministers and presidents.

The rise of an individualistic or entrepreneurial spirit, on the other hand, has ushered in an era of 'outsider politics' which places a premium on prime ministers and presidents who operate in bold strokes. These styles – marked by what Rockman terms 'decisive and clear-cut direction' – expressly discount the legitimacy of consultative and consensual ways of making decisions. Hence, Margaret Thatcher projected herself as a conviction politician bent on stamping out all 'consensus mongering'. John Major presents himself as a hybrid, an outsider who has become very conscious of the need to work with the inside. Major's pre-prime-ministerial career in government involved rapid moves through successively more important posts each of which relied very heavily upon Thatcher's patronage and disdain for Tory colleagues schooled in the ways of the inside. Yet Major – perhaps through a prescient reading of the signs of the times – tried to establish himself as head of a collective government and a builder of bridges to the standing bureaucracy.

Rockman and others have argued that Westminster systems have remained relatively immune from outsider politics. This assertion might hold up in the UK – Margaret Thatcher at least held one cabinet portfolio before becoming the leader of her party. John Major, although relatively new to the cabinet, had held three important posts before becoming prime minister. However, neither Brian Mulroney nor Bob Hawke had belonged to cabinet before becoming prime minister. In fact, Mulroney first won election to the House of Commons just one year before he became prime minister, while Hawke first won his seat in the House of Representatives only three years before becoming prime minister. Paul Keating, of course, served as treasurer under Hawke for eight years before resigning after his first and unsuccessful effort to dethrone his leader. Keating has also proved himself one of the most able parliamentary debaters this century. However, he has so far demonstrated little patience for collective decision making in cabinet and has found difficulty disguising his contempt for the standing bureaucracy. The evidence suggests that the 'insider–outsider' distinction could force us into generalizations about presidential and cabinet leadership and individual presidents and prime ministers that do not hold well under closer examination.

B. Guy Peters (1991) has examined the changes in the styles of executive leadership as it relates to government overload and retrenchment. He finds that the most successful leaders have run against 'government as usual'. But this does not suggest that they have provided an alternative ideology about government that includes an integrated and coherent vision of the state. They have, in fact, only proffered a series of beliefs about government that resonate with voters' disenchantment. In the 1980s, the political debates centred on slogans such as Thatcher's 'enterprise culture' which appealed to voters who had written off the government's ability to solve problems. Later, they shifted toward less harsh distinctions between government and the market. Although it proved a spectacular illusion, Bush's promise of a 'kinder and gentler' form of Reaganism played to the deepening concern that too many people had fallen through the safety nets during the 1980s. Major's emphasis on the social market and the development of a citizen's charter both came wrapped in language which seemed to accept the fact that public services would continue to perform important functions in society.

Still, as Peters notes, voters have not reached the point where they look once more to leaders to pursue comprehensive efforts at problem solving. Executive leaders do not seek – either from their cabinet colleagues or from the public service – detailed information about alternatives. They want to get on with the job of governing without canvassing all the ambiguities and pitfalls. This perhaps works well in clearly defined areas, such as cutting social services or privatizing, in which the government has arguably taken on more than it should have. However, it presents clear problems in areas in which the government has yet to define a role. That is, some problems are 'too massive and/or too inadequately understood' to lend themselves to the type of intuitive decision making that has become the hallmark of executive leadership in the neo-liberal era. Minimalist leadership has operated from the assumption that the number of issues on a government's plate will continue to shrink indefinitely. To date, however, the real world has continued to serve up an endless supply of new, seemingly insoluble problems. These more than cover the slack left by governments' declining attention to agenda items left over from the 1960s and 1970s.

Is Cabinet Government Still Viable?

American scholars and political leaders alike often look longingly at Westminster systems. From afar, cabinet government seems to have avoided the dysfunctions of the US system. It is believed that in Westminster systems the constitutional convention of collective cabinet responsibility constrains prime ministers from acting without adequately consulting their colleagues. The legitimizing forces issuing from such consultation foster more comprehensive and coherent policies. Also, these systems' bureaucracies still run overwhelmingly under the direction of permanent civil servants who, theoretically, remain indifferent as to which party holds power and precisely which policy options will hold sway. In theory, such officials contributed to the rationality of government actions by providing objective advice on alternatives and their likely consequences.

George Jones and Patrick Weller have long debated whether the idealized view of cabinet government still pertains or, instead, prime ministers so exert their prerogatives that collective decision making has greatly diminished (Jones, 1983; Weller, 1983). Jones maintains that prime ministers can never become thoroughly presidential. The very character of Westminster systems requires that they function within the confines of the support they can muster in cabinet. In turn, the cabinet cannot operate as a viable government unless it maintains the support of Parliament.

Jones stuck to his guns, even though the relatively monocratic leadership of Margaret Thatcher seemed to produce myriad counter-intuitive cases. In one assessment of her prime-ministership Jones concluded that she stretched but did not break the normal parameters of cabinet government. That is, the 'constitutional structures and political pressures' of the system kept her from personalizing British executive leadership. Our interviews present a different picture. We have found that many strategically located participants in the policy process became strongly convinced that Thatcher's style of leadership operated out of the normal bounds of cabinet government. This draws us inevitably to two questions. First, why did the Conservative Party and successive Thatcher cabinets put up with the Prime Minister's monocratic approach for so long? Second, notwithstanding the tensions produced by her approach, did her style prove dysfunctional with respect to the substantive consequences of her actions?

To Staff or Not to Staff

Several issues come to the fore in any attempt to look comparatively at the personal staffs which support prime ministers and presidents. Even the settings of the staffs exemplify the immense differences among Anglo-American systems. The US president's personal staff occupies the west and east wings of the White House and much of a huge office building next door. The most senior appointees crowd into cramped quarters in the west wing so as to be as close as possible to the president.

The UK prime minister's staff crams itself into a medium-size town house which the world knows as 10 Downing Street. To maintain the distinction between no. 10 and the Cabinet Office building, a coded security door guards a narrow passageway between the two. In Ottawa, the Prime Minister's Office (PMO) mostly occupies quarters on one side of the office building it shares with the Privy Council Office (PCO) – Canada's equivalent to Britain's Cabinet Office. In Canberra, the Prime Minister's Office lodges itself in a bunker-like suite in the new Parliament House. Members of the Department of the Prime Minister and Cabinet (PM&C) – roughly the equivalent of Canada's PCO – work so far away that they take chauffeur-driven cars to 'the Hill' when briefing the prime minister or taking minutes at the meetings of cabinet or its committees. New Zealand has only in the past few years begun to develop such resources at the disposal of the prime minister and/or cabinet. However, the pervasive influence of the Treasury has meant that there is no vacuum. In Wellington, a single building – dubbed the 'Bee Hive' for its peculiar design – provides the locus for higher-level executive–bureaucratic gamesmanship.

These differences in physical placement and accommodation direct us to a number of more fundamental issues. To UK, Canadian, Australian, and New Zealand observers, the number of political appointees working personally for American presidents seems to have ballooned beyond all proportion. In the US, great debates are fought over whether the White House should be run as a hierarchical organization with a strong chief of staff or a loose federation of White House barons, or some combination of both approaches. The issue of the organization – as opposed to the size – of the prime ministers' staffs has attracted relatively little attention in the four Westminster systems. None have attained the complexity that would cause the prime ministers to multiply the layers of hierarchy in their immediate offices.

On the other hand, discussions about how many personal advisers prime ministers should have have attracted a great deal of attention among practitioners and scholars alike in Westminster systems. We have already mentioned above the concerns registered in some circles that prime ministers have presidentialized their systems when – like Margaret Thatcher – they have paid less attention to the rubrics of cabinet consultation. Observers can become equally alarmed when it appears as if prime ministers have built up their personal staffs excessively.

The various systems also have different ideas about the distinction between the prime minister's staff and the cabinet secretariat. The security door between no. 10 and the Cabinet Office conveys the British view that the former serves the prime minister and the latter supports the entire cabinet. The Canadian arrangement whereby the PMO and PCO occupy the same building and scarcely demarcate each other hints at the degree to which the two have tended to work collaboratively. The new spatial language in Canberra underscores a development during the Hawke Government whereby all cabinet members – not just the prime minister – have tended to rely upon their personal staffs much more than their Canadian or UK opposite numbers. Thus PM&C joins the other two principal Australian central agencies – Treasury and Finance – in learning how to operate once removed from its minister. Wellington has scarcely made a distinction between the prime minister's personal staff, the secretariat for cabinet and the key economics department. The result has been that the latter has maintained the upper hand.

Patrick Weller, Australia's most noted student of prime ministers' advisory systems (Weller, 1985; 1989), does not press alarm buttons over suggestions that cabinet secretariats in Westminster systems owe a special responsibility toward their prime ministers. Many British practitioners and scholars – including George Jones – have, on the other hand, strenuously resisted any effort to characterize the UK Cabinet Office as a prime-ministerial staff. Canadians would probably resist any effort to change the name of PCO so as to incorporate 'Prime Minister.' However, they continue to turn a blind eye to PMO's and PCO's cohabitation.

Meanwhile new spatial language in Canberra – which assigns the Prime Minister's Office to the new Parliament House and keeps PM&C down in Barton (a precinct of functional departmental buildings beneath Parliament Hill) – suggests that PM&C has become less 'PM' and more 'C'. In all such developments and nuances, Weller (1991) sees a convergence whereby prime ministers, ever more the heads of government, tend to shape and mould their personal staffs and cabinet secretariats according to their preferences of style and the exigencies of the moment. This, Weller believes, does not suggest for a moment that they have become presidents. It does, however, indicate that prime ministers have reshaped the institutional resources and frameworks of cabinet government to enhance the responsiveness of these to their own agendas and leadership.

A Framework for Analysis

Students of comparative executive leadership have largely failed to probe the extent to which some of the most intractable difficulties faced by prime ministers in advanced democracies derive from generalized problems with executive leadership. We cannot gloss over the obvious systemic differences which a comparative approach must recognize or the different ways chief executives engage their bureaucracies; however, several areas of convergence come to light when we examine executive leadership across systems. For this reason, we will take pains to set our analysis of executive leadership within a wider, comparative framework.

Under close scrutiny we even find that several of the dominant themes of US presidential studies enjoy considerable timeliness in the three main prime-ministerial systems in the Anglo-American political tradition. For instance, Kernell (1986) has much to say to Britons, Canadians and Australians concerned about the tendency – largely abetted by the ascendancy of television – for prime ministers to make direct appeals to the public. Similarly, Seymour-Ure's comparative study of prime ministers' and presidents' press secretaries in the United States, United Kingdom, Canada and Australia (1991) suggests a high degree of convergence between the four systems. His findings highlight the extent to which prime ministers have employed the same strategies as presidents to concentrate news management in their personal offices, and used direct appeals through the media to enhance their leverage both with cabinet and parliament.

Deinstitutionalization of the executive branch – as recorded in the US by Margaret Wyszomirski (1982) and Terry Moe (1985) – has engendered considerable comment elsewhere. Even George Jones (1987; 1991) concedes that Margaret Thatcher utilized *ad hoc* meetings of cabinet ministers to the point where the British tradition of highly regularized and relatively inclusive cabinet committees has atrophied substantially. Campbell has argued strenuously that Pierre Trudeau overly personalized the upper levels of the career bureaucracy in Canada during his lengthy prime-ministership (1968 to 1984, except for nine months in 1979). In Australia, Gough Whitlam (prime minister 1972–5) and Malcolm Fraser (1975–83) expected the Department of Prime Minister and Cabinet – even though it was staffed by career civil servants – to go beyond simply processing cabinet business to actively advancing the progress of their top priorities through the governmental apparatus. The department thus has learned to adapt to the 'demands and style' of each prime minister (Weller, 1985, pp. 138–9; 1991, p. 13).

Advisory Systems

In the development and utilization of their advisory systems, presidents and prime ministers are constrained by a range of principles and political factors that influence the selection of cabinet colleagues and the nature of their advisers. An assessment of prime ministers' management designs and their implementation of these requires an understanding of the reasons why collective decision making has been significant in Westminster systems. The relative power of prime ministers varies among countries within the Westminster tradition, and usually between the main parties that have experienced office.

All chief executives have personal staffs. What types of officials do they appoint as advisers and how do they organize their work? With regard to appointees, we should keep in mind that increases in the proportion of such officials involves a set of issues different from those debates over politicization of the public service (Aberbach, Putnam and Rockman, 1981). Over the past two decades, virtually every advanced democratic system has encountered an intensification of the engagement of senior officials – appointed or career – in executive–bureaucratic politics (Campbell, 1988). Thus, a career-based secretariat could prove to be a more politically effective resource than a party-political staff full of ideas about how to tame the governmental leviathan.

In all these issues, engagement of the state apparatus constitutes the common goal of chief executives. Both presidents and prime ministers – with varying degrees of collegial involvement of their cabinet members – set out to seize control of, and direct toward their own purposes, the bureaucratic establishment. This enterprise requires some level of institutionalization of guidance mechanisms in the cores of departments and agencies, and the central agencies for the executive branch.

The institutionalization dimension also takes in formal machinery for processing executive branch business. Here much depends on the presence or absence of a constitutional norm whereby executive authority is to be exerted collectively. The former situation has usually resulted – in response to the increasing complexity of government – in the proliferation of standing and ad hoc cabinet committees (Mackie and Hogwood, 1985, pp. 7–9).

In considering the interplay between the desire for chief executives to consolidate and maintain their political support and to engage the state apparatus toward fulfilling their policy agenda, we can conceive of four quadrants (Campbell, 1986, p. 16). Political leaders who achieve some level of 'policy competence' occupy the area bordered by relatively high political responsiveness and effective engagement of the institutionalized state apparatus. It would be the rare chief executive who would not strive in some way for policy competence. However, he or she could drift toward another quadrant by failing to achieve an appropriate balance between political responsiveness and utilizing the standing machinery of government. Those who stress the former at the cost of the latter run the risk of winding up with 'politicized incompetence'. Those who defer to custodians of the state apparatus flirt with a variant of 'neutral competence'. Finally, a government might slip into a weak mixture of both and land in 'nonpoliticized incompetence'.

There are four approaches that can be adopted by a political leadership in its efforts to achieve policy competence. In delineating these styles, we must distinguish between governments that foster countervailing views in the advisory system and those that seek to limit conflict. We must also differentiate between those that rely heavily upon central coordinating agencies – such as the Department of the Prime Minister and Cabinet in Australia – and those that prefer as much as possible that line departments should settle daily matters on their own.

Under this framework, a 'priorities and planning' style emerges when the political leadership encourages competing advice. It simultaneously entrusts central agencies with the development of umbrella strategies and assuring that substantive decisions adhere to these. 'Broker politics' results when countervailing views abound but central agencies play only restrained roles in the integration of policies. 'Survival politics' prevails in the opposite situation, that is when central agencies increasingly draw issues into their

Figure 1   Political leadership, partisan responsiveness and leadership styles

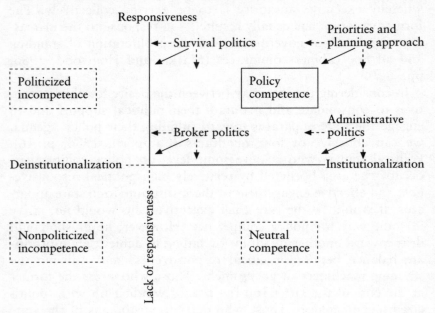

Source: Campbell, 1986

orbit and expressly seek to dampen competition between advisers. Finally, 'administrative politics' develops when the political leadership tends neither to encourage a diversity of views nor to rely heavily upon central agencies for guiding and controlling the rest of the executive branch.

Since the economic shocks in the 1970s, executive leaders have eschewed priorities and planning. For one thing, the age of stringency has brought an end to the candy store of spending opportunities which enticed governments during the 1960s. Also, the public mood has turned mean, focusing leaders' minds increasingly on the need to avoid positions that will undermine their political support. Political capital has proved just as scarce as fiscal capital. Thus, leaders have adopted 'blame avoidance' and 'risk minimalization' as instruments of political survival. The more priorities and planning have appeared elusive goals the more executive leaders have compromised their capacity for policy competence.

Johan P. Olsen has alerted us to the effects of economic conditions on our view of the state and, in turn, what we expect from political executives. He argues that political executives operating within the corporatist–pluralistic model for governance that emerged in Norway during the period of economic expansion and growth of the welfare state lost all sense of proportion (1983, pp. 31–3). Their efforts to respond to societal demands went beyond the integration of broad and institutionalized groupings to the accommodation of extremely particular and *ad hoc* interests. Following strategies of privatization and deregulation, the conservative-centre government of the mid-1980s attempted to recapture the 'institutional state', a style of governance that seeks to define in clear terms the boundary between the state and various sectors of society.

In a subsequent work (1988), Olsen has further developed his thesis in ways which point up its applicability to the comparative study of executive leadership. Here three points emerge. First, political executives must develop their relations with the bureaucratic elite in ways which comport with the formers' preferred model for governance. Instrumental approaches will prevail when general agreement exists over the boundaries of the state; evolutionary modes when the political executive attempts to redefine these boundaries; an emphasis on adaptiveness characterizes the classic corporate–pluralistic state as it adjusts to shifts in societal power from group to group; and political responsiveness becomes the dominant value for the welfare state that – like Norway in the 1960s and 1970s – has become the 'supermarket' for society's 'great necessities'.

Second, political executives can misread their circumstances to the point where a disjunction develops between their leadership style and the received image of the state. Canada's Pierre Elliott Trudeau ceaselessly pressed the sovereign–rational approach in a highly fragmented, consociational and corporate–pluralistic state (Aucoin, 1986; French, 1980; Hartle, 1983). Britain's two Labour prime ministers during the 1970s – Harold Wilson and James Callaghan – failed adequately to address the shift of British thinking about the state from corporate–pluralistic to institutional (Keegan and Pennant-Rea, 1979; Rose and Peters, 1978; Hood and Wright, 1981). Thus, their adaptive strategies were left unrewarded.

Third, Olsen's emphasis on administrative style as related to the boundary between the state and society invites us to make a distinction between moderate and radical views of the proper role of government. In other words, we must allow for thinking which crosses the line between reorienting and dismantling the state. As represented by some of the thinking behind Ronald Reagan's and Margaret Thatcher's form of market-oriented governance, a distinct movement emerged in the 1980s toward recrafting the entire context of the state in ways that would limit it to only a fraction of its former functions (Savas, 1982; Riddell, 1983, Chapter 8).

The Spectre of Public Choice

Just as advanced democracies had begun to recognize the constraints on the role of the state, public choice theorists began to promote a perspective on political leadership that eventually constricted analysts' expectations for executive politics. They anticipated by several years the limits of campaign appeals based on candidates' promises of social programmes for which ultimately voters had to pay. It was not until the late 1970s that mainstream students of executive leadership began to observe that presidents and prime ministers faced new constraints (Rose and Peters, 1978, pp. 33–4). In the world of practical politics, however, the public choice perspective had already linked up with monetarist economics and captured the minds of the two most dominant chief executives of the 1980s – Reagan and Thatcher.

Margaret Thatcher achieved considerable success in pressing the public choice agenda. She so cut spending that the UK government operated in surplus throughout the last years of the 1980s. She privatized numerous government enterprises and introduced a series of reforms designed to make the public service more accountable for its resources.

It is ironic, considering the fact that the initial theoretical progenitors of the approach were American, that public choice perspectives achieved only limited success in the US under Ronald Reagan and George Bush. What is bad for the goose is bad for the gander. The separation of powers and divided government made it as difficult to implement the public choice agenda as it had been to advance the welfare state (Stockman, 1986; Roberts, 1984). The proponents of public choice touted the approach as a cure for the incrementalism of the US policy process.

Among these theorists, William Niskanen stands out because his work had a direct impact on the thinking of Conservatives close to Thatcher before she became prime minister. Niskanen styled the crisis of executive politics as one in which presidents find it impossible to break down the alliances of officials, legislators and interest groups that fuel the proliferation and expansion of government programmes. He asserted that the budget-maximizing tendencies of government officials – appointed as well as career – stood at the root of the problem (Niskanen, 1971, pp. 21–2, 38). The fragmentation of the system sets officials up in a perfect climate in which to pursue their personal utility. This involves seeking higher salaries, better perquisites, greater reputations and more power, dispensing more patronage, increasing programmatic outputs, and it adds up to immense pressures to expand organizations and increase budgets.

In suggesting how political executives might stem budget-maximizing, Niskanen departed from the received wisdom of the time. This held that those seeking to control bureaucracies should acquire more detailed information about the actual operation of policy programmes. He argued that the surest way to take political executives off the scent of budget-maximizers was to get them absorbed by issues associated with comprehensiveness, detail, procedural rationality and control (Niskanen, 1973a, pp. 6–8; cites Wildavsky, 1961).

Niskanen proposed a number of structural changes in the US budget process which would replace *ad hoc* mechanisms with automatic rules that would force tough decisions. This automatization included a committee of congressional budget leaders which would recommend 'target' outlays to both houses and the president, a requirement that Congress would have to offset spending beyond that recommended in the agreed budget with dollar-for-dollar increases in personal income taxes, and the assumption by the Executive Office of the President of a more active role in providing express guidance to the Office of Management and Budget on budget priorities – thereby making '... the proposed budget a more effective instrument of the political interests of the President' (Niskanen, 1973a, pp. 17–19, 55–7).

Although the approach has encountered considerable difficulty in its native land, public choice has found much more fertile soil in parliamentary systems. This is ironic. Several qualities of such systems already make them less susceptible than the American system to afflictions – such as budget-maximizing bureaucracy – which so absorb the attention of Niskanen and others. First, political appointees and career civil servants in the US, especially the latter, tend to focus their careers much more narrowly than their opposite numbers in parliamentary systems (Heclo, 1977, pp. 116–20; 1984, pp. 18–20). This makes them more prone to defending relatively narrow bureaucratic interests. Second, parliamentary systems do not have truly transformative legislatures. That is, legislators lack the capacity to mould and reshape laws and budgets independently of the guidance provided by the political executive as embodied in the leadership of the governing party or coalition (Polsby, 1975, p. 277). The absence of long and reasonably secure tenure in specialized fields for bureaucrats and transformative legislatures inhibits the development of strong client–patron relationships in parliamentary systems.

In the English-speaking world, parliamentary systems began implementing public-choice approaches to budgeting in the late 1970s. As a condition of its 1976 rescue of the pound, the International Monetary Fund prompted the UK's Labour Government under James Callaghan to extend the application of 'cash limits' to public expenditure substantially (Keegan and Pennant-Rea, 1979, p. 205). The Treasury imposed cash limits on the estimates submitted to Parliament (Campbell, 1983, pp. 185–6). Departments received authority from Parliament to spend a given amount of cash, not an open-ended remit to pursue specific programmes. In theory, this procedure greatly reduced overspending. However, not all parliamentary systems concentrate budget power in one department to the degree that the UK does. The imposition of cash-limits – particularly without external pressure – becomes especially difficult if control over economic policy is divided between a finance department and a budget department, as is the case in Canada and Australia. It also would encounter much more resistance if ministers – as has traditionally been the case in Canada and more recently has become the practice in Australia – make budget decisions through collective consultation rather than defer largely to the judgement of the minister responsible for preparing the budget (Campbell, 1983, pp. 189–200; Campbell and Halligan, 1992).

As already noted, the Thatcher Government so tightened fiscal policy that it ran surpluses throughout the latter part of the 1980s. Rational choice perspectives played an important role here. In 1973, Niskanen published a monograph in the UK (1973b) which set out to alert Britons to the need to control the growth of bureaucracy. This work argued that prime ministers should eschew particularistic considerations – such as personal and regional backgrounds – in the assignment of cabinet secretaries and ensure that they do not go native by shuffling them occasionally on a random basis (Niskanen, 1973b, p. 60). In making such proposals, Niskanen showed he did not understand the dynamics of cabinet systems of government. However, his book did work a tremendous effect on Margaret Thatcher, who urged all her ministers to read it when she formed her first government in 1979.

Adapting Niskanen's message to the circumstances of the British executive, Thatcher stressed innovations that made budgeting less *ad hoc* and more automatic (Campbell, 1983, pp. 186–9; Wildavsky, 1983, p. 164). She extended cash limits to several previously exempt programmes; she created a 'Star Chamber' of cabinet – a group of her most prominent ministers – to impose spending constraints in cases where the Treasury and line departments had become deadlocked; she abolished Policy Analysis and Review, that is interdepartmental studies of programmes, which as often as not failed to recommend the tough options necessary to limit the size of the budget.

Some schizophrenia has emerged among those who style the central task of political executives as taming the bureaucracy. Public choice oriented political executives have embraced as a primary goal reduction of the bureaucrats' discretion and latitude for independent advocacy. In this respect, they have tried to re-establish the dichotomy between policy and administration, which dominated thinking about the relationship between politicians and bureaucrats earlier in this century (Wilson, 1941 (reprint); Goodnow, 1900, pp. 92–3; Gulick, 1937, p. 10). Yet many of the same political executives have sought to devise ways of making bureaucracy run more like organizations in the private sector. This would require public servants to become more creative and risk-oriented in managerial terms. As Niskanen argued (1973b, p. 61): 'Bureaucrats . . . would be permitted to offer a wide range of public services. . . . There would be no "strong" departments or "strong" secretaries. The choice of which bureau or combination of bureaus to supply a specific service would be forced to the level of the executive review.'

Peter Aucoin – a Canadian scholar who has closely followed managerial reform in his country over the past 20 years – has argued that the automatic decision criteria and managerialist paradigms of public choice political executives derive from different and potentially conflicting premises (1990a, pp. 125–6). Automatic decision criteria frame the problem of the relationship between political executives and bureaucrats as one of control and seek measures through which the elected politicians might tame the public service by putting it under tighter constraints. Managerialist paradigms, on the other hand, start with the proposition that, intramurally, bureaucracies run too hierarchically, thereby stifling imagination and initiative.

In the US, the two premises have not done much hand-to-hand combat. This is due largely to the difficulty of introducing managerialist concepts in a highly fragmented bureaucratic culture (Campbell, 1986, pp. 192–3; Hansen and Levine, 1988, pp. 267–8). On the other hand, the UK, Canada, Australia and New Zealand have all initiated managerialist programmes with relatively far-reaching objectives (Aucoin, 1989; Boston, 1987; Considine, 1988; Fry, 1988; Scott, Bushnell and Sallee, 1990; Keating and Holmes, 1990; Kemp, 1990). As with the introduction of automatic budgeting techniques, however, the level of fragmentation in the political/bureaucratic system appears to affect the degree to which political executives can guide public service organizations toward managerialist approaches. Here Britain and New Zealand have achieved the most sweeping changes – which is not to say they have all worked: Australia has taken a more paced approach and achieved a great deal and Canada has moved cautiously and made only modest progress (Aucoin, 1990a; 1990b; Hood, 1990; Campbell and Halligan, 1992).

The New Zealand case represents by far the most conscious use of public choice theory as a justification for managerial reform in bureaucracy. In the late 1980s, Graham Scott and Peter Gorringe (1989), then both Treasury officials, explicitly employed agency theory to justify their department's initiatives toward re-organization of the public service. Relying heavily upon the work of A. A. Alchain (e.g. Alchain and Woodward, 1987), they fully embraced the view that bureaucrats serve as the agents of politicians who, in turn, function as the agents of the populace. In this regard, Scott and Gorringe distinguished between strategies for improving 'performance' and those attempting to enhance accountability (1989, p. 6). The latter focus on whether '. . . politicians . . . buy the right services to achieve social goals like wealth, justice and the relief of suffering.' Politicians need not purchase from the bureaucracy all the services which advance social goals.

In all this, bureaucrats often perceive constraints on their agencies. They welcome the opportunities for greater flexibility that managerialism holds out. However, many find themselves tempted to conclude that political executives have thrown them crumbs after sharply curtailing their ability to exercise discretion and to operate as advocates. A civil-service head of a large department in Britain put it as succinctly as any:

> I said to Treasury, and so did many others, 'This is a fine doctrine, but unless you believe it and are prepared to implement it and accept what goes with it, it won't work.' . . . you can't say to someone, 'You're responsible for your budget and you won't get any more money, and you can carry your own account,' if at the same time you are saying, 'I will determine your staff, what they will be paid, how much you will pay for accommodation. . . .' And this is exactly how it worked out. The amount of delegation of eventual control was at most five per cent. (1990 Interview.)

Much of the ongoing debate centres on how we ascertain whether neo-liberal political leadership, notwithstanding efforts to redefine the boundaries of the state and to sharply curtail public spending, has failed to foster and tap competently the creative resources of the standing bureaucracy. Terry Moe – who has greatly influenced thinking about executive leadership in the US during the age of constraint – accurately identifies one school of thought in the profession that gives, in his view, too much attention to 'neutral' competence (1985). This criterion for executive performance focuses on whether an administration effectively engages the permanent state apparatus by getting it to work imaginatively toward fulfilling its core policy commitments.

Moe correctly notes that this concept can take on romantic proportions in the minds of some analysts.

Colin Campbell and Margaret Wyszomirski have amplified this view by asserting that the concept 'neutral competence' remains ill-defined by those who mourn the suspicion and/or neglect of the state apparatus that has characterized recent administrations' encounters with their executive branches: 'Their critique might simply be a lament for a neutrally competent . . . [civil service] that never existed – one in which officials offered their advice and conducted the affairs of state without any personal commitments of a partisan or political nature' (1991, p. 15).

This does not mean that political executives have nothing to gain by tapping into the expertise and institutional memory of the permanent bureaucracy. However, they must engage it or ignore it for the right reasons. Governments that dismiss the capabilities of the permanent bureaucracy become error prone about small things which, over time, can add up to major crises. Yet administrations which defer too much to the ongoing bureaucracy – allowing it to ponder the myriad options interminably – will lose sight of the big picture and doom themselves to electoral defeat. In either case, such governments would betray a misunderstanding of the meaning of 'neutral'. It should not imply that public servants have abandoned all ideas and convictions about the range of possibilities suggesting themselves in a given issue. It should simply convey the notion that their career commitments prescribe a capacity to adapt what they supply – expertise and knowledge about the system – to the needs of their new principals each time the executive branch passes from one party to the other.

In Westminster systems, the amount of attention paid to governments' relations with the permanent bureaucracy has also lulled observers into giving inadequate attention to the dynamics by which prime ministers have interacted with their political advisers and cabinet colleagues. As we have already noted, George Jones, rejoining an old debate which he has been conducting for several years now with Patrick Weller, vigorously denied that Margaret Thatcher was running her cabinet in a 'presidential' way (Jones, 1991).

Weller has led a growing number of students of executive leadership in Westminster systems who assert that the complexity of modern government and the availability of electronic means for making direct appeals to the public have introduced an era of convergence between the devices employed by prime ministers to get what they want from their governments and those used by presidents with their administrations. In this context, he has construed the growth and specialization of staffs reporting directly to prime ministers as fitting within the evolutionary development of Westminster systems toward more central guidance by chief executives.

Jones denies such an evolutionary process. Even in the case of Thatcher, he argues, her party maintained the potential – assuming action on the part of Conservative MPs – to remove her if her approach appeared greatly at variance with the conventions of British government. However, Jones's argument only takes us so far. In fact, the 1990 leadership challenge which unseated Thatcher came initially not from within the most aggrieved institution – the cabinet – but from a group of disenchanted MPs who had rallied around Michael Heseltine and whom Thatcher had forced from the cabinet more than four years earlier. That the members of that cabinet – apart from Nigel Lawson and Geoffrey Howe, both of whom resigned – did not publicly register their concerns with her until she lost the confidence of her party members in the House of Commons hardly means that the seeds of her own demise had not begun to germinate long before. As *The Times* of London had noted as far back as 1984, Margaret Thatcher had neglected cabinet consultation and manipulated ministers to an unprecedented degree:

> Ministers increasingly voice concern . . . about the way key decisions are being taken by Mrs Thatcher and small groups of ministers without reference to the full Cabinet – a practice which they say has contributed to failings in the presentation of policies. One minister said privately last week that Mrs Thatcher probably has used Cabinet less than any prime minister since the war. Some MPs are calling for a return to genuine Cabinet Government. (5 March 1984.)

A Pinch of Personality?

In comparison with literature on the presidency, which supplies an abundance of studies centring on the personalities of presidents, we find relatively little work that explicitly examines prime

ministers from the standpoint of personality. This does not mean
that scholars do not have available biographies of prime ministers which develop profiles of incumbents' personalities and make
links between these and their performance in office (Young, 1989;
Radwanski, 1978; Gwyn, 1980; d'Alpuget, 1982). However,
political scientists normally leave this type of work to journalists
who have the luxury of both knowing a great deal more about
incumbents' foibles and having to adhere to somewhat relaxed
standards for analysis. Some expressly psychoanalytical works
have appeared which reviewers have believed make somewhat
strained connections between prime ministers' personalities and
their performances (Little, 1983; Anson, 1991). Political scientists' efforts to incorporate some material that relates to personality have tended to employ this only within a context in which the
leadership style of a prime minister serves as an especially engaging topic (Campbell, 1980; Weller, 1989).

Personality, thus, proves to be a relatively elusive dimension to
analyses of political executives. As if this did not constitute a
sufficient obstacle, researchers' inclusion of personality factors
has increasingly run up against the strongly institutionalist
perspective of many scholars these days. This view has taken
strong root in the US. For instance, during the previous US administration Barbara Sinclair, a noted scholar of presidential–
congressional relations, issued a strong caveat against factoring
personality into evaluations of George Bush's presidential performance. At a time when Bush was still riding high in the polls,
she directly took on his critics' hand-wringing over whether his
neglect of so many challenging domestic issues reflected a flawed
presidential character:

> The behavior of the president and members of Congress is shaped
> and constrained by the context in which they act; what comment-
> ators interpret as playing politics or a lack of backbone is, given
> the context, often the best strategy . . . That is, it is the best way
> to advance the politician's goals of policy results and electoral
> success. While some may argue that the goal of electoral success
> is disreputable and that what is needed are principled public
> officials indifferent to being voted out of office, this argument
> ignores the crucial role that wanting to be re-elected plays in keep-
> ing public officials responsive to the wishes of the electorate that
> chose them. (Sinclair, 1991, p. 155.)

Very much like Jones's, Sinclair's position fitted within the institutionalist perspective, which currently dominates analyses of political executives. Sinclair appeared essentially to assert: '. . . if George Bush was ignoring problems, the people would not be giving him such high approval ratings;' while Jones's argument seems to boil down to '. . . if cabinet and Parliament believed Mrs Thatcher was operating outside the conventions of collective cabinet government, they would remove her as leader.' The institutionalists view executive behaviour as stemming much more from the exigencies of office and the maintenance of political support than from personality.

In our assessment of recent executive leadership in the UK, we have tried to disentangle what scholars such as Sinclair and Jones have argued. On the one hand, they seem to be maintaining that personality lacks salience because institutional factors largely cancel out its effects. On the other, they seem to base part of their reluctance to include personality in analysis on the grounds that its operationalization presents too many difficulties. The first rationale would absolve us of any responsibility to continue to consider personality as a major element of prime-ministerial behaviour. The second, however, should prompt at least some of us to redouble efforts to develop theoretically cogent ways of incorporating personality factors in analyses of political executives.

The American political scientist Erwin C. Hargrove has done more than any other scholar to mediate between students of the executive leaders focusing on institutional factors and those seeking to introduce a systematic consideration of personality (1993). He argues that a great deal of executive leadership does not, in fact, fit neatly into what we might expect from incumbents' institutional context (p. 5). Such behaviour includes how political executives present themselves to mass audiences, how they devise their initial policy agendas, how they manage decision processes, and how they persuade independent power holders in the policy arena.

Hargrove registers a strong and, we believe, legitimate question about how much observers can leave to the institutional constraints of executive leaders. As a student of the US presidency, he notes that history presents us with several cases of presidents who engaged in behaviour stemming more from their 'internal vulnerabilities' than from their objective circumstances (1993,

p. 20). Owing to the monocratic structure of the American executive, such tendencies when present pose a greater threat than they would under collective formats of political leadership. However, Hargrove's central question bears close examination under cabinet government as well.

In so far as collective governance yields to prime-ministerial rule of a near-monocratic nature, the issue of how a system protects itself from 'inappropriate ego-defensive actions' (1993, p. 30) can present itself with great force. To be sure, Thatcher – through the sheer force of personality – led Whitehall through a time of unparalleled experimentation. Two questions remain, however. First, how much of the change involved Whitehall in paying lip-service to a chief executive who would not take no for an answer? Second, even if Whitehall – or its most consequential parts with respect to administrative culture – did sincerely embrace Thatcherism, how much of this will prove sustainable given both a return to more usual leadership and the changing expectations of the public *vis-à-vis* governance?

Conclusion

This chapter has tapped the comparative literature on executive leadership in an attempt to define what we can expect from presidents and prime ministers in a minimalist age. What difference can they make? We began by noting the degree to which problems with executive leadership in advanced liberal democracies have become the norm rather than the exception. Among cabinet systems of government which follow the Westminster model, we find growing doubts about the viability of collective decision making. Also, serious questions have arisen about how prime ministers organize their policy advice, including whether they have so personalized their resources that they no longer facilitate cabinet government.

We argued that, notwithstanding their different institutional contexts, presidents and prime ministers have tended increasingly to pursue responsive competence at the expense of policy competence. We probed at length the effects of public choice theory in all this. Chief executives, more or less explicitly, have increasingly drawn upon this perspective to justify their approaches to governance. Perhaps more important, analysts frequently excuse detached leadership. They do so for the tautological reason that the times, the public mood and/or institutional constraints make more positive governance very difficult to achieve.

Consistent with this perspective, the public choice approach has shown particular distaste for assessments of executive leadership that pay attention to the personal style of presidents and prime ministers. We adopt quite a different view, as will become obvious in the next chapter.

4

Leadership under Thatcher and Major and the Legacy of Neo-liberalism

After winning her third mandate in 1987, Margaret Thatcher seemed to have established a dynasty for her party. Indeed, soon after the election, she began to make it clear that she fully intended to lead her party into the next election, thereby suggesting that her leadership would prove essential to the continuance of her party's mission to 'turn Britain around'.

The facts now suggest that Thatcher's perception of her situation had become delusional if not messianic. And, just as many pundits believed that the 1987 election results seemed to enshrine the Thatcher hegemony, the executive–bureaucratic community seemed to have become resigned to the Thatcher style of governance. Ministers had learned to live with a situation in which the cabinet and its standing committees simply ratified deals that the Prime Minister had reached in *ad hoc* and private negotiations. Officials lowered their sights, accepting the fact that ministers sought little by way of policy analysis and that Thatcher thought their job was to run the public service like Marks and Spencer.

Examining what went wrong, we find the short answer in the process whereby any type of executive leadership ultimately wears thin. It does so because the chief executive ultimately becomes tired and/or sloppy and – in time – accumulates a sufficient number of resentful colleagues that the long knives begin to glisten even in the light of day. The less obvious answer proves somewhat more difficult. It is to be found in the fairly illusive region of executive leadership associated with personality.

If chief executives eventually wear down, then we can assume that they become increasingly subject to forms of behaviour that emanate from – employing Hargrove's term – internal vulnerabilities. The relatively collective nature of its executive leadership leaves governance in Britain less exposed to this phenomenon than it has become in the US. None the less, Thatcher's style approximated to the monocratic nature of US presidential leadership as much as executive leadership can within the context of the Westminster model.

In the literature of the US presidency, discussion about the effects of personality on behaviour have centred on whether incumbents have developed and maintained positive views of their jobs and whether they pursue them in an active way. Ironically, the seminal proponent of positioning presidents in quadrants associated with the interaction of these 'positive–negative' and 'active–positive' axes – James Barber – has consistently attracted scorn for oversimplistic application of his paradigm (Barber, 1972; George, 1974; Qualls, 1977; Barber, 1977). The subsequent critiques of institutionalist and public choice theorists have exacerbated Barber's problems with the rest of the discipline. Yet most mainline presidency scholars pursue analyses that explicitly take into consideration the positive–negative and/or active–passive tendencies of incumbents (Hargrove, 1993; George, 1980, pp. 146, 155; Neustadt, 1990, p. 206). In fact, one derives from their work the sense that they believe that well-adjusted and productive presidents (invariably Franklin D. Roosevelt and John F. Kennedy) differ immensely from neurotic and ritualitistic ones (characteristically Lyndon B. Johnson and Richard M. Nixon) in the degree to which they derived psychic income from their positive engagement in the process of governance.

To address the case of Margaret Thatcher in the light of this literature, we must treat two problems – neither of which stems from the fact that we are examining the personality dimensions of executive leadership in a Westminster system while employing concepts developed in the US. First, political scientists have revealed in their portrayals of active–positive styles a bias for the type of interventionist and expansive governance that characterized executive leadership during the apogee of the welfare state. This raises the issue of what a well-adjusted activist would look like in the era of stringency and the contraction of the state. Second, and relatedly, analysts failed to differentiate between types of activity. If activeness depends on engagement in one's job, it will take different shapes depending upon the dimensions of his or her position that a chief executive chooses to stress.

Campbell has addressed these two issues by distinguishing between four types of engagement in executive leadership (1991). 'New order' chief executives pursue fairly ambitious and positive agendas which will enhance the role of the state in ways that comport with the views of those supportive of interventionism. Generally, these leaders employ more readily than others charismatic appeal to the general electorate. They also attract into government those who want to change society and serve the public. 'Executive' presidents and prime ministers pursue a different kind of leadership. They wish either to consolidate the achievements of a 'new order' predecessor or, if they have based their appeal on rolling back the state, to help the country toward tough decisions about the desirable extent and degree of intervention. In either case, 'executive' incumbents believe that their job requires them to make government run more efficiently and effectively and keep it down to size.

'Being there' chief executives focus much more on the symbolic dimensions of leadership than on policy and the operational parts. They see themselves as more heads of state than heads of government. Notwithstanding his huge success in rolling back the size of government in the US, Ronald Reagan's central policy objectives called upon little by way of positive governance. His monumental inattention to detail clearly contributed to the immense disjunction between his administration's pious wishes concerning efficiency and effectiveness and actual practice. Reagan threw himself hugely into the Presidency, but largely in the roles of the high priest of the national liturgy, the leader of the free world in the struggle against the Evil Empire and the general-purpose icon for neo-liberalism.

Finally, a 'let's deal' political executive focuses on the cut and thrust of political bargaining. Here political objectives might seem minimalist, commitments to the operational side of government marginal and affective attachment to the symbolic dimensions of office secondary. 'Let's deal' leaders start out wanting to resolve impasses. When this gets increasingly difficult, they may tend to get absorbed with winning battles.

Britain has not proved fertile ground for 'new order' prime ministers. Winston Churchill struck a charismatic chord in his prime-ministership during the Second World War. However, he proved very much a 'being there' prime minister during his second administration. Clement Attlee presided over a huge amount of change. But his style proved far from charismatic and the 'new order' politics that his government followed rested substantially upon the consensus about the role of the state which had emerged during the war. It did not require a lot of pushing and shoving. Macmillan, Eden and Douglas-Home all fit within the 'let's deal' mould, Macmillan having immense success, the others encountering failure. Wilson, Heath and Callaghan operated 'executive' governments – so much so that, like their American soulmate Jimmy Carter, they tended to focus upon competent engagement of the state apparatus at the cost of their electoral futures.

Our assessment of Thatcher will argue that she started as an 'executive' prime minister. However, unlike Wilson, Heath and Callaghan, she soon departed from this approach. Temperamentally she lacked the patience to follow through in a concerted way with running the government. Further, she had little regard either for routine cabinet decision making or for the permanent bureaucracy. Finally, she proved much more attentive than the others to political danger, sensing instinctively when circumstances forced her to take bold actions, deviating from the counsel both of her ministers and of Whitehall.

Some might mistake Thatcher's migration from executive leadership as a move to 'new order' politics. Yet neither the objectives that she set out nor her personalization of decision making would sustain this analysis. She became increasingly a 'being there' prime minister. The more she employed the regal 'we' when referring to herself the more she imbibed the heady wine of symbolic politics. To be sure, Thatcherism incorporated particular policies – a special relationship with the US, scepticism toward Europe, privatization, fiscal stringency and running down the welfare state. The radicalism of her Government's policies – such as the ill-fated Community Charge – continued unabated. But increasingly Thatcher sold herself as an icon more than a chief executive, the tough lady who had shown Britain how to regain its spine.

In her article in the American magazine *Newsweek* (27 April 1992) Thatcher uses language whose form parallels very closely that messianic language employed by Jesus in the last discourse as rendered in St John's gospel. For instance, we find this caution against false prophets (i.e. John Major): 'If a man gets up and says, "Look really, I'm a very modest man," would you believe him? What about the person who says, "I care far more about people than she did"? Look at the record, and make a judgment.' Or take these reflections on Thatcherism as against what John Major has to offer: 'There isn't such a thing as Majorism . . . We restored the strength and reputation of Britain. We did it on fundamental principles. They bear my name, but they are far older than I am . . . Thatcherism will live. It will live long after Thatcher has died, because we had the courage to restore the great principles and put them into practice.'

These words reflect the degree to which Thatcher had turned herself into an icon. Her hubris had gone beyond extravagant claims about bringing an end to socialism. For instance, it exceeds her ruminations about the need for more time in a *Financial Times* interview in 1986 (19 November):

> If people could be sure that we would never have another socialist government, increasing state control, increasing control of ownership . . . then I think the prospects for this country would be really bright . . . and if only we could get rid of socialism as a second force and have two [parties that] fundamentally believed that political freedom had to be backed by economic freedom . . . I think you could get another realignment in British politics . . . After two more victories.

Margaret Thatcher began to see her message and the fate of the nation as organically linked. Within this context, her messianic vision of her role for the nation began to override her instinct for political survival. Eventually, her party faced this and jettisoned her. Yet Thatcherism still holds considerable sway in the Conservative Party and among many Britons. Messianism does not necessarily make a vision illusory.

In the initial months of the Major Government, observers derived a sense that the new prime minister fitted the mould of executive politics. He aimed to return to collective government and seemed to telegraph favourable views of the Whitehall bureaucracy. However, the reality proved somewhat more complicated. Whatever Major's intentions, Thatcherism still worked powerful influences in the cabinet and the Conservative Party. This fact has become most manifest in the herculean struggles within the government over the level of integration with Europe that Britain should pursue. Major has found it essential to the maintenance of his power base to curry the favour of Thatcherites by appointing their darlings to the cabinet and ministerial positions. He has also done a very poor job of keeping them under some semblance of control.

Several of our respondents have emphasized how the continued presence of a Thatcherite cadre has altered the behaviours of executive–bureaucratic politics in Whitehall. The result: an error-prone government in which ministers frequently embrace faulty options without much consultation with officials and grudgingly correct course only when the failure of their policies has become undeniable.

Some officials characterized the residual Thatcherism of the Major Government as stylistic rather than messianic. That is, they saw many current ministers as relative newcomers who viewed Whitehall with a high degree of scepticism. The respondents did not always see this as meaning that ministers pressed radical views. They simply did not have the cultural ties to the mandarinate that most British cabinets display. In the words of one Cabinet Office respondent in 1993:

> . . . they're different in the sense that they're not long-term, long-established, traditional, knights-of-the-shire grandee types, they're more professional . . . the concept of the old-fashioned grandee in a department, the minister who did it through a sort of *noblesse oblige*, that doesn't really exist. I mean the newspapers try and talk about the more sort of estate-agent culture, the realtor culture on the government benches, more people have come in from commerce and the city and that sort of entrepreneurial background.

Other officials rendered less benign interpretations of the Thatcherite style. To be sure, they did note a cohort-shift during the last years of the Thatcher period – a group of young, relatively inexperienced ministers took over almost entirely from the more conventional group which Thatcher had selected at the outset of her Government. One respondent did an especially good job taking us through the consequences of this transformation – the emergence of a highly ideological and wilful form of executive leadership. With reference to an early Thatcher minister whom some viewed as the Prime Minister's ideological mentor but who,

none the less, brought his own independent experience to Whitehall an interviewee said:

> ... we were all very fond of [him] ... there was nothing he liked
> better than an argument or a discussion. You could have two
> hours of argument and then he'd say I don't want to come to a
> conclusion let's carry this on next week.... Although ... he came
> with a very clear ideological position of his own, he was very
> much in the tradition of secretaries of state who were interested
> in debate about the merits of policies and their practical conse-
> quences. (1993 Interview.)

Our respondent made it clear that this type of creative tension
now rarely occurs in his department. But the erosion of this
dynamic was gradual. The first step saw the emergence of ministers slightly younger than Thatcher, who owed their ascendancy
to her indulgence but still brought with them a sense of how to
get things done in Whitehall. In our respondent's department, the
minister in question '... came in very much in the mould of a
politico who feels that he's got a mandate to do something. If
you are going to do something you have to do it quickly and
press it through with vigour otherwise – his feeling was – you
get bogged down in a morass of consultation and different
opinions ...'
The official acknowledged that the Major Government sought
a more consensual approach, both with regard to consultation
within cabinet and the relations between ministers and officials.
However, the Prime Minister's weak leadership soon led to a
disintegration of cabinet coherence and trust between ministers
and officials. Especially after the 1992 election, Major had imparted too much trust to inexperienced Thatcherites, who then
ran roughshod over their departments. For instance, he witnessed
in his Education Department the spectre of his secretary of state
and minister of state pressing idiosyncratic positions associated
with their religious affiliations:

> ... there are still in this department people at moderately senior
> levels who find it difficult to get a hearing because all their in-
> stincts argue for putting both sides of the case ... there have been
> references in the press which I think are quite worth pondering
> about this Christian Democratic tendency in the Conservative Party

at the moment. And we have here at the moment a secretary of state who makes quite a lot of the fact that he is a Catholic and a minister of state who certainly makes a lot of the fact that she is an Evangelical Christian...I don't know enough about the Christian Democratic tradition in Europe to know whether it's taken a slightly different shape from here....It does seem to be a rather ideological version of Christian Democracy that is being sponsored...under Mrs Thatcher the criterion was the political views of the person concerned....I have actually heard of one example of the minister of state turning down someone [for appointment to a commission] whose political views were actually probably closer to her than the person she favoured because the person she favoured had religious views closer to her own.

It is very possible that by the time this book is published the Conservatives will have sorted out what they want to be. One option is that they will replace John Major with a moderate who can achieve the executive politics which the current prime minister has attempted but failed to attain. The other is that they will embrace an ideologue to whom executive–bureaucratic politics would be an anathema. In either case, we should find it instructive to revisit briefly the last executive politics government, that of James Callaghan. Should a moderate inherit the leadership from Major he or she might derive some benefit from the lessons to be learned from the last engagement of this style, which, as we noted above, dominated the executive–bureaucratic landscape for most of the post-war period before the Thatcher premiership.

Should an ideologue assume the prime-ministership, we shall see a frantic attempt on the part of the Conservatives to convince the public that a return to Labour in the next election would mean a re-establishment of the executive politics of the pre-Thatcher era. For the purposes of this inquiry it becomes important for us to look at that legacy. Does it warrant its seeming status as the thesis that provoked the antithesis?

James Callaghan and a Legacy not to be Disparaged

James Callaghan faced greater constraints on his style of executive leadership than perhaps any prime minister since the Second World War. Callaghan inherited his mandate when Harold Wilson resigned as prime minister and leader of his party in 1976. To understand what Labour faced at that time, we must take stock of the degree to which decaying industrial capacity and fractious unions limited the likelihood of new and imaginative government programmes. Even allowing, however, for the perennial economic difficulties Britons faced, Wilson had yielded the prime-ministership to Callaghan at the least opportune of times.

At the outset, Callaghan met increasing pressure from the US Treasury to seek assistance from the International Monetary Fund (IMF) to save the pound from collapse. The ultimate arrangement with the IMF imposed on the United Kingdom continued and intensified commitments to wage controls and cuts in public expenditure. Under this regime, Callaghan focused a great deal of attention on economic policy. However, pressures bore down on him from the British political environment as well. With a maximum of three years left in the mandate, he did not have time for comprehensive planning. Yet he could attempt to prove to the public that Labour could manage the economy better than the Conservatives. Efforts to get unions to limit wage demands formed the keystone of such a policy. Callaghan benefited somewhat from an interventionist stance in the Cabinet Office, the effectiveness of the now defunct Central Policy Review Staff (CPRS) as a source of independent advice and the partisan counsel of the Policy Unit in no. 10. The latter – a fixture in the Thatcher and Major governments as well – had been operating for only two years. Further, a trend in cabinet government whereby prime ministers keep some key issues from the entire cabinet until thorny matters have been handled by the ministers whose assent is crucial increasingly allowed Callaghan to hold many decisions close to his chest.

The circumstances of Callaghan's government preordained that he would adopt the politics of survival. By nature, he fitted as well within the 'executive' leadership style as one could imagine. He tried to minimize general cabinet discussions on the economy and confrontation in the committee on macroeconomic policy. He convened an exclusive seminar on economic policy to which only the absolutely essential people were invited. But, as often happens when an executive leader embraces survival politics, Callaghan's approach ultimately misfired. As was the case with Jimmy Carter after the malaise speech of 1979, the reflex to do the best thing combined with the dire circumstances and produced a recipe for electoral defeat. Unfortunately for him, the volatile cocktail did so at the most inopportune time – the run-up to an election.

In the summer of 1978 the Treasury fully expected an October election. As a result, it advised a fairly serious 'phase four' of the Government's pay restraint policy. The Cabinet mainly opposed continued wage controls but was persuaded that a phase four would make a good plank for an October election. Additionally, the Cabinet wanted at all costs to avoid a mandatory ceiling for wage increases. However, the Treasury pressed for a specific level simply because it believed that without a ceiling phase four policy would lack credibility with voters.

No one anticipated a rigid follow-through with the pay policy after the election. In fact, the Treasury had not really prepared itself to ensure that phase four was implemented. Under phase three, the Treasury pursued a firm policy of requiring departments and the private sector to follow its guidelines. About the time that Callaghan had tentatively set for calling the election, polls showed the first signs that his Government had lost favour with the electorate. Callaghan suddenly got cold feet. To the astonishment of his colleagues, who expected him to break the election news to them, he announced to his Cabinet that it was off. Now saddled with a 5 per cent ceiling on pay increases that was both unenforceable and unexpected by the Treasury, Callaghan passed irrevocably into the winter of labour discontent that destroyed public confidence in his party.

How could a prime minister botch his economic policy so badly? We had noted above that the difficult circumstances under which Callaghan took office severely limited the options throughout his government. Even with the improvement in the economy by 1978, conditions still warranted a firm hand. The 1974–9 Labour Government saw a period of uncertainty about the economy so intense that Treasury officials clearly viewed their task as more political and psychological than technical: 'We have gone through a particular kind of experience over the last three or four years here when inflation did get out of hand badly. The thrust has been political and psychological, in a sense, rather than economic.' (1978 Interview.) With respect to pay policy, the Treasury had just reached the point where it was prepared to use pay restraint more according to economic than political or psychological criteria. However, it was far from abandoning specific limits:

> [Direct] incomes policy . . . started as a one-off shock exercise in round one back in '75. Having proved successful with that round, they [Labour] tried it again and then moved into a slightly different idea, not of regarding what had happened as being a once-and-for-all shock exercise but now 'Let's try a transition gently into something freer.' The present operation is not only a further step in that transition, tightening the thing down further, but – as we made absolutely clear in our white paper – really this government is now persuaded that some permanent framework of a direct attempt to influence the way that leg of the economy goes is part of the scheme of things. (1978 Interview.)

Pressure building to eliminate the pay programme consolidated the Treasury's resolve. The impending election provided the coat-tails upon which the programme could ride. Of course, the Department's strategy had it once again using political and psychological warfare. To most informed observers, the Treasury had over-dramatized what should have remained a simple exercise to advance further the progress already made in controlling wages. We again find a parallel today in the Treasury's Johnny-one-Notism concerning the inflation rate.

Why did Callaghan buy the Treasury line? Several of the respondents interviewed at the time stressed the degree to which Callaghan would take problems to himself and allow them to be blown out of proportion. During the British deliberations over entrance into the European Monetary System, he plunged the Treasury into confusion. The Chancellor, against the Treasury consensus, favoured entrance. Everyone knew that the Prime Minister would make the ultimate decision. However, the Treasury simply could not figure out which way he was leaning. This uncertainty contributed to the confused way in which the Department handled the issue.

On the pay front, Callaghan even allowed his Cabinet to work itself into a lather over the implementation of existing pay policies. A committee on pay, consisting of the Chancellor and the secretaries of state for Prices and Consumer Protection, Employment and Industry, met more than a hundred times in one year.

This was of a piece with Callaghan's emphasis on detail – a quality that served him well on occasion, for instance the avoidance of a crisis over the Falkland Islands in 1977. In aggregate, the trait, coupled with the relative urgency of the times, slipped him irrevocably into survival politics. He tended to pursue each issue alone and with considerable commitment of time. A well-placed journalist contrasting Callaghan with Wilson stressed the former's extremely cautious nature:

> You just cannot predict what he will do. He prefers to take his briefing material home to ponder over things in solitude and then to reach a decision which is as much guided by his political instincts as the advice he has received. On the other hand, you could predict what Wilson was going to do if you knew what his officials were saying. Wilson liked to appear decisive. He loved to be stopped in the hallway and presented with some options and to make a decision on the spot. (1978 Interview.)

A Treasury official added another element to the comparison of Wilson and Callaghan. Callaghan would frequently become mesmerized by the long-term implications of what he decided. This tendency, according to the respondent, derived from a relatively simple patriotism that saw Britain at a crossroads at every turn. As a former Second World War petty officer, Callaghan perhaps saw too much incomprehensible peril in the future:

> Callaghan is much more of the lion than the fox I would say than Wilson. Although I believed Wilson prided himself on being a strategist, funnily enough, I think he was much more likely to do the short-term easy thing. Callaghan quite often takes a longer view – as someone said to me the other day, perhaps because he became prime minister rather at the end of his life. He is not thinking too far ahead about his own future. He is a patriot and takes a long-term view. (1978 Interview.)

Our official gave us a clue as to why Callaghan destroyed his own re-election plans by embracing the Treasury's strategy for a continued pay programme. The Treasury's interest in maintaining some sort of permanent structure got him thinking of Britain to the detriment of re-election.

Some supreme ironies present themselves in our assessment of the legacy left to Margaret Thatcher by James Callaghan. Conservatives still pillory the Labour Party for the Winter of Discontent. Few voters recall that this period was brought on by Callaghan's extreme fiscal caution, not profligacy.

An even more remarkable dimension of Callaghan's Government is that it adhered to a relatively automatic device for control over government spending increases due to inflation, which has become in many observers' minds, incorrectly, the hallmark of Conservative governments. This instrument involved cash limits covering some two-thirds of government spending. The first of these, employed under Wilson in fiscal year 1974, responded to the rapid escalation of land and property costs and applied to government construction programmes. As we have shown, Callaghan took the helm just as the IMF had prescribed very strict expenditure control as one of its conditions for assistance to the collapsing British economy. By this time an extended cash-limits programme fitted the government's central economic strategy nicely. This included pay limits beyond which wages could not increase. With inflation in 1975–6 approaching 25 per cent, the Treasury could no longer sustain the traditional process in which overspending departments submitted supplementary estimates for parliamentary approval. In the view of one respondent: 'The advantage of cash limits is that people understand cash. If they are given a certain amount of cash and told that's what they have got for the year, that's the thing everyone understands.' (1978 Interview.)

The Treasury attained much greater success with employing cash limits as a restraint device than it did with pay. First, cash limits applied to annual votes based on estimates to be submitted to Parliament rather than to the Public Expenditure Survey (PES). The Treasury thus arrived at cash limits in a process operating independently of collective cabinet consideration of long-range expenditure plans. Second, the chief secretary held authority over cash limits very close to himself. Virtually no discretion over cash limits resided in the review divisions. Third, cash limits left departments little room for appeals. In the case of base-line figures for current costs, departments could ask for more cash if there was exceptional inflation in particular areas of the marketplace. Under such circumstances, the Treasury found itself in an awkward position. Often it lacked detailed information about costs within various sectors.

Cash limits turned the tables on departments. Relying on forecasts of inflation, they crossed into a base of knowledge presided over by Treasury economists: 'The Treasury will say to the divisions and departments: "These are the factors that you ought to apply for the movement of prices for the year ahead . . ." Whereas they know better than we do what is happening to their prices, they don't know better than we do what is going to happen. The cards are in our hands on that.' (1978 Interview.)

Fourth, the Treasury adopted a conscious 'bloody-mindedness' about cash limits and severely restricted exceptions on the grounds that they would negate the entire purpose of the instrument: 'If you say "yes", particularly in the early years, the departments are watching this like hawks. They collect all the precedents. You make sure that nobody at a junior level agrees to something allowing other departments to say, "Well, if you let them, why not us?"' (1978 Interview.) Cash limits thus greatly enhanced the role of the Treasury *vis-à-vis* departments. By extension, they greatly increased the leverage of the prime minister, the chancellor and the chief secretary in relation to spending ministers. Wilson introduced this system. Callaghan extended and entrenched it. Thatcher took gratuitous credit for it.

Thatcherism in its Early Phase

One of the least endearing qualities of Britain's Iron Lady was her determination. In the early years of her government, this trait seemed to lead to much greater success for Margaret Thatcher than most observers would have predicted. Specifically, she shepherded her resources in an exceptionally astute way. She disciplined herself to focus only on the matters that would continue to earn the respect of the electorate for her ability to manage the affairs of the United Kingdom as well as could be expected. Most of her behaviour – tough language notwithstanding – comported with the executive style of leadership which had prevailed during the administrations of her three immediate predecessors.

Notwithstanding her executive approach, Thatcher's use of governmental machinery departed to a considerable degree from that of Edward Heath, the Conservative prime minister from 1970 to 1974. Heath created the Central Policy Review Staff to serve as a source of advice alternative to that of Whitehall, with particular responsibility for keeping the cabinet aware of the direction of the mandate. He also assigned to some ministerial positions and advisory posts a number of Conservatives who had prepared plans for instituting throughout Whitehall improved methods for policy analysis. Before long, Heath's innovators had put in place Programme Analysis and Review (PAR). Under this system, the Treasury, with the assistance of the Central Policy Review Staff, would direct departments through comprehensive studies of the effectiveness of programmes that required closer scrutiny than routine budgetary review allows for.

One might have expected Thatcher to continue Heath's efforts to improve comprehensive planning and analysis in Whitehall. The Conservative Party might have seemed to some to continue such a bias. For at least two years before the 1979 election, the Shadow Cabinet had pretty well settled on the contours of its policies for the next government. Two Conservative think tanks, the Centre for Policy Studies and the Conservative Research Department, provided each shadow minister with a mass of material with which to prepare for the assumption of a portfolio. Also, the think tanks supplied the new Government with a large pool of potential advisers for ministers.

Thus those who placed a great deal of emphasis on the density of activity in Conservative preparations for office might have come to the erroneous conclusion that Thatcher would operate essentially as Heath did. In retrospect, Thatcher never really indicated an interest in comprehensive evaluation comparable to that of Heath. The Conservative election manifesto, in fact, contained few commitments to new policies. Thatcher and her closest advisers in the shadow cabinet recalled, of course, how bold promises have a way of haunting governments.

Thatcher departed from Heath in a still more fundamental way. Heath took a passionate interest in the operation of the policy process in Whitehall. When he became prime minister, Heath found a tutor in Sir William Armstrong (later Lord Armstrong of Sanderstead; he died in 1980). Armstrong, as Permanent Secretary of the Civil Service Department and head of the British civil service, won Whitehall acceptance for many of

Heath's reforms. He so identified himself with the Prime Minister that the two became inseparable. Thatcher had come under a different spell even before forming her Government. Her mentor, Sir Keith Joseph, Secretary of State for Industry, instilled in her an unshakeable trust in monetarist economics. Stated simply, the Prime Minister believed that control of money supply and government spending would force economies upon industry and the individual that ultimately would revitalize productivity and competitiveness.

Several respondents interviewed in 1980 and 1982 pointed out ways in which the decision-making process had changed under Thatcher. Along with a studied detachment from microeconomic issues, she already tolerated much less collective decision making through formalized cabinet committees. One official put the contrast between Thatcher's attitude toward committees and James Callaghan's rather starkly:

> Under the last administration, we had a committee . . . that looked at incomes and this wretched committee used to meet about twice a week and they used to get into the most incredible, mind-blowing detail on whether or not some group out there in the private sector should have so many percentage points and how much was in productivity and how much etc., etc. So you don't have any of that. It is true that the Prime Minister does have *ad hoc* meetings with ministers. She often likes to have a small group look at a problem, the ministers directly concerned . . . Then . . . if this is of any importance, she will take it to cabinet or to a cabinet committee. (1980 Interview.)

One official put Thatcher's style especially well by saying she operated much as a lawyer (which she is) with the luxury of choosing her clients and focusing at any time on one or two big cases she knows she can win. The same official cited the instance of Britain's budget problems with the European Economic Community. Here she became interested in the issue only through her concern to reduce public expenditure. The Treasury played a pivotal role in the discussions through its natural interest in this and related economic issues; the Foreign and Commonwealth Office entered by virtue of its responsibility for relations with Europe; the Cabinet Office assumed a coordinating function. Of all the other departments that might conceivably have played a part, only the Ministry of Agriculture, Fisheries and Food (MAFF) gained entry. As our official indicates, MAFF got into the discussions because, in the end, it was making the concessions necessary to negotiate a new deal with Europe:

> In the case of MAFF, we're really rubbing their noses in it and saying 'Agree to this' and they come back and say 'Well, we can't go that far, we have our own farmers' and 'That's really kicking New Zealand in the teeth' and that sort of thing. New Zealand is an interest of the Prime Minister's. The thing gets modified. But, eventually, they sign on the bottom line. (1980 Interview.)

By de-emphasizing collective decision-making and staying away from matters that did not bear directly on her macroeconomic policies, Thatcher pursued a somewhat selective form of executive leadership style. In theory, she tried to devolve responsibility for day-to-day decisions to individual ministers. As one respondent put it: 'I think there is some sort of shift toward ministers being responsible for their own department and getting on with it.' (1978 Interview.)

Thatcher's approach deviated from recent trends in British cabinet government in two ways. It suggested that ministers, who in the past few decades fought the enhancement of prime-ministerial power with appeal to collective decision making, should spend more time on their departmental business. Here macro-economics should return to the private domain of the prime minister and the chancellor of the exchequer. Only if other issues impinge on this domain in a serious way should the prime minister and chancellor get involved. According to one observer, one concession to this norm brought two other cabinet ministers, Sir Keith Joseph and Michael Heseltine – then considered a true believer – into the macroeconomics inner sanctum. In her first year, in fact, Thatcher kept the Cabinet almost completely out of conflicts over public expenditure and general discussions of the state of the economy. Following her form of executive style of leadership, she operated largely under the assumption that matters of detail would fall into line once her Government won widespread acceptance for its economic strategy. On expenditure budgets, initial cuts won ready acceptance because they were anticipated and not so severe as feared. Ultimately, the new

Government hoped, the salutary effects of its economic strategy would change even willy-nilly assent into cooperation. This might well lead to a situation whereby disputes over expenditure budgets, whenever they arose, would rarely rise to the Prime Minister. The whole thrust of Thatcher's view of ministers' obligations toward their departments would dictate that they assume personal responsibility for checking the expansion of bureaucracy and their programmes.

The Conservative Government complemented Labour's cash-limit programme by placing the Public Expenditure Survey in an entirely new perspective. Over the years, expenditure budgeting under PES took on an entrenched character. Departments viewed four-year projections as pledges of continued support complete with written-in provisions for expansion. Thus expenditure budgeting commitments greatly affected the outlines of fiscal policy and general economic strategy. The Thatcher Government resolved to stem this process. As one respondent noted, the flow in the relation between economic, fiscal and expenditure policy moved much more in one direction. The Government's monetary policies clearly took precedence over expenditure commitments: 'The principle which sums it all up is that finance determines expenditure rather than the other way around . . . They start from an objective for the growth of the money supply and regulate everything to put into that.' (1980 Interview.)

Although the Treasury before Thatcher had successfully applied cash limits to non-human resources, wage settlements for various public service groups had largely escaped the regimen. The bitter 1980 negotiations with public service unions, however, produced settlements much more consistent with cash limits than thought possible. The Government had linked public service settlements to cash limits by making it clear that agreements beyond an accepted percentage increase would mean that departments would have to find economies by reducing services. It chose 6 per cent as its 1981 wage ceiling. Early indications suggested that unions would not accept this constraint on their bargaining, especially since the private sector enjoyed new-found freedom from limits. Although a number of settlements were made at 7 per cent or more, economies kept the total wage bill increase to 6 per cent.

With regard to the emphasis placed on various techniques related to the promotion of effectiveness and efficiency, the British government has fluctuated greatly under different administrations. Starting in 1970, Heath introduced Programme Analysis and Review (PAR). This method for in-depth study of existing programmes centred on effectiveness evaluation. Both Wilson and Callaghan retreated somewhat from the innovative and bold approach to the effectiveness promoted under the Heath Government. During their governments, PAR eventually fell from grace.

Thatcher followed the lead of her Conservative predecessor and brought a new technique, this time styled 'scrutinies', to Whitehall. Introduced by her special adviser Sir Derek Rayner, scrutinies focused on the efficiency with which departments administered their programmes. As we will see, this thrust amounted to one quite different from that behind PAR.

To understand the origins of PAR one must look to the optimism of the 1960s about government decision making. At that time, the belief prevailed that modern science, especially vastly improved information systems, had ushered in a new era in which decision makers could achieve much greater rationality. Harold Wilson had relied heavily on the widely accepted potential of modern science in a speech to the 1963 Scarborough Conference. He asserted, 'Britain must harness Socialism to science, and science to Socialism.' (Rose, 1976, p. 382). In practice, the Conservative Party took the promise of science much more to heart. This fact largely derived from the working acquaintance many bright young party activists had with the introduction of modern management science to business.

One thing became clear as the Conservatives cooled their heels during the years of Labour government from 1964 to 1970: when they took charge again, they would have to do battle with Whitehall mandarins. These, for the most part, tended to view management science as a passing fad. One Conservative recounted some of the antediluvian thinking that prevailed in Whitehall at the time when he and his associates worked in the party to prepare it for the technological revolution: 'I remember at the time [1964] being told by a senior official in the Ministry of Health, when I was chatting with him about the possible applications for computers in British hospitals ... "Well of course before we start spending money on computers in the health service we have got to be sure that they are here to stay."' (1978 Interview.)

The main thrust toward incorporating plans for new management technology into the Conservatives' preparations for their next government came from a privately financed body, the Public Sector Research Unit. Headed by Ernest Marples, the shadow Minister for Technology, and staffed by David Howell, briefly a minister in the Thatcher Government, and Mark Schreiber, eventually a writer with *The Economist*, the Unit made an exhaustive effort to explore public-sector applications of modern management techniques. It embarked on a three-month tour of several countries that focused on various governmental institutions and techniques designed to improve policy decisions.

Ultimately, the Unit took improvement in reviewing public expenditure as one of its main interests. A strategy emerged whereby the next government would bring along as advisers a cadre of executives from the private sector, whose absence from their home companies would 'hurt'. These executives would spearhead PAR. Here each department would undertake a fundamental review of two programmes, the selection of which would depend on three criteria: (1) the volume of resources allocated to them, (2) the length of time since they had been evaluated from the standpoint of first principles, and (3) the relevance of their objectives to the priorities of the government.

When the Conservatives came to power in 1970, the PAR system was only partially instituted. The Government did bring in six managers from the private sector and mandated several studies. However, it failed fully to install the linchpin of the system. Under the original concept, the Central Policy Review Staff would have selected and coordinated PAR and shouldered responsibility for advising the cabinet on responses to the results of the various studies. However, this plan would have encroached on the territory of the Treasury, the Civil Service Department (which Thatcher disbanded in 1981) and the Cabinet Office. As one Conservative involved in the process recounts, Whitehall was well prepared to protect itself from an overly experimental approach on the part of the new Government:

The cabinet secretary, Burke Trend, and the head of the civil service, William Armstrong, had talks with me. They said, 'This is all very interesting, your views. We watched them develop while you were in the opposition. We agree with you. We have been

thinking along the same lines. In fact, we have all sorts of plans
setting up essentially the same things.' I became very suspicious.
(1978 Interview.)

As it turned out, Whitehall inserted into the Conservatives' plans
several important safeguards of entrenched prerogatives. The
provision that the Treasury rather than CPRS would take the
lead on PAR worked especially well to secure the traditional role
of the Department within the public expenditure field.

Margaret Thatcher's early efforts to reform Whitehall focused
somewhat more narrowly on efficiency than Heath's emphasis on
effectiveness. We have already seen that she upheld the view that
ministers should take more responsibility for the day-to-day administration of their departments. If they took this part of their
obligations more seriously, Thatcher believed, they would more
readily identify various savings that could cut both the cost and
the size of their bureaucratic establishments.

To promote the ministers' search for economies, Thatcher installed Sir Derek Rayner in no. 10 as a part-time adviser on
efficiency. Sir Derek then also served as vice-chairman of the
retail chain Marks and Spencer. He had done a stint in government before: in 1970, Edward Heath took him on as one of the
six executives from the private sector who were to help introduce
modern management principles to the civil service. Concentrating
his efforts on the reorganization of defence procurement, he even
served in the Ministry of Defence as Chief Executive for Procurement in 1971–2.

Sir Derek Rayner's initial work set a relatively modest compass. At his suggestion, ministers commissioned some 29 projects
in which departments conducted their own studies of areas where
administrative costs might be reduced. Clive Priestley, a Civil
Service Department under-secretary on secondment, and David
Allen, a Treasury economic adviser, monitored the various
scrutinies. During the first batch, Sir Derek kept fairly close tabs
on the officials (nearly all of them principals, six rungs down the
hierarchy of permanent officials) conducting the scrutinies for
departments. A report did not filter back through the division
being studied. Rather, it went directly to a department's permanent secretary, the minister who had assumed responsibility for a
specific scrutiny, and Sir Derek. The pilot projects proved very
successful.

The basis for a marriage of convenience between Sir Derek and like-minded officials took shape soon after his arrival at no. 10. From the standpoint of some officials the thrust for efficiency provided a streetcar for careers that otherwise would have been overtaken by the Treasury's increasingly 'bottom-line oriented' approach to budgeting and managerial policy. The Civil Service Department assumed responsibility for spotting economies resulting from such moves and for asking the Treasury's expenditure divisions to press departments with similar operations to produce comparable savings. Indeed, CSD, detecting the emerging growth sector, regrouped so as to provide more concerted follow-throughs on Rayner's scrutinies.

The desire to avoid bureaucratizing the Rayner method became the hallmark of the CSD initiative. As one CSD respondent noted, standardizing such exercises would defeat their purpose by evoking only routine responses from departments:

> That's the dilemma of standardization because it stops being fresh. You tell people you must do annual scrutinies of their activities and really examine closely what your activities are for. Round it comes to that time of the year and the weary chaps who have been bogged down with day-to-day tasks say, 'Oh, I've got to do this tomorrow ... the form A23/B/C50 has got to be returned to the establishment officer by the 25th of May.' Once one is relying on that kind of thing it's lost. (1980 Interview.)

For his part, Sir Derek tried to prevent his scrutinies being swallowed up by CSD. While he respected some of the passengers, he thought their lifeboat had become too leaky.

Part of Sir Derek Rayner's vision of central-agency machinery for advancing efficiency in the public service had all of the old CSD moving back to the Treasury. His view hinged on the assertion that financial and managerial responsibilities formed part of a seamless garment that should not be divided. As he noted before the Treasury and Civil Service Committee of the House of Commons:

> The principle that the permanent secretary is also the accounting officer for the department's votes reflects the principle that finance is inseparable from good policy advice and implementation, good organization and good management ... Any headquarters organization must surely be weakened in its functions of central control

if the two parts brought together so clearly by the permanent secretary are separated in the centre of government. (Minutes of Evidence, 1980, Q 991.)

On 12 February 1981, the Government transferred the Financial Accounting and Audit Division of the CSD to the Treasury. It also established a Financial Management Coordination Group, an interdepartmental body chaired by a Treasury deputy secretary (Hennessy, 13 February 1981). The committee's mandate involved developing policy toward the following goals (Treasury and Civil Service Committee of the Home of Commons, 1981, 6):

1   more effective planning and control of the cash cost of programmes of public expenditure;
2   further development of financial responsibility and accountability in line management;
3   better matching of the financial information needed for the Public Expenditure Survey and the Estimates with that required for management;
4   the strengthening of internal audit in departments.

The die was cast for dismantling the CSD. However, the Government also embraced in this document the principles that would ultimately lead to the creation of the Financial Management Initiative and Next Steps.

The Steeling of the Iron Lady

We have argued above that Margaret Thatcher's style changed over time from a selective form of executive government – one respondent likened it to the approach of a lawyer working case by case – to an increasingly idiosyncratic vision that began to take on the qualities of a crusade. As our interviews progressed through the span of the Government, to what degree had our respondents identified this gradual constriction of the Iron Lady's Government into the narrow parameters of Thatcherism? How did they perceive this rare phenomenon, the development of a governmental approach into an ideology, in the light of the British constitutional tradition of cabinet government and the cultural integrity of the permanent civil service?

Several of our respondents dwelt at length on the peculiar nature of the Thatcher approach. One permanent official working in no. 10, whom we interviewed in 1989, stated approvingly that Thatcher had adopted a vertical form of organization with a 'stronger sense of accountability back on finance to both Treasury and the prime minister'. Whereas the three previous governments had placed considerable emphasis on consensus coordination, focusing on policy objectives across the board, Thatcher had stressed that ministers and departments should state their objectives and concentrate their efforts on achieving these. Our official thus painted a stark contrast when explaining why Thatcher had disbanded the Central Policy Review Staff:

[That was part of] the various bits which underpinned our collective discussion. I think to some extent, that was all part of the apparatus of consensus coordination, a feeling that everybody had some responsibility for things and nobody had sole responsibility for anything, which this Prime Minister and the general administration criticized and felt that they didn't want to continue. From that point of view, we're operating in an environment where the departments in policy terms have been made more vertical . . . CPRS spent most of its time looking at policy objectives across the board. We tend to assume that policy objectives will be stated by the minister and his department.

Many officials elsewhere in Whitehall saw the greatly diminished emphasis of cabinet consultation as a significant (even if not regrettable) departure from Whitehall practice. Some of these almost left the impression of collective government meltdown:

. . . it is the style of this Government to do less business through formal cabinet committees and meetings in no. 10. [The Cabinet Office] secretariat gets a bit less involved than it did . . . They come in occasionally, *ad hoc* rather than on a continuous basis. There are bits of business going to ministers which are contentious between some ministers and can best be solved in a formal cabinet committee. (1986 Interview.)

On the other hand, some respondents who found themselves lucky enough to be pressing policies in which the Government had a lot at stake positively applauded the Thatcherite approach.

For instance, one permanent official involved with the Government's 1987 reforms of the Supplementary Benefits Scheme praised both his minister, Norman Fowler, for organizing his departmental resources toward action and the Government for knowing how to bring about reform speedily:

> Fowler doesn't like working in strict bureaucratic terms. He tended to like having people whom he got to know and trust . . . the idea of set teams of the experts in that area appealed to him . . . The way we used to work in the seventies was more 'here is a problem, tell us what you think about it.' We would refine it and put it back to them. And, you had a long process which meant that things were exposed as you went along. But, the danger was that you never actually got anywhere. You had a splendid interactive process, but no product. Whereas now, we have rather the reverse. We have an action-oriented government which makes up its mind, announces its intentions . . . by and large, I prefer the present atmosphere. (1987 Interview.)

Campbell has discovered that time lags often appear between changes in the performance of chief executives and others' perceptions of these. For instance, senior officials in the Carter Government persisted in describing their President's approach as 'cabinet government' even though to many observers it had become a pious aspiration with little empirical reality (Campbell, 1983, 37–9). We ran, thus, into many respondents who continued to give Thatcher high marks for her selective form of executive management. For instance, one very senior Bank of England official described her as an expert at 'mixed-scanning' (Etzioni, 1968, 283–8), selecting from the myriad issues she faced those which really counted: 'Given the whole canvas of government concerns, it has focused well on those matters in which it can actually do something and make a difference.' (1986 Interview.)

Closer to the heart-beat – from those working in no. 10 – we found some respondents becoming a bit extravagant in their claims about Thatcher's style. One member of the Policy Unit, a person who entered no. 10 as a career civil servant and left as a political operative, saw in her what the US had lacked through the Carter and Reagan administrations: 'The reason she is a great PM is – the way I put it to Americans – "Imagine someone with President

Reagan's ideological certainty and President Carter's attention to detail. It's a pretty devastating combination."' (1989 Interview.)

We could not question that once Thatcher locked into an issue no minutiae would escape her attention. However, one monumental lapse in her mixed-scanning approach suggests that she did not come close to the attention to detail that Carter maintained. If we look at her and her Government's handling of the events leading to the Argentinian invasion of the Falkland Islands in 1982, we find a succession of documented omissions and failures of judgement which together added up to near dereliction of duty (Franks Report, 1983, pp. 26–7, 33–4, 40–5, 79, 82–3).

Thatcher had given scant attention to the looming crisis. She never even mandated her ministers to 'scan' the matter for her. She scribbled 'we must make contingency plans' on a copy of a cable (3 March 1982) from her ambassador a month before the invasion. But her private office did not get round to conveying her comments to the Foreign and Commonwealth Office, the Ministry of Defence and the Cabinet Office until 8 March. Obviously the matter lacked priority. Thatcher had set up a situation in which the political leadership became virtually impenetrable for those trying to warn of the impending invasion.

Relatedly, no. 10 respondents conveyed the view that Margaret Thatcher always remained on top of the government's strategy. Yet the possibility arises that those close to her mistook ideological conviction – hers and theirs – for policy coherence. We received from no. 10 strong assertions of the Prime Minister's commanding position on policy:

> The PM's style is very strong, 'dominates' might be too strong. But the powerhouse of ideas and strategy come from no. 10 and her. To a large extent, she was and remains custodian of the strategy. Without the force coming from no. 10, it would be difficult to imagine that the Conservative Government would have done those things it has done. (1986 Interview.)

The approach presaged lots of problems for our respondent's previous agency, the Central Policy Review Staff, and for cabinet consultation. In the former case Thatcher, understandably in the official's view, abolished the agency because it did not work within the context of monocratic governance: 'Everything tended to revolve around her attitude and approach to government. So, by definition, CPRS needed to focus on the PM . . . that is one of the reasons why we went wrong . . . CPRS had become too institutionalized and was not really responding to her requirements.' The official also echoed George Jones in asserting that Thatcher's monocratic approach fell short of presidentialism, notwithstanding his awareness of the belief among many permanent civil servants that her style raised issues of constitutional propriety:

> I don't buy the argument that the PM had pushed us toward presidential government. We have a very strong-willed PM who is clear where she is going. But, we still have a cabinet system of government and things are still decided by groups of ministers . . . The PM tends to have *ad hoc* groups meet rather than official cabinet subcommittees. Lots of civil servants will tell you this is highly improper constitutionally.

The likes of Michael Heseltine, Nigel Lawson and Geoffrey Howe would beg to differ. Heseltine (then Defence Minister) left the Government early in 1986 in the aftermath of his dispute with Leon Brittan (then the Trade and Industry Minister) over the future of Westland, the helicopter manufacturers. Thatcher employed a number of manipulative tactics in opposition to Heseltine's moves in favour of a purchase by a European consortium. Her tactics included alternating between *ad hoc* groups and the appropriate standing committee in search of the right balance of ministers, having her press secretary convey to the media distorted accounts of ministers' preferences, and expunging from cabinet minutes any record of dissent. Heseltine subsequently claimed that during the crisis she read out to the Cabinet the results of a meeting of ministers that never took place (*Independent*, 19 November 1990).

In October 1989, Nigel Lawson resigned from the Cabinet over the Prime Minister's effort to renege on an agreement she had made in spring 1989 with other EEC leaders that the UK would ultimately enter the European Monetary System (EMS). Geoffrey Howe's November 1990 departure from the Cabinet proved to be the final straw. In his parting shots, he noted that Lawson and he had forced Thatcher into the Spring 1989 agreement on the EMS with threats of resignation. He also observed that cabinet government under Thatcher had become '. . . trying to pretend there was a common policy when every step forward risked being subverted by some casual comment or impulsive answer' (*Independent*, 14 November 1990).

No permanent officials registered concern about Thatcher's style in constitutional terms. Thus they did not live up to the suspicions harboured by the no. 10 official cited above. Yet a number stressed the potential dysfunctions of her approach. One permanent secretary highly regarded by her shared some fairly serious reservations about the non-strategic nature of the Government and its lack of collective consultation:

> . . . a great vacuum exists in the Cabinet Office since the absence of CPRS . . . one wonders what the options would be for reviving this function under the current government. Certainly Treasury has no interest in filling the vacuum – its view of policy making starts with fiscal policy and does not include bringing ministers into accord on strategic issues. Fundamentally, one doubts that the existence of a strategic body would establish a market among ministers for its product. The approach to strategy derives from the Prime Minister's style, not from a collective body. The current government has minimal interest in strategy. (1986 Interview.)

Another official who had had the carriage in his department for two major cabinet blow-ups in the mid-1980s opined that the increasingly conspiratorial nature of the Government suggested cabinet government no longer functioned to a significant degree. That is, the abandonment of collective processes meant that very deep ideological differences in the Government simply festered and deepened:

> . . . [on each issue the official handled] cliques within cabinet emerged, with people being invited to some and not to other meetings, usually due to the interference of the PM . . . Even the inner group might have an inner group. It has been quite conspiratorial . . . This type of behaviour is engendered partly by fear of leaks and partly by ideological splits. I think it is a sign of a cabinet that is falling apart at the seams. (1986 Interview.)

We noted earlier that Margaret Thatcher did not extend her ambivalence about collective governance to her view of ministers' responsibilities for managing their own departments. However, a closer look suggests that management – as construed by Thatcher – perhaps meant an emphasis upon administrative detail that went beyond the ken of most ministers.

Michael Heseltine, while Secretary of State for the Environment, became a virtual paragon of the administrative minister. In 1980, he set up in the Department of the Environment the Management Information System for Ministers (MINIS). This programme antedated by two years the Financial Management Initiative (FMI). The latter, of course, became the imputed vehicle for the implementation of Thatcher's efforts to get ministers to focus on administration.

MINIS proved to be a highly structured process which gave Heseltine abundant insights into what his department was doing (Whitbread, 1987, pp. 94–9). Under the system, under secretaries developed detailed statements of their goals. The top management committee of the department – including the permanent secretary and the deputy secretaries – would vet these objectives. Finally, Heseltine would review each in an individual session with the under secretary in the presence of other senior officials. Here Heseltine's direct involvement tended to concentrate minds.

The closer we look at the experience the more it appears that it simply comported with the almost unique conditions of the department at that time. These included the combination of a minister with a seemingly limitless fascination with detail and a department with – in the words of a permanent secretary – many 'corporations' (1986 Interview). The latter provided an array of programmes which made the semblance of free-standing operations a palpable (however illusory) possibility. Of course, Heseltine encountered considerably less success with managerialism in his next cabinet post, Secretary of State for Defence (Cooper, 1987, pp. 124–6). And, as the Westland episode illustrated fatally, the real game proved to be internecine struggles between those in the Cabinet who remained faithful to Thatcher and those who chose to contest her fiat.

By the time of our sessions with officials, after the introduction of the Financial Management Initiative, managerialism had become a four-letter word in the privacy of interview sessions with officials. This proved the case notwithstanding the fact that public documents continued to give obeisance to the great strides being made by FMI toward its offspring 'Next Steps'.

The fact that few ministers could bring themselves to acquire a detailed knowledge of their departments played, in the eyes of officials, a critical role. One respondent from the Ministry of Agriculture, Fisheries and Food ascribed a tremendous amount of ritualism to FMI in his department. He asserted that Thatcher's belief in managerialism meant that 'her ministers are stuck with it and must meet every single under secretary group.' Yet, this inevitably set up a situation of overload in which 'all this superficial discussion is peripheral, based on massive amounts of information', which no one individual could digest (1986 Interview).

A Department of Transport respondent likened FMI to ministers taking detailed decisions about nuclear disarmament: 'There is a problem about how to get ministerial decisions on things which are extremely detailed. It is a bit like disarmament negotiations . . . you can state what you want in principle, but as soon as you begin to discuss it you get into appalling complexity.' (1986 Interview.) A strategically placed official in the Department of Trade and Industry questioned out loud whether administration was in any way a central concern of ministers:

> There were very mixed feelings in this department initially in this process. Mixed in many ways, not just hostile. Some people found it obvious and thought 'all right, if this is the name of the game I have no difficulty with that.' At the other end, you get people who thought it didn't really work. That is, the actual priorities ministers put on them, . . . I mean, a minister wanting a bill to get through. He isn't actually saying, 'are you employing one or more chaps, can you afford them?' He is saying 'where are the notes on the clauses, when will the bill be drafted?' (1986 Interview.)

Several of our respondents, in fact, gave their own ministers low scores as managerialists, without necessarily implying that they did not function well as political executives. A deputy secretary in Environment contrasted Nicholas Ridley's approach to MINIS with Michael Heseltine's highly routine approach, which – as we saw above – included individual sessions with the heads of under secretary commands: 'I don't mean to run down Nicholas Ridley at all. He's an immensely influential minister, more so than Heseltine in many ways. But, he doesn't do it like that.' (1989 Interview.) Similarly, an assistant under secretary in Defence observed that George Younger, Heseltine's successor as secretary, did not attempt a detailed review of management: '. . . [his] style was very much more to insist that certain parameters are followed, like no increase in the bureaucracy, but to leave the management within broadly defined terms to the department' (1989 Interview). An assistant secretary in the Welsh Office asserted that his minister (Peter Walker) likewise chose not to involve himself in matters concerning greater efficiency or value for money. He used weekly meetings with the permanent secretary to keep abreast of his department. This meant that he had to undergo a crash course during the annual Public Expenditure Survey: 'He just has to be briefed up to the eyeballs for when he's got his key meetings with the chief secretary' (1989 Interview).

We will discuss later in the book the degree to which – notwithstanding ministerial indifference – senior managers in many departments and agencies went ahead and tried to utilize FMI principles as much as possible. This became the case with a permanent secretary responsible for an agency reporting to the chancellor. He had struck out with both Geoffrey Howe and Nigel Lawson in his efforts to engage them personally in the FMI process:

> A doctrine was introduced that ministers should be managers as well as policymakers. Heseltine was interested along with some others. But, the Treasury ministers were not . . . Geoffrey Howe was conscientious enough to grant meetings each month to discuss management. However, they were useless because Howe didn't really understand or know anything. He listened to what you had to say, sympathized, nodded his head – but, he took no part in decisions . . . I once tried it with Lawson, but he fell asleep. From there on, Lawson took no part in management whatever. (1989 Interview.)

This suggests that the Treasury, an important proponent of other departments' adherence to FMI, could not bring its own ministers to practise what they preached. It also does not bode well for agencies once-removed from ministers' immediate departmental core – a category which under both Thatcher and Major has absorbed over half the civil service. Clearly, organizations such as the Inland Revenue and Customs and Excise encountered difficulty in bringing Treasury ministers to consider management issues. How might we expect decidedly less vital agencies created under the Next Steps initiative to fare?

What officials did with managerialism constitutes a different matter from how it fitted into the general frame of Thatcher's prime-ministerial style. The issue, thus, receives more detailed treatment elsewhere in this book. We can observe, however, that many of our officials had developed jaundiced views of the notion that ministers would become more effective political executives through a command of administrative detail. An under secretary in the Department of Environment used strong terms: 'I think FMI is a huge con trick at the moment. The civil service has acquiesced because it keeps the Prime Minister and ministers off their back.' (1987 Interview.)

A permanent secretary argued that the previous Labour governments had transformed the fiscal context of Whitehall departments through the introduction of cash limits. The resulting shortage of resources gave greater salience to squabbles over management costs. But, the official maintained, 'there isn't really a constituency for efficiency except the PM and her interest is inevitably spasmodic' (1989 Interview). Under the circumstance, the permanent secretary found it difficult to spread the word on FMI, especially since politics readily overrode efficiency in any crunch: 'It's no good telling the office that ministers want them to concentrate totally on good management, if what the minister really wants them to do is find a way of persuading the Treasury to permit an increase in police management: not because it is right on merits, but because it's politically irresistible.'

A Look at John Major

Just as often as it hurts, the truth comes under the strangest circumstances. This certainly applies to two columns written by Peter Jenkins of the *Independent* the day before and the day of the 1992 election (8 and 9 April). Jenkins, who died shortly after the election, gave John Major a report card which did not disguise the expectation that he would not form the next government. Assuming that Jenkins had no idea that his chronic condition would take his life soon after the election, his words strike us as an especially bold instance of speaking the truth to power.

Jenkins asserted that Neil Kinnock ran Major ragged in the campaign, raising serious doubts about his ability to continue as prime minister: '. . . the more the country saw of Mr Major the more it saw through him.' He styled Major as an only superficially reconstructed Thatcherite, one who has equivocated on Europe, even engineering a pyrrhic victory at Maastricht by institutionalizing Britons' footdragging in relation to Europe. Jenkins, who never disguised his pro-Europe sympathies, believed that Major had failed to wean Britain of the illusion that it only needed Europe selectively and could compete without continent-style, 'government driven' industrial strategies. His Cabinet consisted of men (no women) most of whom, like himself, rose to prominence by attaching themselves unquestioningly to Margaret Thatcher. His rewards to those who supported him in the leadership contest – for instance to Norman Lamont, who became chancellor – lavished responsibility far beyond the apparent aptitudes and proven abilities of the beneficiaries.

Jenkins confessed to having hoped for more from Major. From the outset of his prime-ministership, he had appeared to be 'a competent and diligent technician and a thoroughly amiable man'. But the election campaign had brought the harsh reality. It had '. . . cast doubt upon the scope of this vision, exposed once more the poverty of his language, and raised doubts about his capacity to catch the imagination of the country and move it forward.'

One might find parallels between this assessment of Major in spring 1992 and those of George Bush which gained currency in the US at the same time. We, of course, cannot ignore one difference: Bush came to power while voters were still suspending their disbelief about neo-liberal ideology because things were going well. As Campbell and Rockman noted in their assessment of Bush's situation when he took office: 'He is a pastel political personality serving in a mostly pastel time that offers him a limited range of shades from which to choose' (1991, p. viii). Major inherited a dream unravelling as quickly as voters awoke to the illusory nature of the Thatcher vision. Peter Jenkins saw a mismatch between the political circumstances and Major's persona and style: '. . . [his] style is of such a pastel hue at a moment when politics is entering the broad-brush phase of an election run up' (*Independent*, 4 November 1991). Both men took over from icons. Each of them knew that he could not summon the royal jelly necessary to keep the spell bound. The best they could do was assure that the awakening would not be rude.

The problem was that each man assumed leadership when being as 'visionless' as possible seemed to fit the times. Regarding those expecting some sort of recognition of the growing sense of societal problems left unaddressed, non-commitment hung over the heads of these potential critics like a manuscript an Oxford don has been preparing for twenty years but has never quite finished. It is often better to keep your critics in a state of anticipation of a capacity to make a breakthrough than provide grist for their mills. The much shorter time-frames of politics, however, pre-ordain that those awaiting results ultimately stop deferring their criticisms. The results of the 1992 American election relieved Bush of the need to face this unhappy fact. The 1992 British ballot dealt less kindly with Major.

As the leader starts to indicate that he recognizes the need for change those content with visionless politics begin to stir. When they awake they register in shrill screams the prospect that their illusion has no future. The previously vague sense of malaise among those who went along but did not believe becomes a rock; the smug self-satisfaction of the core faithful suddenly rigidifies into a hard place.

In near prophetic terms Bert Rockman so characterized Bush's potential plight before it became a reality:

The weaknesses of the visionless presidency are also its strengths, and vice versa. Its priorities, even more than most presidencies, are especially dictated by events . . . there are few ties that truly bind, whether in the form of policy or party commitments. The absence of principle, of course, cheapens the currency of policy positions that are escalated to seemingly high principle then readily aban-doned . . . Doing nothing neither arouses support nor stirs oppo-sition. So far, the benign context of this agendaless presidency has been its saving grace. But that context has begun to recede, and as it does so, we probably can expect precisely the kinds of con-flicts that damaged the Carter administration from within. Sooner or later, Bush's bona fides as a Republican will be questioned by the 'ideas' wing of the party . . . To cover himself, he will . . . flip in one direction and then flop in the other . . . Such a situation will make him look foolish . . . (Rockman, 1991b, pp. 21, 23–4).

Bush walked willy nilly into this academic prognosis. Major renewed his mandate even though he had not risen to an almost identical occasion. At the end of the day, the voters' visceral fears of a Labour government won. Yet, as events since the election have proved, victory at the polls did not liberate Major and his party from its struggle with self-imposed paralysis.

Like George Bush, John Major inherited a 'being there' regime when there was no there there. This was both because the there of his personality paled next to the conviction and compulsion of Margaret Thatcher's and the there of Thatcherism was becoming manifestly 'back when'.

Bush dealt with this conundrum by trying to distinguish himself as a 'let's deal' president. He failed because he could not execute. He did not achieve the 'flexible rigidity' of a dealer *par excellence* – that is the ability to be resourceful about means without abandoning ultimate ends (Quirk, 1991, p. 72). Like aspiring athletes who continually zig when they should zag and zag when they should zig, Bush seemed too often to have become rigid about means and flexible about ends (Quirk, 1991, p. 75). Further, he got his gearboxes almost totally wrong. He failed to establish a semblance of teamwork among his cabinet secretaries. In staffing the White House, he resorted to people who did not know the difference between means and ends and the level of political combativeness appropriate for each (Campbell, 1991).

Major took a different tack. He tried to become an 'executive' prime minister. In the early stages of his government, hopes rose that he could carry this off. Just before the challenge to her leadership which led ultimately to her resignation, Margaret Thatcher had lost the confidence of her Cabinet. Her increasingly strident views on Europe had undermined her support. Her pique had reached the point where she began to discuss publicly the possibility of going to the people with a referendum on Britain's role in the EEC (*Independent*, 17 November 1990). This struck horror in the hearts even of anti-Europe MPs. As a member of the No Turning Back Group said: 'It is an appalling suggestion. How can she talk about the sovereignty of Parliament and then suggest a referendum?' (*Independent*, 20 November 1990). In the circumstances, the restoration of cabinet government became a motif of all three of the main contenders for the leadership. In so far as this criterion worked an effect on the selection of the new leader, John Major's manner certainly provided reassurance.

Early accounts of Major's handling of the Cabinet glowed. Ever conscious of his humble origins, the self-effacing Prime Minister started his first cabinet meeting by musing, 'Who would have believed it?' (*Independent*, 17 December 1990). He ran notably relaxed deliberations. His consultative solicitousness extended even to backbenchers. In an early decision, he reversed himself and extended special assistance to AIDs-infected haemophiliacs but not without first informing Tory MPs. By all appearances, his concept of the 'club' extended to his non-cabinet parliamentary colleagues. One cabinet secretary explained the contrast between Margaret Thatcher and John Major in exuberant terms (*Independent*, 21 January 1991). He noted that in cabinet sessions Major 'sums up, but he doesn't prejudice the question, so that changes discussion.' Thatcher normally came to cabinet with preordained proposals which had emerged from a series of private meetings with the lead minister or some *ad hoc* group. When proposals required special preparation, Major was resorting much more to standing cabinet committees than had Thatcher.

Several officials interviewed in 1993 spoke at length about the implications of Major's more consensual style. One such respondent contrasted it sharply with Thatcher's, arguing that it has floundered only because of the intractability of the problems faced by the Government and the weakness of its 1992 election mandate:

> ... there's been a noticeable change ... it happened overnight, and it was change from directional government, which is what Mrs Thatcher's regime had come to be, where she had her policies and the role of her ministers was to carry them out; to a problem-solving government, where each minister is part of a team and they've got problems and they're not quite so sure that any one person knows the answers, and the prime minister holds together certain ministers who are working to solve problems. That's been the change, and it's run all the way through the machine. More cabinet work, more interdepartmental coordination, not necessarily working terribly well sometimes, but I think that's largely because of the big problems, and the very small parliamentary majority is giving the government trouble.

One official, lower down in the Whitehall hierarchy and a member of the new managerial generation of mandarins, almost lamented the loss of strongly directional leadership from the prime minister. In the process, he hinted that one encounters a trade-off for officials between clarity and individuals' capacity to maintain some degree of meaningful input, even, perhaps, integrity:

> ... there is greater comfort and people feel more able to put up their own genuinely held views. Integrity-comfort, if you like. I am not sure, if any timidity existed, that it ever got as far as getting rid of integrity. That would be an awful charge. But, anyway, people might feel more comfortable then. But, civil servants desperately need ministers. They need a clarity of view to come back on what ministers are asking them to do. There are occasions where ministers collectively are trying to decide what they are asking officials to do now in a more consensual government. It does not give the civil servant that quick clarity on just where the thing is going. Therefore, things can take a lot longer and get into wrangles that perhaps would not have occurred in the past. I do not think that all civil servants like that. I could say paralysis. Again, that would be a wicked word to put on tape. You know what I mean? (1992 Interview.)

Only the likes of Margaret Thatcher and the especially self-assured Australian Prime Minister Paul Keating would eschew lip service to the concept of collective decision making. However, prime ministers might find ultimately that – no matter how sincere their personal commitment to a consultative style – events soon press in to the point where such decision making no longer becomes viable. Major, however, took pains to maintain cabinet dynamics. For instance, he received very high marks for his negotiating a compromise on the poll tax through the Cabinet – consulting earlier and oftener than Thatcher would have, allowing for genuine exchanges between ministers in cabinet meetings, and concluding agreements and sticking to them (*Independent*, 7 May 1991). Indeed, Major received the imprimatur of the most flattering source imaginable. A 1992 profile of Sir Robin Butler, secretary of the Cabinet and head of the civil service, claimed that he derived satisfaction from Major's restoration of 'the club' and 'genuine collective discussion' in cabinet (*Independent*, 7 March 1992). Major's style truly had struck a chord in some important circles if the chief mandarin had registered pleasure with his consensuality.

By all indications, Major's personal manner at the outset of his premiership suited both his 'executive' concept of leadership and cabinet government. Unlike Thatcher, Major supposedly made decisions in a highly deliberate manner, even taking a sheet of paper and listing pros and cons on different sides of a ledger (*Independent*, 28 November 1990). In his first cabinet session, he assured his colleagues that they could put anything they wanted on the agendas for meetings (*Independent*, 17 December 1990). While chancellor, he once responded to the observation that people did not know whether he was a Thatcherite or not with 'Oh good' (*Independent*, 21 February 1991). His former officials in the Treasury reported that he would avoid making decisions if possible. He frequently asked in response to a set of circumstances, 'What if we do nothing?'

The more we examine the Major Government, the more it appears that his variant of an 'executive' style has seen his Government lunge from one untenable position to the next in the search for policies that might distinguish it from Thatcherism without antagonizing Thatcherites. Until autumn 1992, the Government's inability to ease the immense burden of interest rates loomed in many observers' minds as an especially serious case of indecision. When Major appointed Norman Lamont as his chancellor some commentators asked out loud whether Lamont would devise his own policies (*Independent*, 4 January 1992). Or would he simply follow those that had been enshrined by the new prime minister while he was chancellor?

Just before the 1992 election, Major gave an interview to Peter Jenkins (*Independent*, 27 March 1992) in which he constantly returned to the more arcane dimensions of his economic strategy. Consider this stirring discourse on the merits of the Tory's tax proposals as compared with Labour's:

A further point is that by introducing a 20p band we have opened up the possibility of reducing income tax by less than a penny at a time widening the 20p band rather than by reducing the 25p to 24p. So there is now a new possibility of making gradual progress towards the 20p and I am pretty confident – indeed I am totally confident – that we will be able to make a fair amount of progress during the course of this parliament towards the 20p. I cannot promise we will get there and I don't.

Add 'Prime Minister' here and there and the answer begins to sound like a briefing from a Treasury official. John Major – the man who came to office with an academic preparation less than that of any prime minister this century, who reached the pinnacle of his career in banking as a public affairs officer and who passed rapid-fire through cabinet posts courtesy of the patronage of Mrs Thatcher – had mastered his Treasury brief and stuck with it.

Interestingly, several of our respondents spoke of the Prime Minister as someone whose Whitehall personality development had stopped when he was chancellor of the exchequer. One respondent even noted that, as well as being short, his experience in cabinet had never really exposed him to the side of Whitehall that thinks 'policy':

> . . . the Prime Minister instinctively is a Treasury man . . . first of all, because he's cautious. Secondly, because his experience has been so strongly in the Treasury and the Department of Social Security – which is revenue-raising and has to be very careful with money because the figures are so big. So Social Security is Treasury-minded in a way too. And his experience basically was there, not in the Home Office, Department of Environment, Foreign Office – although he was there briefly – which are departments which don't so much think numbers and cash. They think policy issues without cash. He's a banker. So, for all those reasons, I think he's instinctively a Treasury sort of man. (1993 Interview.)

Major's rise to the top in politics – notwithstanding the difficulties encountered by his family during his childhood and his lack of academic achievement – seems to have been very much due to his psyche. While selling his Citizens' Charter in 1991, the Prime Minister frequently reminded voters of his humble origins. Some of this shamelessly played on their heart strings. For instance, in his speech to the annual party conference, Major made the connection between the Conservatives' pursuit of greater choice in services and his resolve not to abandon the less advantaged: 'I know how they feel – I know what it's like for a family when a business collapses. What it's like when you're unemployed and when you have to search for the next job. I haven't forgotten – and I never will.'

Indeed, Major's past and rise to the top have mightily influenced his adoption of the 'citizen charter view' of governance – the belief that public services have cheated ordinary citizens of the type of choice and value-for-money that they require to advance their lives. To Major, ordinary Britons find themselves trying to climb up a ladder of life. Government services should encourage and facilitate this process. They should no longer sustain situations which do not place the onus on individual enterprise and resourcefulness. In the language employed in his interview with Peter Jenkins on 27 March 1992 and utilized in his first post-election speech to Parliament, Major sees no barriers for those who set their sights high:

> Let me tell you what I mean by the classless society and a society of opportunity. What I mean is that people from wherever they start can achieve by their own efforts whatever it is in them to achieve. That there is a ladder of opportunity they can climb and that there are incentives on that ladder, not penalties. And the artificial distinction between the value we put on the work of the blue-collar worker and that of the white-collar worker, I think they are old-fashioned, old hat and socially and economically damaging . . . I want everybody to have the same chances and opportunities.

We have subsequently seen the Government go back on many of its election promises about maintaining the structure of opportunities in society. Major, after all, appointed Michael Portillo, the staunch Thatcherite and apologist for the poll tax, as chief secretary and allowed him to impose fixed ceilings on social expenditure. Major perhaps gave us an insight into the Hobbesian dimension to his ladder of opportunity when he justified to Parliament why he did not initially appoint any women to the cabinet, by saying they would have to 'reach the top on merit'.

We cannot fully understand the tremendous investment made by the Conservatives in the Citizens' Charter concept without taking into account the role of Chris Patten in developing Major's message in the build-up to the 1992 election. Patten assumed the chairmanship of the Conservative Party when Major became prime minister in 1990. A practising Roman Catholic, he maintained an almost continental notion of society which viewed citizens' fortunes as organically interconnected. Patten saw the future of the party as balancing Thatcher's advances in the restoration of market forces in various sectors of the economy with a greater sense of social cohesiveness (*Independent*, 14 February 1991). The Conservative Party would follow the lead of the Christian Democrats and maintain its appeal by promoting the 'social market', a combination of neo-liberalism and sensitivity to the needs of the ordinary citizen. By early 1991, Major was beginning to echo Patten (*Independent*, 13 March 1991). Patten had come out with this un-Thatcherite pronouncement: '... people ... express their individualism best in groups larger than themselves ... family ... church ... club ... school ... the collective, the social is important to working out of your individuality.' And Major followed in the same vein: '... the individual achieves his or her full identity in families, clubs, in schools, in churches, in enterprises, in public service.'

We see, thus, the intellectual origins of the Citizens' Charter. We still have to account for three things. First, the pragmatism of current British politics does not readily accommodate organic views of society. Second, now that Chris Patten has left the Government Major lacks an intellectual guiding light, no matter what his personal commitment to the social market. Third, even with Patten present in the Government, Major never achieved a level of 'executive' leadership that would provide an effective gearbox to implement an initiative of these proportions. Put simply, the Citizens' Charter amounted to a brilliantly crafted campaign slogan and little more.

One key no. 10 official gave high praise to Chris Patten for his role in developing the Conservative manifesto for the 1992 election and in giving intellectual thrust to the Citizens' Charter. She also pointed out that Patten's failure to win a seat in 1992 and his departure for the governorship of Hong Kong left a vacuum: 'He was hugely important in the whole manifesto process and I think that's the best way to describe his input. He also was a strategic policy voice in cabinet which was enormously useful ... so there is that gap.' (1993 Interview.) The loss of the Conservative Party's intellectual beacon has led to a situation – as noted at the outset of this chapter – in which some ministers have pursued idiosyncratic views of Christian Democracy. Such ministers have tended to canonize markets and neglect almost entirely the social costs of government disengagement from the provision of services. By construing the remaining government operations as 'businesses' and styling citizens as 'customers' they have delivered a brand of Christian Democracy which denies almost completely the 'social' dimension of social markets.

We have made a harsh assertion here. However, virtually all

the evidence points this way. Early on, Tory sources characterized the Citizens' Charter as 'gesture politics' of the type that
embarrassed some ministers in its crude appeal (*Independent*, 27
November 1991). Indeed during the formulation of the programme, the evidence from leaked documents suggested that much
of Whitehall was fudging responses to the initiative, arguing that
their services already employed an implicit charter, or that changes
would require new legislation or the sharing of information that
would undermine ministerial responsibility (*Independent*, 6 July
1991). Many of the programmes introduced by departments fell
within this category. For instance, the Inland Revenue produced
a form titled 'You and the Inland Revenue – helping you to have
your say'. It proved to be a rehash of a leaflet published in 1986.
When asked whether anything new appeared in the form an Inland
Revenue spokesman felt compelled to answer, 'No.' (*Independent*, 14 August 1991.)

The Prime Minister tried to keep his ministers enthusiastic about
the Charter and to engage Whitehall's senior mandarins in bi-
annual seminars at no. 10. But the general response remained
patchy and most of the papers submitted to the Policy Unit fell
short of acceptable standards. Most departments continue to guard
even the most innocuous information from public scrutiny, even
invoking the 1989 Secrets Act in cases where it clearly does not
apply (*Independent*, 31 March 1992).

It may appear to some that being an 'executive' president or
prime minister presents less of a challenge than the other styles
we have discussed. Such leaders do not require as much of the
'vision thing' as a 'new order' leader does. If they do a good job
at day-to-day governance, they do not need to call upon the soul-
destroying super-charisma necessary for 'being there' leadership
in the electronic era. Neither do they have to engage in the more
distasteful forms of 'let's deal' leadership.

In fact, leaders often find success with the executive style elusive. Few have poured more effort into the quotidian dimensions
of governance than Jimmy Carter or brought greater intellectual
acuity to the task. But to say that Carter never learned how to
distinguish the forest from the trees almost understates the case.
John Major seems to fall on the other side of the continuum. He
aspires to an executive style but seems in many instances incapable
of connecting himself. His biographers have pondered why he

encountered so much difficulty in school (Anderson, 1991, pp. 20–3; Pearce, 1991, pp. 6–7). Pearce notes that Major has received recognition from those who know him as '. . . a highly intelligent person, . . . with photographic recall and flip-wrist mastery of a brief . . .'.

Similarly, Campbell has puzzled over a similar gap between obvious intellectual potential and a lack of engagement in the case of Ronald Reagan. He finally consulted some experts on learning, who asserted that Reagan's problem was that he was bright but shallow:

> Pointing up that 'we read with our acumen', one expert suggested that Reagan probably would tire even in an attempt to cope with a fraction of the formidable memoranda that Carter devoured. In other words, his shallow comprehension urges would fail to respark his interest when it waned. Another identified a five-step cumulative process leading to full comprehension of written material. While a person with a studious disposition like Carter's would by nature go through even the most laborious steps to grasping material, the upper levels can be delegated. (Campbell, 1986, p. 69.)

With this in mind, Major (as quoted in Pearce's book) seems to answer our question. Giving due credit to the role of his family difficulties and apparently delayed maturation, Major still presents himself as highly selective in his engagement in academic study:

> I was bored beyond endurance by the sciences . . . I liked English, I *loved* History, I quite liked Maths and I much enjoyed Economic History. On the good subjects I suppose I did a modicum of work. When I did any work at all I did quite well. Mostly I didn't . . . I really didn't work is the truth. I really didn't do any work at all. It was almost a badge of honour not to in a curious way. (Pearce, 1991, p. 6.)

We are not arguing here that John Major is a Ronald Reagan trying against his instincts to be an executive style leader. However, his level of intellectual engagement certainly falls considerably short of Carter's. And it has not been sustained highly enough for him to carry off the executive style.

Conclusion

In this chapter we have argued that the new leadership styles that have accompanied neo-liberalism – ones characterized by antagonism toward the conventional institutions of governance – can prove to be as self-deluding and replete with unintended consequences as the highly interventionist view of governance that prevailed throughout much of the 1960s and 1970s. Often the appearance of success which graced neo-liberalism until a few years ago rested on leaders' distortions of the circumstances that prevailed when they first rose to power. We have noted, for instance, that the seeds of more disciplined governance were first planted by Labour prime ministers. Indeed, the Winter of Discontent, for which Labour is still maligned, originated in the innate fiscal caution of James Callaghan.

Margaret Thatcher started out as a prime minister with the personal resources, especially toughness, which would have enabled her to revolutionize the way in which Whitehall did business. But three defects ultimately became drags on her performance. First, she tended to engage herself excessively with issues that had risen to the boil, neglecting others which, though less controversial, still required some attention. Second, she tended toward monocratic governance, paying little heed to the conventions of cabinet government. Third, she let her successes go to her head, replacing leadership by the solidification of her status as a national icon.

Thatcher's legacy left John Major in a perilous situation. The lustre began to wear off neo-liberalism just as he took office. But his party could still invoke the ghosts of winters past to scare the public into giving him a mandate of his own. Major would have liked the public to believe that he was defining a new form of neo-liberalism. In fact, he just wanted to appear amiable as his Government pursued essentially the same agenda for 'building down' the state defined by Thatcherism. Indeed, his passive leadership style provided just the context in which radical proponents of Thatcherism could thrive in his own Cabinet. Until the 1992 election, Chris Patten helped Major employ the continental concept of social market to provide a veneer of humanity to his appeal. When Patten left for Hong Kong, Major still faced three main problems. First, how could he get himself out from under the shadow of Margaret Thatcher the icon? Second, how long could he conceal from the public the fact that Thatcherism with a smile is still Thatcherism? Third, how could he do all this while trying to play a more positive role as a principal in EEC dynamics than that sought by Thatcher?

5

The Decline of Coherence and Consistency as Political–Administrative Goals: a Comparative Perspective

Chapters 3 and 4 have examined the dramatic shifts of emphasis in executive leadership in Anglo-American systems and the manifestations of this in the UK. We now turn to the ramifications of these changes for the coherence and consistency of governance – first, in the US, Canada, Australia and New Zealand (this chapter) and then in the UK (Chapter 6).

The coherence and consistency of policy making encompasses a phenomenally diverse and complex range of issues. Campbell and Szablowski (1979) defined five general functions associated with coordination and control across departments and policy sectors. These include:

1 the development and adaptation of the strategic plans of a government/administration and the formulation of substantive policies which adhere to these;
2 the development and integration of economic and fiscal policies;
3 the allocation of budgets and the development of policies associated with the management of governmental resources;
4 the selection and management of senior public service personnel;
5 the conduct of relations between the national government and states/provinces.

Not all these functions merit equal attention. In fact, some ebb and flow in their importance or simply do not pertain within a political system. The highly planning-oriented governments of the 1960s and early 1970s focused quite naturally on strategic goals and took pains to ensure that substantive policy decisions comported with these (Campbell, 1983). Even in these salad days, however, coherence and consistency captured the attention of heads of government and their cabinets much more readily in the early periods of administrations. The closer governments got to the end of their mandates, the more they would make decisions according to *ad hoc* criteria corresponding to efforts to enhance electoral appeal. The neo-liberal governments of the 1980s tended to employ top-down discipline in efforts toward coordination (Aucoin, 1988). Thus, they typically canvassed narrower spectra of options than the earlier expansive governments. Still, these governments would descend to improvization once electoral exigencies bore down on them.

We can make similar observations about shifts in the emphasis of the other functions listed above. The 1980s saw a succession of regimes that characteristically stressed the importance of macroeconomic policy (Keegan, 1984; Roberts, 1984). This approach reflected in part the rather harsh economic conditions which prevailed throughout most of the decade. We should keep in mind that the public mood entered into the equation. The publics of the five countries covered in this chapter and Chapter 6 – respectively, the US, Canada, New Zealand and Australia, and the UK – all sent strong signals that they had had enough of expansive government. Thus, macroeconomic policies which set the stage for tight fiscal frameworks seemingly fitted the adverse economic conditions *and* the public mood (Rose and Peters, 1978).

Within this setting, the allocation of resources became automatized in several of our systems. That is, rules and procedures began to greatly constrict the opportunities and forums for appeals and special pleading (Niskanen, 1973a; 1973b). The formerly collective dimensions of the process began to atrophy. Political executives began to turn a deaf ear to agencies responsible for management reform, especially if these took a shop-steward approach to public service (Lee, 1981). Instead, they went to agents of change who would promote efforts to make government function more like private sector organizations. It did not matter whether these people came from the outside or simply represented the elements of the permanent bureaucracy that were anxious for the further establishment of a different type of managerial culture.

Some may view senior personnel policy as a subset of management policy. However, it can potentially work profound effects upon the entire thrust of the public service culture. The 1980s have generally produced a diminution of the role of permanent civil servants in determining the selection and career management of their cadre. In the US, the chasm has deepened between appointees and permanent civil servants (Levine, 1988). Officials at the point where the rubber hits the ground – five or six rungs from the top of agency hierarchies – increasingly come from outside or are careerists who have earned sufficient trust from the political leadership that they probably would not survive a change of administration. The Westminster systems have all resorted to a greater number of political appointments as a means by which prime ministers and cabinet members can gain greater control over the bureaucracy (Weller, 1991). However, these officials rarely work in line positions.

Campbell and Szablowski's inclusion of federal–state/provincial relations as a core function in achieving coherence and consistency derived from the centrality of this activity within the context of Canadian federalism. Still the role receives some attention in the other systems. The UK variant obviously confines itself to relations between the national government and local authorities, which have become more intensely centripetal as a result of Margaret Thatcher's success in curtailing the authority of the latter (Jones, 1988). A similar pattern emerged in New Zealand, also a unitary system.

Along the lines followed in reference to budgeting, the other central governments generally have tried to automatize relations with states/provinces. This has meant that they have attempted to disentangle themselves from matters of programmatic detail and to impose clear limits to their fiscal obligations. Less fine-tuning and the greater use of aggregate devices such as block grants have placed less of a premium on institutional apparati for federal–state/provincial relations. Only Canada's federal–provincial machinery has escaped this trend (Bakvis, 1991). Significantly, Australia has, over the past few years, undergone mounting pressure for more routine consultation between the Commonwealth Government and the states.

We would not expect each of these functions to receive separate embodiment in distinct bureaucratic agencies. However, the degree of differentiation reached an apogee in the late 1970s. Canada went further than any of our countries, with fully eight central agencies: a predominantly appointive Prime Minister's Office, which functioned as the political agent of the prime minister, and seven career-staff operations: the Privy Council Office, which functioned as the cabinet secretariat and the key policy coordination agency; the Federal–Provincial Relations Office; the Finance Department, which took the lead on macroeconomic policy, the fiscal framework and advice on microeconomic issues; the Treasury Board Secretariat, the principal custodian of the budget process and promoter of management reform; the Office of the Comptroller General, an agency designed to promote effectiveness auditing; the Ministry of State for Economic Development, which advised ministers on budgetary issues concerned with economic programmes; and the Ministry of State for Social Development, which similarly advised ministers in connection with social programmes. None of the other systems came close to this degree of differentiation. During the 1980s all the systems – even in Canada – have eliminated central agencies and/or concentrated functions in one or two at the expense of others.

Some general patterns have emerged which suggest the type of thing that we would identify to visitors from Mars as essential elements of a central agency community. The head of government needs a policy advisory staff and this will largely or exclusively consist of partisan appointees. He or she and the cabinet require a secretariat which will support the process whereby the administration devises its strategy and attempts to make decisions that accord with this. The government will want to be able to call upon an economics policy powerhouse that houses in one place those advising it on the state of and prospects for the economy and the key derivative policies associated with managing the economy. However, we Earthlings – at least the Anglo-American versions – would not be able to agree whether we need a separate agency to oversee the budget process. Few would urge upon our guests a separate agency for management policy. No one would argue for a separate agency to manage senior personnel. However, many would stress the pitfalls of not having the functions firmly established within one of the central agencies with true power. Only Canadians would advise in favour of a Federal–Provincial Relations Office. However, they would recognize that this is because a fragmented society requires special institutions just to keep itself glued together.

The nature of the central agency system appropriate to a given administration in a specific country at a particular time will vary greatly (Campbell, 1988). All the best intentions in the world will not dispel the clear limitations in the US system of coherence and consistency. All presidents – even those fortunate enough to belong to parties that control both Houses of Congress – face daily the realities of the separation of powers. Some scholars have come to identify circumstances in which different parties control Congress and the Presidency as 'divided government'. However, a strong school of thought emerged as early as the 1960s whereby comity between the two branches of government was acknowledged as exceptional even when both are controlled by the same party (Burns, 1963). The system thus places clear limits on the art of the possible for administrations seeking integrative policies.

The US executive branch comes across as extremely fragmented in comparison with other executive–bureaucratic complexes. This may strike some as ironic owing to the monocratic status of the president. He labours under no tradition of collective responsibility. Indeed, those who exercise the authority of the administration do so in the president's name. Cabinet does not act as an executive agent (Fenno, 1959).

This greatly limits the potential benefits of cabinet dynamics toward the improvement of greater coherence and consistency. Since so much of what the executive branch does requires the president's formal approval the circuits to the Oval Office easily become grossly overloaded (Hess, 1988). Since so much discretionary authority rests in one person, Congress takes every opportunity to define narrowly how agencies must respond to specific circumstances. This multiplies exponentially the pleas to the president to intervene in response to special pleading, or to seek corrective legislation or regulations.

Finally, the US lacks the ameliorative effect of a unified civil service system (Heclo, 1977). Departments employ widely different means of recruiting and training their personnel. Career officials move from unit to unit within agencies relatively infrequently, much less transfer from department to department. They often develop narrow foci in highly specialized policy fields. Their networks will include congressional staff, scholars, members of think tanks, lobbyists and representatives of public interest organizations as much as fellow civil servants. All presidents encounter difficulty with their appointees 'going native' – that is succumbing to the insularity of their departments. They also frequently experience frustration with attempts to break down 'iron triangles' – the often incestuous relations between officials, congressional staff and members of policy networks outside government (Aberbach, Putnam and Rockman, 1981, pp. 94–100).

Setting aside the obvious conditions that impinge upon the US system, we find that heads of government and their cabinets face a host of circumstances which will counsel one or other approach to the task of achieving coherence and consistency (Campbell and Wyszomirski, 1991). First among these demands a shrewd judgement from leaders about the type of advisory system they and their cabinet colleagues can sustain. Even if it is always presented itself as the optimal approach to governance, a quest for comprehensive rationality in an administration's decisions does not fit every leader. Leaders such as Franklin D. Roosevelt, John F. Kennedy and Pierre Elliott Trudeau brought two advantages to their jobs, which allowed them to maintain exceptional coherence and consistency. All three benefited from outstanding intellectual acuity. Further, they each proved immensely successful at attracting first-rate minds into their administrations. All three thrived on countervailing advice. All three devised advisory systems that fed their insatiable appetite for policy options and coordination.

Very few leaders can aspire to this level of performance. Most leaders should lower their sights accordingly. They will find it highly profitable to narrow the issues upon which they focus to those whose successful resolution will fulfil the expectations of their electorates and respond to circumstances that demand the attention of the head of government for their resolution. Elaborate and expansive central agency systems will not serve this more modest agenda well. Intense cabinet consultation within the framework of limited aspirations will lend itself to time-serving and the spinning of wheels.

Finally, heads of government in all five systems have struggled throughout the 1980s and into the 1990s with the limiting conditions of public disaffection with governance and the associated fiscal constraints. We have to ask whether even a Roosevelt,

Kennedy or Trudeau would operate as they did if they had come to power in this age. They probably would not. The times have greatly constricted the parameters within which leaders can achieve coherence and consistency. The current age calls upon a very different creativity – the ability to do less but do it well with ever shrinking resources (Rockman, 1991b, pp. 4–11). The age of deciding what more to do with ever-expanding resources has long passed. In fact, Trudeau lived – not too successfully – through this very transition.

The rest of this chapter will consider more closely how Anglo-American systems other than British have grappled with the decline of coherence and consistency in policy making. This will set the stage for a detailed examination of the erosion of the two – both as objectives and empirical realities – in the UK variant of cabinet government.

The United States

As we have already suggested, the US presents a special case in this assessment. The exercise of executive authority focuses very strongly upon the president. And close analysis finds at best sporadic attention to routinized machinery for interdepartmental coordination (Porter, 1980).

The development and adaptation of strategic plans for administrations suffers a great deal under these circumstances. Also, administrations generally experience difficulty adhering to the commitments that do emerge. The functioning of the process depends very much on personal factors and lacks institutional buttresses (George, 1980). In many respects, each administration finds itself reinventing the wheel.

Cabinet rarely operates as a collective decision-making body. In fact, confusion abounds as to exactly what 'cabinet government' might mean. Jimmy Carter, for instance, frequently employed the term. However, he viewed cabinet as a collection of chief operating officers in a conglomerate of subsidiaries (Campbell, 1986, pp. 59–64). He did not expect them to have group dynamics. He preferred, instead, that they run their organizations as much as possible without reference to the White House or to one another.

The Carter approach led to a steady stream of domestic policy fiascos (Lynn and Whitman, 1981). This was due in part to the fact that cabinet secretaries did not coordinate with one another. More fundamentally, it stemmed from the fact that Carter did not keep to his part of the bargain. He found it extremely difficult to stay out of detailed policy issues once these broke through the barriers and crashed into the Oval Office.

It has become increasingly clear that the US presidency suffers from inadequate attention to collective coordination. As indicated above, intellectually vigorous presidents who thrived on the cut and thrust of face-to-face exchanges with mixed groups of cabinet secretaries and advisers appear to have become a thing of the past (Neustadt, 1990). The system does not seem to produce incumbents with the agility and the self-confidence of Roosevelt and Kennedy, although Bill Clinton seems to fit into this category of leader. More profoundly, the task of governance no longer seems to provide presidents the luxury of guiding their administrations through informal and *ad hoc* means. Things have simply become too complex and interconnected.

As the American cabinet system inches toward more formalized consultation it encounters an intractable difficulty. Unlike the other systems covered here, the US cannot draw upon a constitutional convention which would legitimize collective decision making. Those arguing for more routinized cabinet deliberations must base their appeals on the potential instrumental utility of a regularized cabinet system. This compounds the difficulty of successfully implementing reforms.

Although its performance has proved uneven at best, the National Security Council (NSC) constituted a significant step (Nelson, 1981; Destler, 1981). Instituted by congressional mandate at the request of Harry Truman, the NSC emerged as a significant force in the immediate post-war years. In fact, it and the secretariat that supported it became strongly institutionalized during the Eisenhower administration. The Treasury Board in Canada is the only cabinet committee among the Westminster systems to enjoy a statutory base. However, in the US instance, the NSC's being legitimized with a legislative instrument does not prevent presidents from using it very selectively. Kennedy virtually ignored it. He believed that Eisenhower's institutional approach to foreign policy overcooked issues. Johnson and Nixon exploited the NSC staff. They placed little value on collective deliberations, preferring to run foreign policy from the White House.

Ford and Carter demonstrated greater respect for their cabinet officers in the foreign policy field. The NSC process actually came back to life under Carter. And it functioned reasonably effectively during Reagan's first term. We now know that it operated too during the second term. However, the Iran–Contra scandal suggests that ideologues in the NSC staff ultimately hijacked the collective decision-making process. Bush's patchy attention to issues took its toll on the NSC process during his presidency (Berman and Jentleson, 1991). The December 1989 Panama invasion came in the aftermath of the administration's embarrassment over its inept handling of a coup attempt earlier that year. The existing evidence suggests that the administration performed very poorly indeed in responding to the early indications that Saddam Hussein was preparing to invade Kuwait.

The Bush administration followed a practice which virtually preordained the ineffectiveness of the NSC. The President rarely convened principals and allowed much of the business of the NSC to take place on frequent video hookups between deputy agency heads. This meant that many issues never received consideration in formal meetings of agency heads. Further, many of the discussions in the video hookups skirted round issues because the participants never knew who was looking on but remaining out of view. Bill Clinton seems to have taken the reduction of institutional buttresses of the NSC process one step further. Formal meetings of NSC principals actually chaired by the president have become rare. The head of the NSC staff – the assistant for national security affairs – does not have a daily time slot in which to meet with the president.

On the domestic side, cabinet committees have developed only very gradually. The Economic Policy Board under Ford did quite a solid job coordinating between economics agencies (Porter, 1980). It drew upon the support of a White House secretariat, which performed well as an agent of neutral brokerage. Carter instituted an Economic Policy Council. From the beginning, the group included far too many participants. Further, the assistant to the president for domestic policy – Stuart E. Eizenstat – operated more as a principal in meetings than as a neutral broker. In fact, he frequently corrected public comments by W. Michael

Blumenthal, the treasury secretary. This habit seriously undermined the latter's role as the US's 'finance' minister.

During his first term, Reagan went further than any of his
predecessors in differentiating cabinet business. He eventually
created seven cabinet councils. Only two of these, Economic Affairs,
and Commerce and Trade, met with any regularity. The system
received some credit for defusing middle-range conflicts between
departments. However, the White House – largely through the
Legislative Strategy Group headed by James A. Baker III – tended
to draw the really big issues into its vortex and limit participation
to key players. For instance, this applied both to the 1981 tax
measures and to the 1983 social security reforms. The system
pretty well fell apart during the second term. The President
compressed the seven cabinet councils into two – Economic Policy
and Domestic Policy. Bush continued this structure but, in fact,
did not operate it with any consistency. Clinton has opted for a
National Economic Council and a Domestic Policy Council.
Neither meets with any regularity. The aggressive style of the
head of the NEC staff has meant that it has often changed its
neutral-broker, cabinet secretariat role to one of advocacy.

Presidents have employed two strategies to compensate for the
perennial deficit in the system's capacity for collective coordination. Both of these have involved the top-down imposition of
coherence and consistency (Nathan, 1975; 1983). The first entails
the use of the White House staff to shadow departments and
ensure that cabinet secretaries do not stray from the president's
priorities and agenda. The second sees presidents reviewing nominees very closely for sub-cabinet political positions in departments from the standpoint of ideological tests.

Republican presidents have used these devices much more than
Democrats. This probably reflects the relatively undisciplined nature of the Democratic Party. Whatever the reason, the last twenty
years have seen no fewer than three Republican chiefs of staff –
H. R. Bob Haldeman (Nixon), Donald Regan (Reagan) and John
Sununu (Bush) – seriously damage the standing of their bosses by
arrogating to themselves immense discretionary decision-making
authority and then abusing this power. Both Nixon (second term)
and Reagan (each term) enforced very strict loyalty tests on
appointees. The former failed owing to the fact that he faced
a public increasingly fearful of his 'imperial' style. Reagan

succeeded. Thus he greatly added to his administration's capacity for coherence and consistency, even though these strengths were based on hierarchical control rather than collective decision making. The Clinton administration has upheld diversity as a goal more than loyalty. That is, the President has paid a great deal of attention to the degree to which his appointees reflect various segments of American society. Concern has focused on appointing greater proportions of women and people from racial and ethnic minorities than in previous administrations. Here Clinton has run into two problems. First, he has tended to give grey-haired, white, male members of the establishment the plum posts within the cabinet. Second, he has made nominations in the service of diversity that have not come up to Washington standards both regarding experience and political conventionality.

The development and integration of economic policies in the US involves the interaction of three central agencies, the Department of the Treasury, the Office of Management and Budget (OMB) and the Council of Economic Advisers (CEA). The Treasury comprises the classic collection of 'Finance Department' functions including international economics, monetary affairs, economic analysis, tax policy and domestic finance. It does not, however, cover budget review, a function which was hived off from the Treasury in 1939 and put under the direct control of the president. The agency that performs this task – OMB – used to be the Bureau of the Budget (BOB).

BOB was created in 1921 (Berman, 1979). Before it moved to the newly created Executive Office of the President, it had existed as a separate organization residing in the Treasury but reporting to the president. It obtained the name Office of Management and Budget in 1970 as a result of an effort by the Nixon administration to give greater focus to management within the budget review process.

The 1946 Employment Act mandated the third central agency – the Council of Economic Advisers – to be involved with economic policy (Porter, 1991). The legislation stipulates that the CEA, supported by a small staff of professional economists, should advise the president on the means necessary to accomplish full employment. Currently, the Council's three members – who now call upon the support of some 15 economists, normally on secondment from academia or the think tanks – shoulder responsibility for major presidential economic statements and reports and involve themselves in administration discussions of the economic implications of various policy initiatives. Concerning the latter function the CEA has, since the first push toward deregulation under the Carter administration, played a very substantial role in advocating market-oriented economics. Interestingly, Bill Clinton's appointee to the CEA chairmanship, Laura D'Andrea Tyson, has been a high-profile advocate of more protectionistic trade policy. Meanwhile, Mickey Kantor, the head of the Office of the US Trade Representative, has established himself as a strong advocate of free trade, at least in connection with the North American Free Trade Agreement and the GATT.

The interaction between these three central players in key economic decisions normally reaches a high degree of intensity. This is due to the clash of missions and cultures between the career-staffed Treasury and OMB – each of which takes dramatically different views of the economy – and the relatively scholarly CEA. To add to the cacophony, other organizations operating from the Executive Office of the president frequently adopt views at odds with the inner circle of economics central agencies. During the Carter administration, these organizations included the Domestic Policy Staff (DPS), the Office of the US [Special] Trade Representative (STR) and the Council on Wage and Price Stability (CWPS). During the Reagan and Bush administrations, the successor to the DPS, the Office of Policy Development, played a more circumspect role in economic policy; the CWPS faced disbandment – its mandate did not fit into supply-side economics; STR continued to play a substantial role in economic issues with trade implications; and the National Security Council (NSC) staff – largely through aggressive efforts to link trade issues to national security – began to operate significantly in international economics. Regarding the NSC staff role, it reached such proportions by the middle of Reagan's first term that the administration created an NSC senior interagency group on international economic affairs, chaired by the Treasury secretary. The Clinton administration followed along these lines. The head of the National Economic Council (NEC) staff attends meetings of the NSC and the deputy head of the NSC staff covers sessions of the NEC.

The evolution of this complex array of organizations has reflected a tendency for Americans to try to resolve problems by

creating new institutions, most of which have attached themselves to the president. And, as indicated above, the US has not
proved good at improving coordination between agencies that
have difficulties working together. One coordinative apparatus
was actually fairly successful from its creation under Lyndon
Johnson until the end of the Carter administration. Called the
'troika', three layers of trilateral committees – bringing together
the CEA, the Treasury and OMB – worked at reconciling differences in the three agencies' economic projections. The need for
a complex of committees to negotiate forecasts highlights the
extent to which even economic projections, controlled by one
department in our other systems, became subject to interagency
negotiations. As has proved the case with the increased politicization of forecasting in other systems, rigorous analytic criteria
have taken a back seat to political exigencies in the devising of
economic projections in the US. During the Reagan administration, this trend became especially problematic as supply-side economics gained sway. This ascendancy shifted the interagency
battleground from arcane issues associated with the functioning
of models to ideologically motivated debates about desirable
economic targets. Even under Bill Clinton, however, the troika
remains far from recapturing its former standing as the best
ongoing economics analysis seminar in Washington.

With a ballooning deficit whose implications have reached glo-
bal proportions, participants and observers alike rightfully can
register concern about the coherence and consistency of the US
budgetary process and the effectiveness with which the US public
service is managed (Stockman, 1986; Roberts, 1984). However,
much of the difficulty is due to the separation of powers and the
resulting ability of Congress to override the executive in the
appropriation of funds. Also, the context of divided government
– which, it is important to note, operates whether or not different
parties control the executive and the two Houses of Congress –
provides excellent cover both for presidents and congressional
leaders who talk tough about fiscal stringency and then give special
interests what they want. The separation of powers provides a
perfect context for avoiding blame (Weaver, 1986).

With respect to management, the anti-statist political ethos of
the US exacerbates the effects of the separation of powers on the
bureaucracy (Rockman, 1984, pp. 49–52). Not only departments

but offices and bureaux within them almost invariably serve three masters – the president, Congress and client groups. The adeptness of the bureaucracy at brokerage makes it almost impervious to centrally guided efforts at administrative reform (Szanton, 1981; Hansen and Levine, 1988). Management reform, when it occurs, will probably emerge spontaneously within organizations. The US is a highly managerial country and some of this rubs off on the leadership of bureaucratic organizations, some of whom earned MBAs some time during their preparation for higher-level management. This analysis holds even regarding the reformist extravaganza that Vice-President Gore's National Performance Review respresents. Notwithstanding the gargantuan effort, the administration made virtually no provision for an implementation apparatus. In the end, it left change to the innovative proclivities and aptitudes of individual departments and agencies.

Institutionally, the central capacity for rigorous budget examination has experienced considerable erosion, beginning in the 1960s (Berman, 1979). Congress supported the 1921 creation of BOB within the Treasury because it recognized that the president could best monitor the budget process to ensure coherence and consistency. During the implementation of the New Deal, it became obvious that the president required an agency operating directly under his control rather than at arm's length. However, the initial view of the BOB – even when it moved to the Executive Office of the President – was that it would provide neutral advice. In the 1920s, this largely focused on the application of sound management principles to the utilization of public resources.

Throughout the 1940s, 1950s and 1960s, 'neutral' gradually became hard-nosed assessment of the likely effects of new policy initiatives and the consequences of existing programmes. The evolutionary process culminated in the effort during the mid-1960s to extend, throughout the bureaucracy, Planning, Programming and Budget Systems (PPBS), which Robert McNamara had first introduced to the Pentagon early in the Kennedy administration. Scholars and practitioners alike tend to view PPBS as prone to information overload and ill-suited to the *ad hoc* decision processes of the US bureaucracy. None the less, the introduction of analytic approaches ancillary to PPBS revolutionized the capacity of the US bureaucracy to back its policy advice – when called on to do so – with rigorous assessment (Heclo, 1977, p. 150).

Notwithstanding the Kennedy and Johnson administrations' emphasis on analytic criteria, their impatience with the pursuit of their programmatic priorities planted the seeds for a diminution of assessment in budget decisions which reached full growth by the 1980s. Both presidents, many of their close advisers and many commentators on the role of BOB began to believe that 'neutral' analysis had become a rear-guard effort to stall the advance of New Frontier and Great Society Programs (Berman, 1979, Chapter 4). A consensus emerged in Washington that something had to be done to make the BOB more responsive to the timing and priorities of the president's political agenda. Richard Nixon introduced the structural innovation which has accomplished this goal and gone beyond it effectively to undermine the credibility of OMB as a source of 'neutral' assessment. He added a layer of political appointees – called [political] associate directors or PADs.

Nixon did not intend to weaken the analytic credibility of OMB. And he, as noted above, was simply following a consensus view that the budget department had to become more attuned to political exigencies. Indeed, OMB retained much of its integrity throughout the Nixon administration. During the Carter administration it enjoyed, if anything, a resurgence. This was due to Carter's insatiable appetite for assessment and the relatively technocratic bent of his PADs. Thus, the institutional toll of the PAD system did not become fully apparent until the Reagan administration. Here David Stockman refused to engage the career officials in OMB in a serious assessment of policy options, using them instead simply to fill in expenditure details on deals which he worked out with Congress. James Miller proved more benign toward career officials. However, the overarching commitment of the administration to keep career officials out of consideration of priorities meant that they still lacked a market for their analyses.

Richard Darman – the budget director under Bush – made things worse for OMB officials. He tended to use his PADs selectively, much less career bureaucrats. The state of OMB at the end of the Reagan/Bush years might prompt some to suggest that it be renamed BEB – Back-of-an-Envelope Budgeting. Under Clinton, OMB has seen a revival. Much as during the Carter administration, both PADs and career officials have developed a strong sense of working for the President. In the build-up to the 1994 budget statement, this sense intensified as a result of the President's decision to review outstanding issues in individual sessions with cabinet secretaries.

During the 1960s and early 1970s, the view developed that management policy should receive the same type of institutional profile as did budgeting (Berman, 1979, Chapter 5; Rose, 1976). This served as one motivating factor behind the hiving off of the Treasury Board Secretariat from the Finance Department in Canada in 1966 (Glassco Commission, 1962). It also operated behind the creation of the Civil Service Department in the UK in 1968 (Kellner and Crowther-Hunt, 1980, pp. 78–99). Australians were slow to make their move. However, the 1976 division of the Treasury into two departments – with Finance taking responsibility for the expenditure budget – clearly sought to provide an environment in which management issues would receive greater attention.

Over the years, BOB had experimented with various approaches to giving management review greater importance. None of these efforts produced the desired results. Nixon's 1970 insertion of an 'M' into the budget department's name was more than symbolic. The accompanying reforms built up a 'management' side to the budget department. Under the new structure, departments' budget proposals would receive scrutiny from two desk officers, working in separate budget and management divisions. This arrangement lasted only for a few years, although the small 'special studies' divisions which serve the examination divisions reporting to each PAD continue to this day as vestiges of the original design. As noted above, the fragmentation of the US bureaucratic system makes central guidance of the management system difficult – even if it enjoys the full support of the president. Thus, even special initiatives run out of OMB to work on particularly nettlesome management issues have found change elusive.

This certainly applies to the President's Reorganization Project under Carter, and Reform 88 and the Grace Commission under Reagan.

As we write, Vice-President Gore's National Performance Review seems doomed to meet the same fate. The project relied on 'volunteers' from various departments, who have now returned to their home bases. Even the final report of the review cites many 'documents', which proved, in fact, to be works-in-progress that were never finished. The report provided virtually no guidance as to where the apparatus for the reform movement would be lodged. The OMB appointee responsible for supporting the Vice-President in implementing the report soon went off to the White House to assume a post which only very tangentially would encompass reinventing government. Perhaps most tellingly, OMB dismantled its staff units concerned with management and moved their personnel into budget divisions.

Established under Carter, OMB's Office of Information and Regulatory Affairs has played an important role during the Reagan and Bush administrations in cutting the number of government reports that must be published on a regular basis and reducing the proliferation of regulations. However, much of its thrust has amounted to abdication rather than management reform. And the office became – especially during the Bush administration, when it staffed the President's Council on Competitiveness chaired by Dan Quayle – highly permeable to special pleading on behalf of large corporate interests. Indeed, in some cases, such as the dilution of the provisions of the 1990 Clean Air Act, the office engaged in processes which effectively neutralized the legislation that had given at least a modicum of credence to the Bush administration's claim that it remained willing to cooperate with Congress. Under Clinton, the office has had to find a new role in a climate in which government intervention is no longer necessarily an evil while the administration wants to eliminate needless reporting and red tape. Notionally, it still reports to the vice-president.

Selection of senior public service personnel takes us into an area where we once again see the effects of the fragmentation of the US system. On the career side, departments recruit their own senior personnel without much reference to the centre. Officials come up through the ranks in professional positions or they enter the public service at mid-career directly into senior posts. Superiors make little effort to diversify the work experiences of aspirants to senior posts. Moves from unit to unit within departments are infrequent and transfers to other agencies rare.

Political appointees occupy virtually all the posts in the first four layers of departmental hierarchies and about half those in the fifth. Republican administrations since Nixon's second term have exerted a relatively high degree of central clearance of appointments through the White House. This practice bore especially clear results during the Reagan administration – imposing an unprecedented discipline on appointees. Carter exerted virtually no central control over agency appointments below the cabinet level. Bill Clinton, on the other hand, has attempted to administer a great deal of central control over such selections. The fact that he has employed diversity criteria in many appointments has landed him in a great deal of trouble in several cases where the public stances and writings of candidates provided grist for the mill for conservative senators seeking ways to embarrass the President. More generally, the White House clearance process has not functioned very efficiently.

In the 1970s, a fairly active literature emerged about the seemingly irreconcilable split between the behaviours of political appointees and career officials (Heclo, 1977). This work played a role in Carter's embracing the concept that part of the appointive culture could merge with the uppermost levels of the career bureaucracy and operate in a unified cadre. The Senior Executive Service (SES) emerged as a result of these reforms in 1979. The Office of Personnel Management was to have assumed a number of central functions in the selection and management of the SES. It too had come into being in 1979 and received a mandate to give a higher profile to public service management at all levels.

The first head of OPM under Reagan did not accept the premise that political appointees and top career officials should function within the same cadre (Campbell, 1986, pp. 193–5; Hansen and Levine, 1988). He believed, in fact, that a sharper distinction should be made between those responsible for policy – in his view appointees – and those who should focus more narrowly on administration – career officials. The senior managers he brought with him to OPM shared this view (Sanera, 1984). Under the Bush administration, successive directors of OPM softened this approach. Still, the hard-line perspective of the Reagan years – assumed as it was so soon in the implementation of the SES – put paid to hopes of reducing antagonisms between appointees and career officials. President Clinton and his appointees have developed more collegial relations with career officials than those which prevailed from 1981 to 1993. However, the patchy performance of the administrations has undermined career officials' confidence in the ability of their masters to deliver.

Although the US is a federal system, it does not accord to coordination between the Washington and state governments the

attention that relations between Ottawa and the provinces receive in the Canadian bureaucracy. No committee of cabinet
oversees federal–state affairs. No central agency tries to mesh the
approaches of various departments to their relations with states.
Partly this is because states in the US enjoy much less leverage
vis-à-vis the federal government than do provinces in Canada.
However, the fragmentation of the US executive branch plays a
role as well.

During the Carter administration, 'intergovernmental relations',
the term normally applied to units in departments responsible for
federal–state matters, began to take a higher profile. In the White
House, a key Carter confidant – Jack Watson – headed up an expanded intergovernmental relations office. Other central agencies
and many line departments had also augmented the staffs working in this area. The Reagan administration reversed most of
these advances. In the White House, for instance, the governmental affairs office was downgraded to a deputy assistant to the
president command. Elsewhere, units responsible for this area
merged with other operations such as 'congressional affairs'. The
Reagan and Bush administrations have concerned themselves much
less than the Carter administration with micromanaging domestic
policy issues in general. The downgrading of intergovernmental
affairs in most departments reflects this more general trend. President Clinton has given no indication that he will adopt another
approach.

Canada

In an examination of cabinet coordination in Canada one soon
finds hints that the relative fragmentation of the system makes it
much more difficult to attain and maintain coherence and consistency in Ottawa than in other Westminster systems. Discipline
in the party caucuses of the Canadian Parliament actually exceeds that found in London. Thus, a great many regional grievances do not receive an airing by individual MPs. Governments
have compensated for the strictures on the public venting of internal party differences by designating ministers as the guardians
of specific regions in cabinet (Campbell, 1985, pp. 62–3; Bakvis,
1991). This practice, which dates back to before Confederation

in 1867 (Morton, 1955, pp. 113–25), at least gives voters some degree of confidence that regional views will receive some consideration in the privacy of cabinet's and its committees' deliberations. None the less, the representational imperative has introduced a relentless pressure toward overlarge cabinets. The dysfunctions stemming from cabinet's size even received attention from those seeking to streamline government early in this century (Wilson, 1981, p. 329).

Throughout most of the 1980s, the cabinet ballooned to some 40 members. In a dramatic reversal of this state of affairs, Kim Campbell reduced the number of cabinet ministers to twenty-five when she took power in June 1993. Subsequently, Jean Chrétien reduced the size of the cabinet to 22 when he formed his government in November 1993. He also instituted sub-cabinet portfolios in Canada for the first time. Eight in number, these 'secretaries of state' assumed helping roles within the cabinet-level portfolios – for instance multiculturalism and the status of women within the Department of Canadian Heritage and science, research and development within the Department of Industry. Only time will tell how effective subsequent prime ministers will be at resisting the representational imperative and reinflating cabinet's size.

With the pressures upon Canadian cabinets to become too large, the need to introduce division of labour to the cabinet decision-making process emerged fairly early as a concern. Even before the Second World War, standing committees attempted to bring economics ministers together so as to better coordinate their policies (Granatstein, 1981, p. 253). By the time of Lester B. Pearson's governments (during the mid-1960s), the differentiation of cabinet committees began to develop toward the intricacy which now characterizes the structure (Doern, 1971, pp. 52–3). However, Pierre Trudeau did more than any prime minister before or after him to advance the process. A rationalist trying his best to optimize coherence in a highly fragmented system, Trudeau relied heavily on committees as screening devices for policy proposals (Campbell, 1980). He also used an inner group, the Priorities and Planning (P&P), as an executive committee in which ministers would map out the government's agenda, attempt to adjust it annually, and review individual policy proposals – from the standpoint of how they fitted with priorities – before they went to cabinet for final approval.

Over time, Trudeau's P&P worked less effectively as an executive committee for the cabinet. The gradual decline of its contribution to the distillation of policies in relation to the government's chief commitments corresponded with the relentless pressures of the representational imperative. Eventually, the committee grew too large and too many of its members derived their positions more from the leverage of their political constituencies than from the importance of their portfolios to the operation of the government.

Brian Mulroney encountered a succession of frustrations when implementing the executive committee concept. Indeed, he tried three formats: P&P, an 'Operations Committee' (Ops), and an 'Expenditure Review Committee' (ERC). The fact that he rarely chaired sessions of these bodies certainly impaired their effectiveness. In addition, his reluctance to abolish failed bodies made it difficult to know where in cabinet key decision-making power resided. For instance, in 1989, four cabinet committees – P&P, Ops, ERC and the Treasury Board – all assumed responsibility for different iterations in the expenditure review system.

Kim Campbell abolished P&P and ERC when she became prime minister. Jean Chrétien's format takes this initiative a step further by eliminating the Operations Committee, a body that performed various roles over the years but which, under Campbell, was to have focused on the weekly agenda of cabinet and on packaging the government's programme for the public. Chrétien believes that the relatively small size of cabinet will allow it to conduct its affairs effectively without the guidance of an executive committee.

Career officials have played a more aggressive role within the integrative process in Canada than have their opposite numbers in the US and UK. From the very beginning, they have attended cabinet committee meetings and offered their views whenever appropriate (Granatstein, 1981, pp. 86, 92, 145, 253, 332). In the case of key ministers – such as the Finance Minister, who belongs to most committees – officials will represent their departments whenever the ministers cannot cover meetings. This has caused some resentment among less well-placed ministers. And prime ministers have occasionally attempted to curtail official participation in committee meetings. Yet the practice has sustained itself at least since the Second World War. It normally leads to a degree of 'group think' between the inner circle of ministers and senior deputy ministers. This brings the benefit of a fair degree of comity in the upper reaches of the executive–bureaucratic complex (Robertson, 1971, pp. 449–51). However, it also brings the liability that ministers are insufficiently independent of officials and vice versa. This impedes the capacity of governments to correct themselves.

We have yet to see whether officials will attend committees in the streamlined systems devised under Campbell and Chrétien. Certainly the reduced number of committees will make it easier for ministers to cover their obligations personally. Under the old system, some prominent cabinet members, such as the Minister of Finance, would nominally belong to as many as ten committees. Now they must cover only four at the most.

The official responsible for recording the actions of cabinet – the Clerk of the Privy Council – acquired the additional title of Secretary to the Cabinet in 1940. This formalized the gradual process whereby the Privy Council Office (PCO) had developed into an agency responsible for facilitating cabinet decision making. It did not reach the next step – serving as a separate source of advice for cabinet deliberations – until the Pearson prime-ministership. Trudeau presided over the most intense period of growth and differentiation within PCO (Van Loon, 1981). The search for a counter-bureaucracy closely attuned to the preferences of the Prime Minister guided Trudeau's eagerness to enhance the role of PCO. The Prime Minister and many of those closest to him believed that only a large PCO could animate intractable government departments. Both Joe Clark (Prime Minister 1979–80) and Brian Mulroney (1984–93) indicated in their campaign rhetoric that the PCO had become politicized and that they would shake it up when they took office. Neither prime minister actually followed through on these threats. Jean Chrétien has registered public reservations about the power of PCO. At the outset of his administration, he stated in clear terms that he wanted advice directly from his ministers rather than filtered by PCO.

PCO serves as the most sought-after perch in the Canadian bureaucracy. It contains roughly twice as many secretariats as Britain's Cabinet Office. And these units have on average twice as many staff as those in the Cabinet Office. The tendency for PCO officials to establish their careers in the agency stands in critical contrast to the UK Cabinet Office.

The relative stability of PCO careers raises the issue of whether it begins to develop its own agenda, especially on matters concerning the organization of the machinery of government and the public service. One piece of conventional wisdom arising on occasion from PCO argues that changes of prime minister offer the optimal time to initiate and implement sweeping changes. When the Progressive Conservatives assumed power in 1979, PCO successfully convinced the new prime minister – Joe Clark – to completely revamp the cabinet committee system and introduce a new budgeting system. Virtually nobody in the new Government had previous experience in cabinet. Further, the Government lacked a majority in the House of Commons. Ministers faced the burden of following a moving target – that is learning roles in the midst of a radical transformation – and preparing for an early electoral challenge to their mandate. One might argue that PCO should have restrained its innovative zeal.

The changes instituted by Kim Campbell in June 1993 trace their origins to a desire among certain members of the Mulroney ministry, PCO and some especially respected observers (for instance, Gordon Osbaldeston the former clerk of the Privy Council) to reduce the size of the cabinet and streamline its operations. Worthy as their ideas were, one must raise once again the issue of timing. June 1993 did provide the opportunity for a new prime minister. However, Kim Campbell had to lead her party in a federal election some time before November 1993. Some have argued that the changes contributed to an aura of reformism in the new administration. In fact, however, it is virtually an axiom of electoral behaviour that voters pay little or no attention to issues associated with reorganization of government or reform of the public service. Further, the reorganization lacked finality. The changes required parliamentary enactment – something that proved impossible as Campbell chose not to have Parliament summoned during the entire time of her prime-ministership. Finally, some of the features of the reorganization betrayed a lack of political sensitivity. For instance, the Government created a Department of Public Security which merged the former Department of the Solicitor General – responsible for the Royal Canadian Mounted Police, courts and the penal system – with the operational parts of immigration programmes (which used to be in the Department of Employment and Immigration). In a nation which relies upon immigrants for its growth and prides itself on its diversity and openness to outsiders, one can imagine the hue and cry surrounding the proposition that immigration belonged to law enforcement provoked among certain segments of the public. Jean Chrétien created a Department of Citizenship and Immigration. This comported more with the Canadian view of immigration within the development and maintenance of society.

Although prime ministers have over the past thirty years used the PCO as a counter-bureaucracy, they have not gone as far as their Australian opposite numbers, who actually renamed the agency 'Department of the Prime Minister and Cabinet'. This does not mean that PCO operates more distantly from the chief executive than does PM&C in Australia. It derives more from the fact that Canadian prime ministers have found it relatively easy to get what they want out of PCO without formally renaming it. Relatedly, the prime minister's immediate staff – called the Prime Minister's Office – has remained a fairly small operation. With some notable exceptions under Mulroney, its officials have been political appointees. And these have tended to concentrate their activities on the explicitly partisan activities of the prime minister, such as press relations, parliamentary liaison and nominations to appointive offices. Over the years, PMO has usually contained a policy unit. However, this has never achieved the prominence – nor, for that matter, effectiveness – of the comparable operation in 10 Downing Street.

Prime Minister Mulroney had allowed an accretion of staff resources in ministers' offices which led to the perception that these had become counter-bureaucracies to departments. The fact that each minister had a chief of staff – a political appointee receiving remuneration at the level of assistant deputy minister – drew special fire from some observers. Chrétien has abolished the position of chief of staff and severely restricted the resources ministers can tap for their own offices. This move, the Government hopes, will make the reporting lines between ministers and officials in their departments less attenuated.

The most ambitious PMO-led effort to keep the Prime Minister's agenda on track occurred after the 1974 election, which gave Trudeau his third mandate. In close alliance with PCO, PMO pursued a thoroughgoing effort to devise a list of priorities for the mandate. These were considered in a meeting of the Priorities and Planning Committee and embraced as the core commitments of the Government. PMO and PCO then led a process whereby each department was to respond – demonstrating how its planned policy initiatives and existing programmes fitted within the priorities. In the event, the grim reality of stagflation, which became acute by spring 1975, took the Government's attention off its original priorities. However, key players had also come to the conclusion that the massive priorities exercise was about to collapse under its own weight. So the policy unit was almost totally dismantled in the summer of 1976.

A similar type of process was rejoined in the first two years of the Mulroney Government. It relied less than the Trudeau venture on cabinet deliberations and more on PMO's monitoring of cabinet committees and PCO's handling of issues. Relying as it did on the judgement of PMO officials in Ottawa with little experience, the Government began to look hopelessly error-prone. In time, Mulroney began to come round to the view that he had to entrust more to PCO. He eventually called upon Derek Burney, a career diplomat, to occupy a new PMO position – chief of staff. Burney's arrival on the scene contributed greatly to the appearance of improved coherence, which allowed the Government to restore its image in time for the November 1988 election.

The Canadian cabinet consultation system runs best when prime ministers fully engage themselves within the process. In recent history, Pearson and Trudeau sustained the frequency and salience of cabinet dynamics. Joe Clark was not prime minister for very long. However, it appears that he became beguiled by the apparatus and lost sight of the tough decisions that the head of a minority government must make as soon after an election as possible.

Brian Mulroney delegated much of his committee work to the Deputy Prime Minister and convened full cabinets only sporadically. Both practices departed from normal procedure in Canada. They also caused difficulty for the operation of the Government. If a prime minister delegates, two factors will determine the effectiveness of this tack. First, has he or she chosen a competent person? In the case of the first deputy prime minister who served Mulroney until 1986, the answer was no; in that of the second, it was yes. Second, does the prime minister stay out of matters he or she has delegated even when the person entrusted with the responsibility has resolved an issue? In fact, we find that Mulroney encouraged a ceaseless truncation of the collective decision-making process. Whatever was decided by committees, the best connected people knew that they could ultimately get their way by making direct appeals to the Prime Minister. A paradox emerged here. Mulroney probably delegated more than any prime minister should. However, he lacked the self-discipline to stay out of detailed matters, especially in cases that encountered heavy political fire.

The desire to restore the salience of cabinet deliberations stood at the core of the reforms that Kim Campbell adopted in June 1993. Of course, her absorption with preparing for the election campaign and the fact that she did not convene Parliament meant that the Cabinet scarcely operated during her three-month tenure. Jean Chrétien brings a wealth of experience to office: he has served as minister in virtually every important porfolio. Further, he received his socialization in the executive–bureaucratic arena during the Trudeau years. So we might expect that he will engage his Cabinet fully.

We find in Canada a halfway house between the use of a conglomerate department, such as the UK Treasury, to run economic policy and the competitive format which prevails in the US. Only two major players involve themselves in the central economic policy roles, the Finance Department and the Treasury Board Secretariat. And the latter, which presides over the expenditure budget, has found its role increasingly focused on technical functions. Until the early 1960s, Finance enjoyed an unquestioned hegemony similar to that of the UK Treasury. However, the Department of Trade and Industry played a very important role in microeconomics. This was due to the importance of economic development at this stage in Canadian history and the political prominence in cabinet normally accorded the minister responsible for this function.

The mid-1960s saw two factors emerge which affected the role of Finance. First, the 1962 Glassco Commission – employing as its rallying cry 'let the managers manage' – argued strongly that innovative management cannot occur unless budget review functions separately from the agency responsible for macroeconomic policy. It advised that the secretariat supporting the cabinet committee that presides over the budget – the Treasury Board

Secretariat (TBS) – should move to the Privy Council Office. This – along with the provision of a separate non-departmental minister to replace the finance minister as chairman of the Treasury Board – would underscore the role of TBS as a secretariat serving a cabinet committee. Previously, the Treasury Board staff was simply a division within the Finance Department. In implementing the Glassco Commission report, the Pearson Government chose instead to create a freestanding secretariat. The TBS thus gained both a separate minister and an autonomous institutional structure under an independent permanent head called the secretary. Before long, it became a threat both to Finance and PCO (French, 1980).

A different set of developments presented the other factor that began to impinge upon the hegemony of Finance in economics. As noted above, Trudeau developed a strong belief in counter-bureaucracy as a way of bypassing departments which failed to respond to his agenda adequately. Thus Finance, and Trade and Industry (renamed Industry, Trade and Commerce) began to face competition from bureaucratic structures responsible for specific parts of economic policy. By 1978, these included Regional Economic Expansion; Energy, Mines and Resources; Consumer and Corporate Affairs; and Small Business. This added greatly to the complexity of collective decision making. The Economic Policy Committee of cabinet took new prominence and its deliberations became protracted and intricate.

Further, economics expertise became greatly distributed in Ottawa. This proved to be a matter of considerable significance in Canada. Finance had since the 1930s attracted some of the top economists in the country – opting for true expertise, in contrast to the UK Treasury, which preferred gifted amateurs assisted by non-PhDs who happened to take economics degrees. Any effort to break Finance's monopoly of economics advice would weaken its ability to prevail in this field. For instance, between 1978 and 1981 a former Finance assistant deputy minister who became deputy minister of Energy, Mines and Resources – M. A. Cohen – was able to attract many of Finance's senior economists to his new department (Doern and Toner, 1985, p. 41). At the time when taxation of petroleum production became the central issue in revenue policy, Cohen was able to use his economics brains trust to offer stiff competition to Finance when devising both the National Energy Policy and the annual budgets.

Tensions over economic policy emerged in the central agency community throughout the mid-1970s. In 1975, PMO and PCO joined forces to override Finance's opposition to mandatory wage and price controls. This action resulted in the resignation of John Turner as finance minister. Part of the difficulty stemmed from the development in PCO of an aggressive secretariat for the Economic Policy Committee under the leadership of Ian Stewart, an official with no experience in Finance who ultimately became its deputy minister. However, Finance was finding it difficult to adapt its normal approach – proclaiming policies *ex cathedra* – to the new executive–bureaucratic politics which had developed under Trudeau. Indeed, countervailing gambits became the order of the day in relations between central agencies.

With respect to the expenditure budget, PCO developed the habit of letting cabinet committees make commitments to programmes without first giving TBS the opportunity to review the consequences for the expenditure budget. It was not until 1976 that the president of the Treasury Board gained the authority to request cabinet documents when they entered PCO for processing so that TBS might assess their implications for expenditure.

The most serious conflicts between the central agencies emerged in the summer of 1978 when Trudeau – staffed mainly by PMO – imposed $2 billion of expenditure cuts without so much as consulting either the finance minister or the president of the Treasury Board. He then challenged ministers to come up with $300 million of additional savings, which they could reallocate to priority economic development projects. The resulting cacophony of calls for cuts and more money led to the creation of a Board of Economic Development Ministers supported by a Ministry of State for Economic Development. The apparatus would preside over the process whereby savings in 'envelopes' associated with economic development would be reassigned to programmes in the same sector that were placed higher in ministers' list of priorities. The logic behind the programme assumed that ministers might more willingly take some sacred cows to slaughter if they could see that the freed resources would go to programmes in the economic development envelope rather than back to the general treasury (Borins, 1982).

This format – dividing governmental programmes into envelopes, assigning expenditure decisions concerning them to a cabinet committee and supporting ministers' deliberations with a separate secretariat – prevailed in Canada until John Turner closed out the Liberal Government during his brief prime-ministership in 1984. It relied on faulty game theory. That is, ministers proved just as reluctant to identify savings if the benefits went to an envelope related to the work of their departments as they would have been had the money gone to the general treasury. Further, by segmenting the Treasury Board's former authority over the expenditure budget, the system multiplied the fora in which ministers could engage in logrolling and pork barrel politics (Hartle, 1983).

In its heyday, the system included ten envelopes assigned to four committees, two of which were supported by their own central agencies. Under the scheme, TBS had direct responsibility for only one set of envelopes – those that came under Government Operations. The secretariat supporting the Foreign and Defence Policy Committee worked in the Department of External Affairs. While TBS retained a role as ringmaster for annual expenditure budget aggregates and supported cabinet's Government Operations Committee, much of its day-to-day activities began to focus on technical matters including adherence to the rules of the process. Even with the abolition of the separate secretariats in 1984, cabinet committees have clung to their prerogatives over budgetary matters. Further, Finance has enjoyed a renaissance under the Mulroney Government, which has led not only to its recovering its former hegemony over economic policy but also to its absorbing much of TBS's original responsibility for advising cabinet on expenditure policy.

Much like British chancellors, Canadian finance ministers have always been somewhat-more-than-equals in cabinet. The finance minister keeps the prime minister informed as he develops the annual budget. On the other hand, the cabinet would not vet his plans. Further, the finance minister belongs to most cabinet committees. This allows the finance minister (or, as is frequently the case, a minister or official representing him or her) to comment on the economic implications of virtually every government initiative the Finance Department might want to affect.

The dynamics of cabinet government under Mulroney accentuated the role of the finance minister. Beginning in 1986, all matters going to the Priorities and Planning Committee received forward consideration by a steering group called the Operations Committee. (This committee is not to be confused with the committee of the same name under Trudeau that was responsible for fairly minor envelopes. It has been abolished by Jean Chrétien.) Beginning in 1989, an Expenditure Review Committee assessed all proposals emanating from policy committees to see whether they comported with the government's general priorities and efforts to reduce the deficit. The Deputy Prime Minister chaired each of these committees, although the Prime Minister was nominally chairman of the Expenditure Review Committee. It happened that from 1991 to the end of the Mulroney Government, the Deputy Prime Minister, Don F. Mazankowski, also served as finance minister.

Thus, the system had come full circle since Glassco. This 1962 commission made much of the constitutional convention in Canada, whereby expenditure control comes under the collective purview of the cabinet. It strongly urged that the function should be removed from a minister whose absorption with macroeconomics and the fiscal framework inevitably meant that he or she could not focus on budget detail and the means whereby the cabinet could develop an environment in which public servants could manage their resources more effectively. The Mulroney Government went beyond the overload which so concerned the commissioners by bolting Finance onto the person who also served as his surrogate for the day-to-day management of the cabinet.

The various provisions of the Chrétien structure give little indication that TBS will be able to resume its pursuit of the Glassco vision. To be sure, under Chrétien the finance minister does not serve as deputy prime minister – not yet, that is. Further, the position of president of the Treasury Board went to a former mayor of Toronto with virtually no experience in federal politics. More telling were special mandates given to this minister and another – the latter being styled 'President of the Queen's Privy Council, Minister of Intergovernmental Affairs and Minister Responsible for Public Service Renewal and . . . Interlocutor with Metis and Non-Status Indians'. In a classic instance of turning a gamekeeper into a poacher, the Government assigned the president of the Treasury Board a specific mandate to oversee a major government initiative to spend more funds on infrastructure. It airily added that a unit within the PCO would assist the minister to perform this function. However, we could ask what a cabinet secretariat is doing with an operational arm? Further, we might wonder about the degree to which the minister's absorption with infrastructure projects will inevitably turn part of TBS into a ministry of public works. Regarding the 'President of the Queen's Privy Council', besides imparting to this individual perhaps the longest title given to any previous minister in Canada or anywhere else, it continues the process whereby the tentacles of PCO have undermined TBS's mandate (received when it was created in response to Glassco) for management reform in the civil service.

Management policy has since the 1960s played an exceptionally important role in Canadian central agencies. This does not mean that these organizations have achieved greater success than their opposite numbers in other countries, but Canadian central agents have set their sights on managerial objectives to an unparalleled degree. We can partially attribute this emphasis to the legitimizing effects of the Glassco Commission's 'let the managers manage' motif. However, unlike any other of the bureaucratic cultures we are examining here, many Canadian central agents involved in management policy earned MBAs before entering government. Many joined the public service after acquiring management experience in the private sector. For instance, in 1977 – a time when better management principles were pursued with special energy – both of the two senior officials responsible for management policy, the secretary of the Treasury Board and the comptroller general, had taken MBAs, and the latter had served as a vice-president of Xerox of Canada immediately before assuming his post.

Oddly, the tremendous thrust toward managerialism which characterized the 1970s stalled by the time the management-oriented Progressive Conservatives took power in 1984. Much of the emphasis in the early days of the post-Glassco period had been on classic efficiency issues – whether programmes could operate more cheaply. By the mid-1970s a strong evaluative component entered into senior officials' thinking. A planning branch developed in TBS; it headed interdepartmental assessments of the effectiveness of programmes, thereby seeking to determine whether they should continue with fewer resources or close down entirely. The creation of the Office of the Comptroller General (OCG) in

1977 sought to generalize effectiveness evaluation so that it would become a principal element of departments' auditing procedures.

The systems put in place in the 1970s mean that departments can draw upon mounds of material assessing the effectiveness of what they do. However, the fragmentation of budgeting since the late 1970s has provided little incentive for ministers to use the available data when reaching tough decisions about the allocation of resources. Further, a chronic impermeability of departments to management reform has surfaced during the 1980s (Savoie, 1994). Although by the late 1980s TBS and OCG put in place an apparatus for increasing departments' budgetary discretion, only a few agencies participated in the programme. While the creation of executive agencies, commercialization and privatization have all been mooted, progress remained sporadic. In 1991, the Mulroney Government introduced a bold initiative, under the banner Public Service 2000, which sought to devise ways of rewarding creativity and responsiveness in departments and agencies. Unfortunately, it then undermined its own covenant by implementing a series of cut-back exercises. This put the public service in a survival psychosis which left little room for the imaginative implementation of Public Service 2000. Also, the Government chose in several instances to embarrass career officials publicly rather than adhere to Westminster practice and accept responsibility for gaffes and misjudgements. The rationalization of the machinery of government under Prime Minister Campbell exacerbated the pressures experienced by the public service. Chrétien's appointment of a minister responsible for the renewal of public service perhaps sends a signal that the Liberals will try to rebuild the bridges between the political leadership and the career civil service. However, the task will prove gargantuan.

The TBS's loss of leverage in the central agency community has certainly contributed to these disappointing results of attempts at administrative reform. However, a decline in the cultural coherence of the Canadian public service has occurred as well. In the middle part of the century, the modal deputy ministers belonged to the Canadian upper class. Many were connected by family ties to the business elite. Many had studied at Oxford (often as Rhodes scholars) and/or had taken PhDs from prestigious American universities. And since several mandarins ultimately ran for office and became ministers, many officials who remained in the public sector and ultimately became the permanent heads of departments called upon personal friendships with members of the cabinet for leverage in the executive–bureaucratic arena. Indeed, Jean Chrétien has retained a retired mandarin who had also served in the Trudeau Government, Mitchell Sharp, as a special adviser. Chrétien had learned the ropes in Ottawa under the tutelage of Sharp when he served him as a parliamentary secretary. Pierre Trudeau, on the other hand, believed that mandarins, especially those such as Sharp who had moved into politics, had become establishmentarian. He aggressively pursued a strategy of replacing elitism with meritocracy (Campbell, 1983, pp. 251–4).

As a result of Trudeau's actions, a new breed of deputy minister emerged: permanent heads received their positions in their early to mid-40s rather than early 50s, rose to their levels more on the basis of what than whom they knew, and pinned their hopes more on the careers of pure politicians with whom they had become strongly associated than on the old school ties of former colleagues who had gone into politics. (The practice of recruiting cabinet members from the public service greatly decreased in importance during the Trudeau years.) All these developments have meant that deputy ministers and the bureaucratic cultures over which they preside have become much less homogeneous than was the case when Trudeau first came to office. The Mulroney Government has sustained the thrust of Trudeau's approach to senior personnel development.

During the period of transformation of the top mandarinate, the PCO, has maintained a strongly interventionist role. The secretary to the cabinet normally chairs the Committee on Senior Officials (COSO) – the body that develops short-lists for all positions at deputy minister level and upper-strata posts encompassed by the associate and assistant deputy minister levels. The PCO contains a secretariat which supports COSO and develops policy concerning the selection and development of lower-level senior officials within departments. Concerns have arisen from time to time that some cabinet secretaries had become so impregnated with the criteria of the prime minister of the day that they could not adequately protect the prerogatives of the career civil service in recommending advancement to senior positions. Thus, Gordon Robertson – a paragon of the pre-Trudeau mandarinate – retained the chairmanship of COSO for a few years as his successor

– Michael Pitfield, a 37-year-old protégé of Trudeau – attempted to establish his bona fides as *de facto* head of the civil service.

Similarly, Paul Tellier – who recently resigned as cabinet secretary to assume the presidency of Canadian National Railways – had appeared to some critics of both the Trudeau and Mulroney administrations too eager by half to adapt his views to the government of the day. For much of Tellier's tenure as cabinet secretary, which began in 1985, Jack Manion – a throwback to the old mandarinate (in the gradualness of his career advancement if not in his connections with the Canadian establishment) – functioned in PCO as a deputy minister responsible for COSO and senior personnel policy and management.

Some commentators attributed the emergence of the Federal–Provincial Relations Office (FPRO) as a separate central agency in 1975 as a sinecure for its secretary Gordon Robertson. This suspicion gained greater credence when, after the Parti Québecois formed a government in Quebec in 1976, the Priorities and Planning Committee of the cabinet absorbed the functions of the Federal–Provincial Relations Committee. However, the FPRO survived some seventeen years of changes of government, secretaries and emphases on the part of the government to become a permanent part of the central agency landscape, until it was reintegrated in PCO in 1993.

To be sure, FPRO owed its continuance partially to the political convulsions over national unity which regularly afflict Canadian federalism. Some special office has to advise the government how best to cope with these recurrent crises. In addition, the regular run of governance issues in Canada's fragmented political system calls for the careful management of diplomacy between federal departments and their opposite numbers in the provinces. FPRO served as the switchboard for the myriad negotiations between levels of government. Virtually every federal department dedicates substantial resources to relations with the provinces. And most provinces have established central agency units to handle relations with the federal government. FPRO's survival has stemmed in no insignificant degree from the need for a gearbox in the mind-boggling complex of relations that characterizes Canadian federalism. That this function has now returned to PCO in no way means a reduction in its importance.

Australia

As with the UK and Canada, Australia has given a great deal more attention than the US to the machinery for cabinet consultation and related secretariats. Unlike the UK and Canada, however, it has demonstrated relative restraint in the creation of specialized cabinet committees and has limited the size of the ministry. We can partially explain this by the constitutional convention, which applied until 1987, under which each minister had to head a department (Wettenhall, 1989, pp. 95–6; Halligan, 1987). This checked the growth of the ministry, as the creation of new departments would prove much more difficult than layering ministers within existing agencies or appointing ministers with extra-departmental functions, as has been the practice in both the UK and Canada. Moreover, Australian society offers a much less fragmented base than the one upon which the Canadian federal government operates. In so far as a representational imperative functions at all in Australian cabinet making, its effects fall considerably short of those encountered by Canadian prime ministers as they assemble their government teams.

Bob Hawke made a dramatic departure from constitutional convention in 1987 when he appointed junior ministers who would assist portfolio ministers but not attend formal cabinet sessions. This move allowed him to reduce the number of departments from twenty-eight to seventeen. Some of the resulting mergers brought together strongly related governmental functions, for instance Employment, Education and Training, and Industry, Technology and Commerce. However, the officials responsible for integrating the departments wrestled to overcome substantial differences in bureaucratic cultures, the most serious of which were those between diplomats and trade representatives in Foreign Affairs and Trade and medical professionals and social service administrators in Health, Housing and Community Services. Some departments appeared simply as residual categories for functions that did not fit elsewhere. Bringing together Arts, Sports, the Environment and Territories, and Immigration, Local Government and Ethnic Affairs seemed to strain the bounds of credulity as the thrust of the reorganisation set out to house related functions under one roof. Paul Keating – prime minister since 1991

– has juggled parts of some of the portfolios. For instance, he gave Arts a higher profile by placing it with Administrative Services. He also split the Department of Transport and Communications in two. However, this brings the size of the cabinet to eighteen; this indicates considerable discipline when we consider that eight years have passed since the original reforms.

The cabinet in Australia, unlike that in Canada under Mulroney, meets on a weekly basis. However, inner groups have tended to serve as executive bodies to filter and mediate issues before they reach cabinet (Campbell and Halligan, 1992, pp. 78–9). During the Hawke and Keating governments, the Expenditure Review Committee (ERC) has performed this function. Its size and membership have varied. However, it has always included the prime minister, the treasurer and the finance minister. Under Hawke, the other members of the committee came equally from key economics (hard) and social policy (soft) ministries. The current ERC appears to favour soft portfolios as it adds only the ministers for Employment, Education and Training, Social Security, and Industrial Relations to the core group, that is the prime minister, treasurer and finance minister. This focus might reflect the Prime Minister's absorption with the long-term unemployment crisis, which has gripped Australia over the past few years.

ERC has taken as its central task the imposing of strict fiscal discipline on line departments. It achieved especially notable success in the period between 1986 and the fiscal blow-out associated with the 1990 election. During this time, 'economic rationalists', if not a household term, became part of the general parlance that characterized the tremendous power of the ERC ministers and their chief officials (Pusey, 1991). Other important committees that have operated under Hawke and Keating include Structural Adjustment, which has tried to make Australian industry less subsidy-dependent and more market-viable, and Social Policy, which has attempted to monitor the effects of fiscal stringency on less advantaged groups.

A remarkable feature of ERC has proved to be the intensity of its effort. With the exception of the build-up to the 1987 election, Bob Hawke chaired sessions of the Committee. During the most critical phases of the budget process, three weeks before the May economic statement and the August annual budget respectively, the Committee would meet nearly every day in marathon sessions that could extend into the small hours of the morning. Paul Keating essentially delegated the chair of ERC in the 1993 budget cycle to the Treasurer. This led to two difficulties. First, some ministers manoeuvered around ERC and made direct appeals to the Prime Minister. And the final budget contained some proposals whose political viability could clearly have borne a great deal more scrutiny. Since the Labor Party does not control the Senate, it ended up having to negotiate its budget with Democrats and Greens in the upper house. Further, it faced an unprecedented revolt from some backbench labourites in the House of Representatives who became emboldened once they smelt blood.

In the wake of this débâcle, the Treasurer, John Dawkins, resigned. Before his departure, however, he negotiated new procedures for the budget process, which took effect in the 1994 cycle. The Government will publish a fiscal framework in mid-February. It will also enter into early negotiations with those in the Senate whose support will be essential for the passage of the budget. These senators will even be able to make expenditure proposals that will receive consideration from ERC. The Government will condense its May economic statement and August budget into a single document, to be issued in mid May. All of this constitutes a major departure from the normal relationship between the executive and legislative branches during budget preparation in Whitehall. Only time will tell whether ERC will operate as effectively under this system as it did when the budget process functioned in secret.

Cabinet ministers in Australia devote somewhat more time to strategy exercises than their opposite numbers in the UK and Canada. There is one clear reason for this. Australian governments must go to the polls every three years rather than every five. This tends to put cabinets on a constant campaign footing. A trade-off reveals itself here. Australian cabinets find it quite compelling to work on political strategy. Therefore, their deliberations might focus more on the mid-term than on the long term. However, the 1986 Labor commitment to fiscal stringency did demonstrate that governments can take the long view even when electoral exigencies have begun to focus all minds (Keating and Dixon, 1989). In addition, Hawke's wholesale reorganization of government departments after the 1987 election demonstrates the degree to which the shortness of Australian mandates does not proscribe dramatic action. Early on in its new mandate, the Keating Government had identified three principal policy objectives – more coherent handling of long-term unemployment, the development of a new industrial policy for Australia and new initiatives in regional development.

A debate has emerged periodically over the name to be given to the cabinet secretariat in Australia (Weller, 1983). Since 1971, it has gone by the title Department of the Prime Minister and Cabinet (PM&C). This title would be an anathema for some British constitutionalists as it suggests that the secretariat serves two masters – not just the cabinet but the prime minister as well. Of course, the British Cabinet Office in practice remains highly sensitive to the needs of the prime minister. PM&C came by its title honestly in that the initial cabinet secretariat took the name 'Prime Minister's Department'. True to their direct fashion of dealing, Australians have had no trouble acknowledging a key dimension to any cabinet secretariat in the prime-ministerial system.

The PM&C blossomed beyond a traditional secretariat role during the 1970s. Two prime ministers during that period, Labor's Gough Whitlam and the Liberals' Malcolm Fraser, the latter in particular, placed a high value on the capacity of PM&C to provide independent advice on policy issues. Indeed, to this day, officials associate Fraser's reliance upon PM&C as of a piece with his mistrust of cabinet and desire to decide most important issues personally. Under Hawke and Keating, PM&C has shown less of a reflex for micromanagement. However, it has played a pivotal role in the process by which the cabinet develops its central strategy and ensures that specific initiatives fit within it. Currently, PM&C has taken the lead in developing and integrating the government's central strategic programmes regarding long-term unemployment, industrial policy and regional development. It also has assumed responsibility for the pursuit of Keating's commitment to make Australia a republic by the year 2000. Officials generally observe that Keating employs the PM&C as an extension of his personal staff more than Hawke did.

A point of contention has arisen over the role of PM&C. In recent years, permanent heads of departments have come quite disproportionately from PM&C. This trend has spawned the view among line department mandarins without PM&C experience that they will not be able to rise to the top of their departments. Since the mid-1980s, a new career path has revealed itself. This has economists going from Treasury to PM&C on secondment and staying there – often with a period in the Prime Minister's Private Office – until moving on to assume responsibility for line departments or at least taking on important deputies' posts. This development has exacerbated anxiety in some quarters that 'economic rationalists' have taken over recruitment to the upper levels of the bureaucracy. The ascendancy of PM&C – both as a policy unit and as a breeding ground for the best and brightest – has, coupled with the historic Treasury dominance, raised the spectre of elitism. In a society which prides itself on its egalitarianism this involves risks for both organizations. That is, a backlash could emerge if marginalized people in the executive–bureaucratic arena – ministers and officials alike – come to the conclusion that coherence exacts a high price in terms of exclusivity.

The Prime Minister's Private Office has assumed special importance under both Hawke and Keating. We can attribute this in part to the fact that Labor has generally expanded ministers' latitude for developing small advisory staffs working solely for them. When Labor formed the government in 1983, it tended to recruit into these offices roughly even numbers of party operatives with policy backgrounds and career officials on secondment. Over the years, however, it has forged sufficient links with the career bureaucracy that it has tended to call more on them than outsiders. For this reason, the Prime Minister's Private Office has become a proving ground for high fliers marked for key secretary and deputy secretary posts. Keating more than Hawke has tended to develop strong personal attachments to the permanent officials who have joined his personal staff.

The Department of the Treasury in Australia does not enjoy the monopoly of economic policy that its namesake enjoys in Britain. Since 1976, the Department of Finance has assumed responsibility for the expenditure budget and for management, including staff levels. Also, PM&C – drawing largely upon Treasury secondments but benefiting as well from proximity to the prime minister – does involve itself fairly substantially in economics issues. This applies especially to pressure points such as relations with the Federal Reserve Bank and devising the fiscal framework.

Still, the Treasury sustains the type of aura that its counterpart in Britain does. It does not make sense to speak of it as an elite organization in absolute terms. Too many senior Australian Treasury officials come from working-class families, left school at an early age and then regained ground by finishing their high school studies and proceeding to university on Commonwealth government cadetships or completing their degrees at new universities. Australia runs an education system every bit as egalitarian as its society. And this makes for a great deal of forgiveness for the mistakes of those destined to reach the top. However, the Treasury has until recently maintained a corner of the top brain power in the Commonwealth government. And, as in Canada, the PhD serves as a surrogate for social standing among a cadre of officials distinguished more for their native intelligence and grit than for their old school ties.

From 1983 to 1991, the Treasury benefited from the leadership of a minister who, in fact, embodied the egalitarian nature of Australia. In his tenure as Treasurer, Paul Keating displayed a mixture of intellectual acuity and working-class acerbity that often left opposition critics dumbfounded. Having left school at fourteen, Keating had received no formal training in economics. However, he devoured everything his officials provided. In time, he weaned himself off reliance upon his officials, selecting what pleased him from the advice of party operatives, business leaders, union leaders and his private office. None the less, the department drew upon the Keating mystique to advance acceptance of its view of economic exigencies.

As Keating increasingly asserted himself against Bob Hawke, the department gained leverage against its opponents. Keating's 1986 'Banana Republic' speech – delivered without consultation with Hawke and while the Prime Minister was in the People's Republic of China – was a watershed. In asserting that Hawke's policies, if continued, would cause Australia to become a banana republic, Keating invited dismissal from his portfolio. Instead, Hawke yielded to his views, thereby ushering in a five-year period in which the Treasurer sculpted the fiscal framework and wage policies with little challenge from the Prime Minister. Under this regime, the Treasury had to compete with other contenders for their whale's engagement. But no one ever questioned the preparedness of their whale to fight the other whales and win, once directed to their point of view.

The centrality of the Treasury in recruiting and training top analytic minds has provided a streetcar for the spread of economic rationalism into PM&C and outward to line departments. The implantation of former Treasury people throughout senior positions in the public service has meant that ministers are offered a commonality of perspective and advice exceeding what we would find in the other systems considered here. The fact that several ministers have shared the 'economic rationalist' perspective has further advanced coherence in the system, at least in so far as decision makers can reduce issues to economic criteria. The consensus has been eroded in recent years. The Treasury has faced a bit of a crisis. The tapping of some of its top talent for work in PM&C and line departments has taken a toll of its 'bench strength'. Further, the increased demand for economists in the private sector has meant that the Treasury can no longer make unchallenged 'first calls' for top graduates. And it has experienced a certain amount of attrition when officials have left for private sector positions.

Occasionally, one derives from Treasury officials the impression that they view their colleagues in the Department of Finance as the B team. This could stem from the fact that Finance employs fewer officials with advanced economics degrees. Also, Finance people work – much more than their opposite numbers in Treasury – at the coal face, dealing as they must with budgeting and management in operation departments. However, Finance has come into its own in two important ways in recent years. First, it has served effectively as the secretariat for the Expenditure Review Committee of cabinet. Thus, its senior managers – especially officials in the General Expenditure Division – have found a rare opportunity to achieve a very high degree of interaction with cabinet ministers. Second, Finance has spearheaded the efforts of the Labor Government toward management reform in the Commonwealth public service. This role has not ingratiated Finance with the senior managers of line departments. However, it has placed it at the core of the Government's push to achieve cultural change in the bureaucracy.

Departments do not love Finance. However, they have had somehow to come to grips with its various reform initiatives. Change has proved difficult to sell. The task of coping with ever shrinking resources tends to seize the mind more than cultural reform. Indeed, officials in line departments often see efforts such as the

Financial Management Improvement Programme as diversions. To many, the promise of greater discretion over resources means little if in fact their departments have to struggle with chronic underfunding. In addition, the word on managerial reform has not permeated all corners of Finance. Line departments have found a disjunction between the urgings of the cerebral part of Finance – the secretary and the principal advocates of change – and those of supply division officials still imbued with the top-down control orientation to budgeting. Notwithstanding these issues, Finance has fostered a great deal more tangible change in its system than any comparable unit in the US, UK or Canada. This is due both to the rigour of the theoretical grounding of the reform effort and the extent to which it permeated all segments of the public service.

The recruitment and management of the senior executive cadre in Australia has become greatly decentralized, with one exception: the cabinet secretary advises the prime minister on the assignment of individuals to departments as permanent heads. Departments thus run their own competitions for appointments to the Senior Executive Service (SES), although the Public Service Commission performs some monitoring functions. It has become commonplace for officials to move from agency to agency as they advance through the public service hierarchy. This pattern has broken down to some degree the cultural autonomy of departments, especially when it involves economic rationalist implants attracting more of their kind. Also, the Public Service Commission (previously the Public Service Board) has lost its former role of offering a view of succession to the headship of departments independent of the received wisdom in PM&C. The current arrangement, indeed, allows for few checks and balances against a cabinet secretary who has become impregnated with the standards of the government of the day, and recommends for permanent head positions only those who embrace this value system.

Finally, federal–state relations do not loom large in Australian central agencies. Australia does not labour under the fragmentation experienced by the Canadian system. And the balance of power between the two levels of government strongly favours the Commonwealth. The fact that the Commonwealth government occupies considerably more tax room than the state governments gives it fiscal leverage that the federal government in Canada clearly lacks. Departments typically work out programme details with states at a fairly low level. Before he was replaced by the 1991 leadership challenge, Bob Hawke had established a new system of consultations with state premiers. Although Paul Keating used his opposition to this policy as one of the justifications of the leadership challenge, he has subsequently had to engage in the consultative process established by Hawke. Moreover, PM&C now gives greater focus to Commonwealth–state relations in its organizational structure. Generally, states have preferred engaging these new elements of the Commonwealth apparatus in PM&C to bringing matters to line departments. The PM&C role in this field might be a growth sector.

New Zealand

New Zealand may strike some observers as simply a small United Kingdom. However, a number of factors make running this unitary system, based on a comparatively homogeneous society, quite difficult (Boston, 1992, p. 91). Two of these seem to take us furthest in explaining why coordination and coherence have become so difficult in New Zealand. First, its cabinet has some twenty ministers. Each of these has responsibility for two departments on average. The prevailing view has been that ministers should reconcile conflicts between various sectors of government. That is, various functions should receive full embodiment in a department rather than be housed with other functions under one roof – allowing officials to resolve differences without reference to ministers. Separate departments assume responsibility even for such specialized areas as Maori Affairs, Pacific Islanders, Women, Youth, and Consumer Affairs.

Second, New Zealand has perhaps faced pressures for structural adjustment greater than those in any of the other Anglo-American systems. Thus, adaptation in the 1980s did much more than cope with the secular economic decline encountered in these systems. It extended to addressing the profound dislocations which Britain's abandonment of Commonwealth trade relations for those with the EEC brought to a country that had remained economically post-colonial far beyond its years as an independent nation. New Zealand had remained a supplier of agricultural products.

It could no longer sustain its infrastructure and social programmes without assured access of these goods to Britain.

In the 1970s, New Zealand ran a cabinet consultation system which superficially resembled the one that prevailed in the UK, Canada and Australia (Weller, 1985, pp. 118–19). That is, a number of subject-matter committees reviewed policy proposals from various sectors of government before they went to the entire cabinet. In addition, steering groups emerged – Policy and Priorities under Norman Kirk (1972–4) and Cabinet Economic Committee under Robert Muldoon (1975–84) – which functioned as the cabinet's steering committees. However, New Zealand's process proved somewhat more free-flowing than the structures would suggest. For instance, Muldoon's personality loomed very large in his administration. It provided an inducement to collective government so strong that observers quite legitimately asked whether the system would survive his departure. The fact that Muldoon sat on the Cabinet Economic Committee and served simultaneously as treasurer and prime minister emphasizes the salience of this caveat. Additionally, officials had long enjoyed fairly free access to cabinet-level committees. Indeed, they usually convened before the meetings of these bodies to try to agree to a pre-cabinet consensus. In these two traits, the personalization of prime-ministerial leadership and the potential for officials to pre-programme cabinet meetings, New Zealand under Muldoon resembled Canada under Mackenzie King during the 1930s.

Prime ministers under the Labour governments of 1984–90 – David Lange (1984–9) and Geoffrey Palmer (1989–90) – struggled mightily to exert their authority in pursuit of coherence and comity in cabinet. Both men failed. To a degree, we can attribute this to the severity of the adjustments that New Zealand was pursuing at the time. However, both the nature of the economic difficulties faced by New Zealand and the power of the market-oriented faction within the Labour caucus suggest that neither prime minister could have escaped dramatic actions which inevitably would lead to severe disruptions in the usual ways of doing business (Boston, 1987, pp. 6–10). In addition, deficits in the apparatus for collective decision making had begun to take their toll.

The dominant role of the neo-liberal Labour faction in economic affairs emerged as the principal force pressing Lange and

Palmer to abandon the helm. Here the power struggles between Lange and Roger Douglas – the former's finance minister during most of his government – became especially unseemly. Lange forced Douglas to resign in 1988. The caucus's re-election of Douglas to the cabinet six months later precipitated Lange's resignation. Having thus defied prime-ministerial leadership, the neo-liberals tried their hand at Palmer, who opposed their line on some issues but ultimately yielded power as well.

An examination of the coordinative apparatus available to Lange and Palmer soon reveals that it had not developed at all adequately (Boston, 1992, pp. 91–8). The Prime Minister's Department – which split in 1987 into a Prime Minister's Office (a small advisory staff) and a Cabinet Office (essentially a switchboard for arranging meetings and processing submissions) – became manifestly inadequate to its task considering the pressures of the time. It gave the prime minister precious little capacity to canvass advice alternative to that coming from the Treasury. And it lacked the brokerage skills that the now highly fragmented executive–bureaucratic arena required. But structural initiatives pursued by the Treasury as part of the neo-liberal agenda would make coherence still more elusive.

As we have noted, New Zealand has operated with a highly differentiated departmental system. Several ministers assume responsibility for more than one portfolio and the agencies which embody these function in relative isolation from one another. This compounds the difficulty of coordination between ministers even in the best of times. However, some structural innovations had the short-term effect of making matters worse.

To begin with, Lange cut back drastically on officials' participation in cabinet committee meetings. This assertion of ministerial authority came at the cost of retarding the symbiosis which often develops in Westminster systems between the collective political executive and the upper levels of the bureaucracy. It also meant that officials lacked the sense of cabinet's 'mind', which would give meaning to preparatory sessions before ministers considered the issues. The State Sector Act (1988) further reduced the incentives for officials to resolve their differences before matters went to the cabinet. Following the neo-liberal approach to accountability, the Act attempted to narrow the responsibilities of heads of agencies so that they focused on the obligations of the 'chief executive' (styled the agent) to the minister (styled the principal). The accompanying preparation of annual performance agreements between chief executives and ministers greatly constricted conventional Westminster notions. These included officials' general sense of obligation toward the government of the day and/or the professional integrity of the civil service cadre as a whole.

Both Lange and Palmer sought antidotes to the fragmentation of the executive branch. By early 1989, Lange had introduced new guidelines for cabinet submissions. These required departments to circulate materials to agencies affected by their proposals. They also stipulated that the Prime Minister's Office should review submissions before they went to the cabinet. Also, Lange created officials' committees which would shadow the two main cabinet-level groups, the Cabinet Policy Committee and the Cabinet Committee on Economic Development and Employment. In each case, he placed the Prime Minister's Office in the chair rather than the Treasury. Palmer went a step further by re-merging the Prime Minister's Office and the Cabinet Office into a Department of Prime Minister and Cabinet. This new agency would play a stronger analytic role, although it would not aspire to the level of resources enjoyed by PM&C in Canberra.

Cumulatively, these reforms laid the groundwork for improved coordination. Unfortunately for Labour, the Government remained so fractious until the end of the mandate that it did not capitalize on the potential benefits of the new arrangements. The National Party administration, thus, has profited the most from the enhanced capacity for coordination in the centre. Jim Bolger revamped the committee structure, and the Strategy Committee and the Ministerial Committee on Social Assistance became the main groups. In each case, the prime minister chairs meetings and shadow committees of officials review materials before submission. Bolger has also reinstituted the participation of officials in cabinet committee meetings. His Government has also reconsidered the State Sector Act and introduced provisions which make explicit chief executives' responsibilities to consult with other departments.

As the reader might have already gathered, the Treasury maintains a monopoly of economic policymaking similar to that enjoyed by its namesake in the UK. Unlike the latter, the New

Zealand Treasury has experienced an abrupt generational change in its culture. During the late 1970s and throughout the 1980s, it changed very rapidly from a gifted-amateur operation to a powerhouse of professional economists. Further, the allure of private sector careers – a market for economics talent which expanded very rapidly in conjunction with the deregulation of the financial sector in the mid-1980s – changed Treasury officials' time horizons. Few would now consider themselves likely to work in government throughout their professional careers.

Since the New Zealand Treasury developed into a cadre of professional economists much later than either Canada's Finance Department or Australia's Treasury, the brand of economics that now prevails represents a band of the profession narrower than the one we would find in the other organizations. That is, the dominant Canadian and Australian economists acquired their skills in the Keynesian era and 'retooled' as monetarism and structural adjustment emerged as concerns, beginning in the mid-1970s. On the other hand, economists trained in the neo-liberal tradition control the New Zealand Treasury. In fact, Graham Scott (until 1993 the Department's secretary) – and many of his inner circle represented a sub-set of neo-liberalism called 'public choice'. The drive in the Lange administration to reorganize governance along the lines of principal–agent relations took root in public choice theory. Indeed, the Treasury documents which provided the rationales for the reforms drew upon theoretical literature in the field much more than any similar materials in any of the other systems considered in this book (Scott and Gorringe, 1989; Scott, Bushnell and Sallee, 1990).

We have seen that monetarism taken to its extreme can result in an absorption with macroeconomic policy that leads to a neglect of microeconomics. In the case of public choice, analysts have reached the conclusion that efforts to achieve coherence simply obscure the central issue of governance in advanced economies. The fact that government tends to command too high a proportion of GNP stems from the fact that multifaceted guidance points provide excessive entry for special pleaders. Above all these serve the purposes of the heads of agencies whose private utility rests upon the maximization of budgets. At their core, so the theory goes, bureaucrats are budget-maximizers. Public choice, thus, seeks a regime in which making decisions about resources becomes increasingly automatic. It also attempts to disaggregate governance so that the relationship between the bureau as agent of the political executive (its principal) and the political executive as agent of the citizenry (its principal) becomes more direct and less multifaceted. In classic terms, public choice theorists advocate a return to the nineteenth-century concept of a dichotomy between policy and administration. The bureau should limit itself to the latter as much as possible.

Although it has launched management reform programmes similar to the UK's FMI and Australia's FMIP, the Treasury has shown a preference for shock treatments that completely alter the context of administration. These have involved hiving off entire bureaucratic organizations and making them into State-Owned Enterprises, recasting the headships of departments and agencies as contract-based chief executive posts, and introducing performance measures that try to replicate the conditions of the market. In this context, the Treasury has become more a brains trust providing thrust for the reforms than a neutral management consultancy. In fact, the thrust it has provided behind the agency concept has frequently exceeded that of the political executive – at least it does if we construe the latter in the collective sense rather than as the fiat of a true believer in the Treasury line, like Roger Douglas.

Observers have not always found it easy to establish which is principal and which is agent in the relationship between the government and the Treasury. Frequently, it has appeared that the Treasury functions as principal in mega-experiment in which the political executive serves as its agent! The Department has levered itself into this position through its monopoly of economic expertise and its exploitation of the sensitivity of the political executive – given New Zealand's vulnerability during the age of fiscal constraint – to the preferences of the financial community as mediated by Treasury officials.

Under the current regime, the State Services Commission has played a somewhat more modest role than before in the process whereby agency heads receive their positions. Formerly, three agency heads along with two members of the commission would nominate individuals to be permanent heads of departments. Strictly speaking ministers had to accept these nominees without question. But, in fact, the committees would consult privately with ministers and the latter could refuse their recommendations. Any recruit from outside the public service would have to demonstrate exceptional qualifications for a vacant position.

Now ministers take a much more active role in the selection of their chief executives and define in clear terms what will guide the evaluation of their performances. Chief executives receive limited contracts extending for five years rather than the open remits given to permanent heads under the previous procedures. These measures have refashioned the relationship between an agency head and his or her colleagues in the upper levels of the bureaucracy. Obligations have become much more a matter between a minister and the officials and less one of the professional standards and behaviours of the civil service cadre *per se*.

Conclusion

This analysis has assessed the coherence and consistency of policy making in the United States, Canada, Australia and New Zealand. This comparative treatment has sought to set the stage for an analysis of how well the UK system, in comparison with the others, grapples with the decline of coherence and consistency in governance. It has focused on five principal coordinative functions – strategic planning and decision making, economic and fiscal policies, budgeting and management policy, senior personnel policy and, in the case of federal systems, intergovernmental affairs. We have found that all four systems differ considerably in their capacity for integrative approaches in these five sectors. Dysfunctions can stem from several different sources.

First, the relatively fragmented nature of society in the US and Canada makes coordination more difficult in these countries than in the others. Second, disjunctive structures can exacerbate any tendency in society toward fragmentation. Here the separation of powers in the US and the centrifugal nature of Canadian federalism clearly make coherence and consistency more difficult in these countries. In a milder way, New Zealand serves as an example of a unitary system and a relatively homogeneous society in which, nevertheless, the division of functions between departments tends to mirror client relations. The ossification resulting from these arrangements has greatly complicated coordination.

Third, the systems vary greatly in the apparatuses they have installed to achieve higher degrees of coordination. In some cases, we find a good fit between the difficulty of integration and the machinery – as in Canada. In others, we find a bad fit. Here the US stands out. It grapples with the most complex and intractable coordinative problems with the least well-developed apparatus.

Fourth, the operation of the coordinative apparatus varies greatly according to the abilities and management styles of political executives. Chief executives and their cabinets should consider more carefully how they can organize their activities so as to gain the optimum return from coordinative machinery. They must know the limits of the apparatus – some problems defy institutional efforts to resolve them. However, they must recognize as well the long-term dangers of *ad hoc* decision making. Fifth, political executives should take precautions against politicized incompetence, a condition in which ideological preferences and the desire to maintain electoral support lead the political authority to marginalize the permanent bureaucracy. Political executives correctly seek to avoid capture by the 'neutral' competence of the career civil service. However, they risk becoming very error-prone administrations indeed if they do not devise ways of engaging the permanent bureaucracy as part of the integrative process. Truncated integration, that is harmonization that overlooks or overrides the advice of those most intimately involved with programme development and implementation, runs the risk of being highly illusory.

6

A Paragon Lost?

The UK system operates under substantially more favourable conditions for coherence and consistency than the US. No system can produce more harmony than the society upon which it is based can sustain. Thus, it is questionable whether efforts to maintain the level of cohesion found in the UK would succeed in the US. The UK is a unitary political system with relative societal homogeneity. Furthermore, Britons share views of governance different from those that have prevailed in the US. The separation of powers and the federal system reinforce the conscious American preference for structures that err on the side of individual and local rights. We hear much these days about the dysfunctions of 'divided government' in the US. However, it is extremely doubtful whether Americans would take their governance any other way.

Even among the other Anglo-American systems which have parliamentary government, the British system normally reveals itself more capable of cohesiveness than either the Canadian or the Australian. We can say this not only because these two systems are federal. They have also tended to be more experimental than the British system. This has included a willingness to adapt certain features of American governance to their systems.

The Attributes of the Paragon

The British cabinet meets every week. It also divides into a complicated array of standing and *ad hoc* committees. Indeed, Margaret Thatcher – who always took a dim view of the committee system – performed wonders in reducing the number of standing committees to the lower thirties and keeping *ad hoc* groups to about 120 (Hennessy, 1986a, pp. 2, 101). Until summer

1992, the committee structure and membership remained closely
guarded secrets, on the grounds that how cabinet divided its
labour should remain a private matter for members of the government and their officials. None the less, well-placed observers
proved fairly resourceful in piecing the structure together. Most
of it followed fairly obvious lines. These normally included committees involved with planning for legislative sessions and the
management of parliamentary affairs, economic strategy, overseas and defence policy, relations with the European Economic
Community, home and social affairs and security and intelligence. Under these broad headings, different clusters of sub-
committees would coalesce in more sharply defined fields.

The secrecy of the system – not even cabinet ministers could
monitor the apparatus for redundant accretions and efforts to
bypass normal channels – perhaps contributed to its fairly by-
zantine web of sub-committees and *ad hoc* groups. However, the
fact that even Thatcher found it difficult to streamline the structure should alert us to the difficulty of trimming branches here
and there – even if the accretion of new bodies becomes mildly
embarrassing under the new light of public scrutiny. When we
add to the twenty or so cabinet members who head departments
the thirty or so ministers of state who shoulder responsibility for
sections of departments, we see that some fifty ministers will be
looking at a given moment for significant fora in which to press
their policy views. Normally, only cabinet ministers go to meetings of the full cabinet and main cabinet committees. Thus, the
system of sub-committee and *ad hoc* groups helps provide an
outlet for ministers of state.

The British cabinet has conventionally processed the immediate
issues on its plate reasonably expeditiously. And it keeps in reasonably good focus how its various decisions relate to one another.
Some notable lapses have occurred. As we will see in Chapter 7,
the Franks Commission report (1983) concluded that the overseas and defence apparatus of cabinet had failed to monitor adequately the early signs that Argentina would invade the Falkland
Islands. Also, some issues have posed such wrenching conflicts
that the cabinet has not been able to resolve them without major
rifts. This certainly happened in the Westland affair during the
latter part of 1985 and early 1986, which saw two ministers
resign over whether European or American interests would receive

the green light to rescue Britain's only surviving helicopter manufacturing firm. And the cabinet conflicts over British membership in the European Monetary System – which date back to the late 1970s – still appear far from final resolution.

Longer-range strategic planning is one area in which the British cabinet has not operated especially well. A multiplicity of factors present themselves as reasons for this deficiency. First, political executives in advanced democracies generally tend to focus on the short and middle term at the expense of the long. This trait usually becomes more pronounced as an administration begins to suffer the political backlash from its actions, and moves to avoid risky initiatives which – whatever their potential merits – might prove difficult to sell to an increasingly sceptical electorate.

Second, British ministries – collectively and individually – receive a relatively large share of their policy advice from career officials. The longer-range perspective of this cadre reasonably fits the 'think of Britain' mode. It tends to couch advice in terms of ultimate national interest – in so far as this is accessible. However, its calculations often reveal an aversion to risk. In the words of a Treasury official interviewed in 1978 in reference to economic policy: 'You have to have a view of what the British economy can stand. Ministers left to themselves would do things which would not be consistent with the proper management of the economy.' A 'Yes, Minister' syndrome appears whereby officials tell their political bosses what they want to hear and work feverishly behind their backs to neutralize the impact of their decisions.

British prime ministers and cabinets have employed several techniques in efforts to free deliberations from an impasse between political foresight and conventional wisdom. They have rarely adopted the approach of Canada's cabinet, in which a standing Priorities and Planning Committee attempts to devise for each new mandate a detailed strategy for the length of the government, which it then tries to adjust annually according to new exigencies. This would usually exceed the understanding for planning of the British executive–bureaucratic culture. However, more modest attempts have borne some fruit.

Heath took his cabinet on retreats every six months to assess the degree to which it had kept its broad strategic goals in focus. Ultimately, events overtook the process, but it did yield tangible benefits in the first two years of the administration. Thatcher preferred to work with ginger groups of secretaries of state, which would track the progress of core convictions of the government. Such groups operated behind the government's early efforts to impose tight monetary discipline and later initiatives in such fields as privatization and educational reform. Since the approach relied very much on inner groups of 'dry' ministers, it contributed to the accumulation of resentments over Thatcher's selective engagement of cabinet government.

The Cabinet Office has served as the central agency supporting ministers in their deliberations. Its organization has broadly reflected the structure of the cabinet committee system, with deputy secretaries responsible for the key ministerial groups, and under and assistant secretaries supporting more specialized committees. Its professional staff largely serve on the basis of secondment from other departments. Selection of these officials usually shows a bias toward people with experience in the Treasury. If individuals work in parts of the Cabinet Office concerned with macroeconomic policy or Europe then they are probably Treasury-based officials with little or no experience in line departments. If they work in 'home' or overseas and defence policy, they would normally have been 'starred' as potential permanent secretaries – which means that they would have passed through the Treasury at some point in their careers.

The Cabinet Office normally does an excellent job as a secretariat. It keeps the paper flowing, arranges meetings, gives early warning of conflicts between departments, works to give dissenters a sense that the process has taken their views into account and circulates the results of cabinet meetings throughout Whitehall. It did, however, experience some frustration under Margaret Thatcher owing to her preference for bilateral discussions with ministers and recourse to *ad hoc* groups which often excluded people she had given up on. The Cabinet Office has, nevertheless, lacked an ability to canvass alternative viewpoints. This does not mean that it has not promoted views – its officials normally share the ethos of the Treasury, namely 'We know what is best because we are bright.' It is simply to say that we cannot expect from the Cabinet Office much of an aptitude for going beyond the received wisdom that prevails in the upper strata of Whitehall.

Officials in the Cabinet Office have proved quick to differentiate between themselves and those working in a 'Department of the Prime Minister', such as Australia's Department of the Prime Minister and Cabinet. However, the distinction is often semantic. We see this in the words of one secretary to the cabinet:

> In this country . . . we haven't got a prime minister's department. In theory, the Cabinet Office serves all ministers; in practice, it serves the prime minister a good deal more than anyone else . . . He has, at no. 10, very efficient private secretaries . . . But they, when they want advice, almost always look here. I mean I don't want to pretend we are a prime minister's department under another name . . . But we are the department that services him. (1978 Interview.)

Lower down in the Cabinet Office, one finds that officials wrestle with the potential conflict between the requirement that they remain neutral brokers and the pressures to resolve issues. In the words of one respondent: '. . . one of the things I think we are very emphatic on is that the Cabinet Office doesn't and oughtn't sort of develop its own policies. . . . But, there very often is a role for us to do, knocking departmental heads together.' (1978 Interview.)

In fact, officials have stressed the fact that situations arise in which the Cabinet Office has to take charge of a process owing to an impasse between departments. Under such circumstances, it might step out of its purely facilitative role. As one respondent said: '[In interdepartmental committees] . . . generally, the rule is that Cabinet Office must not speak unless they provide the chairman, then they do practically all the speaking!' (1978 Interview.) Sometimes, the Cabinet Office can even choose to work in stealth – excluding departments that might present obstacles to the resolution of an issue. One official reflected upon one such situation, where he and his colleagues had decided to leave a department out of consultations notwithstanding its natural interest in the matter: 'I have been feeling that they have a role here. But the trouble is at the moment that we're doing things that I'm sure they wouldn't approve of and so we don't consult them.' (1978 Interview.)

The further we examined the Thatcher Government, the more respondents indicated to us that the Cabinet Office had receded to a more traditional role focused on keeping cabinet business running smoothly. As one Cabinet Office respondent put it: 'I have failed if cabinet is unable to reach a decision on an issue or if an issue that should have reached cabinet never makes it.' (1989 Interview.) Relatedly, the Thatcher doctrine on cabinet government held that ministers should focus more on their own departments and less on the business of others.

One respondent – working in the European secretariat – believed that many coordinating functions now resided within operational departments (1989 Interview). For instance, he considered the Foreign Office had the lead for overseeing policy and internal consistency, the Department of Trade and Industry for the single market process and the Treasury for financing reviews. Here his unit had become more a consultancy for departments not schooled in the European machinery:

> Some departments, such as the Home Office or Employment, are becoming more interested in learning about the Brussels process than previously. For example, the Home Office is involved because of problems regarding the abolition of frontiers . . . The Department of Employment is interested because of debate about the social dimension of the community – a question of social security and labour legislation.

Some of our respondents believed that the Cabinet Office under Thatcher did on occasion yield to the inevitable temptation to get caught between neutral brokerage and individual advocacy. As a former member of the no. 10 policy unit put it:

> The Cabinet Office could be mischievous. I was very conservative with regard to the Cabinet Office. They were the mechanics, the engine room, not up on the bridge . . . Sometimes, even inside the Cabinet Office, strong policy views developed. And, their staff would try to do a policy unit type job. And, sometimes, they became disingenuous. I remember on one occasion, one senior Cabinet Office official (now even more senior) writing an anti-Treasury brief to the PM and then going up to the Treasury minister after a meeting where Treasury was defeated and saying 'I'm terribly sorry that you lost, we did all we could.' (1989 Interview.)

To varying degrees, prime ministers have sensed the extent to which the Cabinet Office might serve somewhat ambivalently and even launch its own projects. They have attempted to compensate for the resulting deficit in the policy advice on tap. Heath sought a think tank composed of outsiders (it did not matter whether they brought partisan credentials, he simply wanted bright people not impregnated with Whitehall folk wisdom) who would help keep his Government's central goals in focus and facilitate the generation of new policy ideas as required. Negotiations between his transition people and Whitehall mandarins produced the Central Policy Review Staff. CPRS would advise the cabinet generally as well as the prime minister, be located in the Cabinet Office and include a mixture of seconded officials, rising corporate executives on loan from their firms and partisan policy professionals.

The ambiguity of its function, institutional autonomy and make-up notwithstanding, prime ministers Heath, Wilson and Callaghan and their cabinets found creative ways to employ CPRS. There did develop a secular decline in its impact the more it institutionalized its role and departed from its initial focus on the six-month strategic reviews; it was punctuated by quick turnover of advice on issues of immediate interest to the cabinet (Blackstone and Plowden, 1988). The longer it operated the more difficult it found bringing cabinets to strategic issues and contributing its views on how matters before cabinet fitted within this frame. It increasingly justified its existence by launching protracted studies with no real time limits – for instance its exhaustive assessment of the effectiveness of the Foreign Office's representation of British interests abroad, which became a lethal cause of derision. One CPRS veteran stressed the degree to which that particular exercise gave early warning of growing confusion over CPRS's mission:

> It tied up a very large amount of skilled CPRS manpower which was needed for a variety of other jobs including social policy activities ... on a body of work which couldn't by any sense of the term be said to be related to strategic questions ... It isn't for the CPRS to go about measuring the telegram traffic. That's a detailed nuts-and-bolts type of job. (1978 Interview.)

It thus becomes clear that CPRS might have encountered difficult times even if Thatcher had not become prime minister. However, the poor fit between Thatcher's personalized style and efforts to keep CPRS quasi-detached sealed the latter's fate. In the words of one respondent who worked in the CPRS at the time of its abolition:

> Everything tended to revolve around her attitude and approach to government. So, by definition, CPRS needed to focus on the PM, and make sure they were serving her. In my view, that is one of the reasons why we went wrong. Because CPRS had become too institutionalized and was not really responding to her requirements, in the way she was running her administration. (1986 Interview.)

CPRS thought it was servicing this need when it sponsored a major Whitehall examination of the funding of defence and social programmes. Unfortunately for CPRS, word of the unpalatable options being mooted by departments was leaked to the press. Even though it bore no responsibility for the leaks, Thatcher laid the blame for the resulting political embarrassment on CPRS. CPRS had moved to the wrong side of Thatcher's ledger:

> ... the long-term public expenditure report ... [was] taken out of context; because CPRS did not put forward a radical manifesto in the way that was portrayed. All it did, a legitimate exercise for a government agency, was to show where the profiles of public expenditure and tax were going ... All CPRS maintained was that they would need to do radical things if they wanted to go that far. Doing those things was entirely for them to decide ... It was all taken out of context and leaked inappropriately. It made us look as though we were naive, and the PM was embarking on a radical dismantling of the welfare state ... being an extremely acute politician, that was something that she couldn't put up with. (1986 Interview.)

Prime ministers have throughout this century chosen on occasion to bypass the formal Whitehall integrative process and use personal staffs or coteries in their efforts to ensure that substantive policies comport with the central thrust of their strategic objectives. Of course, prime ministers must in fact have identified such goals before seeking better mechanisms for setting the agenda, scheduling the introduction of initiatives and monitoring their implementation. We can, however, go all the way back to David

Lloyd George for an instance of a prime minister doing precisely this and then setting up a framework which would facilitate the follow-through (Turner, 1980). Lloyd George wanted to win the First World War and lay the groundwork for dealing with the post-war period. He stretched constitutional convention to the limit by narrowing effective collective consultation to a small group of advisers who did not even head conventional governmental agencies. He further established a team of advisers from outside government ultimately dubbed the 'garden suburb' because they occupied temporary accommodation in the courtyard at 10 Downing Street.

Prime ministers such as Lloyd George and Winston Churchill who find themselves facing dire threats to the national security enjoy a great deal of latitude to establish structures that enable them to operate monocratically (Mackintosh, 1977). Outside such crisis times, prime ministers who resort to similar devices might prompt some to say that they have attempted to personalize the decision-making process. We have already seen that prime ministers can – as Thatcher frequently did – narrow their consultation in the cabinet to ensure that they obtain legitimization from the core trustees of the government's mandate and then seek ratification from the rest of the cabinet. They can also resort to setting up advisory units to serve the prime minister and no one else.

Heath's transition people wanted to do this when they began their negotiations with the cabinet secretary and the head of the civil service which ultimately led to the creation of the Central Policy Review Staff. When Wilson began his second term as prime minister in 1974 he created a policy unit within 10 Downing Street. But until that time, prime ministers relied on the career-staffed no. 10 private office to monitor policy issues. In the private office, some five civil servants on secondment from other departments – as with the Cabinet Office, the Treasury is normally strongly represented here – keep in direct touch with various corners of Whitehall so that no. 10 can very quickly find the origins and intensity of various departmental positions. The private office can also identify where log-jams have occurred and – in the name of the prime minister – place the necessary sticks of dynamite to get things moving. The proximity of these career civil servants to the prime minister – their rooms are closest to

the prime minister's and to one another's: they fit into two small
offices – gives them an immense role as the eyes and ears of the
prime minister. As one private office member in the early part of
the Thatcher years noted:

> ... someone has to tell the prime minister that this is what you
> have got, and suggest to her the sequence in which she should read
> these in order to make sense of them, to draw together the salient
> points that they are making – hopefully they are moving in some
> kind of direction – bring out points of conflict and so lead the
> prime minister to the point where she is able, without having her-
> self to write an essay, to give specific directions as to what she wants
> done on the issues that are now before her. (1980 Interview.)

In serving as the prime minister's issues switchboard, the private office must maintain its credibility as an agent of neutral
brokerage. Individuals within the office lose their bona fides in
Whitehall if they appear to have taken a role in the development
of the prime minister's priorities and pressed these as if they had
become partisan operatives. Charles Powell – a Foreign Office
official who served in no. 10 under Thatcher long beyond the
usual three-year secondment – left Whitehall for this very reason
when Thatcher resigned.

Following, thus, upon the model that Wilson introduced in
1974, a vibrant policy unit can play two important roles. It can
offer the prime minister a small group close by that can serve as
a brains trust in the process of devising priorities and discerning
the placement and timing of personal interventions in policy
deliberations. Second, it can remove the pressure on the private
office to engage in advocacy and therefore help preserve its capacity for neutral brokerage.

Still, policy units have not found their way easily. Some analysts have seen their emergence as another sign of 'prime-
ministerialization', making the central machinery too sensitive to
the partisan exigencies of a government. In fact, policy units
encounter great difficulty resisting subsumption into the ethos of
the private office:

> We're so secretive here ... Outsiders when they come to no. 10
> are not secretive by nature, especially academics or journalists, or
> people who've operated in politics. The natural thing for them to

do is to tell other people what they're doing and discuss it. But you find that that's not the way things are done here. If you tell one of your colleagues something you shouldn't have, then you're much less likely to be told something by one of the established civil servants next time ... And it's not only from the civil servants. It's from the prime minister himself. Both prime ministers I've worked for had wanted things to be kept very, very secret. (1978 Interview.)

Wilson's Policy Unit, which continued throughout the Callaghan Government under the stewardship of Bernard Donoughue, performed quite effectively. Its operation relied heavily upon Donoughue's deftness at networking in Whitehall – he did exceptionally well at nurturing permanent secretaries – and the intellectual abilities of the Unit's members. Regarding the latter, Donoughue maintained a rigorous standard:

We must be of a stature intellectually and of an expertise that we can take on a departmental representative in a particular area. Our social policy person has to be as good as a senior person in the Department of Health and Social Security; our economist has to be as good, it so happens that he is better, as any senior person in the Treasury. (1978 Interview.)

Margaret Thatcher at first did not want to continue with the policy unit model; she believed that partisan advisers should largely function from individual ministers' offices. However, she saw the potential use of a policy unit around the time that she abolished the Central Policy Review Staff (1983). From that point to the end of her Government, the Policy Unit figured very substantially in almost all policy initiatives – especially those associated with privatization, the deinstitutionalization of professions, and educational reform. Under Major, the Policy Unit has carried on this tradition. However, its head until 1994 – Sara Hogg, a former economics columnist with the *Independent* – chose to focus much of the Unit's work on economic policy. Thus, it has suffered the experience of guilt by association as the central elements of Major's economic policies have unravelled.

When we turn to the development and integration of economic policies, we find in Britain a structural apparatus much more homogeneous than that found in the US. One department –

HM Treasury – controls all of the leading central agency units responsible for economic policy. Further, the chief economic adviser in the Treasury – with the rank of second permanent secretary – heads up the entire economics service of Whitehall. This takes in all officials occupying economics advisory positions in line departments as well as in the Treasury. The combined effect of these arrangements means that most integration of economic policies takes place in one agency, the Treasury. However, even if it requires the participation of other departments the respective economists will belong to a cadre managed by the Treasury.

The Treasury did face threats to its monopoly of economic policy-making in the 1960s and 1970s. When he first became prime minister in 1964, Harold Wilson created a Department of Economic Affairs, which was meant to provide alternative advice, to balance that proffered by the Treasury, on medium-term economic plans. The Department disbanded in 1969. From 1964 to 1969, the Treasury still controlled all the levers for running economic policy. And, unlike the Treasury, the new department did not claim a special relationship with the prime minister. Still, the Wilson experiment had left the Treasury with the strong view that it alone should proffer economic advice. In the words of one senior official there: 'I'm not terribly keen personally on setting up deliberately a countervailing force. That was part of the idea of the Department of Economic Affairs, creating tension and all that kind of thing. But it tends to waste an awful lot of time. If it's institutionalized, sooner or later perhaps one or the other tends to win.' (1978 Interview.)

The creation in 1970 of the Central Policy Review Staff – though focused on providing the prime minister and cabinet with independent advice – had implications for the Treasury. This was especially the case with issues concerning public expenditure, about which the CPRS often weighed in with alternative views.

Some Treasury officials will argue that the concentration of control over economic policy-making in one department derives from constitutional convention. Pointing to the fact that the prime minister is also formally titled First Lord of the Treasury, they will assert that defining the parameters of economic policy is ultimately a matter between the prime minister and the chancellor and not one for collective cabinet deliberations. One Cabinet

Office official with a background in the Treasury said: '. . . the prime minister is the First Lord of the Treasury. Thus, Treasury is in some ways the prime minister's department . . . There has always been a special relationship between the chancellor and the prime minister . . . The economic policy field does not require much organizational diversity because the chancellor makes the decisions on behalf of the prime minister.' (1989 Interview.)

Certainly, the secrecy that shrouds the development of the annual budget, which sets out the fiscal framework within the wider context of economic projections and announces changes in taxation, comports with this view. Similarly, the devising of monetary policy occurs in private discussions between the Treasury and the Bank of England, which occasionally present issues that require the direct participation of the prime minister.

There are exceptions to this emphasis on privacy. We will see when we consider expenditure budgeting that this has occurred in fairly collective formats depending on varying views of the proper involvement of the cabinet in this activity. Furthermore, cabinet committees have played significant roles in the process of legitimizing and implementing the principal elements of the government's economic strategies. Even under Thatcher, a group of ministers – albeit selected on the basis of their commitment to monetarism – would meet regularly to discuss the course of the Government's economic strategy. Cabinet committees also came into play in pushing forward privatization. However, the award for 'most active committee' probably goes to a group on pay – consisting of the chancellor and the secretaries for Prices and Consumer Protection, Employment and Industry – as it functioned under Callaghan. As noted in Chapter 4, this committee met over a hundred times in the final year of the Callaghan Government and attempted to fine tune a host of industrial agreements so that they would fit within the Government's pay policy.

Notwithstanding the structural concentration of economic policy-making in the Treasury, this does not mean that the process is devoid of conflict. Nor does it imply that the Treasury always gives roughly the same emphasis to various segments of the economic policy apparatus. Significant rifts emerged in the Treasury in the late 1970s between Keynesians – who had dominated the Department since the Second World War – and an increasingly powerful group of monetarists. The fact that this ideological clash had resolved itself in favour of the monetarists by 1978 suggests that Thatcher's arrival as prime minister simply gave intense political backing to a transformation that had already taken place in the Department.

The combined effects of these developments meant that throughout the 1980s the Department downplayed microeconomic policy and the units responsible for this. It worked from the assumption that – given that it had got its macroeconomic policies right – the micro would fall into place. The decade saw a running down of the Department's resources assigned to tax policy and to the monitoring of industries and public services. As one Conservative insider put it, an explicit strategy functioned behind this emphasis:

> Monetary policy operates through affecting expectations . . . You do so when you have built up a series of conditioning channels. One can always think of it in terms of the Pavlovian process. In Germany, they've had strict monetary targets for some time. They always have had quite an effective system of communicating informally the implications of these to various sectors. (1980 Interview.)

Although not as severe as in the US, the rise of monetarism in the Treasury also ushered in a period in which forecasts appeared – somewhat more than usually the case – sensitive to the ideological assumptions of their authors. By the mid-1980s, the Bank of England had in fact lost confidence in the integrity of Treasury forecasts. One senior Bank of England official lamented the degree to which Treasury forecasting had become subject to political bias:

> A problem has arisen between the head of the economics unit in the bank – John Fleming – and his opposite number at Treasury – Terry Burns who is the second permanent secretary responsible for economic advice. Fleming – a former don from Oxford – is a reconstructed Keynesian. The disagreements between the two emerge over the bank's duty to present quarterly reports on the economy . . . the tension between the two emanates from the fact that governments and administrations put forecasts in the most favourable light possible. (1986 Interview.)

Certainly, observers generally attribute the dysfunctions of the 'Lawson Boom' to Treasury projections in the run-up to the 1987 election; they seriously underestimated the danger of excessive reinflation (Keegan, 1989). Analysts widely acknowledge that John Major's absorption with reducing inflation to zero after the 1992 election greatly exacerbated the conditions that led to Britain's unceremonious departure from the EMS in September 1992. Britain had entered the EMS in 1990 with the pound at an unsustainably high value. This undermined the credibility in the money markets of efforts to drive down inflation with higher interest rates.

The Treasury contains the key units of the UK government responsible for reviewing the expenditure budget. The budget process runs in a quasi-collective way. Ultimately, the cabinet must agree to the expenditure budget. However, various structures decrease the extent to which it in fact deliberates over spending issues. To begin with, the Treasury minister responsible for the budget – the chief secretary – may request that the budget implications of policy proposals be considered before cabinet committees decide whether they will recommend their adoption to the entire cabinet. As one official explained, this gives the chief secretary an enormous amount of leverage in any cabinet committee:

> The chief secretary is where the buck stops unless the minister wishes to take the issue to cabinet . . . the chief secretary cannot be overruled by the committee. The majority may want to go ahead. If he says no on expenditure grounds . . . even if he is the lone voice, it must go to cabinet. A committee cannot overrule the cabinet secretary. . . Only cabinet can do that. (1978 Interview.)

In addition to this role, the Treasury also takes a strong lead in easing ministers toward consensus on the expenditure budget in its entirety. Here we find three processes – setting spending targets, negotiations between the Treasury and departments and the resolution of conflicts in a committee of cabinet. First, the annual Public Expenditure Survey sets the rules for the budget review. Notionally, the process includes a committee of principal finance officers (PESC) meeting with the senior Treasury people responsible for the expenditure budget to discuss the likely levels of increases and the various exceptions that departments will want to request. Since Thatcher's time, the committee has not actually met with any regularity. However, the rules are explained to principal finance officers and they have the opportunity to brief their ministers about these before they are embraced by the entire cabinet – normally some time in July.

Second, after the announcement of the PES targets, the chief secretary begins a round of bilateral discussions with ministers, seeking to reconcile differences. Third, usually an attempt is made to arbitrate insoluble disputes collectively. For much of the Thatcher period, a Star Chamber – headed by a prominent cabinet minister whose department was not a huge spender – would resolve any issues not agreed in bilateral meetings. Chief secretaries did not resort to this third process in the latter part of the Thatcher years and during Major's 1991 PES. In 1992, however, Major had resorted to a somewhat more formal committee – EDX – which has been chaired by the chancellor. Whatever the mixture of machinery for resolving outstanding budget issues, the cabinet itself rarely has to tie up loose ends. It agrees the guidelines for the expenditure budget in July and leaves it to the Treasury, aided if necessary by a committee of prominent ministers, to bring departments round to the agreed targets.

Management policy has proved to be an area in which the Treasury has not consistently benefited from the dominant role it enjoys in other sectors. When the Civil Service Department (CSD) emerged in 1968 it became a strong advocate of management reform in Whitehall, including the promotion of positive personnel management. To be sure, its concept of public service management simply enshrined the principle that management is important. It did not embrace nostrums such as those that prevail today about the need for the public service to function more like private sector organizations. The permanent secretary of the CSD assumed from the permanent secretary of the Treasury the headship of the civil service. His Department drew upon the leverage of a separate authorization from the Treasury for running costs – that is management services and personnel – in efforts to get departments to reassess their management and personnel systems. Thatcher abolished the CSD in 1981. Its head had provoked her wrath by disputing the aptness of private sector management principles to the public service. And she viewed the Department's efforts toward settlement of wage disputes as too sympathetic to public service unions.

Even without its problems with Margaret Thatcher, the CSD was falling from grace in Whitehall. As a leader of the civil service unions put it, it lacked the influence to deliver the concessions it purported to have obtained from unions for departments and vice versa. All parties increasingly viewed it as a nuisance:

> Our great criticism of the CSD is that they can't make things happen. They can't get their way with departments. Departments regard them as a nuisance. They have their own problems. They have their own work to do. They want the CSD there if, of course, there is a problem like a redundancy or something of that kind . . . So, the poor CSD is really in an impossible situation . . . Every time it goes to the department they say, 'Well you are just acting as a lapdog of the union' . . . We have come to the conclusion that under the circumstances we will have to negotiate much more directly with departments . . . especially the big ones which will not accept some kind of collective responsibility across the civil service for personnel management. (1978 Interview.)

After CSD's abolition, the Treasury immediately reabsorbed responsibility for pay policy and complementing. Here it applied cut and dried market criteria to pay issues. The concept of positive personnel management quickly became a thing of the past: 'The Government does not consider that the pay of civil servants, or any other group, should be determined by the needs of the individual. In general terms, pay is a matter for the market place, and social needs are the province of the social security system.' (HM Treasury, 1982, p. 21.)

Over time, the Treasury involved itself increasingly in general management policy. However, since the demise of CSD, residual units operating in the Cabinet Office (the cabinet secretary is now head of the civil service) have played significant roles in the selection of senior personnel and the advocacy of management innovation. The Efficiency Unit – which has operated in no. 10 under the direct guidance of the prime minister – has generated a succession of management innovations. These have included Rayner Scrutinies, the Financial Management Initiative, Next Steps, the Citizens' Charter and Market Testing. All of theses initiatives have tried to introduce market conditions to public service. With

the exception of Market Testing, the operational units responsible for implementing these programmes have functioned from
the Cabinet Office. The Efficiency Unit has shouldered day-to-
day responsibility for Market Testing. Each initiative has depended heavily upon the backing of the Treasury, which has not
always been forthcoming. Generally, the Treasury has been slow
to impart the discretion over budget lines and relaxing accountability procedures necessary for the full implementation of managerialist initiatives.

The selection and development of the senior cadre within
Whitehall remains once removed from the Treasury. A unit within
the Cabinet Office supports the cabinet secretary in his capacity
as head of the civil service. Defining to what extent officials
should impart information to Parliament and the public has absorbed a great deal of attention in this unit over the years. In
addition, it advises the cabinet secretary about candidates for
advancement to the uppermost positions in Whitehall – permanent and deputy secretary. Thatcher took an unusually active role
in the assignment of these posts. Thus, the cabinet secretary would
usually have to propose alternative candidates to the Prime Minister and she would normally want to interview them before
making a decision. Major has intervened less in this sector of
Whitehall management, which – before Thatcher – remained
largely the preserve of the senior mandarins.

The Seeds of Decline?

This section will assess the prime-ministerialization of cabinet
government under Margaret Thatcher. It will probe two ways in
which the process took place. First, Thatcher personalized the
complex of relations within no. 10 and between it and the Cabinet Office. This worked to the advantage of the Policy Unit. It,
unlike the private office, the Cabinet Office and the ill-fated CPRS,
had no obligations about the appearance of neutral competence
or working for all the cabinet and not just the prime minister.
Second, Thatcher – immersing herself in the role of First Lord of
the Treasury – essentially made the Treasury her own department.

Some might view this as a collapse of cabinet government.
However, we have to ask how much this much vaunted British

tradition had ever taken root. In the later part of the 19th century, when party discipline operated much more loosely than it does now, ministers were able to establish themselves as virtual barons (Mackintosh, 1977, pp. 146–7). Within this context, chancellors began to develop independent power bases and their department – no less powerful than it is now – played increasingly to their tune. David Lloyd George short-circuited this system for a time when he took power half way through the First World War (Turner, 1980). His approach functioned top-down. In fact, its effectiveness rested in no small degree on the fact that it suspended broad cabinet consultation as a constitutional requirement.

Lloyd George hoped to extend this approach to governance into the postwar period. He sought to aggregate ministries into superdepartments. This would allow issues to be resolved intramurally under the leadership of a single cabinet secretary. It would also limit the number of contestants in the executive–bureaucratic gamesmanship. Both steps would enhance the strength of the prime minister.

Between the wars, cabinet dynamics very much reverted to the contours that prevailed before the First World War. However, the Cabinet Office began to assume a more defined role. Its staff largely came on secondment. However, the permanency of tenure for the secretary of the cabinet assisted the process whereby incumbents to this post took on increasing stature (Chapman, 1988, pp. 8–12). At times when prime ministers required a high degree of political responsiveness from those upon whom they relied the most for advice, they would engage 'kitchen cabinets' of advisers. However, when leading in more 'routine' times, they began to rely very heavily upon the secretary of the cabinet. Additionally, prime ministers – especially in the 1950s and 1960s – began to call upon consultative machinery for handling cabinet business. The intensification of these mechanisms gave the Cabinet Office a pivotal role as the switchboard for executive decision making.

The view has emerged in other parliamentary Anglo-American countries that they followed the Westminster model in developing cabinet committee systems and cabinet offices. The fact is that no system led the others in these developments. There was a great deal of cross-fertilization. For instance, Lloyd George's idea for superdepartments had come from a similar proposal designed to address the unwieldiness of the Canadian cabinet system (Chapman and Greenaway, 1980, pp. 78–80). Whitehall itself often became the issue as well as progenitor of innovation in the parliamentary Anglo-American family.

Prime-ministerial at the Core

The No. 10 Policy Unit

At the beginning of her administration, Thatcher wanted to avoid creating a policy unit *per se*. John Hoskyns, a friend of Sir Keith Joseph, worked as a special adviser without the benefit of a staff. He ran into an old problem: he found it very difficult to get papers out of the private office. He also encountered difficulties getting his views on cabinet business to the Prime Minister. In the words of one respondent, Clive Whitmore – then the principal private secretary – once went to Hoskyns to protest about a note that he had submitted for the Prime Minister's box:

> . . . [he said] 'I saw a minute from you to the PM just going into the box about John Hunt's [then the secretary of the cabinet] memo on the head of the CPRS.' Whitmore said that he didn't think it was helpful to put this note in. What had happened was that Whitmore viewed this as an outsider criticizing the cabinet secretary and had sent a copy to John Hunt. John Hunt had said, 'Don't let that go into the box.' (1987 Interview.)

By summer 1983, John Hoskyns had left no. 10, Thatcher had acquired a new mandate, those in the disbanded CPRS with time remaining on their secondments had moved to no. 10 to form the nucleus of a new policy unit, and Robin Butler – the current cabinet secretary – had moved from the Treasury to become principal private secretary. Thatcher now recognized that she needed a small group of advisers available to help her enshrine and implement her agenda. As one CPRS veteran who made the move noted: 'The PM wanted the CPRS to help her translate her political and policy objectives into practice, and to tell her how far we could go or not, what the constraints are.' (1986 Interview.)

The same respondent – on secondment from the private sector – observed that it took a personal agreement with the objectives of the government to make such a transition possible: 'Since I was in sympathy with the government, what I was trying to do in CPRS was the same in no. 10. I think few of my colleagues could have gone to work in no. 10. They would have been horrified.'

This reflex toward embracing the Prime Minister's goals did not confine itself to political appointees or those on secondment from industry. One career official pronounced in explicit terms the degree of his commitment to the Prime Minister: 'My loyalty was always to the PM, even when the issue involved my department. At first my department expected me to take its line. This provided unstated pressure that assumed that I would be my department's representative in no. 10.' (1989 Interview.)

Significantly, Robin Butler read the signal from the Prime Minister that she wanted an interventionist policy unit. All the former policy unit officials whom we interviewed for this study cited the importance of Butler in placing the unit into the mainstream of the no. 10 'paper flow'. One said:

When the Policy Unit expanded and we came in, they tried to be more routine in following the business of government. So there was some difficulty *vis-à-vis* the private office in no. 10 – establishing that the unit ought to see all the papers on a routine basis . . . Robin Butler was in charge of the private office and was very supportive. (1986 Interview.)

By the mid-1980s and through to the end of the Thatcher years, the Policy Unit leapt onto the radar screens of officials throughout Whitehall – especially of those working on major initiatives that would require the attention and support of the Prime Minister. The Policy Unit participated with the Treasury in a number of review groups taking initiatives as diverse as the privatization of the British Airport Authority and the supplementary benefit review. However, officials frequently reported one-off contacts associated with various initiatives. As one respondent noted, 'I occasionally talk to the no. 10 Policy Unit, in particular the Transport adviser, in order to ensure that the department's policies are acceptable'. (1989 Interview.) Another observed: 'One also deals with the no. 10 Policy Unit. They are organized broadly, functionally, and I would want to bring them in on things that had a large political content. And, there is actually someone who looks after transport and energy. He and I have a fairly close relationship.' (1986 Interview.)

In many cases officials indicated that maintaining close links with the Policy Unit became indispensable to serving their ministers. One respondent considered that keeping the Policy Unit 'in the loop' ensured that a major reform package would be guaranteed acceptance: '. . . the minister was continuously involved and the acceptance of Treasury and the no. 10 Policy Unit was acquired all the way through' (1987 Interview). One asserted that the interest of the Policy Unit even extended to the secretary's success at implementing the Financial Management Initiative: '. . . relations with the Prime Minister's Policy Unit are important because they must see the successful implementation of the FMI, for the secretary of state's sake' (1986 Interview).

Only a minority of respondents gave another analysis. In a 1986 interview, one respondent in the Bank of England doubted whether the Policy Unit had any effect on monetary issues. He took this view notwithstanding speculation that Brian Griffith – then head of the Policy Unit – exerted a strong influence on Thatcher's aversion to membership of the European Monetary System. In the respondent's words: 'During one of their investigations into my area of responsibility, I found that the Policy Unit member had only 48 hours to make his submission to the PM. Obviously, anything that slap-dash couldn't qualify as serious input for policy making. Whether it actually influenced the judgement of the PM is quite another matter.' (1986 Interview.)

Some Policy Unit officials spoke frankly about the limits of their small size. They also suggested that departments could co-opt the Unit just as easily as the Unit could exert influence by playing custodians of the Thatcher agenda. One official stressed this in his reflections upon collaborative efforts with departments:

There was also the calculation that if we could accept responsibility for the ideas early on, and we thought they were half ours, we were more likely to push them past the PM . . . sorry, sorry, I don't want you to attribute that to me . . . about pushing them past the PM . . . [departments could] kill you with kindness . . .

[they] said 'We need fresh ideas from the Policy Unit in this study' or thought 'Christ, this is tricky, the PM will hate this, let's see if we can win over the Unit in advance.' (1989 Interview.)

Indeed, Thatcher proved an immovable object concerning some core items in the neo-liberal agenda. Tax reform is one such item. Thatcher believed that she had done her part at the outset of the administration by reducing income tax rates and shifting the burden to an increased Value Added Tax. She remained persistently immune to proposals for comprehensive tax simplification such as those that absorbed the Americans after Ronald Reagan won his second mandate in 1984. This put the Chancellor at the time – Nigel Lawson – in the awkward position of having to make supportive noises about a policy which he knew full well the Prime Minister would never embrace: 'Occasionally, I made it pretty clear what the Chancellor's position was – mortgage interest relief is something where the world knew the Chancellor wanted to remove it and the PM said she wouldn't have it. I think the Chancellor wanted that to be understood.' (1988 Interview.) 'Several times chancellors would discuss a tax reform with the PM but would come back with a black eye. She was not ready to listen and didn't want to disturb the tax system. She was a traditionalist in the tax system.' (1989 Interview.)

Under the leadership of Sara Hogg, John Major's Policy Unit attempted to adapt its missions to the exigencies of the new administration and its Prime Minister's style. Regarding the challenges faced by the Government, the Unit believed that it should connect itself more vitally to immediate policy development – the – preparation of the election manifesto gave focus to this activity. It attempted to complement Major's own consultative style. As articulated by a no. 10 respondent:

When we came, we tried to do two things: one was to re-engage what perhaps had become a little too distant from the immediate development of policy. The need for us to do that was, of course, accentuated by the fact that we were in a pre-election phase and a manifesto had to be developed. . . . And, secondly, we hoped to follow, with recognition of the obvious limitations to such an approach, a non-confrontational model. Of course, there's a stimulus from confrontation. But, we saw it certainly as the Prime Minister's style . . . to try and build bridges with departments rather than constantly seeing oneself as necessarily an antithesis to them ... (1993 Interview).

In operational departments, respondents left us with the impression that the Prime Minister's non-confrontational approach actually did not in fact add up to a lower profile for the Policy Unit. This assessment certainly applied in the two areas which the Unit had singled out for close attention – matters concerning Europe and the inculcation of the Citizens' Charter in Whitehall. However, much as the situation prevailing under Thatcher, it applied as well to review of policy initiatives or expenditure proposals which required special handling in the centre.

Officials thus still found it essential to have the Policy Unit on their side when dealing with issues that might encounter difficulty with the Treasury and/or other departments. Unlike the case of Thatcher's Policy Unit, we did find occasionally the suggestion that Major engaged himself less in the issues than his predecessor did. As one respondent noted, the view had emerged that the Policy Unit was expressing views on behalf of the Prime Minister without his giving them deep consideration:

> ... in the early years of Mr Major's prime-ministership, and throughout last year, it was said that a lot of the letters that emerged from no. 10 said the Prime Minister had agreed to this and that with the matter not actually being very close to the Prime Minister but with it having been run through the Policy Unit instead. They were rather stamping things or not on his behalf. (1993 Interview.)

Such assessments raise an interesting question. In Major's case, does the seeming continued interventionism of the Policy Unit simply reflect an effort to compensate for his passive leadership style? One Policy Unit respondent suggested as much when noting that Major had returned the UK to a non-hierarchical form of cabinet government and then observing that the Prime Minister tended to 'go with the flow':

> ... the way departments engage with the centre can be much more open and fluid than in a strictly hierarchical system of government with a heavy centre and weaker departments. The more I've been here, the clearer it's come to me that cabinet government is a

reality; let's say that the power of departments and departmental ministers is strong . . . this is a huge plus in the system because it creates a plurality at the centre of government that is vital. I should perhaps add that this is the way this prime minister, in particular, liked to work and it very much places weight on the views of his cabinet colleagues. He's a conciliator and therefore goes with the grain of the system of cabinet government, rather than against it. (1993 Interview.)

The Prime Minister wants above all a non-confrontational government. However, especially after the 1992 election, he has so prized peace that he has invited into his ministry views that clash strongly. Furthermore, he has inadequately engaged himself in the process of developing policy issues. The result: a cacophony of voices and little capacity for the resolution of disputes. These circumstances have placed the Policy Unit in the unenviable position of attempting to fill the gap.

Personalization of the Bureaucracy

The long duration of the Thatcher Government enabled the Prime Minister to leave her mark on the upper echelons of the permanent civil service – perhaps more than any prime minister this century. In this regard, a Royal Institute of Public Administration Working Group looked into Thatcher's influence on the upper reaches of the public service. It characterized this as personalization rather than politicization:

> To some extent the appointment process has become more personalized in the sense that at the top level 'catching the eye' of the prime minister . . . may now be more important than in the past. Evidence to our group suggests that personal contacts and impressions play a role in promotion decisions. Downing Street communicates more opinions about the performance of civil servants, even down to quite junior levels, based on impressions made at meetings with the prime minister. (Royal Institute for Public Administration, 1987, p. 43.)

A number of respondents registered the view that Thatcher had at least personalized the selection of senior personnel. One senior Treasury official saw this as all for the better:

... the other thing the government has done is to promote a lot of young people. And, the Treasury shows the effects of that. The management of Treasury from the Chancellor to Peter Middleton (the Permanent Secretary) – and they set the tone – is young, intellectually lively, informal. It has all the old virtues, with a good deal of vitality. It is great fun to be part of it. (1986 Interview.)

Others had reservations. A Home Office respondent asserted that advancement increasingly depended on officials' willingness to cooperate with the government. He drew parallels with the Iran–Contra Affair, which was unfolding at the time of our interview with him (early 1987):

This Government has a tendency to rely on officials who they believe are sympathetic to their position. It is not as bad as what has happened in the US with the Iran–Contra affair. However to a lesser extent the Thatcher Government opens itself to a similar difficulty. What happens is that there are certain officials who unquestioningly do the Government's bidding and they are sometimes rewarded by assignment to particularly sensitive jobs. This is alright, but it creates trouble because they often lack credibility among their fellow officials. It is not a matter of envy or jealousy, but a feeling of surprise or dismay at the level of trust extended to people who are judged as mediocre by the rest of us.

A Treasury official saw the process as part of a broader trend:

... there was a continuing and increasing pressure to be politically accountable. It's a fundamental change, going on for some time – even before Mrs Thatcher. She has continued it – the politicization of officialdom. Your career wouldn't go further if you didn't take a political posture toward your obligations, and to your advice accordingly. (1988 Interview.)

He added a lament for the loss of the neutrality of the civil service:

The way it is put now, fashionably, is to say, 'Officials used to believe they were almost a fifth estate.' It was there as a constraint and a balancing force and in some way representing something other than simply its bosses and the executive ... people like me came into the civil service believing public service was something that conferred an obligation on you irrespective of the administration you served. I think that view is now largely dead.

Significantly, more pointed remarks emerged in the Civil Service Commission, the formal custodian of the professional integrity of the permanent bureaucracy. One senior respondent there regretted especially the unseemly problems in the Ministry of Defence associated with Peter Levene and Clive Ponting. In the first case, Thatcher entirely bypassed the Civil Service Commission to appoint Levene – a close friend of Michael Heseltine, then the minister of defence – from the private sector to head up the defence procurement sector of MOD. In the second, the Government prosecuted an MOD official whose crime was disclosing to a member of the House of Commons Defence Committee an effort on the part of ministers to cover up the circumstances surrounding the sinking of the Argentine cruiser *General Belgrano* during the Falklands War. In the words of the respondent: 'Morale has been badly damaged by both the Ponting and Levene affairs. The service has become more politicized. Thatcher now almost hand picks those who make it to the permanent secretary level.' (1986 Interview.) He added that the attractiveness of the civil service to young people and university dons who might recommend careers in Whitehall had suffered badly:

There are two problematic attitudes at universities . . . Practical candidates fear a lack of stability in public service careers and certain types of people believe that they would not be promoted in Mrs Thatcher's Whitehall . . . the impression is that dons would not recommend a civil service career under this administration. The government is seen as heartless and indifferent to the poor.

Within this context, it appears that the strongest symbiosis between the government and the mandarinate took place in the Treasury. A former permanent secretary associated this with a tendency of the Treasury to adapt itself to the political flavour of the day: 'Treasury views the world through politically coloured glasses . . . If ministers are monetarist, then Treasury has to be monetarist.' (1989 Interview.) However, the respondent also noted that the closeness of the relationship between Thatcher and the Treasury exceeded that between prime minister and Treasury in

other governments. This was due both to her strong interest in
economic policy and to the influence of Professor Alan Walters,
who worked throughout much of the Government as a special
adviser in no. 10: 'No. 10's relationship with Treasury changed
since the PM was more interested in economic policy and hired
her own policy specialists, notably Alan Walters' (1986 Interview).

One political appointee in no. 10 during Thatcher's first term
takes us a long way to understanding the fairly loose line of
demarcation between no. 10 and the Treasury in this period. This
might involve something as seemingly innocuous as calling an
undersecretary over to no. 10 to help ginger up figures to justify
the Government's limiting public service wage increases to 6 per
cent in the 1981 pay round:

> . . . I got . . . [him] to come over. I said . . . 'You know, there's
> something wrong here.' And with the same calculator as I have in
> my briefcase now, with the medium term financial strategy num-
> bers and the cash pay bills for the civil service . . . we worked for
> it . . . The Policy Unit produced a paper for E Committee saying a
> 6 per cent pay rise would be financially feasible . . . [the Treasury
> official and a policy unit official] brewed a breakdown of all the
> different parts of the public sector and which were indexed
> automatically . . . By the time we'd finished . . . , we knew we were
> poised on the brink of a big problem . . . (1987 Interview).

The tightness between no. 10 and the Treasury extended to the
final negotiations on the budget of 1981, which was confined to
Thatcher, the Chancellor, three political appointees from no. 10
(Walters, Hoskyns and David Wolfson), the Treasury member of
the private office (Tim Lankester), the permanent secretary of the
Treasury (Douglas Wass) and the chief economic adviser (Terry
Burns). 'Although Wass argued that the problem [overly tight
monetary policy] wasn't that bad the Policy Unit said she needed
to take extreme measures . . . The PM let the Chancellor decide.
I wrote privately to Howe over technical details, while Walters
carried on the battle with Treasury. (1987 Interview.)

The Thatcher Government, indeed, institutionalized its hold on
the Treasury with two key appointments. The first of these concerned Terry Burns, mentioned above, who assumed the post of
chief economic adviser at the precocious age of 35. In a departure
with tradition, Burns – a confirmed monetarist – came directly

from the London School of Business, not from the ranks of the economics service. The second of these saw Peter Middleton – a disillusioned academic who entered the Treasury as a press officer – jump a full rank to become Douglas Wass's successor in 1983. Middleton's ascendancy in the Treasury had resulted from a bitter battle, waged before Thatcher's arrival, between unreconstructed Keynesians and the emergent monetarists:

> We have still got undercurrents of this Keynesian–Friedmanite dilemma. Those are the extremes . . . On some of these things it becomes difficult to talk because really quite basic gut feelings about the way the economy works are not consistently shared. . . . It came perhaps more forcefully to the top a year ago [1977] when it just happened to focus on the question of whether the exchange rate should be let go in the interest of stopping an inflow of funds . . . It was resolved – not by agreement but by one of those kinds of drifts of opinion where you suddenly found that a majority had become a minority – and so a decision was taken that way. This left a certain amount of unhappiness behind among people who felt it was the wrong decision. (1978 Interview.)

During the 1980s, the Middleton–Burns axis in the Department gained notoriety for producing economic forecasts that bent according to the preferences of the political leadership. For instance, Treasury policies during the build-up to the 1987 election were based on rosy forecasts that meant as much for the favourable reception by the electorate as for economic analysis. Ultimately, Treasury optimism contributed greatly to the uncontrolled 'Lawson Boom', which put excessive upward pressure on the pound for the remainder of the decade.

One former Treasury economist spoke at length about difficulties with Burns's sensitivity to political atmospherics:

> Terry Burns found it difficult to deal with people with a larger professional experience . . . The situation was never as bad as in the US where the forecast will look like it has to be negotiated. But the risk grew with Terry Burns's involvement, because someone with a background in forecasting was nevertheless seen as a political person . . . The Thatcher Government came with clear ideas of how the economy operated, which differed from the forecasters'. (1987 Interview.)

Terry Burns, of course, succeeded Peter Middleton as permanent secretary in 1991.

The Treasury as the Prime Minister's Department

Even in times in which the Treasury does not enjoy an especially strong link with the prime minister, it has a very formidable presence in Whitehall. The Treasury staffs its fast-track ranks by skimming the cream of each year's recruits into Whitehall. That is, it gets more than its share of those who score A – the highest mark – in the civil service selection process. This bias goes far to explain the aura of superior intellect that pervades the Treasury. One former Treasury official felt bound to explain to us in detail why he had started his career in the Department of Health and Social Security:

> In the year I entered, they felt they had to put a disproportionate number of grade A applicants (you were graded A, B or C) into DHSS because historically the Department hasn't been able to hire its senior management from its own ranks, so to help redress the imbalance they put more good people in at the bottom. Around 1972 something like 12 people got As and 6 or 7 of these went to DHSS. (1987 Interview.)

In addition to imbibing the aura of intellectual superiority, the Treasury benefits immensely from its strategic location in the policy network – people have to come to them, not vice versa. In this respect, one former Treasury official spoke initially of how ill-equipped he was to delve into detailed matters concerning the expenditure of the department (DHSS) that he monitored:

> The traditional function of people in the seat that I was occupying was actually to get quite closely involved in detailed issues of how the Department was paying opticians or how its finances for the National Health Service chemists were working and so on. And, those were the sort of questions where it didn't seem to me that I was in any way equipped to know more about it than the people in the Department – I usually would be less. (1987 Interview.)

Later in the interview the official noted that what really counted in the end was the ability to get one's mind round broader financial issues and the use of one's positional advantage:

> Your knowledge of the subject will always be limited compared with the department . . . But, I don't think that necessarily matters – provided you have a general ability to see financial issues and to appreciate value-for-money questions. You can fulfil a useful function in asking questions . . . sometimes it actually is helpful not to know too much about the subject . . . With people like Geoffrey Hulme [a DHSS deputy secretary] and Terry Banks [an undersecretary] at the top of the financial divisions one is dealing with real pros. But, despite their senior positions they are asking Treasury officials for something and not the other way around. They have to persuade you to agree.

Another former Treasury official echoed this view: 'Experts can be dangerous. Firstly, they have their own personal agendas that they have worked out for years; and secondly, they don't like to reveal ignorance . . . One of the best things you can do sometimes is ask the 'idiot-boy' question that requires a sceptical intelligence rather than detailed knowledge.' (1989 Interview.)

A number of officials in line departments saw matters differently. They frequently perceived the Treasury as pushing its own policy alternatives. Interestingly, two officials working in different parts of the foreign affairs apparatus indicated that the Treasury has pressed its own line on the UK's response to the collapse of Communism in Eastern Europe. One noted that the Treasury was anxious to transfer resources from Africa and Asia to the new democratic states: '. . . this is very much not for the record, there was also a bit of a tug-of-war with the Treasury because they would have liked us to shift resources out of Africa and Asia into Eastern Europe but we were looking for additional resources.' (1993 Interview.) Another reported similar problems in connection with Bosnia: 'I think we still see the Treasury leaning over into policy areas and questioning policy issues. For example, the Treasury's saying "Why are we in Bosnia?" or "Why are we committing troops in Bosnia?" Obviously, that's financially of interest to them. But, it does lead to quite a close Treasury interest in policy.' (1993 Interview.)

Of course, the fact that few Treasury officials bring formal training in finance or cost–benefit analysis to their work does not deter them from considering themselves capable of probing others in these areas. Some of our interviewees in line departments stressed that Treasury questioning frequently revealed not just ignorance of detail but arrogance as well. One former Department of Employment official recounted to us the assertion of an especially presumptuous Treasury official:

> I got into a discussion with one of them one day in which the person maintained he knew more about his area than anyone else in Whitehall. The question had to do with the coal industry. This official was in a dispute with the Department of Energy. He maintained that he was privy to better information than was available to his opposite number in the DOE or, for that matter, to management in the coal industry. Therefore, he could judge better on coal policy matters than anyone else. It did not matter to him that coal was just a small part of his responsibilities whereas for the others it was their only job. The rank arrogance of this assertion was really something to behold. (1986 Interview.)

A chief financial officer of a large line department registered near exasperation when noting that the Treasury approaches executive agencies under his department – organizations which should enjoy a greater degree of latitude – in much the same way as it has treated 'headquarters':

> ...in the case of...two or three really big agencies, Treasury may be hyperactive. In our case, I have seen that they have produced somewhat misdirected comments on targets and so on, on a once-a-year basis. But, I don't see that as any different from misdirected comments I see from the Treasury on almost every piece of work. It's in the nature of the Treasury's work that they generate comments and ideas rather faster than they would do if they wanted to get things right. So, they get things wrong quite a lot of the time...(1993 Interview).

The structure of the Treasury did not seem to serve as a check on its officials' getting out of their depth. Indeed, it seemed to exacerbate the problem. Treasury officials themselves gave us the view that the Department runs fairly unhierarchically. They found it quite easy to take matters one or more steps beyond their immediate superiors. This suggests a certain element of free-agency.

Also, as noted by one respondent who had worked in the Treasury on secondment from the private sector, it could lead to blurred lines of authority:

> I remember asking early on, 'What is the extent of my authority in terms of the amount that I can approve for expenditure?' And there was no answer. Effectively, I was told to proceed until I got nervous... There was no violation of protocol to go above people's heads. This was due to the fact that individuals couldn't choose whom they worked for and this gave the flavour that each person operated independently... I always found it strange that whom you worked for was unclear. I remember thinking morning after morning, 'What a weird place!' Because, 'What was the object, what was the reason?' If you put in the effort, 'For whom was it?' There was a confusing element there. (1988 Interview.)

One respondent observed that the spirit of free-agency in the Treasury extends to the Department's proclivity for leaking. Here officials can advance their views by well-placed conversations with members of the media capable of concealing their sources:

> Although the Government has become progressively obsessed with leaks and secrecy, the Treasury – being what it is – people are at it all over the place and there is no way you can plug all those gaps, happily... Peter Middleton [then permanent secretary] is always said to be a master of the art of leaking, but you never catch him out, you never know who did it. (1988 Interview.)

We noted above the lengthy and painful debate within the Treasury in the late 1970s as it began to adopt monetarist views. In some cases, the division of labour within the Treasury has amplified some of these differences. This concerns the distinction between sections of the Department responsible for economic analysis and monetary policy and those focusing on public expenditure. In the words of a former Treasury official who had left for the private sector: '... public expenditure... fits into the Treasury's structure in an anomalous way... Tension exists between short-term demands of public expenditure and longer-term demands of running a sensible framework for nationalized industries.' (1987 Interview.)

Another former Treasury official who had moved to the Department of the Environment drew sharp contrasts between the two main Treasury cultures. He also identified a third, managerialism, which seemed to face a formidable struggle:

> In the Treasury, two main cultures still coexist. They still fail to communicate with one another. People move from one to the other without apparently realizing they are doing it. One is the expenditure control side. This is concerned with a very short-sighted view of how to keep down expenditure – which is always the assumed good. The other is the economic management side which is a more highly rational culture – longer sighted but deeply pessimistic. Those two cultures are still at odds with one another in the Treasury. There is now a third one, a weak culture – called civil service management – which has lived in Treasury since the abolition of the Civil Service Department. That one is struggling. (1986 Interview.)

We should stress that – while the Treasury seems daunting to the rest of Whitehall – it still operates from the same gifted-amateur culture. Officials in line departments can strike it lucky in their relations with the Treasury official responsible for their areas. At its simplest, the person reviewing an official's programmes may be a friend. In the words of one Transport respondent: 'I was always a bit naughty when I was in Railways because the person [who reviewed my area], the assistant secretary . . . , was an old friend.' (1986 Interview.) Or the official might have spent time on secondment in the Treasury: 'I also knew the ropes – how to handle ministers and the Treasury. I knew the people in the Treasury because I'd been down there and frankly knew the right sorts of levers to pull and buttons to push. That was a big advantage.' (1989 Interview.)

The Treasury exerts a considerable influence by colonizing various parts of Whitehall. Just as it receives officials on secondment it sends its own out to occupy positions in line departments. Often these officials assume posts in areas concerned with expenditure review and financial management – an instance of gamekeepers becoming poachers. Also, a disproportionate number of permanent secretaries assumed their responsibilities directly from the Treasury. This can mean that a department can find that the top level of its operation functions very much according to the Treasury ethos. One respondent in Transport noted that his Department normally exerted a fair amount of central control over contacts with the Treasury and that his permanent secretary's style fitted within this tradition:

The Department has always had a strong finance directorate. Alan Bailey is from the Treasury and believes that a strength of the Department of Transport is that it has good central control ... You're much more likely to be able to keep these things under good, reasonably strict control if you have a strong finance directorate which has a real role. If their job is simply to act as the fifth wheel on all the different coaches of the Department driving all over the place, then that's a very difficult role to play ... (1989 Interview).

Some former Treasury officials holding permanent secretary posts when we interviewed them reflected on their situations. What they said sounds somewhat like the reflections of a less senior Treasury official, cited above, who recognized his lack of detailed knowledge of the issue emanating from the DHSS. In some respects then, the promotion of these officials to permanent secretaries constitutes gifted amateurism writ large: 'I intervene when I think I have a contribution to make. I came to this Department late in my career ... I spent the rest of my career in the Treasury, Cabinet Office and the diplomatic service. So, I am not the world's leading expert on the subject matter of this Department.' (1986 Interview.)

It was a shock becoming a permanent secretary. The emphasis on one's brilliance and acuity as one rises to the top is overwhelming. I ultimately did begin to get a reputation in one policy field ... you become a whiz in that field and others depend on your grasp of the subject and this becomes a vehicle to the top. Then all of a sudden, you're a permanent secretary and you no longer have responsibility for a particular part of policy. Rather, you are likely to be in charge of a department where you don't have a substantive grasp of any of its concerns. (1986 Interview.)

One permanent secretary who came up through the ranks in his department contrasted his situation with that of those transferring from the Treasury: 'I had an advantage when I assumed

this position since many permanent secretaries come to an operational department from Treasury with no specific experience at
the sharp end and even less in a specific policy field.' (1986
Interview.)

Collective Review of Expenditure: the End of an Illusion?

When we first conducted interviews in Whitehall (1978), expenditure budgets maintained an aura of collective deliberation. A
committee of the principal financial officers of the largest Whitehall departments – the Public Expenditure Survey Committee
(PESC) – met on a regular basis to hammer out the rules for each
year's budgeting round. During July, the cabinet would review
the work of PESC and settle the expenditure targets for each
department. A series of bilateral meetings between departments
and the Treasury would try to resolve outstanding differences.
However, the cabinet continued to play a part in resolving
disputes.

A confidential departmental document shown us in 1978 gave
an excellent insight into how the process actually worked. The
department did a 'dry run' early in 1978 asking its units to present the consequences should the PESC guidelines call for either
a rise or a decrease of expenditure by 2.5 per cent. The actual
guidelines fitted the dry run well – departments were to assume
a growth of 2 per cent and then identify savings of 2.5 per cent
against the new figures. On 28 June, the chief secretary proposed
an agreed increase of 2 per cent and the Cabinet – notwithstanding some unhappiness – agreed to this figure on 6 July.

For the department, there emerged a problem concerning the
funding for a proposed programme, which the Cabinet had previously approved in principle. The department lost the authorization to start imposing fees on an existing programme: the
Government believed that in an election year it would prove
dangerous to impose charges on a popular service. Thus the
Treasury ordered that any savings identified by the department
would first have to meet the costs of delaying the imposition of
fees for the existing programme.

The department pressed its case throughout the autumn. At
one point, it caught the chief secretary on a procedural point: he

had let the Cabinet dip into the general contingency fund without so much as considering the plight of the department. The department received an apology. But the chief secretary continued his opposition to resources for the new programme. Ultimately, the department won cabinet approval for a pilot project made possible by savings in its existing programmes and some money from a department with an interest in the programme. The episode demonstrates that, within certain bounds, the department could engage the Cabinet in consideration of its plight. This proved especially the case when a lapse on the part of the Cabinet had resulted at one stage in a decision not based on full consultation.

These conditions even applied to cash-limited expenditure, which in 1978 comprised two-thirds of the budget. Under this regime, the Treasury clearly held the strongest hand – it developed the projections of inflation which would apply to expenditure forecasts for particular programmes. However, the Public Expenditure Survey Committee still operated in a sufficiently consultative way that departments could, with at least some good effect, make arguments for exceptions on the grounds that inflation was hitting their programmes harder than others. One Treasury official described the process which prevailed in 1978: 'The group prepares what are called the guidelines to the survey. And it produces a draft first of all. Then we discuss it with the specific expenditure divisions. They will say: "Hey, that won't do for schools. There is a particular factor about schools which you haven't taken into account." You will make an exception there.' (1978 Interview.)

Thatcher dramatically changed the entire context of the annual expenditure review process. First, and most important, she altered the relationship between the development of macroeconomic policy and the establishment of the fiscal framework and the expenditure budget. Her actions made the Public Expenditure Survey (PES) process much more subject to macroeconomic policy-making than it had been before. Second, she cut PES from four to three years. This gave departments less opportunity to enshrine their long-term spending plans. Third, she linked pay increases in the public service to cash limits. This meant that departments which failed to hold the line in wage negotiations would pay: they would have to shed staff in order to keep within the cash limit for salaries and benefits. Fourth, she instituted

limits to the assistance that would be extended to nationalized
and private industries and agriculture. This greatly constricted
government intervention in public and private enterprise. It resulted in turn in a reduction of the parts of Treasury and line
agencies that involved themselves with the state support of enterprise. Finally, she called upon the services of a Star Chamber –
a committee of senior officials – to arbitrate in disputes between
the chief secretary and departments. This drastically cut the involvement of the entire cabinet in deliberations over the details of
the expenditure budget.

By the late 1980s, officials portrayed a PESC that had lost any
semblance of significance as a collective process. A senior Treasury official opined that PES had become a concept, not a real
entity:

> So, the PES Committee . . . became [after the introduction of cash
> limits in the late 1970s] reduced to discussing the rules of the
> game. More recently, the rules have become set. And, there aren't
> great variations . . . So, this committee effectively never meets now.
> I think there are one or two meetings a year to settle a particular
> point about the rules. But, nothing of great importance . . . the
> PESC itself has become rather like the Board of Trade. It exists as
> a concept but not as an entity. (1986 Interview.)

Many officials in line departments now clearly saw expenditure
review as a top-down process with the Treasury constantly turning the screws. One respondent even saw the new emphasis on
performance measures as part of this overarching reality:

> I think the Treasury actually see it – I wouldn't wish this to go
> down, but it's something you obviously can check out elsewhere
> – as an alternative means of trying to screw departments back in
> terms of cash and manpower. In the old days they would say,
> 'You can all manage with a little bit less, can't you?' It was a
> question of beating everybody back a bit so that the overall targets
> on public expenditure were met. The way they move now is to use
> the individual information on performance to actually target spe-
> cific departments and functions. (1989 Interview.)

Another made it clear that the days of negotiating with the
Treasury in order to accommodate anomalies in price increases

had long since past: 'It is argued that the cost of providing scientists with the proper equipment is rising much faster than the cost of living. However, the Treasury does not accept this as a reason for more funding.' (1986 Interview.)

The decline of PESC effectively left only one collective forum for resolving differences over the expenditure budget. In the early Thatcher years, ministers occasionally found that they could persuade the Star Chamber to recognize the political necessity of some expenditure. However, in time it became clear that ministers more often faced a solid opposition to exceptions. In the words of a key Treasury participant: '. . . the Star Chamber has enough senior and weighty ministers on it that if they reach a view, the spending minister sees that they will prevail in cabinet as well. So, almost invariably, they don't think it is worth going to cabinet.' (1986 Interview.) A principal finance officer for one of the big spending departments spoke of the Star Chamber as taking on almost ritualistic significance, changing little of substance: 'By the end of the day, it turns on the determination of cabinet and the PM to hold public expenditure within given parameters . . . The Star Chamber does not weaken, it becomes routine. There is a danger that people would hold up their offers, as it were, until the last minute.' (1987 Interview.)

Some officials told us that ministers to whom Thatcher was sympathetic had found their way around the Star Chamber. They used their direct lines to the Prime Minister to enshrine initiatives the resources for which magically appeared in documents such as the annual budget. A Department of Employment official described how Lord Young had done this in the mid-1980s:

The secretary of state has gone directly to the chancellor. Apparently he promised to reduce unemployment by a certain amount if the chancellor allocated 'X' amount of money. Last year the figure came to two billion pounds [for training programmes] . . . Before this, every proposal of DE's encountered counter claims from other departments . . . Last year the department didn't [even] do a bilateral with the chief secretary . . . The chancellor announced his unemployment plans as part of the overall economic programme . . . The secretary of state has no patience with bureaucratic procedure . . . He is closely affiliated with the PM. (1986 Interview.)

The Star Chamber fell into disuse at the end of the Thatcher decade. For example in Autumn 1990 – just before Thatcher's resignation – Norman Lamont, then chief secretary, resolved all outstanding spending issues in bilateral meetings with ministers. However, bilateral meetings had emerged in the salad days when the UK government was chalking up annual budget surpluses. These, of course, owed much to the influx of North Sea oil revenues, beginning in the early 1980s, and the proceeds from privatizations. With the economic decline in the early 1990s, a reduction in oil revenues and a slower pace for privatizations, the Conservatives began to wrestle with growing budget deficits. The 1992 election campaign exacerbated the problem. It called upon the Conservatives to enshrine their commitment to certain social programmes which voters suspected would otherwise be cut or eliminated. This had the effect of threatening an even wider gap between spending and revenues. It also greatly constricted possible candidates for spending cuts.

The Government acted immediately after the 1992 election to overhaul the PES process so as to provide a mechanism for making the tough choices that it would now have to face. The Cabinet agreed to a tight public spending total for the year 1993–4. The Government then used a new cabinet-level committee – EDX – to work on the details whereby individual departments would meet their 1993–4 targets. The Chancellor – throughout most of the 1992 PES round Norman Lamont – chaired EDX. This feature distinguished the committee from the former Star Chamber. The latter had made the greatest effects when chaired by William Whitelaw, an *éminence grise* of the Conservatives who served Thatcher as home secretary and government leader in the House of Lords.

Several respondents in 1993 heralded EDX as a vast improvement over the system of bilateral meetings which had prevailed in the previous four or five years. Even officials in spending departments recognized that the system of bilateral negotiations had lost its punch by becoming somewhat ritualized:

> ... there's a new ball game in that we thought we knew the rules of the old game pretty well ... bilateral negotiation between the minister and the chief secretary. And, there was a ritual to that which had been worked out over many years. That

problem, of course, there was too much ritual, a lot of wasted time in the ritual. The real negotiation didn't come until the very end. But, it was a one-to-one negotiation, essentially, between each minister or secretary of state and the chief secretary. (1993 Interview.)

Some respondents went so far as to associate the emergence of EDX with the more consultative approach of the Major Government. For instance, a no. 10 respondent cited EDX as an illustration of cabinet committees' new status in the process of resolving disputes in the Government:

I think it is certainly the intention of the Prime Minister to improve the status of cabinet committees. Taking the fact, without commentary or characterization of what happened before, one phenomenon which may have been described to you, for example, is the way in which public spending decisions are now reached which is through a new cabinet committee rather than through bilaterals with the Treasury . . . it is very much in keeping with the Prime Minister's style where a group of ministers assess the spending priorities of colleagues and act as a decision-making filter before that comes to a kind of lasting battle between the Treasury and a minister in which the Prime Minister has to arbitrate all that comes to cabinet. That is the perfect example of cabinet committee resurrection or recreation. (1993 Interview.)

Similarly, a permanent secretary of a line department saw in EDX a healthy return to a more collective way to make decisions about expenditure:

I am a great supporter of the new arrangement. I think constitutionally it is more appropriate than the previous set-up whereby expenditure was settled by what was essentially a bilateral haggle which could not be regarded as having a lot to do with the collective wisdom or will of cabinet. With EDX, at least there is the possibility of a group of ministers weighing the pros and cons of different departmental claims. Before, it was essentially the chief secretary taking a view, seeing what he could get away with or seeing what he thought was the correct balance and putting his proposal to cabinet. . . . (1993 Interview.)

Not all of Whitehall was so sanguine. Many respondents observed that departments found themselves at the mercy of the

General Expenditure Division of the Treasury – the part which deals with aggregate budget figures and reconciles these with the broad fiscal framework – and the types of briefs that the Division puts forward to EDX. They felt especially vulnerable if they lacked ministers on EDX with some experience of the matters that concerned their departments. Also, owing to the relatively closed nature of the process, departments found it very difficult to discover what kinds of submission were being made by others. One respondent – a principal financial officer – conveyed the sense of 'flying blind' which prevailed in some departments:

> I wouldn't have described it as a Rolls Royce operation last year. I mean there was a sense of people making up the rules as they went along. . . . In a sense, on the part of some departments there was a feeling that it was all a bit mysterious, although people knew EDX existed, those departments didn't really know what was going on in it always, as fully as they would have liked to have done. (1993 Interview.)

Other similarly placed officials went so far as to assert that the Treasury had effectively used EDX to centralize expenditure decisions further. One principal financial officer of a very large spending department said:

> It was handled almost in an even more private way than the old system. The different departments didn't actually get to know where the other departments were in the process until I think the last week or so, as I recall. The Treasury was still effectively running the bilateral operations. As for the Treasury claim that they were merely servicing the EDX committee, which itself was dealing bilaterally, I think that understates the Treasury's involvement. (1993 Interview.)

Another respondent noted that the Treasury General Expenditure Division almost totally ran briefings on his department to EDX. Even the Treasury expenditure division responsible for his department was left in the dark. So the process bore all the marks of a classic Treasury effort to run expenditure decisions with *a priori* targets deriving from very tight parameters for the fiscal framework.

... [the expenditure division] felt very cut off from what was going on. The work of EDX was driven very much by the General Expenditure Division. You'd ring up our expenditure division and say what's going on? How do you react to this proposal? And, they didn't know. ... They didn't know because the rules were being made up to some extent as they went along but also because everything was being driven very much by an assessment of the economic position ... decisions were taken very much in terms of the need to save 100 million pounds here or 50 million there. Find it somewhere! (1993 Interview.)

This experience contrasts sharply with the Expenditure Review Committee (ERC), which came into existence in Australia during the time Bob Hawke was Prime Minister. ERC also worked under very compelling fiscal imperatives. However, the Prime Minister himself chaired the committee. This increased the likelihood that issues other than fiscal exigencies would receive some attention in deliberations. The committee operated in marathon sessions – almost the entire day for three-week periods twice a year. This allowed its members to develop an intimate knowledge of the operations of line departments other than their own. Finally, ministers and senior officials of departments without membership on ERC gained considerable exposure to the dynamics of the committee. The end result was very tough expenditure decisions, but decisions that most involved in the process would truly own as collective commitments.

The Reluctant Delegator

From the mid-1980s, the Treasury engaged itself with pushing forward two initiatives designed to advance managerial principles in the public service. The first of these – the Financial Management Initiative (FMI) – sought to encourage managers in line departments to define their objectives more clearly. As a carrot, it offered the promise of greater discretion in the use of resources falling broadly under the category of running costs. The second – Next Steps – aimed to hive off roughly half the public service into executive agencies once removed from the immediate super-vision of ministers. Operating under chief executives with agreed performance contracts and relatively wide latitude in the use of resources, these organizations would have to market their goods and services just like private sector concerns.

In each case, the Treasury neither spawned the ideas behind the initiatives nor took sole responsibility for their advancement. FMI originated with discussions between the no. 10 Efficiency Unit and the Management and Personnel Office on how best to generalize some of the lessons derived from efficiency scrutinies headed Sir Derek Rayner at the outset of the Thatcher Government. Next Steps emerged when the Efficiency Unit took stock of FMI and concluded that organizations would function more managerially if they operated once removed from ministers. Peter Kemp – previously a Treasury official responsible for pay policy – became the second permanent secretary in the Cabinet Office responsible for civil service matters. He, therefore, headed up Next Steps. Notwithstanding his Treasury roots, Kemp very much pressed his own agenda and increasingly antagonized his former colleagues. When William Waldegrave decided to get rid of him in summer 1992, Kemp could not find a satisfactory permanent secretary position anywhere in the public service – much less in his old department.

Behind the reformist thinking and entrepreneurship of those promoting FMI and Next Steps, we find Margaret Thatcher. She proved a tireless patron of the thoughts and initiatives surfacing from the Efficiency Unit, the Management and Personnel Office and, after MPO's abolition, Peter Kemp's Next Steps operation. Throughout her prime-ministership, Thatcher made time for private meetings about Rayner Scrutinies, FMI and Next Steps, which involved those trying to maintain the thrust. Once it became a factor in 1983, the no. 10 Policy Unit would attend these sessions as well. In addition, she would use 'seminars' with ministers – either individually or in groups – to ensure that word was getting to them.

We perceived in officials in line departments a keen awareness of the Prime Minister's backing for the Government's various managerial initiatives. For instance, one respondent working in the personnel field suggested that no one would have taken any note of MPO's work on FMI had it not retained Thatcher's backing: 'If it wasn't for Mrs Thatcher's interest the Management and Personnel Office would just go under. Two of the problems of MPO staff are that they have mostly not served in a line department so they do not understand the problems of implementing the policy that they suggest and, secondly, there are very few of them.' (1986 Interview.)

Notwithstanding the political thrust behind the managerial initiatives, officials found time and again that Treasury efforts confounded as much as advanced their progress. Some of the language became quite pointed – revealing a high degree of frustration with resistance to true discretion. One Environment official who had left his department by the time of our interview put it starkly:

> The carry-through into FMI has been disastrous. The imposition of demands for more materials, more information and more data had not been compensated for by new freedoms. I think the FMI is a total charade, the way it actually operates. It gives the Treasury more power and it doesn't give individual departments the authority and ability to get on and do things . . . Treasury can say, 'Have you really defined the objectives? What are your performance indicators going to be? How will you actually measure the "output"?' But with lots of things we do in the civil service you can't measure the 'output'. (1987 Interview.)

An official in Customs and Excise stressed the view that, rhetoric notwithstanding, the Treasury took a greater interest in controlling resources than in results:

> On the one hand, they say to managers, 'From now on we will delegate it down to you, you make your plans, spend your money, be responsible for your objectives.' On the other hand, they have these controls. They have always been tight with departments. And, they are reluctant to let go of any of the controls. In different terms, they are still overly concerned about inputs and not sufficiently concerned with outputs. (1986 Interview.)

An Environment official gave an example of the degree to which the Treasury had remained focused on fairly minor money issues:

> The Treasury's control still is in money, to a surprising degree. For instance, I had to go to Treasury last week and argue about whether I could pay someone already receiving £31,000 £2,000 higher as

a promotional pay increase. It's rather odd that I have to go to
Treasury and waste time arguing over a marginal pay increase.
(1989 Interview.)

The Treasury recognized the existence of tensions over its continued involvement with detailed controls. However, it seemed
caught between the imperatives of true decentralization and psychological dependence upon tried and true ways. One of their
officials with responsibility for pay issues put it like this: 'We
acknowledge that we will have to move towards greater delegation because flexible pay systems require that you tailor something to each unit's circumstances. However good you are, if you
try to do that from the centre, you're going to get it wrong.'
(1989 Interview.) However, he appeared to take back most of
this bold assertion in his next breath:

> It is important to safeguard control of public expenditure while
> delegating responsibility to management of particular types of units
> for setting their own pay. You can't do that for as long as you
> continue to have substantial grades of similar people employed
> everywhere . . . Such delegation was possible in Her Majesty's Sta-
> tionery Office because it is a commercial trading organization with
> a bottom line.

Initially, the process whereby units within departments became
Next Steps organizations seemed not to have replicated the difficulties encountered with the Treasury during the development
of the FMI. One respondent involved with pressing the initiative
spoke of the Treasury's initial resistance to the idea: 'These changes
are more popular the further one gets from the centre . . . It was
difficult convincing Treasury. My former bosses there fought tooth
and nail against these proposals. Now they stick out their chests
and say how clever they were to have done it.' (1989 Interview.)
However, those pushing Next Steps initiatives found that the
Treasury was willing to extend discretions to new executive agencies that it had not given to departments.

One official in the Employment Service – which was negotiating the terms of its relation with the Treasury and the Department of Employment – provided a check list of the type of powers
that would emerge from Next Steps status:

... the ES [Employment Service] has had to rethink our relationship with the department and Treasury ... ES had to wait for Treasury to move before they were able to recognize themselves as undergoing real change ... Treasury enabled chief executives of agencies to be accounting officers and to have their own parliamentary vote in certain situations. ES was the first to enjoy these privileges ... Having a vote enables one to bid for financial flexibilities such as breaking through the rigidity of annuality, end-of-year accounting ... The second flexibility is called 'in year viament', the ability to move money from one programme to another or from one heading to another ... The third flexibility is retention of receipts ... [this] will encourage line managers to look at the network of rationality. (1989 Interview.)

One might ask why the Treasury – working through departments – could not extend these discretions without hiving units off from the mainline civil service? After all, the Finance Department in Australia achieved considerable success at precisely this, without having to create a new bureaucratic life form. For political reasons, the Treasury needed beasts that waddled, quacked and took well to water but could not be called ducks. Margaret Thatcher found the prospect of reducing the number of civil servants in traditional departments overwhelmingly attractive. Moreover, both ministers and senior officials could see the advantages if half the government operated at arm's length from political authority.

The Conservative managers of the build-down of government could now dodge questions about the dysfunctions of Thatcherism by saying that MPs and citizens should take their issues to chief executives. Mandarins, most of whom never really accepted the idea that they should manage as well as advise on policy, could sequester themselves from the most mundane dimensions of their departments. Peter Kemp envisaged a time when anyone aspiring to become a permanent secretary must first have run an executive agency. However, the opposite was just as likely to develop as the pattern.

Even under the Financial Management Initiative and privatization efforts, respondents told us that they had found their prospects for advancement in their departments cut off because they had become identified with operations rather than policy. Two officials who left government for this reason gave us a sense of their experience. One had run a large functional branch in his department. His permanent secretary no longer saw him as a policy-oriented official when he had a discussion about his future assignment: 'He said he saw me as a manager, but what he was really saying was that the top rungs, the most senior jobs were closed to me ... I'm not saying that I should be a permanent secretary, but I shouldn't be denied on those grounds.' (1986 Interview.)

The other, from the Treasury, had – according to his permanent secretary – become too involved with ministers in various privatization initiatives. He left when the permanent secretary vetoed his selection as principal private secretary to the chancellor:

> It [all the activity in privatization] caught everyone by surprise when it became so significant. I suspect that I was admired for having started things up ... but certain quarters found it undesirable for me to be so enthusiastic about organizing a programme that could do so much. It started to raise five billion per annum. It was becoming significant in macroeconomic terms as well as being a political plaything ... (1987 Interview).

As another former Treasury official noted, the principle of 'out of sight out of mind' would apply to many officials who had gone to work in executive agencies:

> In departments like Treasury as well as operational departments, after returning from going out and running something people would say, 'He's actually got his hands dirty, he's not one of us' ... The problem is that Treasury controls key policy posts ... deputy and under secretary posts go to those with Treasury and Cabinet Office favour ... The central departments would say, 'Who's he, we haven't heard of him ... Hiving off the operational agencies will give the people back in the department a chance to run the divisions and keep policy jobs clean ... Its the policy jobs that command the premium and the real high fliers who want these jobs ... You don't breed them from running a railroad ... Your best chance of reaching the very top will still be to stick to the pure, 100 per cent traditional mainline jobs in Treasury. (1988 Interview.)

A 1993 respondent working in a central agency intimately involved in the implementation of Next Steps seemed to confirm this analysis when accounting for the fairly modest amount of interchange between departmental headquarters and executive agencies which had actually developed:

> ... if you talk to high-flying policy-making civil servants and you say, 'Well, we think that for the future it'd be a jolly good thing if you had a spell in an agency as part of your career development . . .' they would say, 'Well, why? What could we contribute to the agency and what would we learn? It's a world that's completely different from ours. We are policy specialists.'

Can Governance Survive on Reinvention Alone?

Returning for a final set of interviews in summer 1993, we found profound disillusionment over the directions that management reform had taken under the Major Government. The political leaders had become almost evangelical in their belief that they could reduce government much further and make the surviving parts run like Marks and Spencer.

The period of reduction may well have spelt the end of budget-maximizing bureaucrats in line departments. But clout-maximizing offices abounded in the centre. The Efficiency Unit – still attached to no. 10 – had developed from a ginger group of six to an increasingly bureaucratized operation of fifteen. It shouldered responsibility for the Government's market-testing initiative. In 1993, it was in the process of forcing (not too strong a word) departments to come up with £1.5 billion worth of business that could be put out to tender.

After the 1992 election, Major created a new ministry – the Office of Public Service and Science (OPSS) – which would shoulder responsibility for the continuation of the Next Steps process and the Citizens' Charter. He put William Waldegrave in charge of this organization. Anxious to revive from an accident-prone outing as health secretary, Waldegrave seized the opportunity to take the reins of the 'reinventing government' bandwagon. Within OPSS, the bureaucratization of the Next Steps and Citizens' Charter initiatives had grown apace with similar developments in the Efficiency Unit. Significantly, the Government replaced Peter

Kemp – the very unconventional second permanent secretary who had masterminded the implementation of Next Steps – with a tried and true mandarin, Richard Mottram from the Ministry of Defence.

Meanwhile, the Treasury energetically pressed the view that privatization need not be restricted to state-owned corporations. It could extend to government operational units, especially those already functioning as executive agencies. This view crystallized by late 1993 into an initiative whereby the bulk of Next Steps agencies would ultimately be privatized. And the Department of Trade and Industry – under the leadership of Michael Heseltine, the President of the Board of Trade – advanced a vigorous de-regulation initiative. Building-down government had become a growth industry. Ministers and officials at the centre busily vied for pieces of the action.

So we come to the question, 'Can government survive on reinvention alone?' One would certainly have thought so given the emphasis assigned to these various management reform initia-tives. One finds even in no. 10 a sense that reinvention had supplanted the internal consistency of the government's policy commitments as the meat and potatoes of the executive coordin-ative process.

One respondent there practically eulogized the Citizens' Char-ter initiative as a textbook case of policy coordination: '. . . it was a classic policy unit activity because it was cross-departmental. It is something where if you're going to develop an initiative that involves departments, the role of tracking between departments: explaining, endeavouring to create coherence, execution of ideas and policy is something where the bridge function that this unit should provide is crucially important.' (1993 Interview.) When defining Major's approach to strategic planning in the adminis-tration, the official described the role of the Prime Minister's 'seminars'. Unlike strategy sessions in the 1970s, in which min-isters mapped out the handling of the great issues facing the government, Major's seminars focused essentially on his admin-istration's management issues:

He has a series of meetings which do bring in large groups of colleagues of particular cross-departmental areas where he wants to drive policy forward of which the most obvious are the Citizens'

Charter and deregulation. So, he has regular seminars on these issues with either all of his cabinet colleagues or a selected group, plus their permanent secretaries, which is very important. (1993 Interview.)

While the proliferation of management initiatives has been great sport for central agencies, officials in line departments have had to face an increasingly uncertain world. Each initiative has meant huge investments in terms of institutional adjustment. And respondents frequently reported being buffeted by the crosswinds of inconsistent goals. We found this most clearly to be the case with regard to the future of Next Steps agencies.

In summer 1993 we interviewed several people who either served as chief executives of Next Steps agencies or shouldered departmental responsibility for the policies they administered. The sense of disillusionment had become very pronounced indeed. Much of this stemmed from a belief that the additional managerial initiatives – especially the Citizens' Charter and market testing – had impinged upon the discretions originally imparted to chief executives. However, frustrations also focused on the OPSS's and the Treasury's three-year reviews of the agencies created at the outset of the Next Steps process.

At the time of our interviews, fully thirty agencies had come under review and only one had passed through the process. Much to the annoyance of line departments and executive agencies, the reviews had gone back to first principles – asking whether the agencies should be privatized, whether most of what they do should be contracted out, and whether the remaining parts should be market tested. These emphases seemed to many respondents at the operational level to have constituted betrayals of trust. Agency people believed that they had made herculean efforts to realign their organizations; now they were being told that these might be privatized or forced to shed substantial numbers of staff.

Many officials noted what struck them as logical inconsistencies between Next Steps and the new initiatives. A line department official with policy responsibilities for programmes run by executive agencies described especially well the bind in which chief executives found themselves. According to the inspiration behind Next Steps, chief executives were given a mandate to achieve excellence in their organizations by emphasizing teamwork and flexibility: '. . . Next Steps was taken as an opportunity to enhance people's sense of management responsibility and to import management concepts . . . which are directed to getting communication up and down the organization, getting close to the workers and getting everybody close to the customer and creating a team.' (1993 Interview.)

The respondent saw the new initiatives as impinging upon these mandates by reintroducing micromanagement from the centre. He cited the widespread expectation that market testing will relentlessly reduce chief executives' discretion:

> . . . this will become a continuous cycle in which you're only good for your contract or service-level agreement and then you'll be retested. This I think has put some agencies in the position where they feel that the department is now beating them about the ears saying 'You must make a contribution to the market testing programme and therefore you must find something to put to tender.' The agency says: 'Look, I'm supposed to be managing this organization. If I thought there was anything else to market test I would market test it, believe me! I'm not interested in adding figures to programmes to show to Peter Levene [the head of the no. 10 Efficiency Unit].'

Importantly, the same official employed such terms as 'firm if not doctrinaire', 'management ideology', and 'little holy doctrine' to convey the belief in Whitehall that the Government's perspective on reform had become driven by ideology rather than a coherent management theory. Nobody expressed these sentiments better than one respondent assessing reform from the standpoint of a central agency with a crucial role in the process. This official observed that in New Zealand reformers had put in place an entire theoretical apparatus – based on public choice and principal/agent theory – which then served as a point of reference for various management initiatives. In the UK, iterations in the reform process have not taken root in a logically coherent theory:

> . . . people at the top, actually, are very interested in the process of how you manage organizations and are quite keen to do something . . . the striking point between us and New Zealand . . . is if you ask people in this country to have a discussion with you about the application of principal/agent theory to their organizations they'll

sort of say 'What?' If you ask them 'What do you think about Next Steps?', they'll probably say, 'Well that's quite a good idea.' So, it's not at all clear what's the intellectual and theoretical basis for what's being done. Moreover . . . we've actually got a whole series of things all mixed up together and being presented as though they are a single whole . . . If you've got half-an-hour or an hour, I can do it for you. I do it all the time. But the cleverer people who I do this to often say, 'That's an elegant *ex post facto* rationalization.' (1993 Interview.)

To be sure, the respondent's rendering of the New Zealand case is problematic. In that country, the Treasury enjoys utter domination of the bureaucratic landscape. And, when a neo-liberal Labour Party government came to power in 1984, it paved the way for a bureaucratic *coup d'état*. The marriage of convenience between the Treasury (as led by the rational choice economist Graham Scott) and the Labour right (as headed by finance minister Roger Douglas) set up the context in which New Zealand could become the laboratory for agency theory.

What resulted from the extraordinary symbiosis between the political executive and the higher bureaucracy in New Zealand most certainly yielded a great deal of theoretical specificity and coherence. We can say this even though the premier under which most of the ensuing reforms emerged never fully took on neo-liberalism as his own and Roger Douglas ultimately resigned from the Government. Yet, an abundance of specificity and coherence notwithstanding, rational choice comprised an exceedingly monotonic theory of the state when it was applied to the Whitehall system most prone to monocratic leadership – both on the side of political leadership and bureaucratic politics. During the brief history of rational choice, an ideological component of the theoretical perspective has emerged, especially in its tendency to align itself with neo-liberalism. The conditions in New Zealand offered virtually no breaks to this propensity. So the New Zealand case does not serve as an instance of pure theory being brought to bear on management reform.

In the UK, a strongly different relationship existed between theory and practice. While today's gurus of Thatcherism were still in their political diapers, Sir Keith Joseph and Margaret Thatcher were imbibing rational choice under the tutelage of William Niskanen (1973b). As we have already noted, Thatcher even encouraged her newly appointed Cabinet to read Niskanen. But her rendering of public choice really unfolded in a highly iterative way. That is, it was essentially pragmatic. It began with Sir Derek Rayner's scrutinies. In retrospect, these amounted to fairly modest efforts to identify areas of government that might benefit from the application of private-sector management techniques.

Scrutinies ultimately led to the Financial Management Initiative (FMI). The emergence of FMI relied at least as much upon those public servants – especially those who had worked closely with scrutinies – who sought to generalize the benefits of a managerial approach as it did on political leadership. It enjoyed the strong patronage of Thatcher and some sympathetic ministers, especially Michael Heseltine. In a sense, Next Steps constituted a departure from the gradualism that prevailed during the Thatcher years. After all, it sought to reduce the number of civil servants in conventional departments by half. However, Next Steps functions still fitted within the compass of government services. And the employees of executive agencies still belonged to the civil service. We would soon see that its 'radicalism' would pale beside the next wave of reforms.

The current wave of initiatives has, thus, departed from the Thatcher era in two respects. First, it has emerged from a context of multiple ideological entrepreneurship. As noted above, Major operates a seriously fragmented administration. Furthermore, the political brokerage necessary to sustain him in power has placed ideologues in positions of exceptional power. Second, the symbiosis between Whitehall managerialists and the government has broken down. Under Thatcher, the public service – despite a great deal of pain – gradually repositioned itself so that it could pursue more managerial approaches. Now a sense of betrayal and confusion permeates all levels of the public service.

One respondent working in a central agency encapsulated very well the frustration that had descended upon those wrestling with the current reform efforts:

> ... [we have a] problem of layering – that we have piled initiative on initiative. There is competition between different sorts of ideas and managerial and ideological considerations within the government. The civil service leadership is very keen on promoting

mainstream managerial changes which we can defend as not being ideological, because it fits with our non-partisan status. A significant portion of the government is quite keen on ideologically driven policies. Regarding the staff, including some managers, you find them all actually in an uncharacteristically gloomy mood about all this. They feel unloved and somewhat confused. (1993 Interview.)

Indeed, the conclusion of the 1993 report by Price Waterhouse of Executive Agencies identifies precisely the same sense of malaise:

. . . some chief executives have been disappointed to find that their independence is considerably constrained, particularly when a government-wide initiative like market testing affects them so fundamentally. This reflects the essential dilemma – that they are still part of the civil service and ministerial policies have to be followed. Sometimes their priorities may not be the business priorities of the agency and the time frame is certainly not often the same. In addition, even though agencies have delegated powers, over pay for example, this does not preclude Treasury interference.

Conclusion

This chapter has examined how Whitehall's deeds reflect its reputation for policy coherence and cohesion. The closer we look the more Whitehall's standing appears somewhat putative. True collective decision making developed only very gradually in the UK. It probably reached its height in the 1950s and 1960s. Prime ministers have compensated for the weakening of collective government by adding to the coordinative apparatus at the centre. Heath's creation of the Central Policy Review Staff fitted within this pattern – although CPRS divided its loyalty between prime ministers and general service to cabinets. Thatcher's abolition of CPRS and enhancement of the no. 10 Policy Unit institutionalized prime-ministerial latitude in imposing coherence and consistency from above.

Major's Policy Unit has operated less imperially than Thatcher's. However, other dimensions of the Thatcher legacy have remained. Thus, Whitehall functions in a significantly less consultative manner than it did before Thatcher. Major has found it difficult to resuscitate cabinet dynamics; the public service will only very slowly recover from eleven years of command leadership, which stifled even constructive criticism; the Treasury has positioned itself as the linchpin for all that happens in Whitehall; Next Steps has again enshrined the principle that true mandarins need not get their hands dirty; and various ideological entrepreneurs have busied themselves picking the remains of the operational side to Whitehall.

7

Whither Accountability?

We noted in Chapter 1 that it used to be thought that one of the great advantages of the Whitehall model was its provision for clear democratic accountability. Ministers were individually accountable to Parliament for the work of their departments, and collectively responsible for all major government policies; civil servants were accountable to ministers.

Thus three aspects of accountability provide the linkages between Parliament and the executive. The first is that civil servants are answerable to their ministers for all their actions. The hierarchy within departments is simple. As *The Times* once remarked: 'The constitutional position is both crystal clear and entirely sufficient. Officials propose. Ministers dispose. Officials execute.' (*The Times*, 15 February 1977.) Second, ministers are accountable to Parliament for all the actions of their departments. Ministers are not expected to prevent any and every misdeed by incompetent, dishonest or misguided officials, but they are responsible for seeing that errors and misdeeds are minimized and that if they do occur they are rectified as fully and as completely as possible. Finally, ministers are collectively responsible for the government's principal policies – policy towards the EC, waging war in the Persian Gulf or in the Falklands and managing the economy. Political scientists have focused more on the first two of these forms of accountability; the last, collective responsibility, has spawned a vast debate on its own about whether Britain has prime-ministerial or cabinet government (Mackintosh, 1977; Crossman, 1972; Hennessy, 1986b; George Jones, 1987; Foley, 1993). But the first two of these forms of accountability – of officials to ministers and individual ministers to Parliament, for the behaviour of their departments – are crucial in defining the relationship between bureaucrats and politicians at the core of the Whitehall model.

The belief that ministers ought to be, and are, accountable for the actions of the departments over which they preside is fundamental to the British constitution. It is through ministerial accountability that Parliament attempts to control the government departments; at Parliamentary Question Time, before Select Committees and in censure debates, MPs are able to question the conduct and policies of government departments only through their ministers (Armstrong, 1986; Marshall, 1988; Drewry, 1986). Until very recently, ministerial accountability has been not only the main but the only means by which departments can be held accountable. The post of Ombudsman (Parliamentary Commissioner for Administration) was created to examine complaints of maladministration forwarded by MPs, and the courts became more willing to check the exercise of executive power; ministerial responsibility was the only means by which redress of grievances could be secured and executive power held in check. It is no exaggeration to say that the viability of the doctrine of ministerial responsibility in practice determined the health of British democracy. Democracy in the Whitehall model has therefore rested on the ability of the culture to imbue those within it with a respect for accountability. In theory civil servants are socialized to be aware when to seek instructions from superiors and ministers, either on the resolution of difficult cases or for policy guidance. Ministers are accustomed to the idea that they must be responsible to Parliament for the work of their departments.

The doctrine of ministerial responsibility also plays a vital role in shaping power relations within government departments. The fact that ministers are in theory accountable for the policies and work of their departments gives them a moral hold over their officials. The belief that 'in the end it's the minister who has to take the heat for this' (Interview, 1989), as one of our interviewees put it, helps officials unhappy with a policy decision to be reconciled to it. The doctrine of ministerial responsibility creates a very real feeling in Whitehall that civil servants are working *for* their ministers or ministers in general; it is one reason why there are fewer attempts by British civil servants than by Americans to try to mobilize forces outside the executive branch against decisions they dislike. Moreover, ministerial responsibility is a valuable shield for civil servants. Since only ministers are publicly accountable for departmental decisions, then civil servants are not. Individual civil servants should not be 'hung out to dry' for unfortunate decisions or policies, so long as they are acting within the boundaries of proper procedures and departmental policies. The doctrine of ministerial responsibility therefore safeguards civil servants as well as empowers ministers. It is a convention at the heart of the Whitehall model.

Although any discussion of accountability runs the risk of reading like a gloss on the Scouts' Code, it is a living doctrine for officials in Westminster model countries. A Canadian official expressed this view very clearly in the 1970s. 'In my view . . . even if the minister knows only two per cent of all that is going on in the department, he still is responsible and accountable for the whole 100 per cent. I must hold up my per cent of the whole by giving the best possible advice, from a professional point of view.' (Campbell and Szablowski, 1979.)

Of course, social scientists since Weber have cast doubts on the feasibility of such a minister really knowing and understanding what his or her department is really doing. Weber had argued that 'The "political master" finds himself in the position of the "dilettante" who stands opposite the "expert" facing the trained official who stands within the management of administration. . . . Every bureaucracy seeks to increase the superiority of the professional by keeping their knowledge and intentions secret.' (Weber, 1921b, in Gerth and Mills, 1958, pp. 232–3.) Such problems in securing accountability applied to all political systems, democratic and non-democratic alike. However, the Whitehall model at least provided a coherent account of the chain of accountability, from official to minister, from minister to Parliament and from Parliament to the people. Ministerial ignorance of the actions of officials or of the weaknesses in their advice was no defence in this system of accountability. The enormous constitutional significance of the Crichel Down affair, (a complicated and at first glance minor episode in the history of the Ministry of Agriculture to which we return below) was supposedly that the minister, Sir Thomas Dugdale, resigned because he was responsible for the misconduct of his officials of which he was unaware until a political storm erupted.

The clear and even harsh accountability within the Whitehall system contrasted vividly, therefore, with the incoherence of the American model. Rockman notes the problem of establishing clear

lines of accountability in the United States. 'To whom . . . would
the permanent legion of bureaucrats be accountable? The answer
is to no single source of authority.' (Rockman, 1984, p. 48.)
American officials could be said to be accountable to their departmental, politically appointed superiors, to the president, to
the relevant committees and subcommittees of Congress and,
increasingly in the last three decades, to the courts. Accountable
in theory to so many masters, the American bureaucrat could be
accountable in practice – like the original servant of two masters
– to none by playing one master against the other. J. Edgar
Hoover, the long-time director of the FBI, was perhaps the most
perfect modern practitioner of such strategy. At least the Whitehall model provided a clear, coherent account of who was supposed to be accountable to whom.

As we shall see, accountability in Whitehall systems today is
not clearly achieved in practice. But the *concept* of accountability
is not even as clear in practice as had been supposed. We turn
first to some of the conceptual problems with accountability that
have become pressing in Whitehall systems recently.

Accountability: Some General Issues

At first glance accountability is a simple concept: the Oxford
English Dictionary disposes of the concept in a few lines. 'The
quality of being accountable; liability to give an account of
and answer for discharge of duties or conduct; responsibility,
amenableness.'

Yet though accountability may seem to be a simple concept, as
others have made clear, its practice is not (Marshall, 1988).
Important conceptual problems complicate the achievement of
accountability. These problems can be summarized in questions:
'for what, to whom and to what extent?'

Accountability – for What?

It may seem again that the answer to this question is simple;
subordinates are accountable to superiors for carrying out work
to their superiors' satisfaction. But it is not so simple. Subordinates

cannot be accounting constantly for what they are doing and must be allowed a measure of discretion when making decisions. Too much accountability in the sense of superiors constantly checking up on detailed decisions made by their subordinates is undesirable. One of our interviewees complained about how little discretion he was allowed when he was in charge of road building. 'There are formal delegations. . . . They are very pusillanimous delegations. I, for instance, I need a delegation to approve a new road above one million pounds. . . . Well, that's nothing, only five yards of tarmac.' (Interview, 1981.) Although this official wanted to be accountable for the ultimate product, he did not want to be constantly accountable for his day-to-day work. He favoured accountability for the end result, new roads, not for the details of their construction. This is a view that has found increasing favour in modern bureaucracies. Another of our respondents reported that '. . . the system is evolving whereby officers at every level set out and agree to their objectives for the coming year with their bosses and can be held accountable for what happened on those agreed objectives.' (Interview, 1983.) This accountability for results contrasts with more traditional notions in which bureaucrats could at any moment explain why and how their actions accorded with the values and priorities that their superiors had set.

Many civil servants continue to express this more traditional notion of accountability as a reality. 'We are reviewing the way we allocate resources between regions. . . . which is very sensitive politically. So, today as ever, I am reporting to ministers to see if they want to give us any guidance.' (Interview, 1989.) Another thought that the system worked smoothly and almost effortlessly.

As for dealing with ministers and the permanent secretary and so on, it seems to fall in quite well in the ordinary course of business. You advise ministers within what you know are their priorities and their political considerations. Wherever you are, you have to accept the political parameters that the government brings with it. . . . I don't see there is any great problem really. Nor do I think the task has changed very much from what it must always have been. (Interview, 1989.)

Both of these notions of accountability see obedience to political superiors as unproblematic; bureaucrats either adopt a mode of thinking or deliver a product (such as a new road) that is in line with the government's approach. Distinguished British political civil servants do indeed see such obedience as unproblematic. Quinlan, for example, argues (1993) that the civil servant's duty *as a civil servant* can be disentangled from any feelings or obligations he or she has as an individual, citizen, parent or occupant of other roles. We have different obligations in the numerous different roles that we occupy.

Yet in the 1980s, as we have seen in Chapter 2, at least some British civil servants felt a conflict in practice between their professional standards and the wishes of their superiors. Frequent changes in government statistics in the 1980s had the effect of making the unemployment rate seem lower, thereby serving the short-term interests of the government. Many officials felt, however, that the revisions reduced the authenticity of the figures, so causing a conflict between their professional standards and political accountability; they could not resolve it by repeating the mantra that they were merely required to be obedient servants of their political masters. As a government statistician told the *Guardian* 'There's been a whole change of culture in the civil service. But is your duty to your minister or to your country? I consider my loyalty lies to my country.' Another remarked, somewhat apocalyptically, 'Clearly, we're not in the situation of the German civil service in the 1930s but if we accept what we now accept, we won't know when to stop.' (*Guardian*, 9 January 1991, 'Private Lies and Public Servants'.) At the height of the Westland affair, a severe crisis that bitterly divided the Thatcher Cabinet over who should be allowed to buy the Westland helicopter company, civil servants were told to act in a way (leaking confidential material to the press to undermine the standing of a member of the Cabinet) that at least one felt violated the norms of the senior civil service as a permanent, professional bureaucracy.

In brief, bureaucrats in the Whitehall model felt that it was not as clear as we usually suppose what they were accountable for. Ambiguities about accountability for procedures or outcomes were combined with uncertainty about the degree to which they had duties or responsibilities that went beyond serving the government, to produce an unusual degree of uncertainty in the system about the concept of accountability in practice.

Accountability – to Whom?

A second problem concerns the question: to whom are officials accountable? In theory, the answer to this question is clear; officials are accountable to ministers, and ministers to Parliament. In practice, not all civil servants feel that things are, or should be, so simple. For some of our respondents, their accountability was not the legal or constitutional accountability through their seniors to ministers, but to colleagues more generally.

'I think one accounts to the department first, the ministers second. Ministers come and go, the department has a degree of stability about it. In the five years I've been here there've been three Secretaries of State. It is quite surprising. . . . It's not necessarily the hierarchy, it's the peer group you account to . . . it's how you're seen in the eyes of your colleagues . . . it's actually how you're viewed by your colleagues is the thing that would drive me.' (Interview 1989.)

Other civil servants feel a responsibility to ensure that policy is well made, that the policy adopted is as intelligent as possible, a responsibility that can cut across formal or constitutional notions of hierarchy. One permanent secretary had no doubt that a responsibility went beyond simple obedience to a minister and deference to his or her views. 'If I think a minister is not giving enough weight to the advice he is receiving, I would intervene personally to ask him to do so . . . he does often ask me what is my judgement before he makes up his own mind. . . . So I attend quite a lot of meetings where everybody speaks his mind.' Another senior civil servant, a deputy secretary in a different department, also felt a responsibility that went beyond accountability to the minister of the day. '. . . the deputy secretary . . . is the person who has to keep his eye on the long term – where will this get us, are we going to there on this route . . .' Another senior civil servant knew that in practice accountability to ministers was an unlikely prospect in his work, personnel management and training.

'I don't work at all with ministers. I don't see ministers from one day to the next except on a personal basis. If you're not doing policy, if you're not working in a key policy area, very few ministers are interested in government departments as administrative machines. They're interested in government as a source of ideas and brain power.' (Interview 1989.)

In contrast, a senior official in the Export Credits Guarantee Department had seen accountability arrive as a reality as his agency experienced financial difficulties, after years in which politicians were almost unaware of his agency's existence.

> . . . we had the Public Accounts Committee [of the House of Commons] actually calling us . . . and really putting pressure on us. 'Are you truthful in the way you present your accounts or highly optimistic? Isn't it really much worse?' This kind of scepticism. Ministers were becoming concerned because we had a cash flow problem. Instead of contributing to the Public Sector Borrowing Requirement with our surplus at the end of the year, we were going to ministers and saying we will need 500 million more than we will earn next year. So, that affects the budget. And we gained a high profile. All of those things made us more financially aware, more accountable both to the public and to Treasury and to ministers. (Interview 1982.)

Note that accountability for this official, though very real, and much more real than in the past, was not along the simple, clear lines of the traditional Whitehall model. Accountability to the public, to the Treasury and to the Public Accounts Committee competed with traditional notions of accountability to ministers.

One of the most difficult professional problems for civil servants has been how to proceed when there is a conflict between these foci of accountability. For example, one of the issues that most troubled some of our interviewees was whether a civil servant had a duty to follow a prime-ministerial or cabinet line that conflicted with the views of his or her own minister. This was often referred to as 'the Benn Problem', relating to the period in which Harold Wilson and James Callaghan kept Tony Benn in their cabinets while taking care to ensure that he was not able to implement his more radical policies. Some civil servants in Benn's department felt that they were accountable, as one put it to us, 'to the government as a whole' (Interview, 1989), not just to Benn. It was their duty to make sure through informal channels that colleagues in the Treasury and Cabinet Office knew what Benn was planning so that the prime minister and the Cabinet could control him. Sir Anthony Part, Benn's permanent secretary at the Department of Energy, claimed that he took the other view, that he was accountable only to his own minister (Part, 1990, pp. 173–4). 'It also seemed to me important that I should not "sneak" to senior colleagues outside the Department about confidences from the Secretary of State.' Perhaps inevitably, however, the left wing minority in the 1974–9 Labour Government did feel they were surrounded by a conspiracy that included the civil service. One embittered former junior minister gave us an example.

> I wanted to guarantee small loans for small businesses. They [the civil servants] said we don't like it – the banks will give us all their worst cases. I had minutes and letters from civil servants saying it was impossible. I arranged a meeting with a collection of civil servants. A deputy secretary said at the start of the meeting that the permanent secretary had a meeting with the Secretary of State and they were going to set up an inquiry into the idea – they'd gone round to the dozey twit who was Secretary of State to undermine me. (Interview 1990.)

Civil servants could reply that it is the Secretary of State who is responsible for running the Department; our disaffected junior minister still felt that his experience was symptomatic of civil service manoeuvring to restrain left wing ministers.

The rise of Thatcherism confronted civil servants with fresh demands that they should obey the prime minister, not necessarily their own ministers. Members of Thatcher's Policy Unit would contact civil servants in departments and tell them that the advice they were giving their ministers was not in line with the doctrines of the Government. For Thatcherites, constitutional issues were not raised by this practice, for the prime minister was the chief executive. As Thatcher's friend, admirer and cabinet colleague, Nicholas Ridley wrote, 'The United States Constitution is quite explicit in stating that the Executive consists of one person – the President. . . . Many nations have followed the USA in vesting supreme power in just one person – a President. Britain's practice is not so very different . . . the Prime Minister alone carries the responsibility of the Executive, just as the President of the USA does.' (Ridley, 1991, p. 27.) Yet Thatcher was no more able than her predecessors or successors to guarantee unity in her Government; many civil servants again faced the problem of deciding whether to be loyal to Downing Street or to their own ministers.

The most difficult dilemma for all civil servants is to be placed in a situation in which they appear to be assisting unconstitutional behaviour by ministers. Ministers are often tempted to give Parliament misleading but politically useful statements. Should civil servants facilitate such deceptions, or does their ultimate accountability via ministers to Parliament mean that they should frustrate attempts to deceive it? Two recent instances raise this issue acutely. The first involved Clive Ponting, a civil servant whose performance had been much admired by Conservative ministers. Ponting felt, however, that the Thatcher Government was lying to the House of Commons about the circumstances in the Falklands War under which the Argentine cruiser, the *General Belgrano* had been sunk (Ponting, 1985). Was the cruiser approaching British troop transports threatening heavy loss of life, or was it harmlessly escaping to port? The Thatcher Government suppressed evidence supporting the latter view in order to facilitate its claims to the House of Commons that the first interpretation was correct. Ponting leaked secret information to a Labour MP to uncover what he felt was a clear deception of Parliament. He was dismissed, prosecuted under the Official Secrets Act and saved from jail by a jury that, contrary to the urging of a fiercely pro-prosecution judge, refused to accept that giving information to an MP was prejudicial to the interests of the state, as the Official Secrets Act specified.

A similar episode involved even worse government duplicity. Just before the Gulf War, the British Government altered its policy on arms exports to Iraq, facilitating them while continuing to pretend to Parliament that government policy had not changed. As a former Foreign Office official explained to the Scott Inquiry into the Government's conduct, the infamy of Saddam Hussein's Government made it impossible to admit to Parliament that restrictions on arms exports to Iraq were being eased. Yet the Government was determined to allow British exporters to compete for Iraqi orders with arms suppliers from other countries. The solution was to relax arms export controls while answering Parliamentary questions in ways that implied that government policy had not changed (*Guardian*, 17 July 1993). Remarkably, one of the ministers most involved in this process, William Waldegrave, was subsequently made responsible for reducing secrecy in government. Civil servants were apparently complicit not only with this deception, without complaint, but also with attempts to suppress evidence that showed that British businessmen prosecuted for trying to evade the supposed arms embargo on Iraq were in fact cooperating with British intelligence (*Financial Times*, 12 November 1992, p. 16). Had the prosecution succeeded, the accused would have been given severe jail sentences. Willingness to assist ministers overwhelmed any higher responsibility to Parliament or to the administration of justice.

Accountability – to What Extent?

It is perhaps not surprising that in the 1980s and 1990s, some thoughtful civil servants began to question whether they might not need protection from their political masters. Were there sufficient safeguards that civil servants could invoke to refuse illegitimate orders from political superiors? The examples we have discussed here – the alleged deception of Parliament over the *General Belgrano* and arms sales to Iraq, the attempted suppression of evidence that would have exonerated men on trial for serious offences and, in the case of the Westland affair, which we describe below, the release of an opinion from the Law Officers that was clearly required by law, rules and convention to be kept secret – all involved civil servants in what to outsiders must seem to be quite severe ethical problems. Yet senior civil servants in Britain continue to claim that cases in which civil servants are asked to behave unethically, thus justifying a breach of accountability to ministers, are in practice non-existent (Quinlan, 1993).

Not surprisingly, the safeguards for civil servants are also very weak. In the aftermath of the Westland affair, the then head of the home civil service and secretary to the Cabinet, Sir Robert Armstrong, issued a memorandum that gave guidance to civil servants on how to proceed if they were asked to undertake tasks they thought were inappropriate for civil servants or otherwise wrong (Armstrong, 1986). The advice given in the memorandum was to complain to superiors, then if necessary to the head of the civil service. His or her last resort would be to raise the issue with the prime minister. Whether this mechanism provided adequate safeguards for civil servants is an issue that divided our interviewees. Some were confident that any minister would back off from an unreasonable request if faced with such a potentially embarrassing procedure, while others thought that it could be damaging to career prospects to be seen as 'being difficult'. Others noted that in many of the most difficult cases, their superiors had already been involved in the policies in question; to complain to superiors could be to complain to people who had helped to create the policies in the first place. By 1993, the head of the civil service, Sir Robin Butler, could report receiving only one complaint from a civil servant that he had been asked to act improperly. The case in question concerned not an administrative civil servant, however, but a scientific officer angry about changes in planned research (Treasury and Civil Service Committee, 1993, p. 116) Either ethical problems in Whitehall are indeed extraordinarily rare, or civil servants are reluctant to use the formal complaints procedure.

The effectiveness of the complaints procedure in Britain is not the point that concerns us here, however. The existence of a complaints procedure is a reminder that even in the upper reaches of the British senior civil service, there is some recognition that loyalty may not always be enough, that there comes a point at which the duty of accountability to political superiors has to be tempered with a consciousness of higher moral constitutional concerns.

The apparent simplicity of accountability as a concept therefore masks questions that in practice are problematic. The questions to whom, about what and to what extent are civil servants responsible to politicians became more pressing in Whitehall systems in the 1980s, contributing to what was often seen as a crisis of morale in the senior civil service.

A Comparative Perspective

Whitehall systems were not alone in grappling with the problems of the ethics of accountability in the 1980s. Several continental

European systems abandoned the attempt to maintain systems in which officials served ministers of any duly constituted government, in favour of an explicit recognition of the party loyalties of officials; the French changes of administration in the 1980s were followed by extensive reassignments and retirements of senior officials, following the well-established practice in the Federal German Republic.

In the United States issues such as the Iran–Contra scandal raised the question of the degree to which both career officials (such as Colonel Oliver North) and political appointees (such as Eliot Abrams) were operating free from political control or were loyally serving the president, ignoring the constraints set by law on presidential action. Moreover, the American civil service faced the same challenge as the British to its professional judgement, from highly ideological politicians sure of the correctness of their policies (Peters, 1986). In contrast to the tensions between the bureaucracy and President Nixon, who was regularly frustrated by his inability to control the bureaucracy, the political appointees of the Reagan administration were the undisputed masters of the situation. Not surprisingly, many senior officials in the United States were frustrated by the futility of giving their professional opinions to their political superiors. As one put it,

> They didn't want analysis. They pretty much knew what they wanted to do. So an analytic piece which either said 'yes, you're right, go ahead' or 'No, you're wrong, this is going to create havoc' wasn't the kind of thing they needed. They didn't want to hear if it was wrong. And, if it was right, it was a waste of time to do the analysis. (Campbell, 1986, p. 185.)

The greater ideological cohesion of the Reagan administration, the diminished liberalism of the bureaucracy and changes in the structure of the civil service implemented by President Carter all contributed to greater political control of the bureaucracy (Aberbach and Rockman, 1991). Moreover, the proportion of governmental posts filled through political appointment rather than through civil service procedures reached a level at which issues of accountability were very different. Political appointments now encompass three levels below secretaries and have spread to about half of the next level. The degree to which permanent officials participate in policy making has been reduced, by their exclusion from the process entirely, the limitation of their participation in developing pieces of policies, and the denial of their access to comprehensive plans by which the parts will fit into the whole (Nathan, 1975; Newland, 1983, p. 2; Campbell, 1986, pp. 28–88, 217; Hansen and Levine, 1988, pp. 20–6).

The greatest fear for senior civil servants in Whitehall systems is that a similar intrusion of political appointees will reduce the role of the permanent civil service in policy making, a fear that is particularly acute as policy making rather than management has been seen as the most prestigious aspect of the service's work. A recurring concern of our most senior interviewees in Britain was to deny that politicization has occurred, and to ask how far their subordinates had come to believe that personal political commitment to the government was a prerequisite of professional success. But arguments that the senior civil service was being politicized by Thatcher's unusually close involvement in promotion decisions were common in the 1980s. The assurance given by a Royal Institute for Public Administration inquiry (1987) that politicization was not occurring was in fact based on a very narrow interpretation of 'politicization' – one that defined the concept in terms of loyalty to the Conservative Party. There is clear evidence, however, that the Thatcher Government advanced the careers of civil servants whose style was congenial, whose approach to their work fitted the preconceptions of the Government. Civil servants who promised enthusiastic, uncritical implementation were promoted even if they were not known to be Conservatives; those whose professional judgement led them to emphasize difficulties or dangers in the Government's approach were not. As we saw in Chapter 2, the promotion of Sir Peter Middleton to be Permanent Secretary of the Treasury exemplified how enthusiastic obedience was favoured over the Conservative credentials of one rival and the more detached, critical style of another (Lawson, 1992). The almost explicit threat from the Thatcher Government was that if the permanent civil service could not produce officials willing to work loyally for it, it would not only recruit people like Middleton from within the system but would look for people to bring in from outside.

The distinctive feature of the Whitehall model was not that accountability was problematic: securing bureaucratic accountability is a problem in any system. But in Whitehall systems, the bureaucracy was asked to adapt more than its American counterpart to a change in political leadership, taking on the attitudes as well as policies of each duly appointed government in order to carry out tasks such as generating policy proposals, writing speeches and drafting statements, which American cabinet secretaries would entrust to their politically appointed staffs. The ultimate threat to recalcitrant bureaucrats in such a system is that if they are unwilling to deliver congenial policy proposals and analysis to their political superiors, the whole system could be changed to make it more like the American, with a greater role for political appointees and a diminished role for permanent officials.

The threat to replace a permanent bureaucracy with a system of political appointees is an ultimate deterrent to official obstruction. But, like the nuclear deterrent, it is unusable in most day-to-day situations, or even in crises. In recent years, rational choice writers have argued that the problem of accountability is more easily solved than most political scientists have admitted. The problem of securing obedience and support from bureaucracies can be solved by a judicious mixture of rewards and punishments. Politicians do not have to try to monitor an agency's every action and decision, but can respond to any sign of unsatisfactory performance by sanctions such as budget cuts. A congressional committee does not need to hold oversight hearings constantly to check that a federal agency is following its wishes, but can act on reports it receives about an agency's behaviour ('fire alarms') to offer rewards such as an increased budget or punishments such as budget cuts if it disapproves of the agency's conduct (Moe, 1984; Shepsle, 1991).

A peculiar feature of Whitehall systems is how few of the obvious rewards and punishments are available to secure compliance. Though Thatcher was much more involved in personnel issues than her predecessors (or successor), top-level promotions have usually been determined by other civil servants, not by ministers. Major's reported comment to a very senior official on promotion decisions, 'You know these people, I don't', is much more typical than Thatcher's determination to interview the candidates herself before making the decision in person.

Nor are sanctions against entire agencies as attractive an

option as in the American system, making the application of principal–agent approaches problematic. The politicians who are meant to control the agencies are themselves, as ministers, part of the agencies. Punishments such as budget cuts would be masochistic for the relevant minister, and even problematic for the prime minister. As we shall see, the situation may change in the future if the Next Steps reforms discussed below separate agencies from parent ministries. Until now, however, the constitutional meshing of politicians and bureaucrats in the Whitehall model has prevented the adoption of the usual principal–agent mechanisms for ensuring accountability.

In the absence of effective and available sanctions or punishments, the responsiveness of officials to politicians has been secured through professional norms and values. To those who would say that norms and values are a slim foundation on which to base a political institution, we can only reply that much in Westminster model countries, including in the final analysis the protection of democratic rights, has depended on such equally slim foundations. The importance of norms and values in securing accountability in Whitehall model countries gives added importance to the evidence of strains in the practice of accountability that we present in this chapter.

The Problem of Accountability in Practice: Does the Doctrine Survive?

No one thinks that in practice ministers can know in detail everything their departments are doing. Numerous decisions are made and policies pursued about which the responsible minister in practice knows, and realistically can know, nothing. Any view of ministerial responsibility therefore involves assessing whether the practice of ministerial responsibility none the less is real; the impossible constitutional responsibility of ministers for everything done in their names has to be balanced against the fact that, as one inquiry into a failure of administration (the Vehicle and General case) heard, only 1 per cent of decisions reach ministers (Summerton, 1980). A single instance of a minister refusing to accept responsibility for an action of his or her department of which he or she had no prior knowledge scarcely proves that ministerial responsibility is dead as a practice or a doctrine.

The crucial episode in shaping the modern doctrine of ministerial responsibility was the Crichel Down affair. The facts of the affair are disputed, but we offer this summary. In the 1930s land at Crichel Down was taken into government ownership – and compensation paid to the owners – in case it was needed for a wartime airfield. The land was not in fact used for military purposes. Officials of the Ministry of Agriculture, acting under the policy of maximizing wartime (and postwar) food production, combined the parcels of land, which they believed to have been badly farmed by their previous owners, into a new, single, more efficient unit. In the 1950s, Ministry of Agriculture officials, continuing the policy of maximizing production, declined to sell the land back to its previous owners and instead moved to sell off the more efficient farm they had created.

Critics of the civil service provided a different interpretation. According to the 'myth' of Crichel Down, a heavy-handed government bureaucracy took land into government ownership for war purposes and, instead of returning it to its former owners, high-handedly decided to combine the land with other acreage to make a new farm. The blame for what was seen as despotic government behaviour was laid at the feet of the civil servants in the Ministry of Agriculture. The Minister, Sir Thomas Dugdale, resigned, however, accepting that he was responsible for the misconduct of his officials (Nicolson, 1986). In the subsequent parliamentary debate, the Attorney General enumerated three principles governing ministerial responsibility.

The first principle is that ministers are responsible for all decisions that they have made personally, or failed to make when confronted with proper warnings or advice. The second principle is that ministers are responsible for the decisions and actions of civil servants when either the civil servants are following policies that have been approved by ministers or the civil servants are following policies so visibly that attentive ministers should have known about them. Third, ministers are *not* responsible for the actions or policies of civil servants that they had not approved, that they would not have approved had they known about them and of which ministers could not be expected to have known.

The Crichel Down principles do not translate easily into a

decision on a particular situation. The application of all the principles involves making judgements about the balance of evidence
in a situation in which passions are often running high. Nicolson's
study of the affair itself illustrates the difficulty of applying the
Crichel Down principles. Nicolson makes a convincing argument
against the 'myth' of Crichel Down in which it is argued that a
noble Sir Thomas Dugdale resigned because of the misconduct of
his officials, about which he was ignorant. Nicolson shows that
ministers *were* in fact involved extensively in the decisions made
about the disposition of the land at Crichel Down; Dugdale's
own involvement may have been limited but one of his junior
ministers, Lord Carrington, was much more actively involved. (If
this is true, it is a pleasing irony that Carrington was later, as we
shall see, to be forced to resign for errors in which he was involved later in his career!) The civil servants involved were following a policy that was both approved by ministers and was
eminently defensible. The land at Crichel Down, which had been
farmed poorly by its original owners, who had gladly sold the
land to the government, was grouped with other land to make an
effective modern unit in line with the government's policy of
promoting efficient farming. Far from constituting a case in which
ministerial responsibility was applied appropriately or, given that
in the myth Dugdale was ignorant of the decision, too strin-
gently, the Crichel Down episode was one in which civil servants
were treated almost shamelessly badly. Officials who had made
a decision that was both sound and in line with government
policy were pilloried, with little or no opportunity to defend
themselves. As Sir Douglas Wass commented, 'What emerges from
the official papers . . . is how shamefully the civil servants concerned were left undefended to their fate for carrying out government policy endorsed by ministers, how easily some ministers
went along with the dubious claim that some great injustice had
been done . . . and how reasonable the civil servants were to all
in carrying out their responsibilities.' (Wass, 1988.) Nicolson's –
and Wass's – reinterpretation of Crichel Down is not accepted
universally. It does, however, indubitably remind us how difficult
it is to apply Crichel Down principles in particular cases.

The responsibility of individual ministers for the actions of
officials in their departments is not the only form of responsibility that is supposed to prevail in the Whitehall model. The system

is also supposed to provide for collective responsibility. Collective responsibility is the doctrine that makes ministers responsible for all the policies of the government, not just their own departments'. Ministers are expected to resign, or to be fired by the prime minister, if they cannot agree with policy. Ministers usually feel that collective responsibility gives them rights as well as duties. These rights include being informed of major government policies and having the opportunity to influence those policies.

Arguments that collective responsibility – a central constitutional doctrine – in fact no longer applies in practice have become very common. Frequently ministers in modern British governments have dissented fairly openly from the policies for which they are supposedly responsible, to be, as Margaret Thatcher complained about one of her cabinet dissenters, 'semi-detached'. James Callaghan made clear his dissent from the 1964–70 Labour Government's policy of reforming industrial relations. Tony Benn dissented openly from the central economic strategy of the 1974–9 Labour Government. And a series of Thatcher's cabinet ministers made clear their disagreement with her. Norman St John Stevas (a Roman Catholic) was removed quickly because of his fondness for describing Thatcher to journalists as 'the immaculate misconception', but James Prior, operating from a more secure base, remained in the cabinet for most of Thatcher's term while telling all journalists willing to listen how little he thought of his leader's policies.

If individual ministers have been less willing to be bound by collective responsibility, so prime ministers have given them less opportunity to deliberate collectively. Under Thatcher, the number of cabinet meetings – and even cabinet committee meetings – diminished markedly, and instead the Prime Minister met ministers separately to settle issues, a forum in which she was much more likely to prevail. The positions most crucial for Thatcher's policies, notably the Chancellorship of the Exchequer, were kept in the hands of people thought to be ideological allies (though in Nigel Lawson's case theological disputes about monetarism came to divide them): 'ordinary' members of the cabinet had almost no opportunity to influence crucial decisions such as the 1981 budget that cut expenditure during a recession. The Major Government may have praised collegial discussion in principle, but in practice crucial decisions such as the electorally damaging yet futile attempt to remain within the Exchange Rate Mechanism were beyond the reach of nearly all cabinet ministers. The Major Government was characterized by much informal consultation, but little collective deliberation.

We turn now to look at some of the crucial episodes of ministerial responsibility in the Thatcher years. Throughout those years, the Prime Minister's critics argued that she was stretching the constitution; numerous episodes such as the policing of the miners' strike and the treatment of journalists seemed to indicate a disregard for civil liberties (Ewing and Gearty, 1990). Thatcher's critics also argued that the doctrines of ministerial responsibility were disregarded during her Government. Her ministers resigned with some regularity, including some, like Heseltine, Lawson and Howe, who resigned in protest over a combination of policies and the way in which the Prime Minister ran the Government. But ministerial responsibility, the acceptance of blame by ministers for situations in which under Crichel Down rules they were clearly responsible, became a dead letter.

The Falklands Crisis

The Falklands War at first glance appears to be not only one of Thatcher's finest hours, but also proof that ministerial responsibility lives in practice as well as in theory. The initial British reverses – the successful invasion of the islands by Argentina and the consequent capture of the Royal Marine garrison – were themselves reversed. Thatcher showed a degree of determination and steadfastness in directing the liberation of the islands that it is hard to imagine her predecessors or successor displaying. Her calmness during the risky military operations, with their inevitable casualties, displayed her finest qualities. Similarly, the resignations of not only the Foreign Secretary, Lord Carrington, but also his two junior ministers immediately after the Argentine invasion apparently showed that a gentlemanly acceptance of responsibility lived on in British politics. American commentators have admired the acceptance of personal responsibility that Carrington and his deputies displayed, contrasting it unfavourably with the behaviour of some of their own officials during scandals such as Iran–Contra. Was it all quite as glorious as it seemed?

The aftermath of the Falklands War provided one of the rare opportunities to see the workings of British government in detail (Franks Report, 1983). The Prime Minister had promised that after the war there would be a full inquiry to find out whether the invasion of the islands could have been prevented. It was widely known that the Labour Government of James Callaghan had deployed naval forces to the South Atlantic during an earlier crisis, and although in fact the Argentine Government had not known of this deployment, it had been remembered as an example of successful deterrence. If, it was argued, the Thatcher Government had acted with greater vigour earlier in the crisis, for example by deploying naval forces to the South Atlantic, the Argentine invasion could have been deterred and British and Argentine lives saved. A committee of Privy Councillors, from a variety of backgrounds (former Labour and Conservative politicians, former senior civil servants etc.), under the chairmanship of Lord Franks, examined in detail the crisis until the outbreak of war in order to determine who was responsible for the failure to prevent the invasion.

The Franks Report illustrated clearly the responsibility of Foreign Office ministers for British policy on the Falklands during the lengthy negotiations between Britain and Argentina over the future of the islands. Ministers had developed no diplomatic strategy with any hope of success, because they were trapped between the Argentine demands for sovereignty over the islands, the islanders' refusal to pass under Argentine sovereignty and the strong support for the islanders' cause that existed on both sides of the House of Commons. The all-party support for the Falkland Islanders was displayed passionately in December 1980 when a then junior Foreign Office minister, Nicholas Ridley, made a statement that appeared to countenance transferring sovereignty over the islands to Argentina, in return for guarantees that the islanders could preserve their way of life. The rough ride that Ridley received convinced ministers that they could not meet Argentine aspirations over sovereignty. Yet the constant pressure to restrict government spending and the wish of the Ministry of Defence to concentrate military resources within the NATO area, left the islands defenceless. British foreign policy drifted along, with neither a diplomatic solution in mind nor military plans in place to resist an invasion. Foreign Office ministers hoped that something would turn up, or that negotiations with Argentina could somehow be continued more or less indefinitely.

Ministers could not blame the government machine for their problems. The Franks Committee found (para. 284) that 'On every occasion that a new government – or new Ministers – came into office a full range of policy options was put before them. On every occasion Ministers made a decision of policy and chose to seek a negotiated settlement that would be acceptable to Argentina and to the Islanders.' Foreign Office officials had not tried to pursue a policy of their own. If the Argentine invasion marked a failure of British policy (and in fact the Franks Committee concluded that 'we would not be justified in attaching any blame to the present Government for the Argentine Junta's decision to commit its act of unprovoked aggression' (para. 339)), the blame would appear to fall directly on the Foreign Office ministers who resigned.

What, however of the Prime Minister? At first sight, the Franks Report completely exonerated her of any blame. Indeed, as the crisis worsened in early March 1982, the Prime Minister seemed more alert to the developments than her Foreign Office ministers. After the failure of talks with Argentina in New York in April, the Argentine Government adopted a more aggressive approach. This was reported by the British Embassy in Buenos Aires in a cable sent to London on 3 March, which was seen by the Prime Minister and annotated 'we must make contingency plans'. On 8 March her private secretary wrote to the Foreign Office reporting the Prime Minister's comment; a copy was sent to the Ministry of Defence. The letter suggested that a report on contingency plans could be brought to the Defence Overseas Committee by the Foreign Secretary. On 8 March the Prime Minister also spoke to the Minister of Defence, John Nott, asking how long it would take British warships to reach the Falklands. The Ministry of Defence replied on 12 March saying it would take twenty days.

Yet the Prime Minister's personal alertness did not translate into effective use of the machinery of government. The meeting of the Defence Committee that the Prime Minister's secretary anticipated in his letter never took place. In spite of considerable evidence reported to London of the possibility of the use of force by Argentina against British personnel on the island of South Georgia and against the patrol ship *HMS Endurance*, no warships were sent to the South Atlantic. Not until hours before the invasion did ministers realize the likelihood, although in all fairness it should be noted that the Argentine decision to invade was not finalized until 31 March or even 1 April, the day before the actual invasion (paras. 264–6). However, the crucial failings to pursue the Prime Minister's concern in early March replicated a wider inability within the Government to come to terms with the Falklands problem. One crucial encouragement to the Argentines to pursue sovereignty had been the eagerness of the Ministry of Defence to withdraw the patrol ship *HMS Endurance*. The incompatibility of the planned withdrawal of *Endurance* and the firm diplomatic rejection of Argentine demands was left unresolved, even though the Foreign Secretary forcefully drew the contradiction to the attention of the Ministry of Defence.

Thus the acceptance of responsibility for the failure by the Foreign Office ministers to prevent the Argentine invasion masked the failure by the Prime Minister to accept responsibility for a broader failure in the conduct of the Government. The important interdepartmental dispute between the Defence Ministry and the Foreign Office was not resolved properly; the Defence Committee that could have been assembled in hours was never called to make the contingency plans that the Prime Minister knew to be necessary. Thatcher's leadership in the war dispelled any chance that she would be held accountable politically for what was in fact her failure to operate properly the machinery of government for which she was responsible.

Westland

The Westland crisis, a political pantomime staged before and after Christmas 1985, was probably the moment of greatest political danger for Thatcher before her downfall (Defence Committee, 1986; Hennessy, 1986b; Ingham, 1991). The crisis comprised several elements.

The first element in the crisis was the Westland helicopter company. Like many parts of British industry, the company had a proud history, but was unable to compete adequately in world markets. The company sought a partner. Two possibilities presented themselves. The first was a bid from United Technologies, the owners of the American helicopter company Sikorski. Sikorski, the largest helicopter company in the world, provided the safest option for the Westland shareholders because of its dominance in the field. The second option was to accept a bid from a European consortium built around Fiat, the owners of an Italian helicopter firm, Aosta. The European consortium offered Westland less safety but more of an opportunity to survive as a recognizable continuation of Westland, as opposed to being submerged into the giant United Technologies' helicopter arm, Sikorski. The European option was less safe because it was a less permanent, less defined commercial unit than United Technologies.

The second element in the crisis was a profound disagreement about the issue within Thatcher's Cabinet. The Secretary for Trade and Industry, Leon Brittan, represented the Thatcherite orthodoxy on such issues. The future of Westland was a matter for the shareholders of the company; it was up to the shareholders to decide to whom to sell their company. Brittan had Thatcher's strong support for his policy. The Defence Secretary Michael Heseltine saw things very differently. He was much less convinced than Brittan or Thatcher of the reliability of free markets as guarantors of industrial development. Heseltine was also as Defence Secretary anxious to preserve a European helicopter industry so that Britain (and the other European nations) should not be totally dependent on the United States. Thatcher, much keener on the American alliance than on the European Community, could see little point in such concerns. After all, if Britain bought its submarine-launched nuclear missiles from the United States, what significance would it have that Americans owned Britain's helicopter company?

The third element in the crisis was Heseltine's determination. Most of Thatcher's ministers showed a willingness to cave in to pressure from the Prime Minister, and often tried hard to anticipate her wishes. Heseltine in contrast was determined to fight his case all the way to the Cabinet and to the final decision of the Westland shareholders. In addition to political assets, such as his great popularity with the extraparliamentary Conservative Party and his following on the back-benches, Heseltine's position *vis-à-*

vis Westland gave him great influence. For Westland was not just another company that sold its products to a variety of customers. Westland had in effect only one customer, the Government, and, in particular, the Ministry of Defence. The attitude of the Government towards the company was therefore unusually important. In particular, if, as Heseltine suggested might occur, the Government were less willing to purchase from Westland if it accepted the American bid, the prospects of the company and its future value would be very severely affected.

There is nothing extraordinary in conflicts between ministers in British government. Several aspects of the fight between Heseltine on the one hand and Thatcher and Brittan on the other were, however, most unusual. The first was that Heseltine felt that he was denied proper access to the Cabinet or even its committees to make his case. This claim was energetically denied by Thatcher, who argued that Heseltine merely lacked support in the Cabinet for his views; it is hard to know where the truth lies. However, Heseltine's belief that proper procedures had not been followed in the Cabinet made him feel entitled to refuse to accept the normal conventions – that whatever their private disagreements members of the Cabinet do not feud with each other publicly. Heseltine also felt exonerated from breaking normal conventions by Thatcher's practice of using her press secretary, Bernard Ingham, not only to explain the Government's views and policies, a job he was employed to do, but also to brief journalists to write disparaging stories about members of the Cabinet who had disagreed with or otherwise displeased her.

The final element in the crisis was the use of civil servants in the Department of Trade and Industry and the Ministry of Defence to help their ministers manoeuvre for position within the Cabinet by briefing journalists on the supposedly confidential discussions going on between ministers and between the Government and Westland executives. This process reached a climax with the leaking of a letter from the Solicitor General to Heseltine designed to rein in Heseltine's campaign for the European option. The Law Officers (the Attorney General and Solicitor General) had been asked by Brittan and Thatcher to assess the compatibility of Heseltine's letters to Westland with the Government's policy of non-intervention. The Law Officers reported that Heseltine was out of line with the policy of non-intervention. In order either to humiliate Heseltine, or, according to Thatcher and Brittan, to prevent Heseltine's erroneous account of the Government's policy from influencing the meeting of Westland shareholders deciding on the company's future, the Department of Trade and Industry's information officer, Colette Bowe, was told to leak the letter to the Press Association.

The Thatcher Government had been particularly assiduous in prosecuting civil servants who leaked information contrary to the Official Secrets Act. There was no doubt that the letter from the Solicitor General should have been kept secret under the Official Secrets Act. Indeed, there was a particularly strong convention, derived perhaps from notions of attorney–client privilege, that advice from the Law Officers to the cabinet was never published. Who, then, had told the DTI officials to break the law and the rules that so clearly prohibited publication? One answer was the Secretary of Trade and Industry: Leon Brittan accepted responsibility and resigned. But there was no doubt that the decision to leak the document had not been his alone; the DTI information officers had consulted Downing Street officials before they leaked the advice of the Law Officers. Downing Street officials Bernard Ingham and Charles Powell, both civil servants and, in Powell's case, a career civil servant, had approved the decision to leak it. Had they given this approval on their own initiative, or had Thatcher herself made the decision? If the decision was Thatcher's, then she should resign just like Brittan. If the officials had acted on their own initiatives, then they had surely committed a great error and should be subject to disciplinary proceedings.

In the event, Thatcher did not resign and the officials were not disciplined. In a sense, therefore, no one was held to account for what on the face of it was a major break with the rules of secrecy and confidentiality so dear to the Thatcher Government. Thatcher argued that it was all somehow a misunderstanding, 'a genuine difference in understanding between officials as to what exactly was being sought and what was being given' (*House of Commons Debates*, 27 January 1986, p. 655). How Powell and Ingham could conceivably have misunderstood what was involved is hard to imagine. They were never asked, however, as the Thatcher Government refused to allow them to be questioned by the select committees that subsequently held inquiries into the Westland affair. Accountability, it was argued, would be through ministers, not directly the responsibility of officials.

What came out of the Westland affair? Unease about the fact that civil servants such as Bowe had acted – under instructions – in a manner that clearly conflicted with the law, rules and norms sparked a debate about whether or not civil servants ever had a greater responsibility than to obey ministers. Westland was not the first time this issue had arisen during the Thatcher years. The prosecution of Clive Ponting, pressed with enthusiasm by the Government he had embarrassed, was based on the premise that he had no right to divulge secret material in order to show that the Government was lying to Parliament, that he had no duty to the constitutional order that was higher than his accountability to his minister. Naturally, Ponting disagreed (Ponting, 1985; Norton-Taylor, 1985).

The ultimate answer from the head of the civil service, Sir Robert Armstrong, approved by the Prime Minister, was that he had no such right or duty. Civil servants are servants of the Crown; the Crown is in all practical matters synonymous with the government of the day. Civil servants exist to assist ministers. If asked to help in a manner they dislike, they should appeal for guidance to superiors, their permanent secretaries or the head of the civil service, who would raise the matter with the prime minister. Whether the Armstrong doctrine was adequate may be doubted, particularly given the personalities involved. Armstrong himself, after all, had been forced to confess to an Australian court, during an attempt to prevent a former secret service agent from publishing his memoirs in Australia, that he had been 'economical with the truth' (Turnbull, 1988). Thatcher's own role in the Westland affair had been exactly the bone of contention, so that an appeal to her by the head of the civil service would have done little other than clarify her responsibility in the case. The only gain for accountability in the affair was the modest triumph for select committees in forcing the Government to retreat from its plan to restrict further their ability to interrogate civil servants rather than ministers.

So in spite of the resignation of Leon Brittan, the scapegoat of the affair, the Westland affair did little to bolster accountability. Neither the role of the Prime Minister herself nor the conduct of her staff were examined satisfactorily. A government that had relentlessly pursued civil servants who compromised the British obsession with secrecy had flagrantly broken the laws and rules on the instructions of the Prime Minister's office, while she proclaimed that it was all just a misunderstanding.

The Disappearing Terrorists

British ministers are not expected to be administrative geniuses. They are, however, supposed to prevent rank incompetence in their departments.

An example of such incompetence occurred in July 1991. Two Irish Republican Army terrorists awaiting trial for acts of violence were detained in Brixton prison. On their way back to the cells from Mass in the prison chapel, they produced a gun, took a warden hostage, climbed the walls and hijacked a passing car. For good measure they shot the hapless driver of the car they had stolen, an unfortunate member of the general public unlucky enough to be driving by.

No one expects a home secretary to be held personally accountable for all prison escapes. In this case, however, there were clear grounds for holding Kenneth Baker accountable for what had happened, under Crichel Down doctrine. The Chief Inspector of Prisons, Judge Tumim, had explicitly warned the Home Secretary five months earlier that Brixton Prison '. . . did not have the physical defences necessary for the job of containing high risk prisoners' (*House of Commons Debates*, 8 July 1991). This naturally prompted the questions, duly asked by the opposition spokesman, Roy Hattersley, 'Why were men on terrorist charges not moved out of the prison at once? Why is the Home Secretary now taking action that he should have taken last year and how does he justify such incompetence?' (*House of Commons Debates*, 8 July 1991, col. 650). The explicit warnings that Judge Tumim had given the Home Secretary seemed to elevate the escape from the category of an error by officials of which the Home Secretary could not have been expected to be aware to a matter of direct ministerial responsibility. Inevitably, the ghost of Crichel Down appeared. The Labour MP David Winnick asked Baker, 'What does he think that Sir Thomas Dugdale [the Minister of Agriculture who resigned over the Crichel Down affair] would have done if he had been Home Secretary? Given all the incompetence of which we have heard today, does the Home Secretary feel that he has some responsibility for what has happened?' (*House of Commons Debates*, 8 July 1991, col. 657).

Baker had two replies to his critics. The first was to argue that ministers are in fact responsible only for policy, not administration. He contended that '. . . where prisoners are kept is the direct responsibility of the governor.' In reply to another question, Baker again argued that '. . . the Home Secretary is responsible for policy in prison matters. The administration, development and running of the prisons are the responsibility of the director general and of individual governors.' (*House of Commons Debates*, 8 July 1991, col. 657.) Students of administration will notice at once the implausibility of this separation of policy and administration. A decision to hold terrorists in an insecure prison in spite of warnings about the prison's inadequacy is every bit as much a policy decision as a general policy statement that terrorists should not be allowed to escape.

Baker's second reply was that the level of incompetence in the prison service was so grotesquely high that he could not be held responsible. For it emerged after the storm in Parliament that the prison service had been warned by police or intelligence sources that the terrorists in Brixton were planning to escape, were trying to obtain a gun and had identified chapel services as the opportunity for their escape (Tumim, 1991). This warning had not been passed to ministers. Disciplinary charges were made against the head of the relevant division at Brixton and four prison officers on duty at the time; the governor retired early. In the event, however, the disciplinary charges were dropped or dismissed and many felt the former governor had been made a scapegoat. Baker himself was not held responsible for the massive incompetence displayed. According to *The Times*, he thought of resigning but decided not to on the grounds that the escape was an 'operational failure', not a matter on which to criticize a minister (*The Times*, 6 August 1991).

The most striking feature of the episode was that few expected Baker to resign for the mistakes made by his Department, including the mistake of confining terrorists in Brixton prison, the dangers of which he had been warned of. Hattersley, according to *The Times*, thought after all that Baker was right not to resign and the paper's political correspondent clearly shared such an indulgent view. 'In practice few political resignations these days take place on grounds of policy failure.' Resignations are likely to reflect the revelation more of sexual peccadilloes than of incompetence as a minister. 'Few politicians will have seriously expected Mr Baker to resign over the Brixton breakout.' (*The Times*, 6 August 1991.)

From Crichel Down to Next Steps

The replies that Kenneth Baker gave to his critics over the Brixton breakout were closely in line with the doctrine that was evolving over Next Steps agencies. These were parts of the civil service that had previously been integral parts of ministries, but were given quasi-autonomous status. Agencies were to be given general direction by ministers but considerable latitude in carrying out general policies. The relationship between agency and department would be set out in a framework document. Goals for an agency would be negotiated each year between it and its department. The chief executive of the agency would be responsible for the attainment of the goals and would be eligible for bonuses if they were exceeded; alternatively the chief executive could lose bonuses or even be dismissed if the agency failed to attain its goals (House of Commons Library Research Division, 1989; National Audit Office, 1989; Hennessy, 1991; Kemp, 1990; Flynn, Gray and Jenkins, 1990). Although the prison service had not been turned into a Next Steps agency formally (it has been now), Baker had made it known that he planned to treat it as such.

In fact, the Brixton escape pointed to several of the problems that occurred in trying to combine the Next Steps ideas with the tradition of ministerial accountability. As we have seen, the distinction between policy (made by ministers) and administration (entrusted to agencies) is not made easily. The decision not to move terrorists from Brixton in spite of warnings of the risks of escape was every bit as much a policy decision as a ministerial announcement that prisoners were to be given more education. The balancing of the advantages of not moving the prisoners (such as ready access to their lawyers and the proximity to the Central Criminal Court where they would appear) with the disadvantage (the risk that they would escape) was precisely a policy decision. Moreover, once Baker had refused to accept responsibility, no one else could be held publicly accountable. Not only were none of the officials involved 'convicted' in disciplinary hearings, but those hearings were themselves held in secret. The motorist shot in the incident can scarcely have felt that he was given a complete account of why his misfortune had occurred.

In fact, Next Steps agencies will be even less accountable than the prison service was in the Brixton breakout. Ministers have refused to answer parliamentary questions about their view of the day-to-day activities of Next Steps agencies. An MP who feels that a constituent has been mistreated by an agency is told to take the complaint to its chief executive and not to bother the minister. The government resisted until 1992 demands that the replies of chief executives to MPs be published in *Hansard*, thereby making it easier for MPs to know if their complaints about agencies were part of a general pattern and not isolated errors. Chief executives of agencies will appear before select committees, it is true, but the committees will no doubt be told by them that any failings in their agencies are the results of policy directions over which they have no control. On the other hand, ministers may use chief executives to avoid blame for policy failures that should fall on themselves. Ministers can blame chief executives for unpopular policies that are flawed in their design, not their implementation. Thus in 1994 the chief executive of the Child Support Agency was forced to leave her post early after MPs and members of the public had criticized the zeal with which the Agency extracted money from divorced fathers. Yet these problems were due primarily to the grossly excessive targets the Treasury imposed on the CSA in order to save the state the costs of child support by having fathers pay instead. The CSA had been forced into drastic action as it tried to implement the impossible policy goal it had been given (*Financial Times*, 'Child Support Chief Quits Post Early', 5 September 1994).

It might be supposed that the Next Steps agencies would have been the object of vigorous criticism by defenders of parliamentary sovereignty. In fact, the agencies have been almost universally acclaimed; the relevant opposition spokesman made clear that had Labour won the 1992 election, the creation of Next Steps agencies would have continued. It is easy to see why the

Next Steps idea appealed to ministers and senior civil servants. Ministers, particularly in large, sprawling departments like the Home Office, dread that their reputations will be damaged or destroyed by crises or disasters that in their view emerge from nowhere, but for which they are nominally responsible. The culture of the higher civil service in Britain has never prized attention to administrative detail; senior civil servants welcome Next Steps as it frees them to work on the aspects of the job (working on politically charged policy questions with ministers) that appeal to them the most.

It is more puzzling why backbench MPs, including the Select Committee on the Treasury and Civil Service, have shown such enthusiasm for a reform that reduces their ability to hold ministers responsible. Some of the reasons for this apparent anomaly are not strictly related to the issue of ministerial accountability. The Next Steps idea was ably presented by the civil servant chiefly responsible for the programme, Sir Peter Kemp, as the answer to the problem of securing greater efficiency in the civil service. Conservative MPs could view the agencies as the nearest one could come realistically to handing government over to the private sector. The agencies, headed perhaps by managers of proven ability from the private sector rather than by civil servants who have spent their careers in the public sector, were necessarily inefficient. Labour MPs could be reminded that the Next Steps idea had its origins in the Fulton Committee's report, the product of a period of Labour government. The creation of the new agencies would remove the dead hand of the administrative class civil servants from the practical tasks of administration; Eton and Oxford would give way to technocrats.

Yet of greater significance than these factors was the fatalism of back-benchers about ministerial accountability. Next Steps was not seen as reducing their ability to hold ministers significantly to account because they had such limited ability in the first place. At least under the Next Steps system MPs could gain some idea of the general instructions ministers gave agencies and could obtain information on the agencies' successes or failures in meeting objectives. Next Steps was greeted with almost universal approval by back-benchers because they had so little confidence left in their own abilities to hold ministers accountable. Like the political correspondent of *The Times* they believed that nowadays ministers do not resign over policy failures or the errors of their departments. The formalization in the Next Steps Programme of the distinction between ministerial responsibility for policy-making and agencies' responsibilities for implementation merely codified existing practice. Within a few years, the loss of accountability to MPs for day-to-day decisions was becoming ever more apparent. In March 1993, MPs were told that Home Office ministers would no longer deal with correspondence about the daily management of prisons or prisoners' individual cases. When an MP wrote to the Secretary of State for Health about decisions by a Health Authority not to provide treatment for a constituent, the Secretary passed the letter to the Authority but refused to reply herself (*Independent*, 31 March 1993).

Iraqgate and the Scott Inquiry

Further evidence that ministerial responsibility is at best a tenuous doctrine in Whitehall today came from the Scott Inquiry in 1993 and 1994. The inquiry by Lord Justice Scott was established by the Government after the acquittal of executives of a British company, Matrix Churchill, prosecuted for evading controls on the export to Iraq of arms and equipment suitable for manufacturing arms. The executives of the company were able to show that they had cooperated closely with MI6, the British intelligence service, because the trial judge set aside the attempts of the Government to suppress the evidence that supported this defence. Quite scandalously, four ministers, three of them very senior, had signed Public Interest Certificates asking the judge not to allow the defence access to material that demonstrated the innocence of the accused executives. Taking advantage of the wide degree of latitude in the terms of his inquiry, Justice Scott probed not only the willingness of government ministers to see innocent people sent to jail but the entire handling of arms sales to Iraq.

One of the first points to emerge was that ministers with the full cooperation of civil servants had concealed from Parliament a change in British policy on arms sales to Iraq. In 1988, government ministers had decided to allow a wider range of equipment and materials to be sold to Iraq. Civil servants drew up replies to parliamentary questions on arms sales to Iraq that deliberately obscured the fact that the policy had been changed, implying that previous restrictions on arms and equipment sales remained in place. One of the junior ministers involved in these decisions, Alan Clark, admitted that the Government had been 'economical with the actualité' (*Daily Telegraph*, 14 December 1993). (This remark was itself a reference to misleading testimony that was given in 1986 by the then head of the civil service, Sir Robert Armstrong, to an Australian court that was considering whether or not to ban the publication of memoirs written by a former British agent, Peter Wright (Turnbull, 1988); Armstrong had been forced to admit that he had been 'economical with the truth'.)

Whether ministers (aided by civil servants) had actually deceived Parliament could be debated. It was possible to argue that the relaxation in export controls was a relaxation in the stringency with which the policy was administered, not a change in the policy itself. There could be no doubt, however, that the Government had been eager to change its policy in order to assist British exporters, yet equally eager to avoid admitting publicly a softening of policy towards Iraq, for fear of criticism; after all, Iraq had just used poison gas against the Kurds ('Foreign Office "Lied Persistently on Arms"', *Guardian*, 16 July 1993). Revealingly, Justice Scott was attacked in confidential briefings by ministers and civil servants as naive and not understanding Whitehall for his failure to appreciate that the whole point of answering parliamentary questions is to avoid giving Parliament any damaging information. As one official told the *Financial Times*, 'Scott does not seem to understand what I would call a principle of government . . . This is that you don't tell a lie, but you don't have to open up completely.' Another doubted whether the judge 'really understands about the day to day business of government where things, if not quite murky, are not clear cut' (Jimmy Burns and Robert Preston, 'Iraq inquiry judge examines a very murky crystal ball', *Financial Times*, 13 September 1993). Eager to help British companies export to Iraq but aware that this trade would be halted if it was out in the open, a Foreign Office official wrote in a memorandum,

I accept the recommendation that the licenses should not for the moment be revoked, but *if it becomes public knowledge* that the tools are to be used to make munitions, deliveries would have *to stop at once*. Once the UN embargo is adopted *they will probably have to stop*. The companies should be warned of the falling guillotine *and urged to produce and ship as fast as they can.* (John Plender, 'Struggle to Spike a Smoking Gun', *Financial Times*, 12 November 1992, emphasis added.)

As Alan Clark told the Scott Inquiry, 'The House of Commons is very volatile and you get rows and scenes and oo-er.' Clark added that there was 'a corporate convention' that 'you try not to invite too much intrusion' (*Daily Telegraph*, 14 December 1993). As Anthony Sampson argued, it seemed that in the case of export controls on Iraq, ministers and civil servants went beyond what Clark termed 'not inviting intrusion'. Sampson argued that Scott's report 'will provide a unique anatomy of Whitehall that will challenge all our assumptions about democracy. For his inquiry addresses the central question for ordinary citizens and voters: can they trust their elected rulers to tell the truth? And the answer is a clear no.' (*Evening Standard*, 14 December 1993.)

Ministerial Accountability in the 1990s

Is ministerial accountability dead? If so, the consequences for British democracy are severe, for as we have emphasized, it remains a central organizing concept for the British executive as well as a key element in the structure of British democracy.

Those looking for comfort can point to the fact that in some of the episodes we have examined, ministers did resign. The Westland affair ended with the political stage looking like the final scene of *Hamlet* with the 'corpses' of ministers strewn around. The Falklands invasion was followed by the resignations of Carrington and two of his junior ministers. Even Baker was wounded politically and though he survived the immediate crisis of the Brixton breakout, his time in the Cabinet was soon over. Developments largely outside our focus, such as reforms in Parliament, have arguably improved the ability of the individual MP to hold ministers to account better than ever for the behaviour of their departments. Ferdinand Mount, for example, has argued that as a 'remonstrator' complaining about the treatment of constituents,

> The modern MP equals if not surpasses any of his predecessors; backed by the inflammatory power of the modern media, strengthened by the ammunition provided by the new array of Select Committees (now covering virtually the whole range of departmental activities), he has a variety of opportunities to ventilate the grievances of his constituents and those of other people and interests; he can put an oral question, hand in a written one, demand an adjournment debate, weave the rehearsal of the grievance into his speech . . . : he can buttonhole the Minister in the lobby, or write to him at the Ministry, or suborn one of the Minister's quiverful of junior Ministers or his parliamentary private secretary. *Meanwhile back at the Ministry, the civil servants know that to deal promptly and helpfully with any problem arising out of Parliament is the surest way to the Minister's heart; if they keep him out of Commons scrapes, he will be all the readier to listen to their advice on policy.* Thus what might be called the 'machinery of remonstration' is pretty well greased these days, and this is not to be undervalued. . . . Backbenchers are never satisfied but, by all historical and comparative standards, their opportunities to ventilate, and with luck, to remedy their constituents' grievances are far from dusty. If Parliament has declined, it is not in this respect. (Mount, 1992, emphasis added.)

However, even though ministerial accountability survives, it survives with gaping holes. One of the most gaping is the accountability of the prime minister. Inevitably one stage removed from the action that takes place in an individual ministry, recent prime ministers have been particularly successful in evading responsibility for the failings of their governments. The invasion of the Falkland Islands reflected not only errors of judgement of Foreign Office ministers but also and more importantly the need to reconcile conflicting government policies and objectives. A diplomatic stance that was either determined or, less charitably, obstinate coexisted with a military policy that failed to give adequate support for this policy; indeed, it invited aggression by such displays of lack of resolve as the announcement of the intention to withdraw *HMS Endurance*. Yet the Prime Minister escaped serious criticism for a failure to coordinate policies that could be only hers. Similarly in the Westland affair, the Prime Minister either flouted convention and law by authorizing the publication of confidential advice from the Law Officers or, if the action was undertaken by her staff acting alone, failed to discipline them adequately. Again, however, only a minister, Leon Brittan, paid a political price for the Westland affair.

The second hole in ministerial responsibility concerns the status of civil servants. Episodes such as the Brixton breakout demonstrate that contemporary British politicians are fully willing to let individual civil servants take the blame publicly for mistakes that departments have made. The growth of the Next Steps agencies will strengthen this development as chief executives, not ministers, are held accountable for errors in administration and, when it suits ministers, for the consequences of government policies. This may seem both inevitable and desirable. It is inevitable that ministers presiding over vast bureaucracies should refuse to accept blame for actions that they do not know about, and it is desirable that the people who are in practice responsible for errors should be seen to be so. However, civil servants are also entitled to feel that if they are to be held responsible, they should have the right to make decisions and policies. If, for example, individual prison governors are to be held responsible for terrorist escapes, perhaps those governors should have the right to determine where and how those prisoners are detained. If bureaucrats are in practice held accountable for mistakes, they must have the power to avoid those mistakes.

Substituting the accountability of individual officials for the responsibility of ministers may be sensible, but it also undermines the authority of the minister. One of the underpinnings of ministerial power in Whitehall was the doctrine that the minister might be held to account for actions taken in his name. If that doctrine has been weakened and replaced with a belief that officials will be held to account instead, the importance of officials deferring to ministers is also reduced. Ministerial responsibility was similar to the practices of indigenous people that intrigued anthropologists. At face value, they made little sense; at a deeper level, the practices served a useful function in the society. The hidden function of ministerial responsibility was to buttress the authority of ministers over the bureaucracy, and the refusal of ministers to accept their traditional role in the tribal ceremony weakens their authority in the long term.

Many of the civil servants we have interviewed sense that the doctrines of responsibility and accountability have changed. The once veiled civil servants have been pulled out into the public arena. Regan notes that as early as the beginning of the 1980s, civil servants were appearing before select committees more often than ministers were; in the four sessions 1979–83 inclusive, 1,312 civil servants made 1,779 appearances before select committees whereas 171 ministers made only 230 (Regan, 1986). Some civil servants welcome this development, while others deplore it. One of our respondents sensed that civil servants had entered a 'no win' situation in which they were no longer shielded by the doctrine of ministerial responsibility from public criticism, but were also unable to defend themselves publicly and forcefully. Scrutiny by parliamentary select committees seemed to this official to undermine completely the basis on which the British executive branch has been organized.

> If officials are to be answerable not to their ministers but to Parliament . . . because that means that ministers will be responsible for their own actions but not for the advice they receive . . . officials will always be looking over their shoulders at how it will look and how their actions will look when revealed in a public hearing in a select committee. The bonds between the legislature and the executive will change in a fundamental way, which may be the way the thing has got to go but it shouldn't happen by default. (Interview, 1989.)

But other, perhaps younger civil servants did not see increased scrutiny by outsiders as so threatening.

> I think my generation actually welcomes the chance to appear and talk to significant outside interests. If it were a case where we expressed a personal view, we would make it clear. . . . Particularly when I was . . . [he named a previous post he had held] I welcomed the fact that if things went wrong, the media immediately got onto me rather than the minister. So I would do the interviews and assuage the public fire. (Interview, 1989.)

Others simply come to terms with what they see as an important change, but one that it is pointless either to welcome or to decry. '. . . it is a cultural change, I've had to come to terms with going and giving evidence in select committees. Ten years ago that would have been exceptional. Now Whitehall officials know they must be prepared to appear and account for the policy.' (Interview, 1989.)

Conclusion

We agree with our interviewee who argued that if there is to be a major change in the doctrines of accountability in Britain, 'it shouldn't happen by default'. Yet there are clearly so many forces operating on the doctrine today that it cannot survive in its old form. The demands by select committees for more accountability to Parliament by civil servants for the policies they operate and the challenge to ministerial responsibility for the routine implementation of policies that underlies the Next Steps programme are immediate forces for change. But beyond these short-term forces for change lies the problem that has confronted the British executive at least since the creation of the welfare state by the Attlee Government, and possibly before that; large-scale government in Britain, as in most other democracies, was grafted onto a pre-existing set of institutions, institutions that had not been intended to carry the burden now placed on them. The relationship between bureaucrats and politicians in Britain had been defined in the nineteenth century when the government's domestic responsibilities were fewer and smaller. By the 1990s, as we saw in the reaction to the Brixton prison escapes, senior politicians, including an opposition spokesman with an interest in arguing the opposite, believed that it was unrealistic to hold ministers responsible for the efficacy of their departments' work, even when they had been warned of a problem, in this case by the Inspector of Prisons. The credibility of traditional notions of accountability had almost vanished.

Yet if there is no doctrine of accountability working in reality, a huge hole exists in the practice of British democracy. In an excellent recent study published after we had completed our research Diana Woodehouse reached a similar conclusion; current

notions of ministerial accountability in Britain are hopelessly confused and imperfectly followed (Woodehouse, 1994). If ministers
are not responsible to Parliament for their departments, who is
responsible, and to whom? It is alarming indeed to think that if
it is the sheer size and complexity of the state that has undermined traditional notions of accountability, those doctrines have
yet to be replaced with an alternative.

8

The Post-Whitehall Era

The Core of the Whitehall System

It is useful to remind ourselves of what constituted the core of
the Whitehall system. Its crucial component was the belief that
democratically elected but experienced politicians should make
policy as a result of collective deliberation, and that they should
be assisted in developing and implementing policies by a corps of
professional, permanent and non-partisan civil servants, selected
on merit and inculcated with a belief that they should serve faith-
fully any constitutionally appointed government. We have come
to doubt whether either of these descriptions of British government are accurate today, though we leave as an open question for
others to answer how closely British government ever approximated to the text-book image of the Whitehall model, particularly
with regard to collective decision making.

The suspicion that British government is not as much an exercise in collective decision making as text books have suggested
is not new. Mackintosh (1977) and Crossman (1972) had long
argued that Britain had prime-ministerial, not cabinet government, three decades ago. Foley has more recently suggested
(1993) that we have witnessed the rise of the British republic, led
by an elected president. The fact that the debate about prime-
ministerial versus cabinet power is so old is in itself a useful
antidote to the view that the emphasis on the centralization of
decision making in Britain is merely a reaction to a most unusual
and remarkable politician, Margaret Thatcher.

We would argue that the Government created under the leadership of John Major, explicitly designed to be the antithesis of
Thatcher's leadership, continued to show many of the signs and
deleterious consequences of centralized decision making; for all

the brave talk of the collegial character of John Major's Government, the policy of clinging tenaciously to an indefensible exchange rate level within the ERM was made with little deliberation with colleagues, just as Thatcher had made the decision to cling to the poll tax. Indeed, the failure of Major's prime-ministership served to underline how strong the expectation of centralized leadership had become. *The Economist* for once reflected a common perception in Britain when it asked why there was a 'hole in the middle' of government and decided, after discussing a number of possibilities including the performance of the cabinet secretary, Sir Robin Butler, that the answer was Major himself (*The Economist*, 7 December 1993). The British cabinet system had apparently become as dependent as the American executive branch on strong leadership from a chief executive. The general commitment to *collegiality* in the Major Government did not produce *collective decision making*. In the words of a Cabinet Office official, the members of Major's Government discussed issues with each other more frequently than members of Thatcher's but they did not *decide* issues together any more frequently.

We agree with many of the arguments advanced by others to explain the rise of prime-ministerial power. The rise of the career politician, whose importance has been emphasized by King, has indeed significantly affected the balance of power between a prime minister and his or her colleagues (King, 1981). Politicians who are desperately anxious for office are inevitably eager to please the person who has the power to promote or dismiss them, to a degree that people who are less zealous for career advancement are not. One of the many peculiarities of the diaries of Alan Clarke, a Conservative minister of the 1980s (Clarke, 1993) is the lust for office they display in a man apparently incapable of sustained and disciplined interest in government work and who had many other interests on which to fall back; the lust for office of his colleagues from less privileged backgrounds must have been even greater.

The balance of our explanation for the greater centralization in British government is more an institutional or structural argument than one based on the personalities of prime ministers or ministers. Our argument is that the traditional strength of the Treasury in Britain was reinforced by the centralization of decision making in British government as a consequence of both the strengthening of the role of the Treasury and of the governance strategy that dominated late twentieth-century politics in Britain and other Whitehall model systems. The increase in the power of the Treasury reflected the need to control public expenditure in the context of recurring economic crises. It had always been powerful, and in a sense the increase in its importance was its undoing; just as in previous eras war had become too important to be left to the generals, so economic policy became too important to leave to Treasury officials or ministers. We mean this to be more than an amusing aside. The primacy of economic management in the hierarchy of state purposes today can be compared only with the primacy of diplomacy and war for eighteenth- and nineteenth-century states. As the Treasury has always realized, however, economic management takes the Treasury into the work of every single department in a way that war mobilization influenced other policy areas only in the total wars of the twentieth century. It is conceivable – indeed it happens – that a prime minister (Harold Wilson) can tell a home secretary (Roy Jenkins) to get on with his work, and leave him in peace: '. . . there were very few policies that he wished to impose. He left me remarkably free. In making Home Office decisions I hardly thought of 10 Downing Street as a factor.' (Jenkins, 1991, p. 391.) It is inconceivable that *any* modern prime minister could relate similarly to a modern chancellor. As Thatcher insisted on reiterating to the considerable irritation of her chancellor Nigel Lawson, the prime minister, not the chancellor, was supreme head of the Treasury (Lawson, 1992, Chapter 31). The Treasury was ultimately an arm of the prime minister. In Chapter 6, we saw that officials share this view.

The centralization of power in government was also strengthened by the governance strategy that centralized power in order to shrink the role of the state, a governance strategy that both preceded and survived Thatcher herself. The pressures from the International Monetary Fund (IMF) (welcomed by the Treasury) on the Labour Government in 1976 began a process of transferring power from spending departments to the Treasury, a Treasury controlled in turn by the prime minister. Thatcher willingly embraced a process of trying to shrink government expenditures that the IMF had imposed on the preceding Labour Government. In the 'liberal' attitude, government programmes were not the expression of collective public purposes but the results of the machinations of interest groups and self-interested bureaucrats. Left to themselves, government departments would inflate the size of their programmes; only a strong centre could curtail the apparently inexorable tendency for the government to claim an ever larger share of the national income (Buchanan and Tullock, 1965).

The tendency towards centralization has been an almost inevitable consequence, then, of the primacy of the economic purposes of the state and of the prevailing governance strategy. Yet centralization in British government, as elsewhere, raises important problems as well as opportunities. Indeed, the belief that British government is characterized by extensive collegial discussion before policy is made may preclude the realization that centralized decision making raises problems in Britain, as in other nations. Precisely because John Major's ministers thought that they had much more collegial decision making than under Margaret Thatcher, they were less likely to demand collective discussion of the wisdom of the commitment to maintain the value of the pound within the ERM even as the costs of that policy overwhelmed every other government policy and destroyed its political standing. The character of the American presidency as a singular office inevitably raises acutely the dangers of the adverse consequences of centralized decision making. However, at least wise Americans know that every president runs the risk of the disadvantageous consequences of centralized decision making, such as excessive power and influence for sycophantic staff. Even wise Britons imagine that they have a system of government that is collegial and collective; they do not realize, therefore, the degree to which their leaders can succumb to some of the same problems as American presidents do.

One of the well-known problems facing the American presidency is its relationship to the permanent government. As we noted at the start of this book, the British model of bureaucratic–political relations is an unusual arrangement that at first sight flew in the face of both social science and the experience of other nations. Ever since Weber drew attention to the problem of the power of the expert, social scientists have doubted the capacity of elected politicians to control expert bureaucrats, who are in theory their servants. The British reliance on a permanent non-partisan civil service conflicts with the main thrust of social science writing on bureaucracy, with its doubts about the policy neutrality and disinterest of bureaucrats. Bureaucrats, according to their critics, mask value judgements as professional judgements, and self-interests in maximizing budgets or payrolls shape their advice. (Niskanen, 1971; Buchanan, 1991; Buchanan and Tullock, 1965).

It is scarcely surprising to social scientists, therefore, that politicians in few countries place as much faith in bureaucrats as do the British. The British system contrasts not only with the patronage system at the top of the executive branch in the United States but also with the continental European practice (as in Germany) of placing senior civil servants in temporary retirement or less controversial posts if a governing party loses power. The Whitehall system in Britain contained many subsidiary features. Civil servants had generalist rather than technical educations, usually from Oxford or Cambridge, moved frequently between different posts and even departments and often had a professional class social background. These characteristics were, however, merely contingent, accidents of British history and culture; the dependence of elected politicians on the non-partisan, permanent civil service was the core of the system that has been exported to many other countries and admired by many non-British scholars.

It is precisely this core that the leaders of Britain's civil servants have been most eager to maintain. Senior civil servants anxiously contest the notion that success in the civil service has become dependent on party loyalty, that politicization has occurred. While accepting readily the appointment of small numbers of political advisers, senior civil servants seek to maintain the near monopoly on giving policy analysis and advice to ministers that they have enjoyed in the past. While this may seem to be a self-interested defence of a privileged role, senior civil servants argue vigorously that this central aspect of the Whitehall model serves politicians well. The permanent, professional non-partisan bureaucracy offers any constitutionally elected government an ability to move to implement its programme in its first months, while an American administration, for example, is still struggling to choose and have confirmed the counterparts of senior civil servants. Moreover, the permanent and professional British civil service has an ability to 'speak truth to power' that advisory systems staffed by ambitious, eager-to-please political appointees with no job security obviously lack; the performance of the White House staff in many modern administrations lends support to this view.

It is easy to construct an argument that this central role of the bureaucracy in the Whitehall model has survived. A temporary disturbance, a 'leadership effect' occurred under the Thatcher Government when the Whitehall model was shaken by the personal style, the assurance, conviction or dogmatism (depending on one's point of view) of Thatcher herself and the policy style she inculcated in the Government. But, in this view, this was, to quote the famously boring headline from *The Times* in the 1930s, a 'Small Earthquake in Chile; Not Many Injured'. The edifice of the Whitehall model was subjected to a small earthquake that has passed; the buildings of Whitehall were shaken but did not fall. The monopoly of the senior civil service on policy advising has been challenged, but its 'market share', to continue the analogy, remains massively high. The Major Government seems more eager than its predecessor for policy ideas from the senior civil service, and by the early 1990s, departments such as Trade and Industry were edging back towards policy approaches, for example a modest intervention in industry that had been repudiated vigorously in the 1980s. Thatcher's departure tested the robustness of the cultural change that had seemed evident in Whitehall in the 1980s. It can be argued that many of the apparently permanent changes of the 1980s proved to be ephemeral while the core of the Whitehall system, the dependence of ministers on a professional, non-partisan civil service for advice, remained intact.

We do not share this view. A whole host of changes, in Christoph's words, prevent Whitehall from going home again (Christoph, 1992).

First, in crucial areas the monopoly of the civil service on advising ministers has been broken. British ministers have become used to the idea that, although civil servants can produce good ideas, there is no reason to listen *only* to civil servants. While right of centre think tanks during the Major Government were rather short of ideas in the 1990s, they had emerged as a permanent part of the British political scene. While British practice remained well short of the American reliance on informal issue networks outside the government for advice, even in areas at the heart of government such as economic strategy, ministers moved away from dependence on the advice of professional civil servants. The constituting of a formal group of outside economic forecasters by the Treasury during the chancellorship of Norman Lamont may be merely an extension of a practice begun by his predecessors – Nigel Lawson characteristically claims to have invented the idea (Lawson, 1992, p. 389) – but there is little doubt that it constitutes a major change from the exclusivity of Treasury advice that characterized the system in the past. Indeed, the progress of Terry Burns from outsider to chief economic adviser to permanent secretary of the Treasury is itself a significant sign of the reduced dependence of ministers on the advice of permanent civil servants.

Second, the machinery by which civil service advice can be contested at the centre, machinery that Thatcher did not originate but developed, remains in place. The mini White House staff that Thatcher utilized – the Policy Unit, the right to have economic and foreign policy advisers in the prime ministers' office – continues under Major and will now be a normal feature of British government, just as political advisers have become a familiar, uncontroversial part of individual departments. The Policy Unit will remain composed of a mixture of outsiders and civil servants. But past experience shows that the civil servants will not always be able to return easily to their former occupations. The most influential members of the Policy Unit under Thatcher progressed via posts with think tanks to the Conservative back benches and political careers; few have found the Policy Unit a base (like a posting to the Cabinet Office or the Treasury) from which to launch a successful civil service career. Whatever their prior occupation, members of the Policy Unit have become the British equivalents of a White House staff, too closely linked to the prime minister and therefore too political to be readily reassimilated into the bureaucracy. Thus the Policy Unit has become at the heart of British government a unit whose ethos is the very opposite of the non-partisan permanence that is the hallmark of the Whitehall model bureaucrat. Future prime ministers are unlikely to abandon such a useful weapon. Even Major's first director of the Policy Unit, Sarah Hogg, struck his people who had experience of 10 Downing Street under Thatcher as forceful and interventionist in style, frequently involving the Unit in what would have been seen once as the affairs of a

Secretary of State. Yet this was during a period in which Major was supposedly restoring collective cabinet government. One of Thatcher's crucial contributions to British government was to show how, with the aid of a comparatively small staff, a modern British prime minister can intervene decisively in what he or she thinks are crucial policy areas. The authors of the next policy revolution to develop in Britain will not, as did the Thatcherites, need to invent the machinery to implement their revolution.

A third reason for believing that the apparent continuity of the Whitehall model masks change is that whole generations of bureaucrats and politicians have been socialized since the 1970s into very different professional norms. Bureaucrats and politicians learn their roles not only on entering office, but also as they progress up their hierarchies. The generation of even very senior civil servants who started to study their roles before the Thatcher Government has all but passed; the Major Government was dominated by ministers, including the Prime Minister, who had no governmental experience before the 1980s.

British government in the 1990s is dominated by officials and politicians who began their socialization into their roles during a period, the 1980s, in which the subordination of officials to politicians was greater than at any recent time. A crucial aspect of the Whitehall system was that the job security of the professional civil servant allowed him or her 'to speak truth to power'. The debate on politicization that occurred during the Thatcher years focused on whether civil servants were required to be loyal Conservatives. Almost certainly they were not, as inquiries at the time duly reported. However, professional advancement for civil servants had become dependent on their adopting a professional style that removed the emphasis on the role of civil servants as policy analysts or critics, and instead required them to be enthusiastic implementers of government policies, even when, as with Lawson's economic policy or the 'poll tax', the results were ultimately disastrous for both the government and the country. In the Whitehall model, civil servants had been required simultaneously to implement government policies conscientiously and to provide ministers with an honest critique of them. Contemporary civil servants have advanced through a system in which enthusiasm for government policies has been rewarded more than honest criticism. Nothing better illustrates how uncritical enthusiasm for government policies – rather than intellectual quality, professional competence or even partisanship – secured professional advancement than the promotion of Sir Peter Middleton to be Permanent Secretary of the Treasury; we encountered the Chancellor's (Nigel Lawson's) description of this politicized process in Chapter 2.

A fourth development, to which we referred above briefly, is the erosion of the belief that the civil service is an established profession, like all professions delineated from society as a whole by clear boundaries. Until quite recently, applicants to the civil service were told that they were entering a profession, and, in common with other professionals, it was reasonable to assume that they would remain within it for the rest of their lives. That belief has now been eroded. The civil service has encouraged applications from late entrants, and significant departures from the civil service in the 1980s, into finance, think tanks and politics, have reduced the expectation that a job in the administrative class of the civil service is for life. The British civil service is far removed still from the fluidity of government in the United States; it is much changed, however, from the institution walled off from the rest of society that existed in the 1950s.

The civil service is also less insulated from the outside world in another respect. Many British departments are now involved in regular meetings and exchanges with their counterparts in the other members of the European Community. As early as 1980, MAFF (Ministry of Agriculture, Fisheries, and Food) sent 2,500 officials to 1,200 EC meetings a year, while DTI (Department of Trade and Industry) sent over 1,000. As Christoph notes, the role of the official within the EC itself, as well as within the other member states, is very different from that prescribed by the Whitehall model. In a Britain that no longer believes that it knows better, the civil servants who are seconded to work for the Commission or who merely observe their counterparts from the continent and Ireland at work are likely to bring back fresh attitudes about the role of the bureaucrat (Christoph, 1993).

The final development that may entrench the changes we have noted is the rise of the career politician. There are fewer honourable time servers on either the Conservative or Labour benches, and rather more career politicians. Career politicians advance by making a mark; the proportion of ministers willing to serve quietly as the ambassadors of their departments, asserting interests and values that they did not create, has declined significantly from the situation Headey described in the early 1970s (Headey, 1974). We have seen in our assessment of the Major Government a disturbing amount of ideological entrepreneurship among ministers. When a system becomes used to command control from the centre, its sudden absence produces incoherence.

Future ministers may not have as overbearing a boss as Margaret Thatcher or such a weak one as John Major, but they will still need to make their marks by being associated with new initiatives, not merely with continuity. They will be reinforced in this by the political imperatives of Britain's economic circumstances. Britain is at best a country that struggles to keep up with its European neighbours and it is impossible to imagine this situation changing in the foreseeable future. The complacency of the past has gone for good, and in consequence career politicians will be eager to associate themselves with initiatives for change, no matter how futile those initiatives.

How might we summarize these changes in the ethos of policy making in the Whitehall model? One clear implication is that the bureaucracy has lost much of the standing that it once enjoyed. It is less clearly recognized as a full profession carefully demarcated from the rest of society and constituting a self-governing entity that inculcates professional values by rewarding performance according to criteria determined and applied by members of the profession. It is less frequently regarded as a partner in policy making with, to quote Rose (1987), one hand on the tiller of the ship of state while the politicians have another. Bureaucrats still play an important part in policy making and advising, but that part has been reduced in order to make room for politically sponsored policy entrepreneurs and analysts in think tanks, the Policy Unit and, through late career appointments such as Terry Burns's, in the civil service itself. The formal structure of the Whitehall model is intact, but below the surface important changes in norms and practices have occurred.

Changes in Implementation

Comparatively few changes have occurred in the organization of policy advice to ministers even though cultural change may have been extensive. In contrast, great changes are under way in the organization of policy implementation even though the culture of the Whitehall model may be less developed than the extent of these organizational changes might lead us to suppose.

The Next Steps programme, at least before its dimunition in the face of the Citizens' Charter, market testing, deregulation and, finally, privatization, attempted to make several important changes in the Whitehall model.

First, it provided a formal separation between the developers of policy and the implementers, which had not existed previously in Britain. In theory, the British civil service was a unitary service that stretched without a break in its structure from the Cabinet Office in Whitehall to the social security processing centre near Newcastle upon Tyne. Next Steps in contrast emphasized the separation of agencies from the centre and from each other. The agencies not only had in theory more autonomy from their ministers and the senior officials at the top of their parent departments, but were encouraged to be different from each other. One of the central concerns of Next Steps was to allow the agencies to differ in pay, conditions of service and operating culture, so that they could take account of the particular demands of their work and labour markets.

Second, Next Steps asserted the value of a managerial perspective in the running of most of the civil service, in contrast with the generalist, political executive tradition that had dominated Whitehall previously. A crucial concern of Next Steps was to allow the agency executives to be freer of political controls and the professional values of the civil service in order to pursue efficiency. Next Steps was therefore to an important degree not merely Thatcherite in inspiration but the result of that managerialist discontent with the civil service expressed by Balogh (1959) and, most authoritatively, by the Fulton Committee (Fulton, 1968). It emerged, indeed, from a symbiosis between managerialists both in the Thatcher ministry and the higher levels of the bureaucracy. Theoretically, the programme not only 'empowered' managerialist chief executives but 'disempowered' both ministers and senior civil servants.

Third, Next Steps weakened the idea that the civil service is an autonomous profession, with clear boundaries between it and the rest of society. In 1993, the Prison Service, now fully constituted as a Next Steps agency, was placed in the hands of a former television executive. Notwithstanding the success in Britain of television series set in prisons, this was a surprising appointment in the context of the Whitehall model's tradition of treating the civil service as a full profession through which people progressed in their careers as in any other. If the administration of a politically sensitive government 'service' such as prisons can be placed in the hands of an executive with no previous governmental experience, then almost any programme can. Indeed, while such highly visible external candidates take a minority of chief executive appointments, it is striking that in the first years of Next Steps, none had gone to 'fast track' administrative class civil servants.

Next Steps can be portrayed, therefore, as a decisive break with the past, a revolution in Whitehall that provides independence and power for managerialist administrators who eventually become entirely separated from the generalist administrators (and their ministers) who held sway in the past. But there are at least two grounds for caution before accepting this vision. First, precisely because Next Steps attempted to be a radical change, it sowed the seeds for its own undermining. The idea that administration should be entrusted to quasi-autonomous agencies conflicts with two enduring features of British government: the Treasury's wish to 'micromanage' the work of departments and the tradition that ministers are in theory accountable to Parliament for all the activities of their departments. Will the Treasury really allow agencies to exercise real discretion when setting pay, making purchases and placing contracts? Or will they choose to cut the ties entirely and let markets take over? Will MPs really allow a minister to refuse to answer parliamentary questions on the grounds that complaints about the behaviour of an agency should be taken to its chief executive instead? Is not the real 'next step' to get the function in question out of the minister's hair entirely? Those dubious about Next Steps came by their scepticism honestly (MacDonald, 1992).

A second reason for caution about the degree to which Next Steps could have changed the Whitehall culture is that it can be portrayed as a codification of something that was already true informally. As early as 1986, our interviews revealed the presence of a minority of civil servants, particularly in those parts of the government that have become Next Steps agencies, who were already to an important degree separated from the rest of Whitehall. They thought of themselves as managers not policy analysts, they thought of themselves as having a distinctive career track and they felt unappreciated in the general, alien Whitehall culture. They were disproportionately educated in state schools and had not studied at Oxford or Cambridge. To a substantial degree such managerialists constituted a separate and, they would say, inferior class whatever their formal ranks or status. Next Steps was therefore partly a codification of this difference.

Yet Next Steps did mark important changes in the Whitehall model. Whatever our caution about its current life chances, the attempt to make the change marks the fullest recognition yet that the Whitehall model cannot cope with the managerialist demands of modern government. Whether or not the surviving parts of the Next Steps system will work as intended there is agreement on the failure of the old system. Moreover, even if the attempts to make the new system work fail, the attempt itself will have an impact. The Next Steps system did create a new dynamic within the Whitehall model precisely because it created new institutions. Next Steps agencies were not merely a technique like PPBS or MINIS but were institutions. As such they changed the structure of the Whitehall game, even if not in the way that their designers intended.

So Who Cares?

The Whitehall model, like many other aspects of British life, proved that it could not survive the stresses of the late twentieth century. We noted earlier that three groups, academics, practitioners and citizens, had stakes in this fact. We start with the academics.

Academic observers of bureaucratic–political relations must acknowledge that the much admired, text-book Whitehall model has ceased to exist, even in Whitehall. Beyond this simple fact lies an important conceptual point about bureaucratic–political relations.

Why had the Whitehall model been so attractive? One of the fundamental concerns of academic observers of executives has been to promote institutions and practices that advance good governance. While there would be tremendous disagreement about what constitutes good governance, one common assumption in the academic literature on political executives has been the need for elected politicians to be confronted with dispassionate policy analysis and advice. But where should this come from? The Whitehall model was based on the assumption that it came best from an intellectually capable group who were protected from the favouritism of politicians by considerable job security and membership of an informally constituted profession and who were also imbued with the practical knowledge of problems that came from a long career in government. It was said of Jack Valenti when he was a member of President Johnson's White House staff that if Johnson had dropped the H-bomb on Chicago, Valenti would have rushed to please his master by issuing a statement hailing this action as a brilliant initiative in urban renewal. British civil servants in contrast were supposed to be able to stand their ground and tell their political superiors that their pet policy ideas were nonsense. When British civil servants are asked what alternative careers they would have chosen if they had not been civil servants, they usually pick academic life. The academic's freedom, protected by tenure, to describe the world as he or she sees it, is something to which civil servants aspire. Some civil servants still retain the capacity to give unwelcome advice. Sir Tim Lankester when permanent secretary of the Overseas Development Agency insisted on formally minuting his belief that a grant to Malaysia to build the Pergau dam in return for Malaysia's purchasing arms from Britain was unlawful. In general, however, confidence in the higher civil service declined.

Academics increasingly doubt whether bureaucrats will actually play such a role. Why has this erosion of confidence occurred? It has several sources.

Academics were among the first to criticize the competence of the senior civil service. Lord Crowther Hunt, a political scientist at Oxford and member of the Fulton Committee, was an energetic exponent of the argument that the humanistically educated members of the administrative class were ill-suited to advise ministers, even though he came to regret the Fulton Report's use of the word 'amateur' to describe them. Hunt spent his remaining years arguing that a conspiracy by senior civil servants had blocked the implementation of the Committee's main proposals (Kellner and Crowther-Hunt, 1980).

Perhaps inevitably, the Whitehall model suffered from the general loss of prestige the British political system endured because of the UK's poor economic performance. It was bad enough that the previous marriage of democratic politics and intellectual brilliance that the Whitehall model achieved failed to produce better results. Even worse was the analysis popular among political economists that the success of economic rivals such as Japan and France was based in large part on their bureaucracies. Yet how different were their bureaucracies! Whereas the ideal senior civil servant in the British model was someone who reacted to the wishes, proposals and general orientation of politicians, the Japanese and, in some analyses, the French states accorded a higher status to the bureaucracy. In Chalmers Johnson's influential study of Japanese industrial policy, it was the senior bureaucracy that supplied the heroes who charted the way for Japanese success (Johnson, 1982). In studies of the French economic miracle, in many ways the most impressive of the European economic miracles, the officials of the *Commissariat du Plan* laid the foundations for transforming France into a leading economic power in Europe while the politicians of the Fourth Republic bickered endlessly over trivia (Stevens, 1981). In comparison, the role of the British civil servant in developing and criticizing the ideas of politicians seemed decidedly unheroic. If British bureaucrats had been prepared to adopt leadership roles in promoting long-term national economic interests, this argument continued or implied, Britain's economic performance would have been better.

Even more damaging to the status of the civil service in academic circles was the increasing unwillingness of scholars to accept that senior civil servants constituted a disinterested, platonic corps of policy advisers. There had always been suspicion of the senior bureaucracy based on the unrepresentative social origins and educational background of administrative class civil servants. Studies of policy making and bureaucratic–political relations in fact revealed very little tension or unhappiness between politicians, Labour or Conservative, and senior civil servants. Such studies did suggest, however, that civil servants in government departments gave advice that was highly predictable, in line with the 'departmental view' that embodied their interests and values.

The rational choice movement in political science completed the transformation of academic attitudes to the senior bureaucracy. Gone was the vision of the bureaucracy as the group that might 'speak truth to power'. In its place came a picture of the bureaucracy composed (like all other institutions) of self-absorbed individuals promoting their own interests. Bureaucrats maximize the budgets and size of their agencies in order to promote their own self-interest, primarily in increased salary perquisites. Claims that the bureaucrats serve other roles, such as meeting the needs of politicians or functioning as disinterested policy advisers, simply mask the bureaucracy's pursuit of its self-interest.

The success of the rational choice movement in political science is one of the more puzzling features of contemporary political science. Rational choice scholars, after all, had plenty of time to observe the dead end that the deductive approach had reached in economics before importing it into political science. Rational choice scholars not only offered little empirical evidence to support the value of their approach but even disdained the value of empirical work. Perhaps the triumph of rational choice in political science was a reflection of wider social changes that produced the Thatcher and Reagan revolutions; the view of people as self-interested utility maximizers on which rational choice perspectives rested was certainly in line with the politics of what was called 'the me decade'. Yet the triumph of rational choice not only influenced academic writers but spread from them to practitioners. Thatcher herself brandished Niskanen's work on bureaucracy at her colleagues and pressed them to read it.

Once the rational choice perspective on bureaucracy was adopted, much of the established wisdom on bureaucracy was abandoned. For example, the vaunted unity of the British civil service, promoting an *esprit de corps* crossing departmental and agency boundaries, was a disadvantage from the perspective of rational choice. Bureaucracies worked best when there was competition between agencies and when politician 'principals' had greatest freedom to give rewards or punishments to subordinate 'agents' in the bureaucracies. Thus faith in the benefits that advice and criticism from the bureaucracy would bring to policy making, the belief in the value of the bureaucracy's 'neutral competence', was replaced with a pessimistic view of civil servants in which they needed to be bribed or whipped into line with the politicians' values.

The Whitehall model cannot fit well with a rational choice perspective. For the basic features of the Whitehall model reduce the opportunity for politician 'principals' to reward or punish bureaucratic agents. The idea of the civil service as a permanent, self-governing profession denies politicians valuable powers to reward through promotions, pay increases or dismissals. Cuts or increases in departments' budgets punish or reward fellow politicians at the top of those departments, not just bureaucrats. The ethos of Whitehall is one in which team work and collective decision making, not individual initiative, are prized. It is ironic that principal-agent ideas have had their greatest practical impact in Whitehall model countries such as Britain and New Zealand. For it is precisely in Whitehall model countries that the clash between the embedded values on which the machinery of government is based and the rational choice perspective with its principal-agent derivatives is greatest. The rise of the rational choice perspective has been damaging therefore to the standing of the Whitehall model, even fuelling reforms, such as the Next Steps programme, that propose fundamental alterations in it.

The challenge for political scientists within their own discipline is not to argue for or against changes in the Whitehall model. It is to rise above the simplistic accounts of bureaucracy supplied by both the defenders of the model and by rational choice scholars. Bureaucrats can indeed be selfless servants of the state, even to the extent of developing loyally policies that reduce all the goods that rational choice theorists have them maximize – the size of the bureaucracy, salaries and budgets; the Thatcher years provide examples to fit all three. Yet equally the image of the senior civil servant as platonic guardian of the public good, which occurs not only in works by former senior civil servants in Britain such as Bridges (1950) but in admiring studies of the Japanese and French bureaucracies, are implausible. The reality is that bureaucrats can be both the selfish pursuers of status, agency size and salary, which rational choice writers portray and, as their defenders maintain, the guardians of more noble concerns such as long-term national interest and confronting rulers with awkward facts. The challenge for political scientists is to identify those conditions that produce a bureaucracy resembling the nightmare vision of the rational choice theorists as it pursues its self-interest and those conditions that produce a bureaucracy more attuned to national or public interests. No doubt the rational choice perspective has much to contribute in this quest, identifying institutional incentives that produce self-interested conduct. But so also do perspectives grounded in an awareness of the importance of the socialization of bureaucrats and politicians into their roles within historically deeply rooted institutions.

Consequences for Practitioners

At first glance, politicians have been the big winners from the developments we have described. As many observers have noted, the balance of power between bureaucrats and politicians in Britain shifted significantly in favour of the politicians. This may well have been part of an international development. Reporting on their research in the 1970s, Aberbach, Putnam and Rockman (1981) suggested that a blurring of the distinction between elected politicians and senior bureaucrats was occurring. In the 1980s, in contrast, in Britain – and, according to more recent studies including that by Aberbach and Rockman (1991), in the United States – the politicians reasserted their constitutionally dominant position. Indeed, a major feature of both British and American politics in the 1980s was that the barriers to effective political control of the bureaucracy, which had been supposed immense, were in practice overcome. Both Thatcher and Reagan were far more effective than most political scientists would have expected in bending their respective bureaucracies to their will.

Two questions arise from this observation. First, why were politicians able to assert their supremacy over bureaucrats so successfully? Second, what were the costs – including costs to the politicians themselves – of this victory?

The Ascendance of the Politicians

In Britain the ascendance of the politicians over the bureaucrats was based on three factors.

First, the politicians knew to a quite unusual degree what they wanted. British politicians in the 1960s – as Crossman noted in his diaries (1975; 1976; 1977) – came into office with very little sense of how to pursue even those policies to which they had long been committed. In the 1970s, they were so buffeted by events that they became famous for executing U-turns in office, abandoning what they came to realize were impractical plans, in the face of massive economic difficulties. The Thatcher Government was unusual in that it had a number of clear objectives in mind, several of which combined a distant objective with short-term tactics. Monetarism, for example, combined the distant goal of low inflation with the proximate tactic of changing from fiscal to monetary policies. Ministers knew what they wanted to do and, in a wide variety of policy areas – economic policy, education, labour relations and industrial policy – insisted that their officials should adopt their policies. In some of these areas, such as the former Department of Education and Science, ministers destroyed the consensus within their departments, the 'departmental perspective', that had existed previously under both Labour and Conservative governments (Kogan, 1971). In other areas, such as the Treasury, ministers found themselves pushing new policy approaches on civil servants who had lost their confidence in previous (Keynesian) policies. In all these cases, however, officials made some attempts to dissuade ministers from pursuing their new policies. In the Thatcher era, ministers had the confidence to overrule these objections.

Second, ministers approached the bureaucracy with a more realistic sense of the problems they might encounter when dealing with the bureaucracy than had been the case in the past. Many factors made Thatcherites aware that controlling the bureaucracy might be a problem they would need to address after taking office. These included Thatcher's personal antipathy to the civil service, a belief that the Heath Government had been seduced away from its true beliefs by civil service advice, and the suspicions of the bureaucrats' motives inculcated by rational choice perspectives. The actual mechanisms for dealing with this problem were developed slowly; it is not unfair to say that Thatcher herself progressed from a strategy of simply shouting at civil servants to the more sophisticated reforms of the Next Steps programme. Yet the fact that ministers took office thinking about problems of governance, the problems they might encounter in shaping the behaviour of the bureaucracy to their wishes, placed them in a more advantageous position than most of their predecessors within the Whitehall system, who gave remarkably little thought to such issues.

Third, ministers had a very sharp sense of their right to prevail.

Of course in the Whitehall model, ministers enjoy constitutional supremacy over civil servants. The degree to which they feel that they should assert that right varies, however. The Thatcher era was one in which ministers felt that they had the right to prevail, in part because they considered they had a mission to redeem Britain from the state into which it had fallen. If governance for most of the members of the Callaghan Government was puzzling, for Thatcherites it was triumphing – over obtuse educationalists and unions who were, to use Thatcher's own phrase, 'the enemy within', and over benighted bureaucrats. The percentage of ministers willing (if only out of fear of the Prime Minister) to tell more expert civil servants that they were wrong was unusually high.

Finally, the Government displayed a high level of skill in using weapons often neglected by previous governments to change civil servants' attitudes or behaviour. The widespread feeling among senior civil servants that those who wanted promotion during the Thatcher years had to behave differently illustrated the impact of the Prime Minister's intervention in promotion decisions, even if it did not, in the trivial, partisan sense, amount to 'politicization'. The unusually high degree of change in civil service career plans that resulted from the Next Steps agencies no doubt also made civil servants sensitive to the need to be more accommodating to their superiors; the automatic Buggins' turn of advancement through seniority was less common than in the past.

The Costs of Victory

Civil servants exist in theory in the Whitehall model to help ministers, and triumphing over people who are supposed to help you has obvious disadvantages. This is particularly true in the Whitehall model, in which the senior civil service exists not merely to implement policies but to offer policy analysis and advice. In the United States, a president who disregards the bureaucracy's advice may none the less have a significant cadre of advisers in the Executive Office of the President – the White House staff, the National Security Council staff etc. Likewise, American cabinet secretaries not keen to defer to bureaucrats can use their sub-cabinet appointees to keep the administration's strategy on course.

The small number of political advisers assisting British ministers and the modest size of the staff of the prime minister (including the Policy Unit) mean that if the senior civil service is seen as a barrier rather than an aid to good decision making, there is unlikely to be a satisfactory alternative source of advice.

The great risk for Conservative ministers has been that in taming the civil service they lost the value of the only advisory system they had. To the extent that civil servants were cowed by fears that 'speaking truth to power' would damage their careers, they ceased to play the role they were intended to play in the Whitehall model. It is perhaps a matter of personal political attitude whether one believes that, overall, Thatcherite policies did Britain more harm than good. It is less controversial to claim that during the 1980s British ministers stumbled into situations to their own disadvantage, in part because they were not given or did not absorb warnings about the foreseeable consequences of their policies. It was predictable that the combination of military weakness and diplomatic firmness over the Falklands might lead to invasion. It was predictable that as the size of the poll tax to be levied escalated, it would be very damaging politically to the Government, even if such a regressive tax could be defended morally. Few policies were as central to the Thatcher Government as monetary policy. Yet in practice the Prime Minister pursued one indicator of monetary stability while her Chancellor pursued another, incompatible objective (a stable rate of exchange with the Deutschmark). This was a failure to resolve a crucial policy disagreement that in the classic Whitehall model senior civil servants would have demanded be settled. Ultimately the conflict not only led to the fall of the Chancellor, but also contributed to the fall of the Prime Minister herself. Under Major, the problem has seemed to compound itself with policy failures now occurring almost weekly.

In brief, governments that triumph over their advisers do so at great risk. The Thatcher and Major governments have triumphed over the civil service, as the constitution required. But the triumph has not solved basic problems of governance – ensuring that the rulers are confronted with the foreseeable consequences of their policies, addressing inconsistencies between different policies and producing alternative policy initiatives for elected politicians to consider. Indeed, the adversarial attitude the governments generally displayed toward the bureaucracy made it less not more likely that these continuing problems of governance be solved. This in turn might have mattered less if the governments had created a different system, incorporating, for example, a more politicized system in which a larger number of advisers were appointed on a patronage basis. They did not. Instead the governments merely tried to conquer the advisory system they had inherited.

Consequences for Citizens

Until recently, citizens in most Whitehall model countries, and particularly in Britain, have had little notion of the workings of the Whitehall model. The secrecy that has been a feature of the Whitehall model has sheltered its workings from public view. The argument that ministers should be free to debate policy proposals with each other and with their civil service advisers before presenting them to Parliament and the public may not differ in kind from arguments for executive privilege in the United States. Yet the imbalance of power between Parliament and the executive in Britain and Whitehall model countries more generally makes this secrecy more important than the secrecy that surrounds dealings between American presidents and their advisers. For issues that are hammered out in meetings between ministers and civil servants, usually merely ratified by Parliament, are issues that have vital impacts on the lives of citizens. To take one obvious example, economic policies influencing home mortgage rates or the levels of inflation and unemployment are decided by ministers in consultation with each other and civil servants, and are merely debated in Parliament.

The development of the Whitehall model in Britain was more or less coterminous with the growth of democracy. The Northcote Trevelyan reforms began between the first and second Reform Acts and were completed more or less simultaneously with the passing of the Representation of the People Act, which (with one small exception) completed the process of turning Britain into a democracy. It is unlikely that this is mere coincidence. Viewed from one angle, the growth of the administrative state in Britain was caused by the growth of democracy; electoral competition between political parties, no matter that both the Conservatives and Liberals were aristocratically based until this century, resulted in a growth of government programmes that in turn required an expanded administrative apparatus to deal with them. Viewed from another angle, the growth of the Whitehall model reflected the need to restrain the impulses of democratic politicians and educate them in the realities of public policy. Robert Lowe, the Whig politician, supported the expansion of education after the second Reform Act saying, 'We must educate our masters.' Much the same spirit imbued the Whitehall model, with professional civil servants playing tutor to elected politicians.

It would be easy at this point to react against the Whitehall model with democratic indignation. Senior civil servants in Britain, like elites in most countries (including the United States) are not representative of the population as a whole. Our belief that there is some common sense that is independent of the ideology of self-interest has diminished in modern times, and with it must decline a belief that a permanent civil service can operate as an ideologically neutral tutor, challenging in classic Oxford style the unexamined assumptions of its political masters. No matter what they claim, we could argue, permanent civil servants drawn from a certain social background, educated at a limited number of universities and reflecting the self-interest of the agencies in which they work cannot provide neutral analysis of the policy proposals that any minister produces; the common belief of the followers of both Tony Benn and Margaret Thatcher that civil servants criticize more vigorously policy proposals that fall outside the consensus has great appeal. It was, after all, one of Benn's permanent secretaries who defined his job in part as leading his ministers back to the centre.

Yet indignant democrats must face two awkward facts.

The first is that all advisory systems have their disadvantages. The system in the United States has all too often surrounded presidents with insecure sycophants, trying to secure their position on the White House staff by telling the president what they think he wants to hear. The problem of finding suitable people who can be persuaded to move to Washington to take up high-level jobs that in Britain would be filled by permanent civil servants, and who do not offend the Senate politically, grows worse and worse; in 1993, key personnel for the new administration

were even questioned closely – and some were dropped in consequence – about the arrangements they had made to employ
babysitters years before.

The second awkward fact is that the role of the civil service in
the Whitehall model has been so important because the rest of
the British political system has failed so signally to promote serious thinking about public policy. The failure of political parties,
with rare exceptions, to engage in systematic, detailed thinking
about policies is notorious. Although think tanks became more
prominent in the 1980s, London still lacks a richness of informal
policy networks similar to those, encompassing think tanks,
Congressional staff and academics, that are such a prominent
part of the Washington scene. There is of course a large interest-
group community in London, but by its very nature this community is more likely either to react to policy proposals or to promote
narrow interests than to generate policy ideas. In short, the British political system outside the ranks of the civil service provides
very poorly for thinking about policy.

Finally, the influence of the civil service has been acceptable
because it has helped in a small way to alleviate another well-
known problem in the British political system. That problem is
the absence of mechanisms to compel deliberation. If deadlock is
the obvious danger in the American political system, because so
many people have a veto over new policies, the obvious danger
in the British political system is over-hasty action because so *few*
people have a veto. Fortunately, in both cases the obvious danger
is usually avoided, but just as there are indeed examples of deadlock in the United States, so there are examples in every British
government of policies rushed into so foolishly that even the
governments themselves have soon regretted what they have done;
a well-known example in the early 1990s was an unworkable
policy on dangerous dogs rushed through because of popular
revulsion to an attack on children.

Many politicians have accepted, indeed have welcomed, the
idea that their assumptions should be challenged by unelected
civil servants, in part because they do such a poor job of challenging each other's beliefs. British Parliamentary debate has been
much admired, and British politicians are indeed more fluent
than their counterparts in the United States. But while parliamentary debate and Question Time may subject the general principles

of government policy to serious scrutiny, the crucial details of policy are barely tested in Parliament, unless a select committee examines the issues, usually *ex post facto*. Unintended consequences, conflicts between one aspect of a policy and another, the treatment of special cases that it would be embarrassing politically or indefensible to include in a general policy might surface in the United States during congressional committee deliberations. In Britain, only the good civil servant can force ministers to reconsider before they commit themselves publicly – and therefore usually finally – to a policy. So in a sense the civil service has functioned as a partial antidote to obvious dangers in Britain's 'elected dictatorship'.

Yet the role of the civil service may be less acceptable than in the past. British society, for better or worse, has become much less deferential. The willingness of the British to believe that those who, in the language of the Book of Common Prayer, 'are set in authority over us' are working in the interests of all has declined. British political culture has acquired a little of the American suspicion of political authority. Senior civil servants we interviewed often noted regretfully that one of the changes they had witnessed during their careers was a decline in the public's willingness to believe that people in government were at least trying their best to solve public policy problems. In an age when even the British monarchy is more scrutinized and criticized than ever, willingness to accept the influence of the civil service can similarly be expected to be less than ever.

Simultaneously, the administrative structure of the British state has come into question. For a time it seemed as though the British state, for all the antiquity of its structures, had proved to be better able to take on the demands of a large democracy than, for example, the American. Discontent with administrative inefficiency and agency empire building was much less in Britain than in the United States, and, while some of this reflected differences in political cultures, it also reflected differences in the experience of government. Now, as we have seen, the British administrative state is in turmoil. The Next Steps programme constituted a very conscious attempt to redesign the bureaucracy according to a very different model. The current drive toward market testing and privatization amounts still more to radical restructuring. The central constitutional doctrine of ministerial responsibility is in tatters. The Citizens' Charter programme of the Major Government was an attempt to convince the public that they were not subject to the whims of a powerful state indifferent to their needs. Now much of what the government does will be done through contract and private companies – placing the citizen at the whim of market standards for service.

Yet to point to the inadequacies of the workings of the Whitehall model in isolation may seem a little like emphasizing inadequacies in the kitchen of the *Titanic*. The whole of the British political system is in confusion. The nature (if not the future) of the monarchy, the workings of the electoral system, the legal system, Parliament and the party system, all are subject to extensive criticism in Britain today. The British system as a whole, and not just the Whitehall model of political–bureaucratic relations, looks less than it did thirty years ago like a model for new democracies and more like an old car wheezing uncertainly along the highway. Britain has usually evaded constitutional problems as long as possible; the 1911 Parliament Act, a central part of the British constitution, states in its preamble that it is only a temporary measure while the future of the House of Lords is debated further; the Act and the House of Lords remain only partially modified since. The general feeling of dissatisfaction with many aspects of the British political system today provides no assurance that there will be a thorough review of the constitution. Indeed, the evidence of the past suggests that such a review is unlikely.

It would be too optimistic, therefore, to suggest that the Whitehall model will be replaced by a carefully designed new model of political–bureaucratic relations. Whatever the difficulties, strains and contradictions evident in the model, it may continue. Indeed, the proponents of the Whitehall model can argue that its capacity to survive the Thatcher years is evidence of its adaptability. We believe, however, that the Whitehall model has reached a condition such that even if it survives, it will no longer seem an attractive model of governance to the rest of the world.

References

Aberbach, Joel D. 1991. 'The President and the Executive Branch' in *The Bush Administration: First Appraisals*, eds Colin Campbell and Bert A. Rockman. Chatham, NJ: Chatham House.

Aberbach, Joel D., Robert A. Putnam and Bert A. Rockman. 1981. *Bureaucrats and Politicians in Western Democracies*. Cambridge, MA: Harvard University Press.

Aberbach, Joel D. and Bert A. Rockman. 1991. 'From Nixon's Problem To Reagan's Triumph' in *Looking Back on the Reagan Years*, ed. Larry Berman.

Alchain, A. A. and S. Woodward. 1987. 'Reflections on the Theory of the Firm', *Journal of Institutional and Theoretical Economics* 143: 110–36.

Allison, Graham T. 1971. *The Essence of Decision: Explaining the Cuban Missile Crisis*. Boston: Little Brown.

Almond, Gabriel and Sidney Verba. 1965. *The Civic Culture*. Newbury Park, CA: Sage.

Anderson, Bruce. 1991. *John Major*. London: Headline.

Anson, Stan. 1991. *Hawke: An Emotional Life*. Ringwood, Victoria: Penguin.

Armstrong, John A. 1973. *The European Administrative Elite*. Princeton, NJ: Princeton University Press.

Armstrong, Sir Robert. 1986. *Civil Servants and Ministers: Duties and Responsibilities*. London: HMSO.

Aucoin, Peter. 1986. 'Organizing Change in the Machinery of Canadian Government', *Canadian Journal of Political Science* 14: 3–17.

Aucoin, Peter. 1988. 'The Mulroney Government: Priorities, Positional Policy and Power' in *Canada Under Mulroney: An End of Term Report*, eds A. B. Gollner and D. Salee. Montreal: Vehicule.

Aucoin, Peter. 1989. 'Contraction, Managerialism and Decentralization in Canadian Government', *Governance* 1: 144–61.

Aucoin, Peter. 1990a. 'Administrative Reform in Public Management: Paradigms, Principles, Paradoxes and Pendulums', *Governance* 3: 115–37.

Aucoin, Peter. 1990b. 'Comment: Assessing Managerial Reforms', *Governance* 3: 197–204.

Bakvis, Herman. 1991. *Regional Ministers: Power and Influence in the Canadian Cabinet.* Toronto: University of Toronto Press.

Balogh, Thomas. 1959. 'The Apotheosis of the Dilettante' in *The Establishment,* ed. Hugh Thomas. London: Blond.

Barber, James David. 1972. *The Presidential Character: Predicting Performance in the White House.* Englewood Cliffs, NJ: Prentice-Hall.

Barber, James David. 1977. 'Comment: Qualls' Nonsensical Analysis of Nonexistent Works', *American Political Science Review* 71: 212–25.

Berman, Larry. 1979. *The Office of Management and Budget.* Princeton, NJ: Princeton University Press.

Berman, Larry and Bruce W. Jentleson. 1991. 'Bush and the Post-Cold War Worlds: New Challenges for American Leadership' in *The Bush Administration: First Appraisals,* eds Colin Campbell and Bert A. Rockman. Chatham, NJ: Chatham House.

Berry, Phyllis. 1989. 'The Organization and Influence of the Chancellory During the Schmidt and Kohl Chancellorships', *Governance* 2: 339–55.

Blackstone, Tessa and William Plowden. 1988. *Inside the Think Tank: Advising the Cabinet 1971–1983.* London: Heinemann.

Blythe, Robert. 1969. *Akenfield.* Harmondsworth: Penguin.

Borins, Sanford F. 1982. 'Ottawa's Expenditure "Envelopes": Workable Rationality at Last?' in *How Ottawa Spends Your Tax Dollars: National Policy and Economic Development,* ed. G. Bruce Doern. Ottawa: Carleton University Press.

Boston, Jonathan. 1987. 'Transforming New Zealand's Public Sector: Labour's Quest for Improving Efficiency and Accountability', *Public Administration* 65: 423–42.

Boston, Jonathan. 1992. 'The Problems of Policy Coordination: The New Zealand Experience', *Governance* 5: 88–121.

Boston, Jonathan. 1994. 'The Limits of Contracting Out', *Governance* 7: 1–30.

Bray, Jeremy. 1970. *Decisionmaking in Government.* London: Gollancz.

Bridges, Lord. 1950. *Portrait of a Profession.* Cambridge: Cambridge University Press.

Buchanan, James. 1991. *The Economics and Ethics of Constitutional Order.* Ann Arbor, MI: University of Michigan Press.

Buchanan, James M. and Gordon Tullock. 1965. *The Calculus of Consent: Logical Foundations of Constitutional Democracy.* Ann Arbor, MI: University of Michigan Press.

Burns, James MacGregor. 1963. *The Deadlock of Democracy: Four-Party Politics in America.* Englewood Cliffs, NJ: Prentice-Hall.

Callaghan, James. 1987. *Time and Chance*. London: Collins.

Campbell, Colin. 1980. 'Political Leadership in Canada: Pierre Elliott Trudeau and the Ottawa Model' in *Presidents and Prime Ministers*, eds Richard Rose and Ezra Suleiman. Washington, DC: American Enterprise Institution.

Campbell, Colin. 1983. *Governments Under Stress: Political Executives and Key Bureaucrats in Washington, London and Ottawa*. Toronto: University of Toronto Press.

Campbell, Colin. 1985. 'Cabinet Committees in Canada: Pressures and Dysfunctions Stemming from the Representational Imperative' in *Unlocking the Cabinet: Cabinet Structures in Comparative Perspective*, eds Thomas T. Mackie and Brian Hogwood. London: Sage.

Campbell, Colin. 1986. *Managing the Presidency: Carter, Reagan and the Search for Executive Harmony*. Pittsburgh, PA: University of Pittsburgh Press.

Campbell, Colin. 1988. 'Mulroney's Broker Politics: The Ultimate in Politicized Incompetence?' in *Canada Under Mulroney: An End of Term Report*, eds A. B. Gollner and D. Salee. Montreal: Vehicule.

Campbell, Colin. 1991. 'The White House and Presidency under the "Let's Deal" President' in *The Bush Administration: First Appraisals*, eds Colin Campbell and Bert A. Rockman. Chatham, NJ: Chatham House.

Campbell, Colin. 1992. 'Public Service and Democratic Accountability' in *Ethics in Public Service*, ed. Richard A. Chapman. Edinburgh: University of Edinburgh Press.

Campbell, Colin and John Halligan. 1992. *Leadership in an Age of Constraint: The Australian Experience*. Sydney: Allen & Unwin.

Campbell, Colin and Bert A. Rockman, eds, 1991. *The Bush Administration: First Appraisals*. Chatham, NJ: Chatham House.

Campbell, Colin and George Szablowski. 1979. *The Superbureaucrats: Structure and Behavior in Central Agencies*. Toronto: Macmillan.

Campbell, Colin and Margaret Jane Wyszomirski. 1991. 'Introduction' in *Executive Leadership in Anglo-American Systems*, eds Colin Campbell and Margaret Jane Wyszomirski. Pittsburgh, PA: University of Pittsburgh Press.

Cannon, Lou. 1991. *President Reagan: The Role of a Lifetime*. New York: Simon & Shuster.

Chapman, Richard A. 1988. *Ethics in the British Public Service*. London: Routledge.

Chapman, Richard A. and John R. Greenaway. 1980. *The Dynamics of Administrative Reform*. London: Croom Helm.

Christoph, James. 1992. 'The Remaking of British Administrative Culture: Why Whitehall Can't Go Home Again', *Administration and Society* 24: 163–81.

Christoph, James. 1993. 'The Effect of Britons in Brussels: The EC and the Culture of Whitehall', *Governance* 6: 518–37.

The Civil Service, Continuity and Change. 1994. Cmnd 2627. London: HMSO.

Clarke, Alan. 1993. *Diaries.* London: Weidenfeld and Nicolson.

Considine, Mark. 1988. 'The Corporate Management Framework as Administrative Science: A Critique', *Australian Journal of Public Administration* 47: 4–17.

Cooper, Frank. 1987. 'Ministry of Defence' in *Reshaping Central Government*, eds Anthony Harrison and John Gretton. Oxford: Transaction Books.

Crewe, I. and D. Sårlvik. 1983. *Decade of Dealignment.* Cambridge: Cambridge University Press.

Crossman, Richard. 1975, 1976, 1977. *Diaries of a Cabinet Minister*, 3 vols. London: Hamish Hamilton.

Crossman, R. H. S. 1972. *The Myths of Cabinet Government.* Cambridge, MA: Harvard University Press.

Dahl, Robert A. 1956. *A Preface to Democratic Theory.* Chicago: University of Chicago Press.

Dahl, Robert. 1971. *Polyarchy: Participation and Opposition.* New Haven, CT: Yale University Press.

Dale, H. E. 1941. *The Higher Civil Service.* Oxford: Oxford University Press.

D'Alpuget, Blanche. 1982. *Robert J. Hawke: A Biography.* Melbourne: Schwartz.

Defence Committee. 1986. *Fourth Report From the Defence Committee 1985–86, Westland plc: The Government's Decision Making*, HC 519. London: HMSO.

Destler, I. M. 1981. 'National Security II: The Rise of the Assistant (1961–81)' in *The Illusion of Presidential Government*, eds Hugh Heclo and Lester M. Salamon. Boulder, CO: Westview.

Doern, Bruce. 1971. 'The Development of Policy Organization' in *The Structure of Policymaking in Canada*, eds G. Bruce Doern and Peter Aucoin. Toronto: Macmillan.

Doern, Bruce. 1982. 'Liberal Priorities 1982: The Limits of Scheming Virtuously' in *How Ottawa Spends Your Tax Dollars*, ed. Bruce Doern. Toronto: James Lorimer.

Doern, Bruce G. and Glen Toner. 1985. *The Politics of Energy: The Development and Implementation of the NEP.* Toronto: Methuen.

Donoughue, Bernard. 1986. *Prime Minister.* Oxford: Basil Blackwell.

Douglas-Home, Sir Alec. 1976. *The Way the Wind Blows.* London: Collins.

Drewry, Gavin. 1986. 'Ministers and Civil Servants', *Public Law* 514–26.

Dunleavy, Patrick. 1989. 'The Architecture of the British Central State. Part II: Empirical Findings', *Public Administration* 67: 319–417.

Dunleavy, Patrick. 1989. *Democracy, Bureaucracy and Public Choice.* Brighton: Harvester Wheatsheaf.

Edwards III, George C. 1991. 'George Bush and the Public Presidency: The Politics of Inclusion' in *The Bush Administration: First Appraisals*, eds Colin Campbell and Bert A. Rockman. Chatham, NJ: Chatham House.

Etzioni, Anita. 1968. *The Active Society: A Theory of Societal and Political Processes.* New York: Free Press.

Ewing, K. D. and C. A. Gearty. 1990. *Freedom Under Thatcher.* Oxford: Oxford University Press.

Expenditure Committee of the House of Commons. 1976–7. *Eleventh Report of the Expenditure Committee.* HC 535. London: HMSO.

Fenno, Jr., Richard F. 1959. *The President's Cabinet: Analysis in the Period from Wilson to Eisenhower.* Cambridge, MA: Harvard University Press.

Flynn, Andrew, Andrew Gray and William Jenkins. 1990. 'Taking Next Steps: The Changing Nature of Government', *Parliamentary Affairs* 43: 159–78.

Foley, Michael. 1993. *The Rise of the British Presidency.* Manchester: University of Manchester Press.

Franks Report. 1983. *Falkland Islands Review, Report of a Committee of Privy Councillors.* London: HMSO.

French, Richard D. 1980. *How Ottawa Decides: Planning and Industrial Policy-Making, 1968–1980.* Toronto: Lorimer.

Fry, Geoffrey. 1988. 'The Thatcher Government, the Financial Management Initiative and the "New Civil Service"', *Public Administration* 66: 1–20.

Fulton, Lord. 1968. *The Civil Service*, Vol. 1. *Report of the Committee 1966–68 Cmnd. 3638.* London: HMSO.

Gamble, Andrew. 1988. *The Free Economy and the Strong State: The Politics of Thatcherism.* Basingstoke: Macmillan Education.

George, Alexander. 1974. 'Assessing Presidential Character', *World Politics* 26: 234–82.

George, Alexander. 1980. *Presidential Decisionmaking in Foreign Policy: The Effective Use of Information and Advice.* Boulder, CO: Westview.

Gerth, H. H. and C. Wright Mills, eds. 1958. *From Max Weber: Essays in Sociology.* New York: Oxford University Press.

Glassco Commission. 1962. *Report of the Royal Commission on Government Organization*, abridged ed. Ottawa: Queen's Printer.

Goldsworthy, Diane. 1991. *Setting Up Next Steps: A Short Account of the Origins, Launch, and Implementation of the Next Steps Project in the British Civil Service.* London: HMSO.

Goodnow, Frank J. 1900. *Politics and Administration*. New York: Macmillan.

Granatstein, J. L. 1981. *A Man of Influence: Norman A. Robertson and Canadian Statecraft, 1929–68*. Ottawa: Deveau.

Greenstein, Fred I. 1982. *The Hidden-Hand Presidency: Eisenhower as Leader*. New York: Basic Books.

Grover, William F. 1989. *The President as Prisoner: A Structured Critique of the Carter and Reagan Years*, Albany, NY: State University of New York.

Gulick, Luther. 1937. 'Science, Values and Public Administration' in *Papers in the Science of Administration*, eds Luther Gulick and L. Urwick. New York: Institute of Public Administration.

Gwyn, Richard. 1980. *The Northern Magus: Pierre Elliott Trudeau and Canadians*. Toronto: McClelland and Stewart.

Hall, Peter. 1986. *Governing the Economy*. Oxford and New York: Oxford University Press.

Halligan, John. 1987. 'Reorganizing Australian Government Departments, 1987', *Canberra Bulletin of Public Administration* 52: 40–7.

Hansen, Michael and Charles H. Levine. 1988. 'The Centralization–Decentralization Tug-of-War in the New Executive Branch' in *Organizing Governance: Governing Organizations*, eds Colin Campbell and B. Guy Peters. Pittsburgh, PA: University of Pittsburgh Press.

Hargrove, Erwin C. 1993. 'Presidential Personality and Leadership Style' in *Researching the Presidency: Vital Questions, New Approaches*, eds George Edwards, John Kessel and Bert A. Rockman. Pittsburgh, PA: University of Pittsburgh Press.

Hart, John. 1987. *The Presidential Branch*. New York: Pergamon.

Hartle, Douglas. 1983. 'An Open Letter to Richard Van Loon (with a Copy to Richard French)', *Canadian Public Administration* 26: 84–94.

Headey, Bruce. 1974. *British Cabinet Ministers*. London: Allen & Unwin.

Heclo, Hugh. 1977. *A Government of Strangers: Executive Politics in Washington*. Washington, DC: Brookings.

Heclo, Hugh. 1984. 'In Search of a Role: America's Higher Civil Service' in *Bureaucrats and Policy Making: A Comparative Overview*, ed. Ezra Suleiman. New York: Holmes & Meier.

Heclo, Hugh and Lester M. Salamon, eds. 1981. *The Illusion of Presidential Government*. Boulder, CO: Westview.

Heclo, Hugh and Aaron B. Wildavsky. 1973. *The Private Government of Public Money: Community and Policy Inside British Politics*. Berkeley, CA: University of California Press.

Hennessy, Peter. 1986a. *Cabinet*. Oxford: Basil Blackwell.

Hennessy, Peter. 1986b. 'Constitutional Issues of the Westland Affair:

Helicopter Crashes into Cabinet; Prime Minister and Constitution Hurt', *Journal of Law and Society* 13: 432.

Hennessy, Peter. 1989. *Whitehall*. London: Secker & Warburg.

Hennessy, Peter. 1991. 'The Whitehall Model: Career Staff Support for Cabinet in Foreign Affairs' in *Executive Leadership in Anglo-American Systems*, eds Colin Campbell and Margaret Wyszomirski. Pittsburgh, PA: University of Pittsburgh Press.

Hess, Stephen. 1988. *Organizing the Presidency*. Washington, DC: Brookings.

HM Treasury. 1982. Statement on the 1982 Pay Claim by the Council of Civil Service Unions. London.

Hood, Christopher. 1990. 'De-Sir Humphreyfying the Westminster Model of Bureaucracy: A New Style of Governance?', *Governance* 3:205–14.

Hood, Christopher. 1991. 'A Public Management for All Seasons?', *Public Administration* 69: 3–19.

Hood, Christopher and Maurice Wright. 1981. 'From Decrementalism to Quantum Cuts' in *Big Government in Hard Times,* eds Christopher Hood and Maurice Wright. Oxford: Martin Robertson.

Hoskyns, Sir John. 1982. 'Westminster and Whitehall', *Fiscal Studies* 3: 162–72.

Hoskyns, John. 1983. 'The Whitehall Establishment: An Outsider's Perspective', *Parliamentary Affairs* 36: 137–47.

House of Commons Library Research Division. 1989. *Executive Agencies,* Background Paper no. 239 (unpublished.)

Ibbs Report. 1988. *Improving Management in Government: The Next Steps*. London: HMSO.

Improving Management in Government: The Next Steps Agencies. 1990. Cmnd 1261. London: HMSO.

Ingham, Bernard. 1991. *Kill the Messenger*. London: Harper Collins.

Jenkins, Peter, 1987. *Mrs. Thatcher's Revolution*. London: Jonathan Cape.

Jenkins, Roy. 1991. *A Life at the Centre*. London: Macmillan.

Jennings, Ivor. 1966. *The British Constitution*. Cambridge: Cambridge University Press.

Johnson, Chalmers. 1982. *MITI and the Japanese Economic Miracle*. Stanford, CA: Stanford University Press.

Johnson, Nevil. 1977. *In Search of the Constitution*. Oxford: Oxford University Press.

Jones, Charles O. 1991. 'Meeting Low Expectations: Strategy and Prospects of the Bush Presidency' in *The Bush Administration: First Appraisals,* eds Colin Campbell and Bert A. Rockman. Chatham, NJ: Chatham House.

Jones, Charles O. 1994. *The Presidency in a Separated System*. Washington DC: Brookings Institution.

Jones, George W. 1983. 'Prime Ministers' Departments Really Create Problems: A Rejoinder to Patrick Weller', *Public Administration* 61: 79–84.

Jones, George, 1987. 'The United Kingdom' in *Advising the Rulers,* ed. William Plowden. Oxford: Basil Blackwell.

Jones, George W. 1988. 'The Crisis in British Central–Local Government Relationships', *Governance* 1: 162–83.

Jones, George W. 1991. 'Presidentialization of the British Parliamentary System' in *Executive Leadership in Anglo-American Systems*, eds Colin Campbell and Margaret Wyszomirski. Pittsburgh, PA: University of Pittsburgh Press.

Kavanagh, Dennis. 1980. 'The Decline of the Civic Culture' in *The Civic Culture Revisited*, eds Gabriel A. Almond and Sidney Verba. Newbury Park, CA: Sage.

Keating, Michael and Geoff Dixon. 1989. *Making Economic Policy in Australia, 1983–1988*. Melbourne: Longman Chesire.

Keating, Michael and Malcolm Holmes. 1990. 'Australia's Budgetary and Financial Management Reforms', *Governance* 3: 168–85.

Keegan, William. 1984. *Mrs. Thatcher's Economic Experiment*. Harmondsworth: Penguin.

Keegan, William. 1989. *Mr. Lawson's Gamble*. London: Hodder & Stoughton.

Keegan, William and R. Pennant-Rea. 1979. *Who Runs the Economy? Control and Influence in British Economic Policy*. London: Maurice Temple Smith.

Kellner, Peter and Crowther-Hunt, Lord. 1980. *The Civil Servants: An Inquiry into Britain's Ruling Class*. London: MacDonald, 1980.

Kemp, Sir Peter. 1990. 'Next Steps for the British Civil Service', *Governance* 3: 186–96.

Kernell, Samuel. 1986. *Going Public: New Strategies of Presidential Leadership*. Washington, DC: CQ.

Key, V. O. 1955. 'A Theory of Critical Elections', *Journal of Politics* 17: 3–18.

King, Anthony, ed. 1975. *Why is Britain Becoming Harder to Govern?* London: BBC Books.

King, Anthony. 1981. 'The Rise of the Career Politician in Britain and Its Consequences', *British Journal of Political Science* 11: 249–85.

King, Anthony. 1985. 'Margaret Thatcher: The Style of a Prime Minister' in *The British Prime Minister*, 2nd ed., ed. Anthony King. Raleigh, NC: Duke University Press.

Kogan, Maurice, ed. 1971. *The Politics of Education*. Harmondsworth: Penguin.

Lawson, Nigel. 1992. *The View From Number 11: Memoirs of a Tory Radical*. London: Bantam Press.

Lee, Michael. 1981. 'Whitehall and Retrenchment' in *Big Government in Hard Times*, eds Christopher Hood and Maurice Wright. Oxford: Martin Robertson.

Levine, Charles H. 1988. 'Human Resource Erosion and the Uncertain Future of the U.S. Civil Service: From Policy Gridlock to Structural Fragmentation', *Governance* 1: 115–43.

Lindblom, Charles E. 1965. *The Intelligence of Democracy: Decision-Making through Mutual Adjustment*. New York: Free Press.

Little, Graham. 1983. 'Hawke in Place: Evaluating Narcissism', *Meanjin* 42: 431–44.

Lowi, Theodore J. 1969. *The End of Liberalism: Ideology, Policy, and the Crisis of Public Authority*. New York: Norton.

Lynn, Jr., Lawrence E. and David de F. Whitman. 1981. *The President as Policy-Maker: Jimmy Carter and Welfare Reform*. Philadelphia: Temple University Press.

MacDonald, Oonagh. 1992. *The Future of Whitehall*. London: Weidenfeld and Nicolson.

Mackie, Thomas T. and Brian Hogwood, eds. 1985. *Unlocking the Cabinet: Cabinet Structure in Comparative Perspective*. London: Sage.

Mackintosh, John P. 1977. *The British Cabinet*, 3rd ed. London: Stevens and Sons.

Macmillan, Harold. 1969. *Tides of Fortune, 1945–55*. New York: Harper & Row.

Marshall, Geoffrey. 1984. *Constitutional Conventions*. Oxford: Oxford University Press.

Marshall, Geoffrey. 1988. 'Civil Servants and Their Ministers': the Frank Stacey Memorial Lecture', *Public Policy and Administration* 32.

Mather, Graham. 1992. 'First Division Lecture', *The Bulletin*, March.

Mayhew, David. 1991. *Divided We Govern: Party Control in Lawmaking and Investigations*. New Haven, CT: Yale University Press.

Mayntz, Renate. 1987. 'West Germany' in *Advising the Rulers*, ed. William Plowden. Oxford: Basil Blackwell.

Moe, Terry. 1984. 'The New Economics of Organization', *American Journal of Political Science* 28: 739–77.

Moe, Terry M. 1985. 'The Politicized Presidency' in *The New Direction in American Politics*, eds John E. Chubb and Paul E. Peterson. Washington, DC: Brookings.

Moe, Terry. 1990. 'Political Institutions: The Neglected Side of the Story', *Journal of Law, Economics and Organization* 6: 213–53.

Moe, Terry. 1990. 'Presidential Style and Presidential Theory', a paper presented at the Presidency Research Conference, University of Pittsburgh, 11–14 November.

Moe, Terry. 1993. 'Presidents, Institutions and Theory', in *Researching the Presidency: Vital Questions, New Approaches*, eds George Edwards, John Kessel and Bert A. Rockman. Pittsburgh, PA: University of Pittsburgh Press.

Morgan, Kenneth. 1984. *Labour in Power*. Oxford: Oxford University Press.

Morton, W. L. 1955. 'The Formation of the First Federal Cabinet', *Canadian Historical Review* 36: 113–25.

Mount, Ferdinand. 1992. *The British Constitution Now: Recovery or Decline?* London: Heinemann.

Mulcahy, Kevin V. and Harold F. Kendrick. 1991. 'The National Security Adviser: A Presidential Perspective' in *Executive Leadership in Anglo-American Systems*, eds Colin Campbell and Margaret Jane Wyszomirski. Pittsburgh, PA: University of Pittsburgh Press.

Nathan, Richard. 1975. *The Plot That Failed: Nixon and the Administrative Presidency*. New York: Wiley.

Nathan, Richard P. 1983. *The Administrative Presidency*. New York: Wiley.

National Audit Office. 1989. *The Next Steps Initiative*. HC 410.

Nelson, Anna Kasten. 1981. 'National Security: Inventing a Process 1945–1960' in *The Illusion of Presidential Government*, eds Hugh Heclo and Lester M. Salamon. Boulder, CO: Westview.

Neustadt, Richard E. 1960. *Presidential Power: The Politics of Leadership*. New York: Wiley.

Neustadt, Richard E. 1990. *Presidential Power and Modern Presidents: The Politics of Leadership from Roosevelt to Reagan*. New York: Free Press.

Newland, Chester, 1983. 'A Mid-Term Appraisal – The Reagan Presidency: Limited Government and Political Administration', *Public Administration Review* 43: 1–21.

Nicolson, I. F. 1986. *The Mystery of Crichel Down*. Oxford: Oxford University Press.

Niskanen, William A. 1971. *Bureaucracy and Representative Government*. New York: Aldine and Atherton.

Niskanen, William A. 1973a. *Structural Reform of the Federal Budget Process*. Washington, DC: American Enterprise Institute.

Niskanen, William A. 1973b. *Bureaucracy: Servant or Master? Lessons from America*. London: Institute of Economic Affairs.

Norton, Philip. 1974. *Dissensions in the House of Commons, 1945–74*. London: Macmillan.

Norton, Philip. 1978. *Conservative Dissidents*. London: Temple Smith.

Norton-Taylor, Richard. 1985. *The Ponting Affair*. London: C. Woolf.

Nugent, Neill. 1989. *The Government and Politics of the European Community*. London: Macmillan.

Olsen, Johan P. 1983. *Organizing Democracy: Political Institutions in a Welfare State: The Case of Norway.* Oslo: Universitetsforlaget.

Olsen, Johan P. 1988. 'Administrative Reform and Theories of Organization' in *Organizing Governance, Governing Organizations,* eds Colin Campbell and B. Guy Peters. Pittsburgh, PA: University of Pittsburgh Press.

Olson, Mancur. 1982. *The Rise and Decline of Nations: Economic Growth, Stagflation, and Social Rigidities.* New Haven, CT: Yale University Press.

Part, Sir Anthony. 1990. *The Making of a Mandarin.* London: Deutsch.

Pearce, Edward. 1991. *The Quiet Rise of John Major.* London: Weidenfeld and Nicolson.

Peters, B. Guy. 1986. 'Burning the Village', *Parliamentary Affairs* 39: 79–97.

Peters, B. Guy. 1991. 'Executive Leadership in an Age of Overload and Retrenchment' in *Executive Leadership in Anglo-American Systems,* eds Colin Campbell and Margaret Jane Wyszomirski. Pittsburgh, PA: University of Pittsburgh Press.

Pfiffner, James P. 1988. *The Strategic Presidency: Hitting the Ground Running.* Chicago: Dorsey.

Pfiffner, James P. 1990. 'Establishing the Bush Presidency', *Public Administration Review* 50: 64–73.

Plowden, William. ed. 1987. *Advising the Rulers.* Oxford: Basil Blackwell.

Plowden, William. 1994. *Ministers and Mandarins.* London: Institute for Public Policy Research.

Pollitt, Christopher. 1990. *Managerialism and the Public Service: The Anglo American Experience.* Oxford: Basil Blackwell.

Polsby, Nelson W. 1975. 'Legislatures' in *Government Institutions and Processes,* Vol. 5 of *Handbook of Political Science,* eds Fred I. Greenstein and Nelson W. Polsby. Reading, MA: Addison-Wesley.

Ponting, Clive. 1985. *The Right To Know: The Inside Story of the Belgrano.* London: Sphere.

Porter, Roger B. 1980. *Presidential Decision-Making: The Economic Policy Board.* Cambridge: Cambridge University Press.

Porter, Roger. 1991. 'The Council of Economic Advisers' in *Executive Leadership in Anglo-American Systems,* eds Colin Campbell and Margaret Jane Wyszomirski. Pittsburgh, PA: University of Pittsburgh Press.

Pusey, Michael. 1991. *Economic Rationalism in Canberra: A Nation Building State Changes Its Mind.* Cambridge: Cambridge University Press.

Putnam, Robert D. 1973. 'The Political Attitudes of Senior Civil Servants in Europe: A Preliminary Report', *British Journal of Political Science* 3: 257–90.

Putnam, Robert D. 1976. *The Comparative Study of Political Elites.* Englewood Cliffs, NJ: Prentice-Hall.

Putnam, Robert D. 1977. 'Elite Transformation in Industrial Societies: An Empirical Assessment of the Theory of Technocracy', *Comparative Political Studies* 10: 383–411.

Putnam, Robert D. and Nicholas Bayne. 1984. *Hanging Together: The Seven-Power Summits.* Cambridge, MA: Harvard University Press.

Qualls, James H. 1977. 'Barber's Typological Analysis of Political Leaders', *American Political Science Review* 71: 182–211.

Quinlan, Sir Michael. 1993. 'Controversy: The Ethics of the Public Service', *Governance* 6.

Quirk, Paul J. 1991. 'Domestic Policy: Divided Government and Co-operative Presidential Leadership' in *The Bush Administration: First Appraisals*, eds Colin Campbell and Bert A. Rockman. Chatham, NJ: Chatham House.

Radwanski, George. 1978. *Trudeau.* Toronto: Macmillan.

Redford, Emmette S. and Marlan Blissett. 1981. *Organizing the Executive Branch: The Johnson Presidency.* Chicago: University of Chicago Press.

Reedy, George. 1970. *The Twilight of the Presidency.* New York: Mentor.

Regan, C. M. 1986. 'Anonymity in the British Civil Service', *Parliamentary Affairs* 33: 400–21.

Riddell, Peter. 1983. *The Thatcher Government.* Oxford: Martin Robertson.

Riddell, Peter. 1993. *Honest Opportunism: The Rise of the Career Politician.* London: Hamish Hamilton.

Ridley, Nicholas. 1991. *My Style of Government: The Thatcher Years.* London: Hutchinson.

Riggs, Fred W. 1988. 'The Survival of Presidentialism in America: Para-Constitutional Practices', *International Political Science Review* 9: 247–78.

Roberts, Paul Craig. 1984. *The Supply-Side Revolution: An Insider's Account of Policymaking in Washington.* Cambridge, MA: Harvard University Press.

Robertson, R. G. 1971. 'The Changing Role of the Privy Council', *Canadian Public Administration* 14: 487–508.

Rockman, Bert A. 1984. *The Leadership Question: The Presidency and the American System.* New York: Praeger.

Rockman, Bert A. 1991a. 'The Leadership Question: Is There an Answer?' in *Executive Leadership in Anglo-American Systems*, eds Colin Campbell and Margaret Jane Wyszomirski. Pittsburgh, PA: University of Pittsburgh Press.

Rockman, Bert A. 1991b. 'The Leadership Style of George Bush' in *The*

Bush Administration: First Appraisals, eds Colin Campbell and Bert A. Rockman. Chatham, NJ: Chatham House.

Rogaly, Joe. 1993. 'New Partner at the Last Chance Saloon', *Financial Times*, 28 May.

Rose, Richard. 1976. *Managing Presidential Objectives*. New York: Free Press.

Rose, Richard. 1987. 'Steering the Ship of State: One Tiller but Two Pairs of Hands', *British Journal of Political Science* 17: 409–53.

Rose, Richard. 1988. *The Postmodern Presidency: The White House Meets the World*. Chatham, NJ: Chatham House.

Rose, Richard and B. Guy Peters. 1978. *Can Government Go Bankrupt?* New York: Free Press.

Rose, Richard and Ezra Suleiman, eds. 1980. *Presidents and Prime Ministers*. Washington, DC: American Enterprise Institution.

Royal Institute for Public Administration. 1987. *Top Jobs in Whitehall: Report of a Working Group*. London: RIPA.

Rubinstein, W. D. 1993. *Capitalism, Culture and Decline in Britain 1750–1990*. London and New York: Routledge.

Sanera, Michael. 1984. 'Implementing the Mandate' in *Mandate for Leadership II: Continuing the Conservative Revolution*, eds Stuart M. Butler, Michael Sanera and W. Bruce Weinrod. Washington, DC: Heritage Foundation.

Savas, E. S. 1982. *Privatizing the Public Sector: How to Shrink Government*. Chatham, NJ: Chatham House.

Savoie, Donald J. 1984. *Thatcher, Reagan, Mulroney: In Search of a New Bureaucracy*. Pittsburgh, PA: University of Pittsburgh Press.

Schieffer, Bob and Gary Paul Gates. 1989. *The Acting President: Ronald Reagan and the Supporting Players Who Helped Him Create the Illusion that Held America Spellbound*. New York: E. P. Dutton.

Schwarz, John. 1983. *America's Hidden Success: Twenty Years of Public Policy*. New York and London: W. W. Norton.

Scott, Graham, Peter Bushnell and Nikitin Sallee. 1990. 'Reform of the .Core Public Sector: New Zealand Experience', *Governance* 3: 138–67.

Scott, Graham and Peter Gorringe. 1989. 'Reform of the Core Public Sector: The New Zealand Experience', a paper delivered to the Bicentennial Conference of the Royal Australian Institute of Public Administration, Melbourne, Australia.

Self, Peter and Herbert Storing. 1962. *The State and the Farmer*. London: Allen & Unwin; 1963: Berkeley, CA: University of California Press.

Seymour-Ure, Colin. 1991. 'The Role of Press Secretaries on Chief Executives: The US, the UK, Canada and Australia' in *Executive*

Leadership in Anglo-American Systems, eds Colin Campbell and Margaret Jane Wyszomirski. Pittsburgh, PA: University of Pittsburgh Press.

Shepsle, Kenneth A. 1991. 'Studying Institutions, Some Lessons from the Rational Choice Approach', *Journal of Theoretical Politics* 1: 131–47.

Silberman, Bernard S. 1993. *Cages of Reason: The Rise of the Rational State in France, Japan, the United States and Great Britain*. Chicago and London: University of Chicago Press.

Simeon, Richard. 1972. *Federal–Provincial Diplomacy: The Making of Recent Policy in Canada*. Toronto: University of Toronto Press.

Sinclair, Barbara. 1991. 'Governing Unheroically (and Sometimes Unappetizingly): Bush and the 101st Congress' in *The Bush Administration: First Appraisals*, eds Colin Campbell and Bert A. Rockman. Chatham, NJ: Chatham House.

Sisson, C. H. 1966. *The Spirit of British Administration*, 2nd ed. London: Faber.

Stevens, Anne. 1981. 'The Higher Civil Service and Economic Policymaking' in *French Politics and Public Policymaking*, eds Philip G. Cerny and Martin A. Schain. London: Methuen.

Stockman, David A. 1986. *The Triumph of Politics: How the Reagan Revolution Failed*. New York: Harper & Row.

Suleiman, Ezra. 1978. *Elites in French Society*. Princeton, NJ.

Suleiman, Ezra, ed. 1984. *Bureaucrats in Policymaking*. New York: Holmes and Meier.

Summerton, Neil. 1980. 'A Mandarin's Duty', *Parliamentary Affairs* 33: 400–21.

Sundquist, James L. 1983. *Dynamics of the Party System: Alignment and Realignment of Political Parties in the United States*. Washington, DC: Brookings.

Sundquist, James L. 1986. *Constitutional Reform and Effective Government*. Washington, DC: Brookings.

Sundquist, James L. 1988–9. 'Needed: A Political Theory for the New Era of Coalition Government in the United States', *Political Science Quarterly* 103: 613–35.

Szanton, Peter. 1981. *Federal Reorganization: What Have We Learned?* Chatham, NJ: Chatham House.

Thatcher, Margaret. 1993. *Downing Street Years*. London: Harper Collins.

Tower Commission. 1987. 'President's Special Review Board', *The Tower Commission Report* (*New York Times* edition). New York: Bantam.

Treasury and Civil Service Committee of the House of Commons. 1981. Session 1980/81, *The Future of the Civil Service Department: Government Observations*. London: HMSO.

Treasury and Civil Service Committee of the House of Commons. 1993. Session 1992/93, *The Civil Service: Minutes of Evidence*. London: HMSO.

Treasury and Civil Service Committee of the House of Commons. 1994. Session 1993/94, *The Role of the Civil Service: Minutes of Evidence*. London: HMSO.

Tumim, Judge Stephen. 1991. *Report into the Escapes from Brixton Prison*. London: HMSO.

Turnbull, Malcolm. 1988. *The Spy Catcher Trial*. London: Heinemann.

Turner, John. 1980. *Lloyd George's Secretariat*. Cambridge: Cambridge University Press.

Van Loon, Richard. 1981. 'Stop the Music: The Current Policy and Expenditure Management System in Ottawa', *Canadian Public Administration* 24: 175–99.

Van Loon, R. J. 1983. 'The Policy and Expenditure Management System in the Canadian Federal Government: The First Five Years', *Canadian Public Administration* 26: 255–85.

Walker, Jack L. 1966. 'A Critique of the Elitist Theory of Democracy', *American Political Science Review* 60: 285–95.

Walker, Jack L. 1969. 'The Diffusion of Innovations Among the American States', *American Political Science Review* 63: 880–9.

Wass, Sir Douglas. 1988. Review of Nicolson, *The Mystery of Crichel Down*, *Public Law*.

Weaver, Kent. 1986. 'The Politics of Blame Avoidance', *Journal of Public Policy* 6: 371–98.

Weaver, Kent and Bert A. Rockman. 1990. 'Introduction: Assessing the Effects of Institutions', a paper prepared for presentation at a conference titled 'Political Institutions and Their Consequence', The Brookings Institution, 2–3 February.

Weiner, Martin. 1981. *English Culture and the Decline of the Industrial Spirit 1850–1980*. Cambridge: Cambridge University Press.

Weller, Patrick. 1983. 'Do Prime Ministers' Departments Really Create Problems?', *Public Administration* 61: 59–78.

Weller, Patrick. 1985. *First Among Equals: Prime Ministers in Westminster Systems*. London: Allen & Unwin.

Weller, Patrick. 1989. *Malcolm Fraser PM: A Study of Prime Ministerial Power in Australia*. Ringwood, Victoria: Penguin.

Weller, Patrick. 1991. 'Support for Prime Ministers: A Comparative Perspective' in *Executive Leadership in Anglo-American Systems*, eds Colin Campbell and Margaret Jane Wyszomirski. Pittsburgh, PA: University of Pittsburgh Press.

Wettenhall, Roger. 1989. 'Recent Restructuring in Canberra: A Report on Machinery-of-Government Changes in Australia', *Governance* 2: 95–106.

Wheare, K. C. 1955. *Government by Committee: An Essay on the British Constitution*. Oxford: Clarendon Press.

Whitbread, Michael. 1987. 'Department of Environment' in *Reshaping Central Government*, eds Anthony Harrison and John Gretton. Oxford: Transaction Books.

Wildavsky, Aaron. 1961. 'Political Implications of Budgetary Reform', *Public Administration Review* 21: 183–90.

Wildavsky, Aaron. 1983. 'From Chaos Comes Opportunity: Movement Toward Spending Limits in American and Canadian Budgeting', *Canadian Public Administration* 26: 163–81.

Wildavsky, Aaron and Jeffrey Pressman. 1973. *Implementation*. Berkeley, CA: University of California Press.

Wilson, Graham K. 1977. *Special Interests and Policymaking*. Chichester and New York: Wiley.

Wilson, Graham K. 1985. *The Politics of Safety and Health*. Oxford and New York: Oxford University Press.

Wilson, Sir Harold. 1971. *A Personal Record: The Labour Government, 1964–71*. Boston, MA: Little Brown.

Wilson, V. Seymour. 1981. *Canadian Public Policy and Administration: Theory and Environment*. Toronto: McGraw-Hill Ryerson.

Wilson, Woodrow. 1941 (reprint). 'The Study of Administration', *Political Science Quarterly* 16: 481–506.

Woodehouse, Diana. 1994. *Ministers and Parliament: Accountability in Theory and Practice*. Oxford: Clarendon Press.

Wyszomirski, Margaret Jane. 1982. 'The Deinstitutionalization of Presidential Staff Agencies', *Public Administration Review* 42: 448–58.

Young, Hugo. 1989. *One of Us: A Biography of Margaret Thatcher*. London: Macmillan.

Young, Hugo. 1990. 'GCHQ Memorial Lecture', *The Bulletin*, July.

Subject Index

Unless otherwise noted, all institutions referred to below are from the British case.

Author Index

Pirate Alphabet

Alison Hawes

RIGBY

Aa

ahoy

"I see land. Land **ahoy**!" said the pirate.

anchor

The **anchor** makes the ship stop.

barrel

This **barrel** has food in it.

boots

Pirates have big black **boots**.

3

Cc

Captain

This pirate is **Captain** Hook.

cannon

A **cannon** is a big gun.

Dd

deck

The **deck** is made from planks of wood.

dolphin

A **dolphin** can jump out of the water.

5

Ee

earring

This pirate has a big gold **earring**.

eye patch

An **eye patch** looks good on a pirate.

6

Ff

flag

This is a **flag** from a pirate ship.

fishing

This **fishing** boat has two big nets.

Gg

gold

Pirates like to look for **gold**.

galleon

A **galleon** is a big ship with lots of masts.

hat

This black **hat** belongs to a pirate.

hide

This small boat can **hide** in this cave.

Ii Jj

island

There are trees on this **island**.

jewels

Jewels can be red and green and blue.

10

key

This **key** can open a treasure chest.

knot

This pirate is tying a **knot** in a rope.

11

Ll

lookout

The **lookout** is at the top of the mast.

lighthouse

A **lighthouse** tells ships to keep away from the rocks.

12

map

This is a **map** of the world.

mermaid

A **mermaid** has a tail like a fish.

Nn

net

You can catch fish in a **net**.

night

At **night** you can see the moon in the sky.

14

octopus

An **octopus** has lots of legs!

ocean

There are big waves in
the **ocean**.

Pp Qq

parrot

This **parrot** has green and white feathers.

quickly

A speedboat goes very **quickly** in the sea.

16

Rr

rocks

A ship must look out for **rocks** in the sea!

ropes

A sailor is pulling on the **ropes**.

Ss

seagull

The **seagull** is looking for fish to eat.

seaweed

Seaweed grows on the rocks and in the sea.

Ss

silver

This bucket is full of **silver** coins!

shipwreck

The ship crashed on the rocks. Now it is a **shipwreck**.

19

Tt

treasure

This chest is full of **treasure**!

telescope

A **telescope** helps you see things that are far away.

under

Fish live **under** the water.

Viking

Viking pirates sailed in ships like this.

21

Ww

whale

A **whale** can make a big splash.

wheel

You can turn the **wheel** to steer the boat.

The **X** shows where to look for treasure.

Yy Zz

yell

The captain **yells** "Ship ahoy!".

breeze

A **breeze** blows the sails to make the ship go.

24